SIR GARDNER WILKINSON
AND HIS CIRCLE

Sir Gardner Wilkinson and His Circle

BY
JASON THOMPSON

University of Texas Press, Austin

Library of Congress Cataloging-in-Publication Data

Thompson, John Jason, date.
    Sir Gardner Wilkinson and his circle / by Jason Thompson.
        p.   cm.
    Includes bibliographical references and index.
    ISBN 0-292-77643-8
    1. Wilkinson, John Gardner, Sir, 1797–1875.   2. Egyp-
tologists—Great Britain—Biography.   I. Title.
    PJ1064.W55T46   1992
    932'.007202—dc20
    [B]   91-47636

To the memory of my father

Contents

Acknowledgments

IN THE COURSE of this project I received assistance, guidance, and encouragement from many individuals and institutions. Emmet Larkin, William H. McNeill, and Janet Johnson were patient and helpful supervisors during this work's previous existence as a Ph.D. dissertation at the University of Chicago. Others who read all or part of the manuscript and offered valuable suggestions include Jaromír Málek, the late Arnaldo Momigliano, Robert Lucas, Kent Weeks, Gayle McKenzie, Neil Cooke, Arthur Goldschmidt, Jr., Sabrina Alcorn, Carl Royer, and the anonymous reviewers for the University of Texas Press.

Helping with advice, access to research material, or in many other ways were Howard Colvin, Edith Clay, Tom Arthure, Janet Wallace, M. L. Bierbrier, Christine Kelly, K. P. Kuhlmann, Colin Harris, Jeanne Brown, John Alden Williams, Caroline Williams, Jasper Gaunt, Ron Zitterkopf, Steven Sidebotham, Selwyn Tillett, the late Charles F. Nims, Colin Shrimpton, the late Klaus Baer, Maya Bijvoet, Elizabeth Sartain, Elizabeth Rodenbeck, Mary Clapinson, Raymond Stock, Ken Hale, Maria Unkovskaya, David Harley, Jane Ferson, Fen Ferson, John E. Long, and Richard L. Troutman.

I should also mention my debt to the late John A. Wilson. Although I never met Professor Wilson, his book, *The Culture of Ancient Egypt*, first interested me in the subject of Egyptology, and another of his books, *Signs and Wonders upon Pharaoh*, helped me to prepare this work. Nor did I meet the late Warren R. Dawson, yet his manuscript notes about Sir Gardner Wilkinson were useful, as was the valuable *Who Was Who in Egyptology*, a project which he began.

Institutions that were especially helpful include the Griffith Institute of the Ashmolean Museum, the Manuscript Department at the

British Library, the Manuscript Department of the National Library of Scotland, the Center for Research Libraries, the Joseph Regenstein Library of the University of Chicago, the Oriental Institute of the University of Chicago, the Center for Middle East Studies of the University of Texas at Austin, the Archives of the British Museum, the Department of Egyptian Antiquities of the British Museum, the Royal Geographical Society, the University of Chicago's Epigraphic Survey in Luxor, the German Institute of Archaeology in Cairo, the Creswell Library of the American University in Cairo, the Library of University College London, and the Department of History at Western Kentucky University.

Partial funding for the project was provided by an Overseas Research Grant from the University of Chicago, a Travel to Collections Grant from the National Endowment for the Humanities, and a Faculty Research Grant from Western Kentucky University.

Access to material and permissions to reproduce text and photographs were graciously given by the National Trust, the Duke of Northumberland, the Earl of Lytton, John Murray, the National Portrait Gallery, the British Library, and the Royal Geographical Society.

I am especially grateful to Elizabeth W. Fernea, Annes McCann-Baker, and Frankie Westbrook, whose help and encouragement greatly speeded the production of this volume, and to Diane Watts, who prepared the map of Egypt for it.

Angela T. Thompson, Joseph Goldston, and Julian Thompson were patient and supportive throughout the project. I owe them more than I can express.

Many of the above contributed in more than one way. Without such support, the project would never have progressed as far as it did. Any mistakes or shortcomings that remain are entirely my responsibility.   J.T.

Note on Transliteration

Transliteration always poses a problem whenever Arabic words appear in an English text. Here the difficulty is compounded by the presence of words from another non-Western language, ancient Egyptian. In general, Arabic transliterations have been simplified as much as possible, and the diacritics have been omitted. Transliterations from ancient Egyptian follow the spellings in certain standard Egyptological reference works. In some instances, however, spellings that Wilkinson and his colleagues used have been reproduced; also, spellings of certain place-names that have acquired canonical status have been retained.

Introduction

THE REDISCOVERY of ancient Egypt and the establishment of the science of Egyptology were two of the important intellectual events of the nineteenth century. In the aftermath of the sensational discoveries associated with Napoleon's Egyptian expedition of 1798–1801, a new avenue into the past was opened. The impact upon the European intellectual and popular imagination was enormous, especially in Britain and France. With their institution of the Grand Tour, the British initially made the most of the new opportunities for Egyptian exploration. Scores of British travelers, scholars, and writers descended upon Egypt to see the land for themselves, to write about their experiences, and to collect antiquities. At home in Britain, scholars attempted to assimilate the mass of data that was flowing in; they tried to read the ancient language and ventured tentative interpretations of ancient Egyptian history. An increasingly well-informed public watched with interest. Participating in all of these events and mediating between them was Sir Gardner Wilkinson, who has been called the founder of Egyptology in Great Britain.[1]

Such an attribution would have surprised Wilkinson. For one thing, the term *Egyptology* was not coined until late in his life, well after his years of active Egyptological research were over.[2] Then, even when the formal discipline of Egyptology began to take shape, he was initially accorded little place within it. Wilkinson considered himself a gentlemanly traveler and writer, one of the men of letters who were a common feature of the literary landscape of Victorian England. Nevertheless, his contributions to Egyptology were immense. Spending twelve years in Egypt between 1821 and 1833, he was the first person to work there with some knowledge of the ancient language. With skill and energy, he surveyed almost every major archaeological site in Egypt, many of which he recorded in his highly accurate notebooks and sketchbooks. From these he derived an original and comprehensive view of the reality of ancient Egyptian life that he communicated through his writings, especially his *Manners and Customs of the Ancient Egyptians*. No nineteenth-century writer did as much as Wilkinson to make the ancient Egyptians known to the general reading public. For scholars of this century, his most meaningful contribution is the wealth of Egyptological and other data in his notebooks, the full potential of which has never been realized.

Just as Wilkinson was confronted with the problem of deciding how to concentrate his energies in Egypt with so many possibilities to choose from, I was as his biographer also forced to be selective. I chose not to try to account for Wilkinson's every season in Egypt nor to follow his every journey through the land. Instead, I attempted to show the nature and variety of his interests, life-style, adventures, and accomplishments, even when this meant emphasizing non-Egyptological subjects. Some of the Egyptian chapters are therefore organized topically, not chronologically. In dealing with his later years, I devoted large sections to activities with no pertinence to Egypt. Subjects such as his correspondence with John Ruskin are naturally important, especially since it occurred when the art critic was completing the last of his greatest work; interchange with people such as Harriet Martineau, Ada Lovelace, Charles Babbage, Sir Charles Lyell, and others is obviously of interest. But I was also drawn to other aspects of his life—involvement in current issues, local antiquarian activities, and the many pastimes of a gentleman scholar. Without becoming lost in the minutiae of Wilkinson's daily life, I wanted to convey some impression of how this interesting man lived and worked. If portions of the later chapters sometimes seem to drift from place to place, person to person, and interest to interest, then the desired effect has been achieved, for such variability reflects Wilkinson's later years.

As I organized this study of Wilkinson's career, I was often inspired by the venerable life and letters genre of biography that was popular in Wilkinson's time. Not only did that form suggest a suitable metaphor for Wilkinson's life, but it also gave me an opportunity to quote extensively from his and his associates' papers. So rich is the material for studying Wilkinson that a large, detailed book could well be written about Wilkinson's Egyptological work alone—indeed, a study of his work at Thebes[3] could run into several volumes. On the other hand, materials exist for an in-depth study of

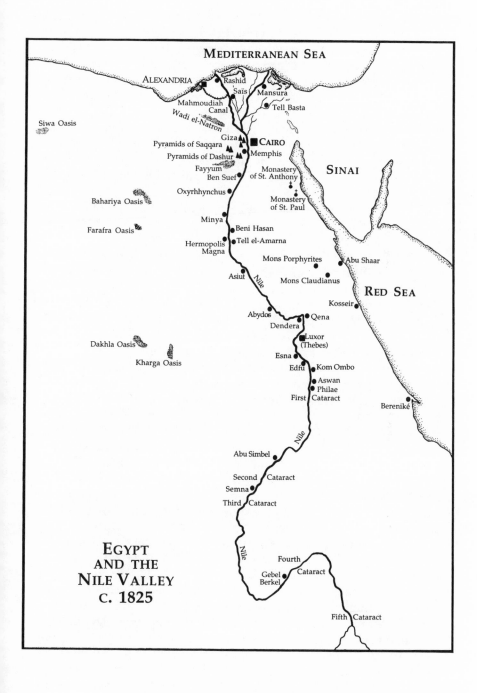

EGYPT
AND THE
NILE VALLEY
C. 1825

Wilkinson as a Victorian gentleman scholar. The intention of this work lies somewhere between those two approaches.

Another important organizational decision was to investigate Wilkinson's network of friends and acquaintances, especially those from his Egyptian years, to the extent that this book is in part a collective biography. The informal group to which he belonged in Egypt was in effect a voluntary association devoted to Egyptian studies. Wilkinson's activities cannot be understood apart from it. Beyond that, Wilkinson was an intensely social person. Following this thread of his character throughout his life, one is led to many people in many different aspects of Victorian life. This is one of the most significant contributions that a study of his life can make to intellectual history. Wilkinson may not be remembered as one of the elite writers of Victorian England, but he was very much a part of the intellectual mainstream.

It is remarkable that no biography of Wilkinson has been written before now, especially since the need for one has been noted repeatedly.[4] There is, of course, the fact that the greatest portion of Wilkinson's personal papers have only recently become available for consultation by the public. Then, too, there is the eclipse of his popularity in the early twentieth century. From being the best-known Egyptologist in Britain, Wilkinson became a name known mostly by specialists. Many twentieth-century tourists in Cairo who happened to glance up and see his name on the façade of the Egyptian Museum must have wondered who he was. In recent years, however, there has been a rediscovery of Wilkinson. With the rise of interest in the history of Egyptology and travel in the Middle East, he has been increasingly mentioned in works on those subjects.

The first scholar to conduct systematic research on Wilkinson was Warren R. Dawson in preparation of the biographical index of Egyptologists, *Who Was Who in Egyptology*, which first appeared in 1951. Drawing upon his great knowledge of pertinent manuscripts and published material, Dawson pieced together a chronology of Wilkinson's life and an assessment of his importance. The entry for Wilkinson in *Who Was Who*, updated by Eric P. Uphill in the revised second edition, is the definitive biographical statement about Wilkinson to date. Dawson's notebooks, now in the British Library, were exceedingly helpful in preparing this work. Leslie Greener also noted Wilkinson's importance in his *The Discovery of Egypt*.[5] This excellent book, however, is mostly concerned with the period before 1800; the unpublished manuscript for the second part of Greener's study of the history of Egyptology, which undoubtedly treated Wilkinson in detail, was lost after Greener's death. One hopes it may yet be discovered. John A. Wilson's *Signs and Wonders upon Pharaoh*[6] provided an Egyptologist's assessment of Wilkinson, especially his work at Thebes and his impact on the British reading public. Whereas Wilson was primarily concerned with American Egyptology, John David Wortham focused on the British in his *British Egyptology 1549–1906.*[7]

During the past fifteen years, coinciding with an upsurge of popular as well as scholarly interest in Egypt, several more books have appeared that emphasize Wilkinson's importance. Brian Fagan's *The Rape of the Nile,*[8] a story of travel and monumental depredation in Egypt, was the first to call Wilkinson to public attention again. Other widely disseminated books, such as Peter Clayton's *The Rediscovery of Ancient Egypt,*[9] have performed a similar service. The importance of Wilkinson's work at individual sites in Egypt has been developed by John Romer in his book about the Valley of the Kings,[10] by M.L. Bierbrier's study of the royal workmen's village of Deir el-Medina,[11] and in Lise Manniche's books about the tombs of the nobles at Gurna.[12] The invaluable reference work *Atlas of Ancient Egypt* by John Baines and Jaromír Málek contains a concise evaluation of Wilkinson's place within the overall history of Egyptology.[13] At the same time several of Wilkinson's circle have also had biographies written about them: Edward William Lane by Leila Ahmed,[14] Robert Hay by Selwyn Tillett,[15] and Frederick Catherwood by Victor von Hagen.[16] Wilkinson and his colleagues, once dismissed as amateurish collectors, are beginning to be recognized for the true measure of their accomplishments. This process should continue in related developments. The third edition of the indispensable *Who Was Who in Egyptology* is in preparation, and scholars anticipate with confidence that a definitive history of Egyptology will appear in the not-too-distant future. *Manners and Customs of the Ancient Egyptians* was even in print again in 1988, reissued in the abridged version of 1854.[17]

Another reason that no one has written a full-length biography of Wilkinson sooner is probably the formidable difficulty of doing justice to the many facets of his life and times. Not only did his work span almost the entire range of nineteenth-century Egyptology, but it was also set within the peculiar intellectual milieu of the eighteenth and nineteenth centuries. Furthermore, his experiences in Egypt and his written account of them raise many questions pertinent to the topic of Orientalism, the subject of some exciting debate of late.[18] His later years of traveling, writing, and engaging in varied pursuits and pastimes open entirely different dimensions for speculation and interpretation.

One especially important facet of Wilkinson's work, and one that has largely been ignored, is its bearing on Middle East studies. Although Wilkinson and his colleagues are best remembered today for their Egyptological work, they are also important sources for early nineteenth-century Egyptian history. As interested and critical outside observers, they documented many of the changes that were occurring during the reign of Muhammad Ali as he attempted to transform Egypt into a modern nation-state. Numerous notebook and sketchbook entries describe aspects of that controversial period. They were also drawn to the medieval city of Cairo, realizing that it contained the greatest collection of Islamic architecture remaining in the world. Their appreciation heightened as they saw the medieval city being destroyed by the forces of modernization, and they strove to record it for posterity.

Wilkinson's role in the initial stages of colonial penetration of Egypt is another important facet. Though Wilkinson and his colleagues never thought of themselves as the advance guard of British imperialism, that is, nevertheless, what they were. With their insistence on the rights of a British subject, even when abroad, with their acquisition of the skills of living in the East, and above all by their accumulation and dissemination of information, they provided Britain with the advantages of an extended, thoughtful reconnaissance of Egypt. This was especially true of Edward William Lane, of course, but in the short run Wilkinson may have been even more influential. He made the Egyptian past comprehensible, removing much of the awe and fear that the past had inspired and replacing it with interest. Those portions of his books that dealt with modern Egypt provided a wealth of information about the land at that moment, especially his *Handbook for Travellers in Egypt*, which guided hundreds of tourists, soldiers, businessmen, and colonial administrators as they moved through Egypt. This in turn leads to the question of cultural imperialism as Wilkinson, a representative of the West, took the heritage of an Eastern culture and defined it in Western terms for Western uses.

Wilkinson's role as artist must also be emphasized. Wilkinson was rarely without pen and sketchbook in hand, so much so that they were an integral part of his life. Over the decades he accumulated a vast collection of sketches, washes, and watercolors. The best of them are minor works of art, but far more significant than their artistic merit is their value as sources, primary sources, for monuments that no longer exist. By knowing more about Wilkinson we can use those sources better.

One could go on indefinitely about the various aspects of Wilkinson's career, but one other that should be mentioned here is the pertinence of Wilkinson's career to two very important questions in nineteenth-century historiography, the transformation from amateur to professional scholarship and the relationship of antiquarianism to history.[19] If one defines an antiquarian as someone who is solely interested in facts about the past and who does not selectively arrange those facts and interpret them to answer questions about the past, then Wilkinson was much more than an antiquarian. Even so, *antiquarian* and *antiquarian studies* are terms with which Wilkinson was comfortable, and they help distinguish him from the scholars who during his lifetime were first recognized as professionals. By comparing his methods with those of the first professionals and following his relations with the professional establishment, we can document an important phase in the development of nineteenth-century intellectual life.

Within that context, it is essential to define two additional terms as they are used in this book: *amateur* and *dilettante*. *Amateur* means merely someone who is not a member of a professional discipline. In that sense Wilkinson was an amateur. The word does not carry its present-day connotations of lack of expertise or commitment. *Dilettante* refers to one of the group of eighteenth- and early nineteenth-century aristocrats who took a connoisseur's interest in classical antiquity. The term is used here without the implication of superficiality that it later acquired. Wilkinson's mentor, Sir William Gell, was one of the great dilettantes, in the positive sense of the term. While Wilkinson was not a dilettante, he was nevertheless strongly influenced by the dilettante tradition.

With so many approaches to a study of Wilkinson's life, one might reasonably conclude that his biographer should be a historian of both modern Britain and modern Egypt, an Egyptologist, an art historian, and a specialist in the many other areas that Wilkinson's life enfolded. I am hardly an expert in all of those disciplines, but it has been my good fortune to research and write at this moment of growing interest in the history of Egyptology and of general European contact with Egypt. I have also benefited from the kind assistance of many people who do have expertise in these fields. This book is therefore designed both to show the diversity of Wilkinson's life and to analyze his greatest accomplishments. Indeed, the two are inseparable.

We now stand at a great remove from Sir Gardner Wilkinson. His are not the books that we would turn to today to learn what ancient Egypt used to be like, because his vision of the past has been mostly—though not entirely—replaced by subsequent scholarship.

His excellent copies of Egyptian antiquities are still consulted, but the conclusions that he drew from them have largely been superseded. Yet he remains interesting to the historian of ideas because his views of ancient Egypt predominated for more than a half a century in England. His work was original and significant. Many aspects of nineteenth-century culture can been seen from the vantage point of his life. A deeper understanding of Sir Gardner Wilkinson and his circle adds to our knowledge of early Victorian intellectual history, one of the outstanding blank spots remaining on the historiographical map of nineteenth-century England.

SIR GARDNER WILKINSON
AND HIS CIRCLE

CHAPTER ONE

The Origins of an Egyptologist

LIKE MANY of his contemporaries, Sir Gardner Wilkinson took pride in his genealogy. He could have boasted of many worthy ancestors, but he was proudest that his mother was the great-great-granddaughter of Sir Salathiel Lovell. Sir Salathiel was the incompetent—though Wilkinson never mentioned that—Recorder of London and Baron of the Exchequer in the reign of Queen Anne.[1] He merits a footnote in literary history for being the target of some of Daniel Defoe's satiric poems, for which he took revenge, after his fashion, by sentencing Defoe to the pillory.[2] Nevertheless, Wilkinson did come from a respectable family that originated in Yorkshire.[3]

John Gardner Wilkinson was born 5 October 1797, probably at Little Missenden Abbey in Buckinghamshire.[4] He was the only surviving child of Mary Anne Gardner Wilkinson and the Reverend John Wilkinson of Hardendale in Westmorland. Neither the infant nor his mother could bear the northern cold, so the family moved south to Chelsea where Wilkinson was baptized on 17 January 1798.[5] That was the first of many moves during Wilkinson's life away from dark and cold toward warmth and light. Mrs. Wilkinson was a person of high intellectual attainments and a happy disposition that remained undampened despite the ill health that she suffered after her son's birth. From her sofa she taught him French and the rudiments of Latin and Greek. She also taught him to draw, the only artistic training that he ever received. From his father, a Fellow of the Society of Antiquaries of London and a member of the African Exploration Society, Wilkinson derived his interests in far away times and places.[6] His reward for doing well at his studies was permission to look at the plates in his father's scholarly journals, a pleasure that he remembered with delight until the end of his life. He especially looked forward to nights when one of his father's associates, the Moroccan traveler James Grey Jackson, came to dine with them.[7] Jackson's exotic stories left a lasting impression on the boy's mind. Another memorable experience was when his father took him to visit a cousin, Captain (later Admiral) Sir Charles Richardson, who was about to sail on the ill-fated Walcheren expedition. The experience of being aboard a warship so excited him that he resolved to make the navy his career. That particular resolution was never fulfilled, but his youthful experiences all contributed to what he later described as his "early predilection for travelling & for antiquarian research."[8] Wilkinson lost both of his parents early, his mother when he was six and his father two years later, but they gave him a good start in life. Besides training him and encouraging his imagination, they left him an annual income that, though not especially large, was enough to provide financial independence. Later it gave him the leisure to travel and write.

After his parents' deaths, Wilkinson became the ward of one of his father's friends, the Reverend Dr. Yates, the chaplain of Chelsea College.[9] Rev. Yates was a well-intentioned man, but he lacked the emotional capacity to care adequately for his young charge. He put Wilkinson into a preparatory school and let him languish there, even during vacations, for several years. The boy found some emotional solace from two otherwise unnamed friends, Mr. and Mrs. Stephens of Chelsea. Lady Wilkinson years later mentioned their importance to the sensitive young boy: "It was to these two early friends that he had been indebted for the kindness which tended so much to compensate him for the early loss of his parents, & the interesting society he there [in their home] met brought him at an early time to appreciate the tastes and pursuits of men of talent."[10] Rev. Yates also resisted Wilkinson's choice of career. Wilkinson still wanted to go into the navy, but Yates had decided upon the church for him; after all, Rev. Yates was a churchman, as Wilkinson's father had been, so the choice must have seemed natural, at least to Rev. Yates. Wilkinson tried to persuade him to change his mind and even got Admiral Richardson to help, but to no avail.[11] The situation improved when one of Wilkinson's uncles intervened and persuaded Rev. Yates to transfer Wilkinson to Harrow, the school that Wilkinson's father had, in fact, wanted his son to attend. That pleased Wilkinson, who entered Harrow at Christmas in 1813, thereby beginning the most fruitful years of his formal education.[12]

Harrow was not a pleasant place in the early nineteenth century. Even a sympathetic witness described its atmosphere as "hard or even barbarous";[13] and Anthony Trollope, who went to Harrow not long after Wilkinson, always remembered it bitterly.[14] What made Harrow work well for Wilkinson was a teacher of unusual ability, the Very Reverend George Butler, headmaster of Harrow from 1805 until 1829, whose notice in the *Dictionary of National Biography* reads, "Few men could compete with [him] in versatility of mind, and in the variety of his accomplishments." Despite his high qualifications, Butler's appointment was initially controversial, following as it did a fierce competition for the headmastership. The students resented him because they had favored another candidate whom they already knew and liked.[15] Even his humane reforms aroused opposition, such as the confiscation of the monitors' canes, a move that angered the older students who relished the privilege of beating their juniors. This did not mean that Butler banished the rod entirely, because Trollope wrote that Butler used to beat him "constantly," and Wilkinson probably felt the bite of the rod occasionally. Nevertheless, Butler did lower the level of brutality at the school. Slowly he won the allegiance of his students, even young Lord Byron, who had plotted to blow up the "usurper" headmaster with a well-laid charge of gunpowder.[16] Butler treated the boys as individuals and showed them thoughtful little kindnesses, such as bringing them food when they were sick. Often he invited them to his home for peaches and Madeira.[17]

The official curriculum at Harrow was classical, although Butler, an accomplished mathematician, introduced Euclidian geometry. In fact, Harrow was momentarily in disfavor because many parents preferred to send their children to schools where they would learn more financially useful skills than conjugating Greek verbs or declining Latin nouns. On a typical day, the students learned several chapters from the classics, both Latin and Greek, in addition to other studies.[18] Wilkinson exhibited sufficient skill to win a prize, a copy of Aristotle's *Nicomachean Ethics,*[19] but just how thoroughly he learned his classics is questionable, because in later years, whenever he was confronted with a classical text, he seems to have resorted to a translation. Although the official curriculum was strictly classical, the headmaster of Harrow customarily tutored some of the boys, of whom Wilkinson seems to have been one, and Butler's tutorials covered a wide range of subjects.[20] Years later, Wilkinson often said that his interests in art and archaeology were inspired by Butler.[21] He may even have heard something of ancient Egypt while he was at Harrow, because Butler studied Egyptian hieroglyphics under the direction of his friend, the Scottish polymath Dr. Thomas Young.[22]

The time at Harrow passed pleasantly for Wilkinson. Besides study, there were other occupations, such as rowdiness, drinking, and fighting the town boys on the cricket field.[23] In summer, when dawn came early, he slipped away at first light to go sketching, returning in time for roll call. Before he left Harrow, he had sketched every church in the neighborhood.[24] Wilkinson threw himself into his studies and other activities, like the debating society, with such application that his physician, Sir Astley Cooper,[25] became concerned and decided that the boy should have a period of sustained mental rest. Accordingly, Wilkinson was withdrawn from the school. Did the hard-working boy suffer a nervous breakdown? It sounds as if he may have, but the evidence is inconclusive. At any rate, Sir Astley prescribed a program of outdoor exercise, primarily horseback riding. Even then Wilkinson was drawn to Harrow and rode down to school at least twice a week where he was the guest of Dr. Butler.[26] Wilkinson always remembered Harrow affectionately. After he made his mark in the world, he gave it a collection of antiquities, things he thought might have interested him during his school days.[27]

His connection with Harrow ended in the spring of 1816 when, at the age of eighteen, he matriculated into Exeter College, Oxford.[28] Wilkinson's three years at the university must have been an anticlimax to the fruitful time he spent at Harrow, because Oxford was not much of an educational experience in those days, especially for someone with Wilkinson's interests. There was, for example, no ancient history program—indeed, there was scarcely a history program at all. A permanent chair of history had been established during the reign of George I, but the first historians at Oxford belonged to what a subsequent Oxford historian called the "do-nothing school" of history. They seldom wrote or lectured. Someone reported in 1790 that the Professor of Modern History did not teach but deputized someone "who would wait on gentlemen in their own rooms." Edward Gibbon's well-known disparaging comments about the university in his *Memoirs* still applied when Wilkinson went there, though things had just begun to change. The prime minister had appointed the historian Edward Nares to a position in 1813, and this signified a more systematic approach to history at Oxford, for Nares took his duties seriously, though he complained as late as 1835 that only two people had attended one of his lectures.[29] Not until the second half of the nineteenth century were professional historical studies solidly established at Oxford. In the meantime, the university could do little to train someone whose interests were the past, distant places, and different peoples.

Even so, Oxford was not a complete waste of time for Wilkinson. Although it left little intellectual imprint upon him, he made friends and traveled to the Continent during the long vacations. He went to Belgium and France in 1817 and to France and Spain the following year.[30] At Oxford he especially enjoyed the various collections of antiquities around town and spent much of his time sketching the Arundel Marbles.[31] He read, though not deeply, on current events, recent history, and political economy. His greatest literary interest, however, seems to have been the poetry of Lord Byron, which he had begun reading at Harrow where he copied some of Byron's manuscripts.[32] Throughout his subsequent travels, Wilkinson was always drawn to places with Byronic associations.

Despite his guardian's wishes, Wilkinson remained firmly attached to his idea of a military career; indeed, there were few other options open to a young gentleman who did not intend to suffer loss of caste by entering trade—and Wilkinson seems never to have considered that. He hated the idea of a clerical career; law or medicine might have been financially rewarding, but Wilkinson had no real vocation for them, and he did not need to worry about money yet. His initial interest in the navy had, however, transposed to the army; he consulted a relative, Captain (later Major General Sir) Lovell Lovell, who advised him to put his name on the waiting list to purchase a cornetcy in the Fourteenth Light Dragoons.[33] Wilkinson appears to have done this toward the end of 1818, shortly after his twenty-first birthday, so he probably had been biding his time until he came of age and could do what he, not his guardian, wanted.

With his commission arranged, Wilkinson soon terminated his connection with Oxford. Some accounts suggest that his departure may have been hastened by ill health,[34] but if he was well enough to want to go into the army or to take the Grand Tour and spend twelve years in Egypt as he subsequently did, then it is difficult to understand how another year at Oxford would have exceeded his endurance. In any event, the exact conditions under which he left are unclear. Lady Wilkinson wrote that he passed his final examinations but did not wait "to put on his bachelor's gown,"[35] and he referred to his education as being "completed" at Oxford;[36] but this all seems to mean that he never took a degree. There is none recorded for him at Exeter College, and his name appears on neither the mathematical nor the classical honors list, so there may have been some deficiency in his course of study. Also, it was quite common to leave Oxford after three years in those days. A degree was probably the last thing on his mind, for he was in a hurry to travel in Europe and Egypt before going into the army.[37] What he was planning was the Grand Tour, the long, leisurely voyage through Europe that completed the education of a young gentlemen and gave him a taste of the world before he turned his mind to more serious things. During the eigh-

teenth century the Tour had occasionally been extended to such exotic places as Egypt and the Near East. The long years of war with France
had interrupted the tradition of the Tour, but it was begun again in
1814, and Egypt, which became fashionable during the war, was frequently included in the itinerary. Wilkinson had wanted to go there
for years,[38] a desire he may have inherited from his father and James
Grey Jackson. The pages of his notebook show him planning his Tour
in the spring of 1819.[39]

On 25 June of that year he was on his way.[40] After a brief excursion
into Devonshire, he passed once more through Oxford to pay bills
and get letters of introduction for the Continent; then he proceeded
to London and spent some pleasant days. He visited his intended
regiment and saw the Prince Regent and the Duke of Wellington at a
review. He then went to Dover and took a packet to Calais, suffering
"most terribly" during the crossing. His behavior was that of a
young man out to see the sights—or "to see the lions," as he put it—
and have a good time. He walked about Paris, taking notes and
making sketches. A French acquaintance, a lawyer with whom he
had traveled in Spain the summer before, urged him to remain in
Paris and study painting under some unidentified "famous artist,"
but he wanted to travel; soon he was passing through Strasbourg on
his way to Germany and Switzerland. He did, however, begin to devote serious attention to the techniques of surveying, mapmaking,
and fortification, thinking they would help him get a staff appointment when he joined his regiment.[41] As things turned out, the army
never benefited from these skills, but they were very useful to him
in his subsequent activities as a topographical antiquarian.

When he started his travels, he began a notebook, the first of many
that he kept throughout his life; indeed, he would almost never be
without one at hand. The first notebooks are mostly filled with
trivia, a note about a bad road here or a description of a stream with
a "romantic effect" there, and he usually noted the quality of the
local wine. But his special attention was to women whom he evalu-
ated everywhere he went: at London he noted, "The women here are
pretty"; at Nancy there was "the prettiest French woman" he ever
saw—a judgment that must have been only relative, because at
Karlsruhe he saw "the only pretty women" he had seen since he left
England. And so on. It all seems to have been a visual matter, at least
in Stuttgart where he noted, "I have not found any bedfellows here."[42]
These notes about women, incidentally, were heavily crossed out by
the censorial pen that was later applied to the notebooks, perhaps by
Wilkinson or, more likely, by Lady Wilkinson.

As Wilkinson became a more mature traveler, his frivolous notes tended to be replaced by serious observations; his generalizations, shallow and jejune at first, gradually became more perceptive, as when he came to Switzerland and wrote, "The Swiss are in reality the happiest people, the French make themselves happy & the English tho' they could be the happiest people render themselves unhappy by fancying they are so." Inextricably intertwined with his observations were his peculiar social attitudes, as in this entry made at Geneva: "The people of Geneva are a very disagreeable race, I speak of course of the natives excluding the better class which with a trifling change & discrepancy in manners & customs is somewhat the same everywhere. I mean the middle class by which one can more accurately judge a people. The young Genevois are an impudent, affectedly independent, & assuming demirepublican would-be-free-thinking conceited puppyish set."[43] Despite all that, he came to like Geneva well enough to spend the winter of 1819–20 there and record a pleasant stay in his journal. Besides his notebooks, he also kept sketchbooks, a habit he began during his Oxford days. Often he would make a rough sketch in his notebook and work up a more detailed drawing in the sketchbooks but could, if necessary, sketch under the most adverse conditions. It was later said that he made some of his best sketches on horseback. The sketchbooks from 1819 show a high degree of detail and accuracy. They are quite pleasing to the eye.

Wilkinson left Geneva in late February 1820 and passed into Italy. At an observation point he paused to look out at Mount Blanc and the passage to Mount Cenis, "the most superb view I almost ever beheld." Soon he saw the "beautiful city of Turin" below. He spent about a month meandering through northern Italy where he indulged his keen interest in Renaissance art, though depictions of Christian martyrs left him cold: "I w^d rather see a pretty woman (if not a Madona [sic] except in a very few cases) or a pretty cow than St Sebastian pierced by arrows or a St Peter crucified downward."[44]

When he arrived in Rome at the beginning of spring, about the time of Holy Week, his tour took on an intensity that it had lacked before, for the splendor of the ruined Imperial City profoundly impressed him. The change is evident in the pages of his notebook where rambling entries about cities, wine, and women are replaced by sustained descriptions of one monument after another, descriptions that were informed by earlier reading he had done in the works of the art historians Forsythe and Winckelmann. He developed the technique that he later used in Egypt, comparing on-site observations with classical accounts. The delight that he used to take in objects like the Arundel Marbles was now multiplied many times over.

"Ruins in every direction," he wrote delightedly of Tivoli, which was "the most beautiful spot I ever beheld." The Pantheon was "the most beautiful of Roman buildings"; and so on through Rome and the Campania. He sketched the pyramid of Caius Cestus and paused in front of the church of Saint Giovanni in Laterano to look at one of the Egyptian obelisks that had been transported to Rome during the Imperial Era; it was, he noted, "a fine pillar or needle of Egyptian granite covered with figures in the taste of that country."[45] Although he intended to travel to Egypt, he little suspected that he would devote most of the rest of his life to studying just that sort of thing. For the moment, most of his attention was taken by the classical antiquities of Rome.

One of the reasons for his absorption in ancient Rome was the acquaintance he made of Sir William Gell, a remarkable man who was about to alter the course of Wilkinson's life. Gell was, in many ways, much the kind of man that Wilkinson later turned out to be.[46] A skilled artist and a classical scholar, Gell combined both talents in his work. At the turn of the century when English travelers in the eastern Mediterranean were rare and scholars tended to stay at home with their books, Gell traveled extensively in the Levant and did work of pioneering importance there. His *Topography of Troy*[47] was a substantial contribution to the debate about the location, or the very existence, of that legendary city. Lord Byron, an acquaintance of Gell's, wrote in "English Bards,"

Of Dardan tours, let dilettanti tell,
I leave topography to classic Gell.[48]

Not long afterward, a diplomatic mission to the Ionian Islands gave Gell an opportunity to prepare his *Geography and Antiquities of Ithaca.*[49] These two works were extraordinary in that they sought to establish the geographical background of the *Iliad* and the *Odyssey* at a time when most people considered Homer's poems to be complete fabrications set in imaginary places. Many other important publications about the ancient Greek world followed. In 1814 he found himself in need of a patron, so he entered the service of Caroline, Princess of Wales, as her chamberlain and participated in some of her pathetic adventures. In fact, he had just returned from testifying at her trial before the House of Lords when Wilkinson called on him. After leaving the Princess's service, Gell made his home in Italy where he began the work at Pompeii which resulted in his greatest book, *Pompeiana.*[50] At the time of Wilkinson's visit, Gell had recently finished a collaborative study of the walls of Rome.[51]

In Rome Gell lived in a Gothic villa amid the ruins of Domitian's palace on the Capitoline Hill that commanded a magnificent view of the city, ancient and modern.[52] After presenting his letter of introduction, Wilkinson was welcomed into a house that one of Gell's friends described as "the resort of all ranks, ages, and sexes, and [the] mornings one continued levee."[53] Another friend wrote, "His house is the rendezvous of all the distinguished travellers who visit it, where maps, books, and his invaluable advice, are at the service of all who come recommended to his notice. The extent and versatility of his information are truly surprising; and his memory is so tenacious, that the knowledge of any subject once acquired is never forgotten."[54] Gell, though badly crippled by gout, received his visitors in comfortable state, "surrounded by books, drawings, and maps, with a guitar, and two or three dogs."[55] His travels, combined with wide reading and extensive correspondence, gave him a vast store of antiquarian and general learning. His friends called him "Classic Gell." Though widely read, his favorite form of intellectual interchange was conversation. "Placing people of all classes on a footing of easy familiarity, and thus unlocking their confidence, he drew from them a perpetual supply of materials for his own combination."[56] But he was not at all secretive with his learning, delighting in sharing it with others.[57] He happily discussed the antiquities of Rome with Wilkinson, turning what might otherwise have been a superficial visit into a fruitful period of sustained application.

Wilkinson's mind, however, was still set upon his intended army career. The waiting period for purchasing his commission, which he had originally estimated at six months, was turning out to be longer because of all the applicants who were queuing for places, places that were fewer as the army was reduced to peacetime size. After two memorable weeks in Rome, Wilkinson started north again, first to Florence, then to France, and finally back to Geneva, where he fell in with one of his college friends, James Samuel Wiggett, a native of Allanby Park in Berkshire. Wiggett was also making the Tour before beginning an ecclesiastical career. They decided to travel together, planning to return to Rome, pass the winter there, then proceed south to Naples and Sicily, and finally to Egypt.[58]

Wilkinson and Wiggett arrived at Rome in the autumn of 1820. Gell had gone to his Neapolitan residence, but Wilkinson got his address there from one of Gell's friends, Edward Dodwell. Once again Wilkinson plunged into a round of sight-seeing, but by winter's end he was eager to be on his way. "Rome now quite dull," he scribbled in his notebook.[59] He and Wiggett booked passage on a boat for the short coastal sail to Naples, but it turned out to be more difficult than they had anticipated. The Kingdom of the Two Sicilies, of which Naples was the capital, was sealed off because of the Austrian suppression of the liberal revolt that had broken out in the kingdom the year before, and the coast guard turned them back.[60] They spent a few weeks touring northern Italy to give the situation time to settle and then tried again, this time by land. They set off past the tombs that line the Appian Way on 13 June 1821, and reached Naples three and a half days later. They could have made it faster but for the circuitous routes they took to avoid customs houses along the way.

Naples in 1821 was a much bigger and more cosmopolitan city than Rome. Situated on its beautiful bay with Vesuvius smoking in the background, Wilkinson found it "a constant fête de St Cloud." Always attracted to festivals and the like, Wilkinson enjoyed himself immensely in Naples. On the streets, "Pulcinello mal contento," a commedia dell'arte song, caught his attention and ran through his mind for years thereafter. He saw Paganini in concert and was presented to royalty, the decadent Bourbons of Naples. Among the many people he met was James Burton, brother of the distinguished architect Decimus Burton, who intended to leave soon for Egypt to do geological work for the government of the pasha, Muhammad Ali. Burton, Wiggett, and Wilkinson made plans to rendezvous in Cairo. Of course Wilkinson toured Pompeii, which was being excavated from the volcanic ash that had covered it during the great eruption of A.D. 79. Already some of the uncovered buildings showed signs of deterioration from exposure to the atmosphere. The local museums were filled not only with bronze helmets and swords, but also with everyday things that probably appealed even more to someone like Wilkinson who liked to imagine how vanished people had lived. One Greek vase showing the death of Priam especially caught his attention. Decades later when he assembled his own collection of Greek vases, its most important piece would be by the same painter, though he never knew of the association.[61] He, Burton, Wiggett, and some other friends climbed Vesuvius and explored the crater of the volcano, which was quiet at that moment. Wilkinson made a charming colored sketch of them all picnicking there, wine bottles and food in the foreground. They left at a good moment, for a sudden release of fiery gas nearly trapped and killed them on their way down. The gas was so corrosive that it changed the color of his notebook.[62]

The crucial element in Wilkinson's visit to Naples was the renewal of his acquaintance with Sir William Gell, who welcomed his young friend and took him to see many of the archaeological sites—

Pompeii, Stabia, and nearby Nola where the Emperor Augustus had died. Wilkinson naturally looked up to the famous scholar, but he was also making a very good impression upon Gell. Gell noted that Wilkinson had a genuine enthusiasm for antiquities, a deep love of classical learning, and the ability to sketch accurately.[63] One day when Wilkinson was plying him with antiquarian questions, Gell said, "You seem to be much interested in these matters. Why do you not take up some branch of antiquarian research, and instead of going to Egypt as a mere wandering traveller, why not turn your attention to its antiquities?"[64] Wilkinson replied that he would gladly do so if only he had sufficient knowledge. Gell offered to supply the knowledge: he proposed that if Wilkinson would give up his idea of going to Sicily and spend the time at Naples instead, then Gell would loan him the necessary books and teach him everything then known about Egypt. Wilkinson eagerly accepted, and Wiggett good-naturedly agreed to wait.[65]

There probably was no one in the world at that time better qualified than Sir William Gell to teach Wilkinson about Egypt. Not only had he read all of the published work, but he also corresponded regularly with men who were well placed to tell him about the latest discoveries, among them Thomas Young and Henry Salt. Thomas Young, George Butler's friend, was making substantial progress toward translating the language of the ancient Egyptians; already he understood something of the nature of hieroglyphic script and had managed to read some royal names in it. Henry Salt, though not a scholar of Young's stature, was the British consul-general in Egypt and could provide Gell with first-hand information about archaeological developments along the Nile. Egypt was much on Gell's mind in those days; indeed, he was contemplating going there himself—"I have determined upon going to Egypt as soon as circumstances permit," he had written to Young the spring before—but events prevented the trip.[66] Wilkinson's appearance must have been a great opportunity for him, for if he could not go to Egypt himself, then the next best thing was to send someone like Wilkinson who could report to him. As for Wilkinson, he was preparing to go to Egypt at a particularly promising time. But if we are to understand why the opportunity was so great at that particular moment and to appreciate the tradition in which Wilkinson was preparing to work, then we must pause to examine the development of Egyptology.

The Origins of Egyptology

NO VANISHED CIVILIZATION ever left as much curiosity in its wake as ancient Egypt. The great stone monuments along the Nile, the elaborate preparations for afterlife, and the stately yet enigmatic representations of themselves in their art, all made the ancient Egyptians seem eminently worth knowing, yet they remained unknowable. Their secrets, it seemed, were boldly displayed in their hieroglyphs, yet hidden, for no one could read them. Having passed into the realms of myth and legend, enshrouded with mystery, ancient Egypt exerted an allure from remote antiquity.[1]

The ancient Greeks were the first to be drawn to it, for the splendor of Egypt, albeit greatly faded by then, penetrated even the gloom of the Greek Dark Ages. When Achilles refused Agamemnon's request to return to battle and declined his gifts he chose these words to emphasize his resolution:

> Nay, not for all the wealth
> Of Thebes in Egypt, where in ev'ry hall
> There lieth treasure vast; a hundred are
> Her gates, and warriors by each issue forth
> Two hundred, each of them with car and steeds.[2]

The primary attraction of Egypt to the Greeks was knowledge. As the antiquarian Diodorus Siculus noted in the first century B.C., "Many of the customs that obtained in ancient days among the Egyptians have not only been accepted by the present inhabitants but have aroused no little admiration among the Greeks; and for that reason those men who have won the greatest repute in intellectual things have been eager to visit Egypt in order to acquaint themselves with its laws and institutions, which they consider to be worthy of note."³ To this end, a series of Greek travelers ranging from mythical to historical traveled to Egypt. Orpheus came, and "brought back from Egypt most of his mystic ceremonies, the orgiastic rites that accompanied his wanderings, and the fabulous account of his experiences in Hades."⁴ Homer also was thought to have traveled there, as were the lawgivers Lycurgus and Solon. Better documented was the visit of the antiquarian Hecataeus. When Hecataeus boasted to the priests at Thebes that he could trace his ancestry back sixteen generations to a god, they scoffed at the notion of divine descent and showed that their high priest had a genealogy that extended three hundred forty-five generations, with no gods among them.⁵ Thus was a Greek's conception of high antiquity extended.

The Father of History, Herodotus, came to Egypt around the middle of the fifth century B.C. when it was a province of the Persian Empire and left the first surviving comprehensive account of it in the second book of his *History.* Carefully distinguishing what he saw from what he heard, Herodotus ranged over many facets of his subject, including history, plants, animals, the Nile, monuments, and the construction and function of the pyramids. "There is," he wrote, "no other country that possesses so many wonders, nor any that has such a number of works which defy description."⁶ The nineteenth-century antiquarians later emulated both his curiosity and his range of interest.

Plato, who also may have traveled in Egypt, wrote of the god Thoth who "invented numbers and arithmetic and geometry and astronomy, also draughts and dice, and most important of all, letters."⁷ Plato possibly derived from Egypt the social ideas that were incorporated into *The Republic.* Diodorus Siculus listed some other Greeks who traveled in Egypt and told what they learned there:

Pythagoras learned from Egyptians his teachings about the gods, his geometrical propositions and theory of numbers, as well as the transmigration of the soul into every living thing. Democritus also, as they assert, spent five years among them and was instructed in many matters relating to astrology. Oenopides likewise passed some time with the priests and astrologers and learned among other things about the orbit of the sun, that it has an oblique course and moves in a direction opposite to that of the other stars. Like the others, Eudoxus studied astrology with them and acquired a notable fame for the great amount of useful knowledge which he disseminated among the Greeks.⁸

It has been noted that the ancient Greeks admitted their intellectual debt to Egypt much more easily than many scholars are willing to do today.[9]

Egypt was conquered by Alexander the Great in 332 B.C., but the Ptolemies, the new ruling family that emerged after Alexander's death, adopted many of the trappings of the pharaohs. Though purely Macedonian, they were portrayed in ancient Egyptian royal attire, had their names transliterated into hieroglyphs, and took a place within the framework of Egyptian religion. Because of their religious activities we have the Rosetta Stone, a decree issued in 196 B.C. by the Council of Priests to record some good deeds that Ptolemy V had done and the honors that the council proposed to pay him in return. This decree, written in ancient Egyptian and classical Greek, eventually became the key piece of evidence in deciphering the hieroglyphs after the ability to read them was lost during the late antique period. An important literary work of the Ptolemaic era was a history of Egypt written by the priest Manetho for Ptolemy II. Unfortunately, it survived only in fragments incorporated into the works of subsequent writers, but Manetho's list of kings became the framework for Egyptian chronology.

In 30 B.C., after defeating Mark Antony and Cleopatra, the emperor Augustus "added Egypt to the Empire of the Roman people," to use the words of his political testament. Egypt, however, became a unique province, outside the normal pattern of imperial provincial administration; it was, in effect, the personal property of the emperor who, conscious of its strategic and economic importance, permitted no senator or member of the imperial family to visit it without his permission. Like the Ptolemies, the emperor ruled in Egypt as the pharaoh, his name written hieroglyphs in cartouches with the appropriate honorifics attached. Wilkinson always thought imperial Roman cartouches were ugly.

The enormous influence of this peculiar province upon the Roman Empire can be demonstrated in several ways. Egyptian religions circulated throughout the empire, and Roman pilgrims often went to Egypt to sleep near the temples, hoping to experience the ancient religion. The cult of Isis was especially popular, despite a nasty scandal during the principate of Tiberius.[10] The Romans also were fascinated by Egyptian obelisks, the tall, slender monuments that are thought to have represented the rays of the sun, and the emperors had several of them transported to Rome and Constantinople. For example, the Lateran obelisk that Wilkinson paused to admire had once stood in front of Karnak Temple at Thebes. It was brought to Alexandria by the emperor Constantine and transported to Rome in

A.D. 357 by Constantius. He had it erected in the Circus Maximus, although it was subsequently moved to the church of Saint Giovanni in Laterano.[11]

Egypt had the greatest influence on the Romans who traveled there, either as tourists or officials in the course of their duties. Such travel was facilitated by peaceful conditions and efficient internal transport that linked Egypt closely with the rest of the Roman world. The panegyrist Aelius Aristides wrote, "Now indeed it is possible for Hellene or non-Hellene to travel wherever he will, easily, just as if passing from fatherland to fatherland. Neither Cilician Gates nor narrow sandy approaches to Egypt through Arab country, nor inaccessible mountains, nor immense stretches of river, nor inhospitable tribes of barbarians cause terror, but for security it suffices to be a Roman citizen, or rather to be one of those united under [Roman] hegemony."[12] Large numbers of Romans traveled in Egypt and left their names on the ancient monuments, just as many Victorian travelers did in the nineteenth century. The pyramids were popular, as was the crocodile pool at Fayyum. The greatest attraction of all, however, was Thebes which, besides its many other monuments, had the two so-called Colossi of Memnon. One of these enormous statues—believed to be representations of the Homeric hero, but actually Amen-hotep III—made musical sounds at dawn, sounds described as similar to a breaking harp string.[13] Romans often rose early to hear this phenomenon and covered the lower part of the colossus with inscriptions like the one that reads, "I came at night to listen to the voice of the very divine Memnon, and I heard it, I, Catulus, chief of the Thebaïd."[14] Even emperors came to hear Memnon. One of the more elaborate inscriptions tells how Hadrian listened in vain one morning, but the statue spoke to him on another day, indeed spoke thrice, as if to atone for its previous silence. Some years later another emperor, Septimius Severus, came to hear the statue. It was mute. In an attempt to propitiate Memnon, Septimius had it repaired, an act that somehow silenced it forever.

Among the several writers of the Roman era who turned their attention to Egypt were the geographer Strabo, the natural historian Pliny, and the historian Ammianus Marcellinus. Another was Plutarch, who supplied the most comprehensive and detailed account of Egyptian religion in his *On Isis and Osiris*. In Plutarch we can see most clearly the assumptions of classical writers about religion. First, they believed that the gods existed and were concerned with people; also, they thought that foreign gods were the same as their own, but with different names; finally, they believed that under the superficial appearances of myth and ritual were deep truths that could be sought and found.[15] From these assumptions developed two important thrusts, both of which were at least purportedly involved with Egyptian religion: Neoplatonism and Hermeticism.

Neoplatonism was a synthesis of elements from Platonic, Aristotelian, Pythagorean, and Stoic philosophies. Its origins were considerably earlier, but it received its classical formulation in the third century A.D. in the works of Plotinus and Porphyry, and it was carried a stage further toward mysticism and magic by Iamblichus in the fourth century. The connection of Neoplatonism to Egypt came partly from the residence of Plotinus' teacher, Ammonius Saccas, at Alexandria, for which reason Neoplatonism was also known as "the school of Alexandria."[16] A more important connection, however, was the references to Egyptian religion in some of the Neoplatonist writings.

Hermeticism, like Neoplatonism, was rooted in Hellenistic times, but the texts that became known as the *Corpus Hermeticum* were all composed between A.D. 100 and A.D. 300 by Greeks in Egypt.[17] The Hermetic writers, who wrote under the collective name Hermes Trismegistus, identified the Greek god Hermes with the Egyptian god Thoth, whom they promoted from his rather secondary rank as god of letters to a paramount position as the essential intelligence of the universe. The texts of the *Corpus Hermeticum*, though claiming to be of remotest antiquity, were in fact a mixture of Platonism, Stoicism, popular philosophy, and probably some Jewish and Near Eastern elements as well. Their subject matter ranged from religion and philosophy to magic and alchemy. Whether any genuine ancient Egyptian elements found their way into the *Corpus* is debated among scholars. The Hermetic writings were, however, given a powerful stamp of authenticity by the Church Fathers who believed that Hermes Trismegistus was a real person who had lived around the time of Moses. Lactantius identified him as one of the most important of the gentile writers who foresaw the coming of Christianity.[18] Augustine also was impressed, writing, "This Hermes says much of God according to the truth."[19]

The Muslim conquest of Egypt in A.D. 642 broke the unity of the Mediterranean world that had so impressed Aelius Aristides and that persisted, at least to some degree, even after the collapse of the Roman Empire in the west. Even so, a few western travelers, primarily religious pilgrims, still managed to make their way through. Bernard the Wise and two companions came in A.D. 870 on their way to Jerusalem. Bernard saw the Pyramids which he, like some others before him, believed to be the granaries that Joseph had built in Egypt. The difficulties that Christian travelers faced in those days are shown in the experience of Bernard, who was imprisoned in Cairo and had to bribe his way out. Because of such conditions, there were few European travelers to Egypt during the European Dark Ages.

Pilgrims began to visit Egypt more frequently during the Crusades. Even after the Crusaders were expelled, pilgrims continued to come, and many accounts of their experiences appeared. The most famous and influential was *The Voiage and Travaile of Sir John Maundevile, K*[t], which appeared in the fourteenth century. Ostensibly a guidebook based upon the experiences of its purported author, a knight from St. Albans, it was in reality a fraud, a compilation of various sources. Even so, it circulated widely. The fictitious Sir John wrote of the Pyramids,

And thei ben made of Ston, fulle wel made of Masonnes craft; of the whiche two ben marveylouse grete and hye; and the tother ne ben not so grete. And every [one] hathe a Gate, for to entre with inne . . . And with inne thei ben alle full of Serpentes. And aboven . . . with outen, ben many scriptures of dyverse Langages. And sum Men seyn, that thei ben Sepultures of grete Lordes, that weren sometyme, but that is not trewe, for alle the commoun rymour and speche is of alle the peple there, bothe fer and nere, that thei ben the Garneres of Joseph.[20]

Perhaps the best of the genuine pilgrims' accounts was the *Evagatorium in Terram Sanctum* of Felix Fabri, a Dominican monk from Ulm. Fabri and his companions began at Jerusalem and went to Egypt through the Sinai. There was a bad moment when they thought the Saracens might seize their wine supply—"If we had been deprived of our wine we should not have attempted the pilgrimage," he wrote—but the danger passed and all went well. In Egypt, Fabri saw the Pyramids, which he correctly identified as sepulchral monuments, and he noted several monuments in Alexandria, including one of the pair of obelisks that later became known as Cleopatra's Needles; the other obelisk, which was eventually transported to London over Wilkinson's objections, was on its side, covered by sand. The visible obelisk was, Fabri wrote, "a very remarkable column, all of one stone, yet of wonderful height and width. On the four sides were carved men and animals and birds from top to the bottom; and no one knows what these figures signify."[21]

Pilgrims' accounts are limited both geographically and intellectually. The pilgrimage route never took them south of the Pyramids, so the vast majority of ancient Egyptian monuments escaped their notice entirely; also, their observations were conditioned by their theological preconceptions.Two notable accounts by people outside these limitations were written by Rabbi Benjamin of Tudela and Abdel Latif. Benjamin of Tudela came to Egypt on his eastern journey of 1165–1171. He entered Egypt not from the north, as most did, but from the south, through Abyssinia. His observations in the south showed him that the annual inundation of the Nile was caused by rain in the Abyssinian highlands. His contribution to the study of the Pyramids was his opinion that they were built by magic, a belief long held by the Arabs. Abdel Latif was a physician from Baghdad who became a teacher in Cairo around 1200. His account is especially significant because he observed many monuments in a relatively undamaged state. The Sphinx had not been mutilated when he saw it, and the Great Pyramid still had its casing stones.

The political and economic relationship of Egypt to the rest of the world altered in the early sixteenth century. In 1501 the Portuguese sank the Egyptian fleet at Calicut, and in 1508 they attacked and destroyed the Egyptian Red Sea fleet. That diminished the importance of Suez as a transshipment point on the Eastern trade that subsequently was conducted, initially under Portuguese auspices, around the Cape of Africa. This did not, however, mean economic isolation for Egypt, for in 1517 the Turks invaded and added Egypt to their empire. The new regime actually put commercial relations with Europe on a more secure basis than they had been before. Places like Venice that had been heavily committed to the Eastern spice trade tended to lose by the change, but countries like England and France that were interested in Egyptian markets gained from it. Commercial travelers became more numerous in Egypt, though religious pilgrims still came.

French travelers were the most numerous during the first part of the sixteenth century, but the English came in increasing numbers toward the century's end. The voyages of the merchant vessel Tyger brought several observant travelers to Egypt.[22] Throughout the century there is a marked shift in emphasis in travel accounts away from incidental observation in the course of a pilgrimage to direct curiosity about Egypt and its monuments. This is apparent in several instances, but most explicitly in an anonymous manuscript entitled "Voyage Made in the Year 1589 from Cairo to Ebrim by Way of the Nile": "For some years I had a lively desire to see the province of the Saïd as far as the end of the land of Egypt, and my sole reason was to see so many superb buildings, churches, colossal statues, needles, and columns."[23] Beginning with Laurence Aldersey in 1586, English travelers began to publish their experiences. Aldersey mentions many of the sights that later became standard in travelers' accounts. Of the Pyramids he wrote, "The monuments be high and in forme 4-square, and every of the squares is as long as a man may shoot a roving arrowe, and as high as a Church. I sawe also the ruines of the city of Memphis hard by those Pyramids."[24] Soon afterward came the account of John Evesham, one of the many travelers who sailed to Egypt aboard the Tyger. Evesham wrote of Alexandria, "The said citie of Alexandria is an old thing decayed or ruinated . . . within the said city there is a pillar of Marble, called by the Turks, King Pharaoe's Needle, and it is foure square, every square is twelve foote, and it is in height 90 foote."[25]

While these things were happening in Egypt, there were also some developments in Europe that heightened interest in Egyptian antiquity. One was the revival of Hermeticism after the *Corpus Hermeticum* was translated from Greek to Latin by Marsilio Ficino in 1460. The manuscript arrived just as Ficino was about to begin translating Plato, but Ficino's patron, Cosimo de'Medici, ordered him to put Plato aside and translate Hermes Trismegistus first. That Plato should be left waiting in favor of Hermes Trismegistus shows the high esteem in which the Hermetic writings were held.[26] The *Corpus Hermeticum* went through numerous editions and was translated into many languages. Its influence was both profound and persistent. Even after Isaac Casaubon conclusively proved in 1614 that it had been written not in remotest antiquity but in the early Christian Era, scholars continued to regard it as a document of ancient Egypt. Athanasius Kircher wrote in 1652, "Hermes Trismegistus, the Egyptian, who first instituted the hieroglyphs, thus becoming the prince and parent of all Egyptian theology and philosophy, was the first and most ancient among the Egyptians and first rightly thought of divine things; and engraved his opinion for all eternity on lasting stones and huge rocks. Thence Orpheus, Musaeus, Linus, Pythagoras, Plato, Eudoxus, Parmenides, Melissus, Homerus, Euripides, and others learned rightly of God and of divine things. . . . And this Trismegistus was the first who in his *Pimander* and *Asclepius* asserted that God is One and Good, whom the rest of the philosophers followed."[27] Casaubon was ignored even into the nineteenth century when Wilkinson accepted, with slight reservations, the high antiquity of the Hermetic works, thereby causing himself much fruitless speculation.[28]

During the seventeenth century a new category of visitor appeared in Egypt, the gentleman traveler. These were well-to-do men with classical educations and occasionally even some knowledge of Arabic. They took notes and made sketches. George Sandys, famous for his translation of Ovid's *Metamorphoses,* came to Egypt in 1610. As he passed through Alexandria he visited Cleopatra's Needle, and he was the first to notice another obelisk lying in the sand beside it. Passing upriver, he made the first accurate drawings of the Pyramids at Giza. Deeply influenced by the Hermetic writings, he copied some hieroglyphs, but his preconceptions rendered his representations of them quite fantastic. Another notable seventeenth-century traveler was the Oxford professor John Greaves who came to Egypt with definite scholarly objectives. His *Pyramidographia* (1646) is the first scientific study of the Pyramids. He measured them accurately, discarded the notion that they were Joseph's granaries, and assigned the correct motive for their construction: "this sprang from the Theology of the Egyptians, who believed that as long as the Body endured, so long the Soul continued with it."[29]

Even more travelers came to Egypt in the eighteenth century when curiosity about Egyptian antiquities began to increase. Among the British travelers, three stand above the rest: Richard Pococke, Frederick Norden (a Danish naval captain who later made his home in England), and James Bruce. Pococke and Norden came during the 1730s. Traveling separately and unknown to each other, though their boats passed one night on the Nile, they were the first British travelers to venture far south of Cairo and see the monuments of Upper Egypt. Thebes impressed them, especially the Valley of the Kings. Pococke and Norden both published accounts of their travels; the plates in Norden's book are better, but Pococke's show a wider range of subjects and convey more feel for Egyptian life.[30] James Bruce, one of the increasing number of gentlemen who were coming to Egypt as part of their Grand Tour, traveled there in the late 1760s and early 1770s. An important innovation by Bruce and other eighteenth-century tourists was their practice of hiring professional artists, usually Frenchmen or Italians (English artists not being good enough), to accompany them. Bruce's artist was an Italian named Luigi Balugani, a good artist who died on the journey, but received only scant notice as "my clerk" when Bruce published his book. Partly because of Balugani's efforts, Bruce's book contained more accurate reproductions of ancient Egyptian art than anything that had preceded it, but it was received with disbelief.[31] The pictures, it was thought, were too perfect; it seemed that they had to be highly idealized representations. This was unfair to Bruce, but the criticism could have been justly applied to the work of many other eighteenth- and early nineteenth-century copyists.

Surveying the course of eighteenth-century Egyptological activity in Great Britain, we may discern a peak followed by a decline. The peak coincided with the publication of Pococke's and Norden's books and with the establishment of an Egyptian Society in London. This society was founded in 1741 with the object of "promoting and preserving Egyptian and other ancient learning."[32] The president, or "sheik" as the society called its presiding officer, was the Earl of Sandwich, who had traveled to Egypt as part of his Grand Tour. Pococke and Norden both were members, as was the distinguished antiquarian William Stukeley, who, though he had never been to Egypt, took a great interest in the society and delivered several papers before it. Despite such participation, the society met for less than a year and a half, and the pages of its big minute book, now in the British Library, were never filled.[33]

The failure of the Egyptian Society did not mean complete cessation of all British interest in ancient Egypt, for many of the society's members were also members of the Society of Antiquaries. Occasionally they addressed Egyptological matters within the latter organization, but overall interest nevertheless slackened. Part of the problem was lack of adequate information. Also, internal conditions in Egypt were too difficult for the kind of systematic study that was needed. An occasional aristocratic Tourist with a large retinue might travel in relative comfort and safety, but most foreign travelers had to take care where and how they went. Another problem was the interruption of the Tour, first by the Seven Years' War and the American War of Independence and later by the lengthy wars with the French Republic and Napoleon. Finally, the European public was not conditioned to demand adequate information, because ancient Egypt had not yet made a deep impression upon the popular imagination. A good book like Bruce's inspired disbelief, not interest. What was needed was an event that would focus popular attention on Egypt. That event came at the end of the century when Napoleon Bonaparte invaded Egypt.

It is usually considered that Egyptology began with Napoleon's Egyptian expedition. If that is true, then Wilkinson and Egyptology were born at almost the same time, for he was only seven months old when Napoleon and his army sailed for Egypt in 1798. From what has gone before, however, it should be clear that people had been studying Egypt for at least two centuries before Napoleon, though Napoleon's expedition was nevertheless a landmark, for it awakened the sustained interest in ancient Egypt that has continued until the present.

Napoleon brought with him to Egypt not only a powerful army but also the famous Commission on the Sciences and Arts. The men of the commission were experts in many fields: engineering, surveying, hydraulics, mathematics, languages—in every skill that was needed to make them capable organizers and administrators of a new colony. Among them were scholars and artists whose function was to study Egypt's past. By an order of 22 August 1798, Napoleon created the Institute of Egypt as headquarters for all of his scholars, and he outlined its purposes: "(1) the progress and propagation of the sciences in Egypt; (2) research, study, and publication of natural, industrial, and historical data on Egypt; (3) advising on various questions concerning which the government shall consult it."[34] This endeavor represented the ideals of the French Enlightenment. It was the beginning of systematic study of ancient Egypt.

Napoleon's army was quickly victorious. Moving under the army's protection, the French scholars could observe in safety. Of course there were some problems. They had to move when the army moved and stop when it stopped. That often meant spending long periods of time in places of no interest, then hurrying past important sites. But the opportunity was unprecedented. Napoleon's scholars knew it, and they made the most of it. As they followed the army up and down the Nile Valley, they recorded in words and pictures the monuments of ancient Egypt. Soon not only the scholars, but also the rest of the army became interested in the work. The hydraulic engineers became especially excited about antiquities and soon forsook waterworks to help make sketches and surveys of monuments instead. When no pencils were left, bullets were melted to make drawing lead. This rank and file interest in antiquities led to the expedition's most important discovery, the Rosetta Stone.

A French soldier, whose name is unrecorded, was building a fortification near Rashid, or Rosetta as it was called by Europeans, when he uncovered a black basalt stone covered with three inscriptions. One was in Greek, the other in hieroglyphs, and the third in the script now known as demotic. This was a multilingual inscription, the best aid for deciphering an unknown language, for the known language, in this case Greek, could be used to decipher the unknown. The soldier's supervising officer recognized the importance of the stone and sent it to the Institute of Egypt. The *Courier d'Egypte,* a French newspaper published in Cairo, soon reported, "This stone offers great interest for the study of hieroglyphic characters; perhaps it will give us the key at last." It was indeed a key, though the difficulties of hieroglyphic script in general, and of that inscription in particular, delayed translation for many years. Meanwhile the Rosetta Stone tantalized the imaginations of the many who tried to translate it but could not find the correct approach.

Despite Napoleon's early victories, his Egyptian expedition failed. Severed from France by the disastrous Battle of the Nile shortly after his arrival and thwarted in Syria, Napoleon abandoned his army and returned to Paris to seek new opportunities for himself. The army surrendered not long afterward to the British. The new conquerors of Egypt appreciated the work of the French scholars and left them mostly undisturbed, though many of the antiquities, among them the Rosetta Stone, were shipped to London where they formed the nucleus of the British Museum's superb Egyptological collection. But whether the artifacts went to England or France, copies were made for scholars everywhere to consult. A stream of information about ancient Egypt suddenly poured into Europe.

The first notable book to result from the expedition was *Voyages dans la Basse et la Haute Egypte* by Vivant Denon, one of the expedition's scholars and later director of the Louvre. Published in 1802, Denon's *Voyages* became enormously popular and was immediately translated into many languages, including English. The *Edinburgh Review* noted, "Few publications, we believe, have ever obtained so extensive a circulation in the same space of time as these travels."[35] Wilkinson read it repeatedly. Denon's book prepared the way for the great multivolume *Description de l'Egypte*, which was edited by Denon's colleague, Edmé Jomard, and began to appear in 1809.[36] The *Description* created a sensation. Its many plates, clearly and excitingly executed, provided the most extensive panorama of ancient Egypt ever published.

These revelations about ancient Egypt stimulated desire for more, and now it was much easier to conduct systematic investigations on the spot because conditions for Europeans in Egypt improved enormously after Napoleon's expedition. The British army of occupation soon left, after which the pasha of Egypt, the remarkable and enigmatic Muhammad Ali, developed a much more effective government than anything that had preceded it. One of Wilkinson's acquaintances, R. R. Madden, described the change in a passage reminiscent of Aelius Aristides: "Travellers, so far as their personal safety is concerned, have reason to speak in the highest terms of the security afforded them by the measures of Mohammed Ali, for their protection in every part of Egypt. I do not know of any European country where one may travel with greater safety than in Egypt. Robberies, and murders for the sake of plunder, are almost unknown."[37] Young gentlemen again made Egypt part of their Grand Tours, businessmen came in larger numbers, and occasional scholar-travelers sought out the monuments that had recently been revealed to them. The British Consulate became more influential as its role expanded to assist growing numbers of British merchants and travelers and to protect British interests.

In 1815 an enthusiastic amateur Egyptologist was appointed consul-general in Egypt. This was Sir William Gell's acquaintance, Henry Salt.[38] Salt, a former student at the Royal Academy, had been making his living as a portrait painter when George Annesley (Viscount Valentia) hired him as secretary and draftsman for an expedition to the East in 1802. During that expedition Salt visited Egypt and Abyssinia, among other places. When he returned to England, the government sent him back to Abyssinia on a diplomatic mission. The mission failed, but Salt wrote a successful book, *Voyage to Abyssinia*, that was published in 1814. The following year Lord Castlereagh appointed him consul-general for Egypt, and he took up his post the year after that. When he passed through Italy he met Johan David Akerblad who wrote to Thomas Young, "I had the pleasure a few months ago to see Mr. Salt on his passage to Naples, where he embarked for Malta and Egypt. He is certainly a very active man, and though he may not discover the duplicate of the Rosetta Stone, he will probably succeed in other researches in the very interesting country where he resides, in a character which undoubtably enables him to do more than any common traveller."[39]

Though he has subsequently received little credit for it, Salt did indeed use his time and position well in Egypt, for the sketches he made there are the first drawings by an antiquarian that are sufficiently accurate to be considered reliable Egyptological evidence.[40] But most of Salt's energies went into collecting antiquities, which he pursued on a large scale. His motivations were a genuine interest in ancient Egypt and the desire to make a fortune in the wholesale antique trade. Nowadays we take a dim view of such diplomatic traders, but there was nothing unethical about it in Salt's time; for example, Sir William Hamilton had made a name for himself as a connoisseur of ancient vases while selling them at a good profit during his long service as minister plenipotentiary in Naples.

Salt employed a large team to work permanently at important archaeological sites and to range up and down the river in search of special opportunities. The most famous of his agents was the traveler Giovanni Battista Belzoni, who obtained such treasures as the colossal bust of Ramses II, now in the British Museum, and the alabaster sarcophagus from the tomb of Seti I, which he discovered and which was known as Belzoni's Tomb for a long time thereafter.[41] Salt and Belzoni eventually quarreled, and Belzoni later wrote a book portraying Salt in an unfavorable, even ludicrous, light. But Salt had many other employees, such as Giovanni d'Athanasi, the manager of his permanent operation on the west bank at Thebes, on whom he could rely. When he marketed his first big collection, Salt found that London would not support his work as cheerfully as he had been led to believe, forcing him to sell at a loss.[42] Undeterred, he was busy accumulating his second collection when Wilkinson met him.

Salt had a formidable rival in the French consul-general, an Italian named Bernardino Drovetti. A clever diplomat whose counsel was highly regarded by the pasha, Drovetti also was a ruthless collector of antiquities. Like Salt, he headed a large, well-organized team of collectors. The two consuls or their employees frequently clashed over some especially prized antiquity. Sir Richard Burton described their rivalry in his memoir of Belzoni: "Nile-land was then, as now, a field for plunder; fortunes were made by digging, not gold, but antiques; and the archaeological field became a battle-plain for two armies of Dragomans and Fellah-navvies. One was headed by the redoubtable Salt; the other owned the command of Drovetti, or Drouetti, the Piedmontese Consul and Collector, whose sharp Italian brain had done much to promote the great Pasha's interests."[43] Actual combat seemed likely when two of Drovetti's agents, enraged over the removal of an obelisk that they considered theirs, accosted Belzoni near Luxor, assaulted his servant, and held a shotgun on him. Such aggressive competition could not continue indefinitely, so the two consuls arranged a modus vivendi described by an independent French collector in 1822: "They concluded a peace treaty. Like kings who, in accommodating their differences, want to preclude all causes that could renew them, they took a river for the border of the respective possessions that they granted themselves in Egypt. For two or three years now, it is the flow of the Nile that has separated them."[44] But the situation actually was more complex than that, as an English traveler commented that same year: "The whole of ancient Thebes is the private property of the English and French consuls; a line of demarcation is drawn through every temple, and those buildings that have hitherto withstood the attacks of *Barbarians*, will not resist the speculation of civilized cupidity, virtuosi, and antiquaries."[45] There were still problems, but the rival consuls had at least learned to coexist.

The exploits of Salt and Drovetti sometimes make sad reading these days. An archaeologist, or anyone who cares about the past, resents grave robbers and artifact hunters, for these people do irreparable damage to the remains of the past. It seems tragic that for

more than a century the Nile Valley was subjected to the depredations of people like Salt and Drovetti, their hired plunderers, and
others even more destructive. This, however, was the prearchae-
ological age. Many professional collectors were well-intentioned
people who thought they were performing a useful service to scholarship while making money. It is, nevertheless, pleasant to note that
Wilkinson and his circle tended to hold themselves aloof from such
practices.

Even in ancient times people broke into tombs, for human nature
has never allowed wealth to lie long interred. Almost as soon as anything was entombed, grave robbers began trying to extract it. A series of documents from the reign of Ramses IX (ca. 1120 B.C.) records
the experiences of a commission appointed to investigate systematic
grave robbing in the necropolis of Thebes, the area where Wilkinson
later lived and labored. One reported, "The tombs and chambers in
which the beatified of old, the citizenesses and citizens, rest on the
west bank of Thebes: it was found that the thieves had broken into
all of them, and dragged their occupants from their coffins and sarcophagi, so that they were lying on the desert, and had stolen their
funerary furniture, which had been given to them, as well as their
gold, silver, and the fittings which were in their coffins."[46] The commission found that many high officials, including the governor of
Western Thebes, were implicated in the robberies. Amon-pa-nefer, a
stonemason accused of grave robbing, told how he had bribed an official to let him go free. Amon-pa-nefer went on to confess, "And I, as
well as the other robbers who are with me, have continued to this
day in the practice of robbing the tombs of the nobles and the people
of the land who rule in the west of Thebes. And a large number of
the men of the land rob them also."[47] Tomb robbing is almost as old
as tomb making.

During the millennia between Amon-pa-nefer and Napoleon, the
antiquities of Egypt suffered many depredations, not just from looters
but also from intolerant Christians and from Muslims who attacked
statues and murals that they considered graven images. Gangs of
militant monks who lived near Alexandria were especially notable
vandals, though their destruction usually was visited upon temples
of living cults, such as that of Serapis, whose temple they destroyed
sometime around the end of the fourth century A.D. Also, builders
tended to see ancient monuments as convenient quarries. The casing stones, which once made the Pyramids smooth and unbearably
bright at mid-day, were used to build medieval Cairo. The so-called
Labyrinth, the mortuary temple of Amen-em-het III, considered by

Herodotus to be an even greater wonder than the Pyramids, was completely consumed by generations of lime burners. While Wilkinson was in Egypt, stone for the factories that were built at Muhammad Ali's orders was frequently taken from temples. Finally, people often lived in tombs and temples, thereby subjecting them to the wear and tear of daily life. But what happened after Napoleon was systematic pillage and destruction on an unprecedented scale.

There is some consolation in the fact that many of the antiquities that were taken from Egypt during the nineteenth century eventually found their way to museums where they could be protected and appreciated—indeed, many artifacts were probably saved by being removed from Egypt—but even in those cases there was a loss that could never be made good. Archaeologists want to know the context within which an object was found, for that is itself evidence of paramount importance. To that end they keep careful records, because the very process of excavation destroys the context. But the collectors could at best give only vague reports of the provenance of their objects and often not even that, for many antiquities were purchased from Arabs who naturally did not want to reveal the source of their livelihood. This is not, however, to say that the Arabs were the only ones so elusive. Wilkinson's young friend Alexander Henry Rhind recorded a conversation with "two distinguished travellers of those days, whose names are well known in connection with Egyptian research." These men, one of whom was probably Wilkinson, recalled trying to persuade one of Henry Salt's agents to show them an untouched tomb that he had recently discovered. He refused, and even their offers to pay him well could not change his mind.[48] Indiscriminate collecting eventually led to the sad situation that Rhind described: "For many of the Egyptian sepulchral antiquities scattered over Europe, there exists no record to determine even the part of the country where they were exhumed. Of many more it is only known from what necropolis they were obtained. And of a very few can it be stated from what tomb, and under what circumstances they were discovered."[49]

A more pleasant story in the development of Egyptology is the decipherment of the hieroglyphs, which became the great mystery as knowledge and curiosity about Egypt increased. Even during classical times the hieroglyphs were the subject of speculation, much of it erroneous, though Egyptian priests could still read them and could have explained them to anyone who asked. For example, the classical writers all followed the mistaken but already popular notion that the hieroglyphs were a symbolic language; typical in this respect was the historian Ammianus Marcellinus who wrote in the fourth century A.D.,

> For not as nowadays, when fixed and easy series of letters ex-
> presses whatever the mind of man may conceive, did the ancient
> Egyptians also write; but individual characters stood for individ-
> ual nouns and verbs; and sometimes they meant whole phrases.
> The principle of this thing for a time it will suffice to illustrate
> with these two examples: by a vulture they represent the word
> "nature," because as natural history records, no males can be
> found among these birds; and under the figure of a bee making
> honey they designate "a king," showing by this imagery that in a
> ruler sweetness should be combined with a sting as well; and
> there are many similar instances.[50]

The opportunity to correct these mistaken notions ended in the sixth century A.D. when the emperor Justinian closed the last of the temples in Upper Egypt. The priests who had served the temples dispersed, never to be replaced. More than a millennium passed before anyone could read hieroglyphic script again.

Serious speculation about the significance of the hieroglyphs developed during the Renaissance. Spurred by the revival of Hermetic literature and the assumption that hieroglyphs expressed profound Hermetic truths, scholars sought to understand them. The most notable effort was by the Jesuit scholar Athanasius Kircher (1602–1680) who published several volumes about hieroglyphs. Frequently ridiculed by modern writers, Kircher was a meticulous student who, despite great odds, achieved at least marginal results; for example, his work on the Coptic language was valuable once scholars had the key to the hieroglyphs. His approach, however, was fundamentally mistaken and doomed to failure.

After the rush of interest during the Renaissance, the hieroglyphs attracted little attention until the discovery of the Rosetta Stone.[51] There was a remarkably astute work in 1737 by William Warburton who attacked Kircher's symbolic ideas and posited instead that hieroglyphs were an alphabetic script that had developed from pictographs. Demotic script, he guessed, was a shorthand for hieroglyphs. Furthermore, he rejected the notion that hieroglyphs were a philosophical and mystical language, suggesting instead that they were an everyday language used for ordinary purposes.[52] But such level-headed comments were obscured by the symbolic and Neoplatonist ideas that still predominated. William Stukeley, in his ca-

pacity as secretary of the Society of Antiquaries, expressed the trend
of contemporary thought:

> The hieroglyphics of the Egyptians is a sacred character. . . . The
> characters cut on the Egyptian monuments, are purely sym-
> bolical. They are nothing than hymns & invocations to the de-
> ity. . . . To give a few instances. A feather so often appearing,
> signifies sublime. An eye is providence. . . . A boat, the or-
> derly conduct of providence in the government of the world.
> A pomegranate imports fecundity, from the multitude of its
> seeds. . . . I believe the true knowledg [sic] of the hieroglyphs
> was immersed in extremest antiquity. So that if any skill of
> interpreting them, remain'd with the priests, to the time of
> Cambyses; after that time, the just understanding of them was
> lost. . . . The perfect knowledge of 'em is irrecoverable, with the
> most ancient preists [sic].[53]

There the situation rested for a time, but after Napoleon's expedition, many raised the old questions: What did the hieroglyphs
mean? Could they be deciphered? Taunting the questioners was the
existence of an ever-growing body of hieroglyphic texts and the
Rosetta Stone, which obviously was a key to translating those texts,
but a key that no one could turn. It was frustrating. The Greek section of the stone could be read easily, but the demotic and hieroglyphic portions remained as enigmatic as ever.

The problem was a misunderstanding of the nature of demotic and
hieroglyphic scripts. The hieroglyphs were thought to be an ideographic, not a phonetic script; according to that premise, each hieroglyph represented a separate word or concept. Considering the
appearance of the hieroglyphs and the supposedly authoritative statements of the classical writers, it was a plausible premise, but an entirely mistaken one. Demotic also was misunderstood, for it was
thought to be an alphabetic script, but it is really a simplified form
of the hieroglyphs, though so simplified that its nature and origin
were not apparent to uninstructed eyes.[54] Laboring under such mis-
conceptions, scholars were unable to make any progress toward deciphering the language of the ancient Egyptians, and at length they
began to despair. Matthew Rapier of the Society of Antiquaries
wrote in 1812, "Seven years having now elapsed since the last communication on the subject, there is little reason to expect any further information should be received."[55]

The first significant progress was made by Thomas Young, one of

Sir William Gell's correspondents and the man who had instructed George Butler in hieroglyphic studies.[56] Young had already made a name for himself in medicine, natural philosophy, mechanics, mathematics, languages, and especially in physics for his formulation of the undulating wave theory of light. In 1814, at age forty-one, he turned his attention to Egyptian hieroglyphs. Working with a copy of the Rosetta Stone, Young soon achieved important results. Through careful observation, he realized that the demotic and hieroglyphic scripts were closely related. This discovery, which he reported in 1816, removed a big impediment to translation—the misconception that demotic was alphabetic.

That work, important though it was, did not help translate the hieroglyphs themselves, but Young also made an important discovery in that area. He noticed that certain sets of hieroglyphs seemed to correspond to the names Ptolemy and Berenice. Although he still thought hieroglyphs were ideographic, Young hypothesized that they might have been adapted to express the Greek names phonetically. By matching Greek letters and corresponding hieroglyphs, he established the correct phonetic value of several hieroglyphic characters. He reported this discovery in the article on Egypt that he wrote for the 1819 edition of the *Encyclopaedia Britannica.*[57] This important advance pointed the way to the nature of the hieroglyphs. Young's discovery was not, however, immediately accepted. Jean François Champollion, who later took all the credit for deciphering the hieroglyphs, initially rejected Young's discovery, erroneously maintaining that the hieroglyphs were "signs of things, and not sounds." But Young's ideas nevertheless attracted some followers, among them Sir William Gell and George Butler, to whom he regularly communicated his findings. When Wilkinson left for Egypt, the hieroglyphs were still undeciphered, but knowledgeable observers like Gell knew that decipherment was only a matter of time.

Wilkinson was therefore preparing to go to Egypt at a propitious moment. He would indeed be but one more of a long series of travelers, but none of his predecessors had enjoyed the opportunities that had opened or were about to open to him. Poised between a rich tradition of antiquarian scholarship and unprecedented opportunities, he was about to participate in laying the foundations of modern Egyptology.

Sir Gardner Wilkinson. Portrait by Henry Wyndham Phillips, 1840s.
Photograph courtesy of the Griffith Institute, the Ashmolean Museum,
Oxford.

In this picture of Gurna from A. H. Rhind's *Thebes, Its Tombs and Their Tenants,* Wilkinson's house is the one with the towers in the background. Yanni's house is the one in the foreground with the flag. The brickwork just below Wilkinson's house is connected to the tomb where Hay's artists lived.

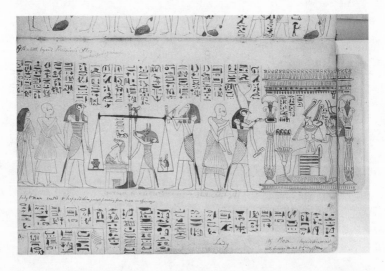

Page from one of Wilkinson's Egyptian notebooks showing the weighing of the heart in Theban tomb A.15. Later reproduced in *Manners and Customs of the Ancient Egyptians.* Wilkinson Manuscripts, Bodleian Library, Department of Western Manuscripts.

This sketch from the Hay portfolio shows Hay (foreground) and two of his artists and their servants taking their ease in a temple or tomb that they have converted into a habitation. British Library, Department of Manuscripts. By permission of the British Library.

No. 279. A party of guests, entertained with music and the dance. From Thebes, and now in the British Museum.
Fig. 1 and 2. 4 and 5, 6 and 7, 8 and 9. Men and women seated together at the feast. 3. A servant offering a cup of wine.
10, 11, 12. Women singing and clapping their hands to the sound of the double pipe, 13. 14, 15. Dancing women.
16. Vases on stands, stopped with heads of wheat, and decked with garlands.

A dinner party scene from the tombs at Thebes. From *Manners and Customs of the Ancient Egyptians.*

Page from a letter from Wilkinson to Sir William Gell mentioning Champollion's death. Wilkinson Manuscripts, Bodleian Library, Department of Western Manuscripts.

Sir William Gell.
Pencil drawing by
T. Uwins, 1830.
National Portrait
Gallery, London.

Edward William Lane. Marble statue by Richard J. Lane, 1829.
National Portrait Gallery, London.

Robert Hay. Photograph courtesy of Guglielmo Hay.

Joseph Bonomi. British Library, Department of Manuscripts. By permission of the British Library.

Algernon Percy, Fourth Duke of Northumberland (formerly Lord Prudhoe). Photograph courtesy of the Duke of Northumberland.

Caroline Wilkinson c. 1863. Photograph courtesy of Robert Lucas.

Wilkinson and Harb at Brynfield toward the end of Wilkinson's life.
Photograph courtesy of Robert Lucas.

CHAPTER THREE

Egypt

WILKINSON SPENT THE REST of the summer and the early autumn of 1821 in Naples, studying under Sir William Gell's direction. From the shelves of Gell's large library, he read the accounts of travelers in Egypt, including the sensational one by Belzoni that had been published after Wilkinson left England. He also studied the writings of the Neoplatonists, the Hermetic *Corpus*, and Kircher's publications.[1] In addition to Egyptian books, he read about Turkey and Arabia, and supplemented his factual reading with some of Voltaire's oriental works.[2] He, James Burton, and, later, Sir William Gell began studying Arabic under the direction of Padre Giuseppe Campanile, who had traveled in Kurdistan.[3] Writing to a friend, Burton made this assessment of Wilkinson and the preparations they were making for life in the East: "Mr Wilkinson is a young Oxonian, an excellent scholar, and full of ardour. We are fagging together in the different routes but leading to the desired end of our intended journey—Herodatus and the Koran—Trigonometry and drawing—swimming and smoking—the latter of which perfect qualifications for a musselman. Of course beards etc will not be forgotten." He went on to joke about doubting that he would go as far as being circumcised.[4] Wilkinson, incidentally, was circumcised, a fact that did indeed help him to pass for a Muslim.

Gell also taught Wilkinson the method of hieroglyphic transliteration developed by Thomas Young and showed him his own hieroglyphic notebooks. He took Wilkinson to some local museums where together they practiced sketching Egyptian antiquities; "drew some hieroglyphics in blocks," Wilkinson wrote of one such trip, referring to royal names in cartouches. Gell drew hieroglyphs elegantly, though his hands were so swollen by gout that it seemed impossible that he could hold a pen.[5] Wilkinson drew quickly and clearly, but as yet with no real understanding of what he was drawing. There was one bad moment when a museum official refused to let them draw an Egyptian statue. They protested, an argument ensued, and they were finally expelled from the museum. Wilkinson always considered it a distinction to have been turned out of a museum with Sir William Gell.[6] When he afterward drew the statue from memory he added the note, "Fragment of red granite in Studii at Naples which the Asses at the Museum will not let us draw."[7] Despite such annoyances, the work went well. Because of the training he gave Wilkinson, Gell was justified in boasting, as he later did, that Wilkinson went to Egypt better prepared to study its antiquities than any traveler there since antiquity. Wilkinson soon afterward mentioned his debt: "For whatever I have done or ever shall do in hieroglyphics, I am entirely indebted to the kindness of S[r] W. Gell, whose assistance & useful instructions, though I fully appreciated, I do not know how to acknowledge."[8]

Wilkinson and his traveling companion J. S. Wiggett sailed from Naples 26 October 1821 aboard a Neapolitan brig. Burton had originally intended to accompany them, but decided to delay his departure. The weather seemed promising for the short first leg of their journey, the run to Malta, but the wind failed, and they were becalmed. Each passenger was responsible for his own provisions, and Wilkinson and Wiggett, who had anticipated only a short voyage, ran out of food while off the coast of Sicily. The captain took no pity on them, refusing either to give or to sell them anything to eat. They would have been in a bad way had not some of the other passengers shared food with them. This put the captain in a bad light, and when the ship finally reached the Maltese port of Valletta, he tried to entangle the two young men in difficulties with the customs officers. Unfortunate consequences might have followed, but the other passengers told the authorities about the captain's outrageous behavior, the wine was passed, and the heartless captain was threatened with confiscation of his vessel. Only the forgiving intercession of Wilkinson and Wiggett persuaded the officers not to execute their threat. That, at least, was Wilkinson's account of the episode.[9]

The departure of the British brig that was to take them to Alexandria was delayed by contrary winds, so Wilkinson passed the time practicing his Arabic. In the pages of his notebook we find him reviewing such utilitarian Arabic phrases as "pluck the fowl," "go fetch many fowls," and so forth. He met Mr. Sadic Gibraltar, the son of Sir William Gell's good friend Ismael Gibraltar, a Turkish naval officer. Gibraltar gave Wilkinson the latest news from Egypt as well as some practical advice, including a warning that travel there would be easier and safer if he dressed as a Turk.[10] Once the wind changed after a week or so, the trip to Alexandria took only eight days; Wilkinson, however, suffered from seasickness, so it must have been with relief that he caught his first glimpse of Egypt on 22 November 1821.

That first glimpse, all travelers agreed, was distinctly unimpressive, especially in comparison to expectations.[11] The great landmarks of the past, such as the lighthouse, were mostly gone, and few structures—Pompey's Pillar, the minarets of the mosques, and the pasha's granaries—broke the monotony of the low, sandy shore. They sailed into the western harbor where Franks, the generic term that the Arabs applied to all Europeans, had only recently been admitted, having previously been restricted to the inferior eastern harbor, or the "harbour of the infidels," as it was known.[12] Once he landed and passed the importunate donkey men and the bored customs officers, Wilkinson found himself in an environment for which none of his previous experiences had prepared him. Later he would come to see Alexandria as a rather insipid place, its charm diluted by Western influences, but at first glimpse it seemed wondrously exotic. He wrote to Gell,

> Everything appears quite novel in Alexandria, & totally different from Europe. The variety of costume, the appearance of the houses with their wooded lattice windows, many of which are very [   ] & highly ornamented, the bazaars, the minarets of the mosks, the palm trees, the camels, the noise of the clamorous Egyptians, & the gravity of the smoking Turks cannot fail to strike the stranger; & the barren appearance of the country, with its low flat shore, which you scarcely perceive from the sea before you reach it, fully realises the notions previously formed of the African coast.
>
> You walk in the streets, voices assail you from every direction; asses driven at full gallop have scarcely passed on your left, when others strike you on the right at the moment you hear a shrill cry shemálak, followed by *riglak, dahrak,*[13] *oah, haw;* or while mounted on one of those quick little animals, in a narrow street, you are carried as you look round against the enormous burden of a stately camel, & precipitated into the muddy street, or caught in the arms of the still less cleanly driver. You bear it patiently.[14]

Guided by notes that Gell had given him, he toured the ancient monuments of Alexandria, just as centuries of travelers had done before him, taking notes, making sketches, and copying inscriptions. He visited Pompey's Pillar and copied the Roman inscription on its base. He also went to the "obelisks called of Cleopatra," one upright and the other fallen, though partially excavated from the sand that had covered it, and recorded their inscriptions: "The obelisks here have, as you know, the names of Dr Young's Mespheres (Thothmes 3) in the central lines."[15] He also observed that the inscriptions on the fallen obelisk were somewhat worn. Gell had asked him to examine the foundations of the fallen lighthouse, but bad weather prevented that excursion. As he went about, he contemplated the transformation of what had been one of the great cities of the eastern Mediterranean but was now a small coastal town of perhaps five thousand inhabitants. Soon he was anxious to start upstream. "Alexandria offers little more than interesting associations," he wrote to Gell. "At Alexandria all is comparatively modern; it is at Thebes that I expect really to enjoy the antiquities of the Egyptians."[16] By the second week in December he was on his way, though Wiggett lingered in Alexandria.

Alexandria is more than forty miles west of the closest navigable channel of the Nile, so Wilkinson's first task was to reach the Rosetta branch of the river. There was constant sea communication between Alexandria and Rashid, but sandbars made the passage dangerous. Years later, when he wrote his travelers' handbook for Egypt, Wilkinson advised taking the overland route to Rashid. On this occasion, he took the newly opened Mahmoudiah Canal, which linked Alexandria with the Nile a few miles above Rashid. Poorly engineered, the canal was unnavigable during a large portion of the year. "Ugliest and most wearisome of canals," Sir Richard Burton later called it.[17]

To sail up the Nile, Wilkinson hired a *maash*, one of the species of riverboats that European travelers on the Nile favored in the eighteenth and nineteenth centuries. Other possibilities were the *canjah* and the *dahabiyah*.[18] Although he took a *maash* on this occasion, Wilkinson usually traveled in a *dahabiyah*, which was ideal for a single Englishman traveling with a small retinue. These peculiar vessels with their steep sides and full triangular sails made a pretty picture on the water, but the shallow draft that allowed them to ride over sandbars made them somewhat unstable, prone to tip over if an unexpected gust of wind caught the crew unprepared to lower the sails quickly enough. Even so, when all went well they were a convenient way to see the Nile and a good base of operations for a traveling scholar. Each of these riverboats was commanded by a *rais*, or captain, and a small craft like Wilkinson's had a crew of three or four men. There was at least one cabin large enough for the traveler, and the crew usually slept on deck or on shore at night when the boat anchored close to the riverbank.[19] British travelers always flew the British flag so Muhammad Ali's gunboats would not compel them to stop for an examination of their cargo.[20] Such craft have vanished from the river now, but one may still derive some impression of their appearance and characteristics from the *felucca*, which is ever prepared to carry tourists about. The *felucca* is rigged similar to the older types of riverboats and responds just as readily to the slightest breeze.

On such a vessel Wilkinson set off on a pleasant, if uneventful journey up the Rosetta branch of the Nile Delta. "Werdán is prettily situated, & Nigeéleh, & a few other places offer some points for the pencil of a draughtsman," he wrote to Gell.[21] He had some hopes for Saïs, which Gell had especially requested him to examine, but after stopping there he reported, "I confess [I] was sadly disappointed. Much remains to be done there before the positions of the temple of Minerva & other buildings can be ascertained, & without extensive excavation it is impossible to arrive at any satisfactory conjectures on some of the sites."[22] Sailing upstream, he spent his time writing descriptions of peoples and places, making occasional sketches, and taking thermometer readings every morning. In the evenings, the crew danced on the deck.[23]

On 19 December 1821, his boat drew near Cairo. First the Pyramids came into view through the relatively clear air of the early nineteenth century. Then far away on the left he saw the numerous minarets of Cairo against the limestone backdrop of the Mukattam Hills. At that time, the city still lay about a mile to the east of the river, its northwest corner just below present-day Ramses Square, so the traveler landed at the port of Boulaq where the customs house was located. It was not until two days later that Wilkinson set off across the open fields dotted with country estates that separated Cairo from the Nile. He entered through the Ezbekiah Gate and, passing by the elite quarter around the large lake that once filled Ezbekiah Square, plunged into the heart of the city.

If Wilkinson had thought Alexandria was exotic, then Cairo must have seemed like another world. Much larger than Alexandria, it contained perhaps a quarter of a million inhabitants, though the number fluctuated in response to epidemics that periodically decimated the population. It had not yet experienced the Western influences and the forces of economic and social change that soon transformed it. Wilkinson was seeing the medieval city of Cairo, the *Arabian Nights* city, largely unchanged for centuries. He made his way through narrow, crooked streets framed by countless Moorish arches wrought in exquisite detail. Some streets were so narrow that a loaded camel could scarcely pass through, filled as they were with "a confused medley of men, camels, and asses."[24] He came to appreciate what he called a superior breed of ass that coped well with the situation.[25] Along the sides were shops more like cupboards than places of business. In front of each was a bench, or *mastaba*, further hindering passage through the crowded ways; there men sat and talked while enjoying their pipes. Corbeled upper stories projected overhead and shaded the streets from the harsh sun. So close did they come in places that people could have reached across and clasped hands. The windows of these upper floors were covered with the intricate screens of turned wood called *mashrabiya*. After dark, pedestrians were required to carry lanterns in the unlighted streets; they seemed like ghosts as they passed in the night. The unpaved streets were, James Burton said, composed of "the accumulation of the ages."[26] When the occasional rain came, they became impassable. Dirt and garbage were everywhere; one saw grandeur and delapidation in the same glance. High overhead soared the minarets, of which no Eastern city had so many as Cairo.[27] Suddenly, unexpectedly, Wilkinson would see one framed in a narrow space of sky as he followed a winding street. At night the minarets were suffused with soft light from lanterns hung from them. Wilkinson and his colleagues are important sources for visualizing this vanished city— "Saracenic" Cairo they called it—that changed greatly during their lifetimes.

One of Wilkinson's first stops was at the Cairo residence of Consul-General Henry Salt, which was located in the Frankish Quarter of town, just east of Ezbekiah. We may be sure that Wilkinson brought a letter of introduction from Sir William Gell because of the facetious verses that Gell wrote and circulated among Wilkinson and his friends. "Saline Verses Addressed to Egyptian Travellers from Tentyra," Gell entitled his little poem:

If you travel in Egypt tis reckon'd a fault
To be seen on the Nile without letters for Salt,
But be sure when you shew your credentials to say
What dropp'd from your intimate friend Castlereagh
Whom you met at the travellers club t'other day.
Who seem'd quite consoled when he thought that at Cairo

That good fellow Salt rul'd instead of old Phaaroah
Who he felt quite assur'd would take *you* by the hand
When he knew how allied to the Marquis you stand
That Sidmouth & Harrowby both were your cousins
And you reckon'd your friends in the household by dozens.
Add that Hamilton once forc'd upon you a letter
But to burn it dear Liverpool hinted was better
Than that persons connected like you with the Court
Should be troubl'd with things of such little import.
Not a word of Mountnorris—that interest is past
Sense of favours conferr'd is not likely to last.
And hint not oh hint not one word about painting
Unless you would set the great Consul to fainting
But lock up your papers & hide all your drawing
If you would be safe from his pilf'ring & clawing
And whatever you do hold your head up in Alt
Or you're likely to profit but little by Salt.[28]

These verses, whatever they lack in poetic merit, tell something about the kind of person Salt was, but the characterization is correct only to a point. Salt probably was finely attuned to personal connections and influence, because he, a gentleman of limited means, had made his way by trading patron for patron until he won the consulship, something he viewed as a means to greater ends. His primary goal was financial security for himself and his family, which he hoped to achieve through large-scale trade in Egyptian antiquities. He was, as Gell implied, ashamed of his portrait-painting past and wanted to put it behind him—a pity, because it was his artistic ability that made his copies of antiquities so good.[29] Like many an unsure person, he masked his insecurity with an air of self-importance—hence the "Saline hero," as Gell called him—that made it difficult to appreciate his better qualities. But Gell was wrong when he implied that Salt was jealous of the antiquarian pursuits of others, because he was always helpful to Wilkinson and other travelers and he made Wilkinson's first years in Egypt much easier than they otherwise would have been. Wilkinson shortly afterward said as much in one of his first attempts at publication when he acknowledged "the kindness of Mr Salt, our Consul General here, who has ever been ready to give me assistance in my pursuits; whose fame as an antiquarian is well known, & with justice highly appreciated by the literary world."[30] Perhaps what Gell's poem reveals most is the peculiar attitude that he and some others had towards Salt.

Soon after Wilkinson arrived in Cairo, Salt took him to meet the pasha, Muhammad Ali.[31] Though nominally the vassal of the sultan at Istanbul, Muhammad Ali was, in fact, the undisputed ruler of Egypt. He was, at that moment, consolidating and extending his power. Europeans were always granted an audience, for he was interested in winning their goodwill and learning new ideas to apply to his ambitious modernization program. Wilkinson and Salt were invited to sit, and coffee was served, though no pipe was offered to them. That was reserved for equals. Even so, Muhammad Ali was relaxed and cordial, his conversation touching a wide range of topics from military affairs to local news. As the visitors departed, courtiers slipped up and asked for *backshish*, a bribe or gratuity. Wilkinson's opinion of Muhammad Ali would subsequently range from admiring to deprecating, but on this occasion he merely recorded a dull visit.

Salt also accompanied Wilkinson to the Pyramids at Giza. When he had first seen them as his boat approached Cairo, Wilkinson wrote, "Nothing during this journey of three days strikes the traveller more than the first appearance of the pyramids. They seem to comprise all that is most beautiful & imposing; they are the representatives of the grandiose & majestic amidst all human works, the types of Egypt & of all Egyptian vastness of conception."[32] He climbed and measured them, including the Second Pyramid, where he carved his name on the top.[33] The Second Pyramid is by far the most difficult to climb because it still has its smooth casing stones near the apex. Wilkinson was fortunate in having for his guide Henry Salt, who had commissioned the extensive explorations at Giza conducted by Giovanni Battista Caviglia a few years earlier. Caviglia made several important discoveries, including the steps that ascend the Sphinx and the pavement between its paws.

Another person at the Consulate who was helpful to Wilkinson was Osman Effendi. Sadic Gibraltar had told him about this man, a Scot who lived as a Turk and a Muslim. His name had been Donald Thomson when he came to the East as a drummer boy in General Fraser's disastrous expedition in 1807. Wounded, captured, and given a choice of death or conversion to Islam, he chose conversion and became the slave of a wealthy Turk who renamed him Osman. After initial hardships, he won the favor of his master who married him to a woman from his harem and gave him money. On a visit to Arabia he met the explorer J. L. Burckhardt and accompanied him to Mecca. When they returned to Cairo, Burckhardt used his influence to obtain Osman's freedom. When Burckhardt fell fatally ill, he left his property to Osman who buried his friend in the Bab al-Nasr Cemetery, just outside the northern wall of the city. Osman began buying real estate in Cairo and soon prospered as he never could have hoped to do in Scotland. Several Europeans offered to help him return home, but he politely refused them all, pointing out that he would be but a poor man there, whereas he was doing quite well in Egypt.[34] He achieved a high, indeed deferential, degree of respect among the Turkish and Arab communities, hence his title, *effendi*, which means "gentleman." At the British Consulate he became an interpreter, or *dragoman*. Travelers' accounts frequently mention how he was indispensible in helping them cope with the manifold difficulties of life in Egypt, whether renting a boat, buying a slave, or staying out of trouble. "In short," one of them wrote, "nothing is to be arranged without Osman, who keeps the rogues in order."[35]

Osman took Wilkinson to buy Turkish clothes and showed him how to wear them.[36] First it was necessary to select a pair of voluminous Turkish trousers that were held up by a drawstring at the waist. Then came a shirt with loose, hanging sleeves. Over the shirt went two silk jackets: the first fitted closely and could be buttoned, but the second was designed to be worn open. It was trimmed with lace, the longer the better. Both of these jackets were tucked into the trousers, before a third jacket, this one loose and trimmed with silver and gold, was put on. For dressy occasions, a long robe went over everything. An embroidered pouch for the Quran hung on the right side and a Turkish sword on the left. For headgear there was a linen cap, which was worn under a woolen cap, which in turn was worn under the turban. Shoes were made of red morocco; one wore a thin pair of slippers inside of them. When visiting someone's home, the outer shoes were removed and left at the edge of the carpet. Good taste called for dressing all in the same color. With the clothes selected, it was then necessary to shave the head and face, except for long, drooping mustaches. The costume took a long time to put on, and someone unaccustomed to it found it oppressively heavy at first.[37] Wilkinson had little to say about his new clothes, but his acquaintance Henry Westcar, whom Osman helped into Turkish garb two years later, described the difference it made:

> Under his [Osman's] auspices I became to appearance a Turk, my head shaved, a mameluke turban & a proud look, I walked along the streets & the first day I proved the difference of the change, when dressed in frank clothes every ragged arab that passed woul[d] run against & the soldiers elbow you & make you get out of their way, when I was a Turk & with my pipe bearer before me

all got out of the way & the Arabs who were sitting down got up as I passed & saluted me then I was a great man.[38]

Having taken care of the necessities of life in Egypt, Wilkinson was eager to sail upstream and examine the antiquities of Upper Egypt. Wiggett arrived in Cairo in early January, and a month later he and Wilkinson started up the Nile. Primarily guided by Norden's *Travels in Egypt and Nubia* and the map made by Colonel William Martin Leake,[39] Wilkinson now saw for himself the monuments on either bank in Upper Egypt as he sailed past places like Meidum, Beni Hasan, Antinopolis, Abydos, and Dendera. He made many sketches, drew floor plans of temples, and occasionally noted mistakes in the works of Norden and others. He saw his first crocodile, always a notable experience for travelers on the Nile. When he reached Thebes, where he would later do his most important work, he visited some of the best-known sites, though he mostly concentrated on the two great temples on the east bank, Luxor Temple and Karnak Temple. Wiggett recorded his visit to the temple at Medinet Habu on the west bank by chiseling his name on a wall.[40] Other than some careful drawings Wilkinson made in Karnak Temple, there was too much to see for any concentrated work. Above Thebes were Esna, Edfu, Kom Ombo, Aswan, and Elephantine. At the island of Philae, near Aswan, they paused to examine the large temple complex built by the Roman emperor Trajan. Part of the temple was subsequently converted into a Christian church, and many of the pagan murals were plastered over, which Wilkinson noticed had ironically protected rather than obliterated them: "During our stay here we cleared the walls of one side adyta [adytum] from the mortar of the Christians, & found most of the colors of the figures very well preserved."[41] When they passed the rock at Abusir, by the Second Cataract, Wilkinson, like many others, including Belzoni and Burckhardt, carved his name on it with the date, 14 April 1822.[42] The farthest penetration on this trip was Semna, several miles above the Second Cataract.

Impressive ruins stand on both sides of the river at Semna. Having seen those on the one side, Wilkinson and Wiggett wanted to cross and see the others. They had left their *dahabiyah* below the First Cataract. There was no ferry, so they had to rely upon two Nubians who took them across on a crude raft. One Nubian swam in front and pulled while the other pushed from behind. The raft rode exceedingly low in the water, so the two passengers were partially immersed and sat facing each other "like the 2 gods in the name of Remeses." Being near the cataract, the currents were tricky, causing Wilkinson to think of the opportunity they were offering to the crocodiles, but they crossed and recrossed safely, quickly drying under the hot sun.[43] There, in Nubia, for the first of many times in his life, Wilkinson watched the beginning of the annual rise of the Nile.

They began a leisurely descent of the river, returning to Thebes on 5 July. This time Wilkinson wanted to take a more careful look at the antiquities that lie profusely around that spectacular site, especially on the west bank. He spent a week at the Tombs of the Nobles on the hill of Gurna, but Wiggett was suddenly attacked by a violent case of dysentery. He became so desperately ill that they made for Cairo as quickly as possible, arriving in mid-August. No medical skills could be found in the capital to alleviate Wiggett's suffering, so Wilkinson set off in a *dahabiyah* to Alexandria to fetch Henry Salt's physician, Dr. Alessandro Ricci, for Ricci was known to have cured Muhammad Ali's son of a similar affliction.[44] Wilkinson was traveling at night when a sudden squall hit and capsized his boat, throwing him overboard and nearly drowning him. He later learned that at that very moment Wiggett's attendants were despairing of their patient's life, a coincidence that caused him to reflect upon the nearly simultaneous end of the two travelers.

Whether Dr. Ricci came or not is unclear, but Wiggett recovered enough to be taken to Alexandria where he was put aboard a British warship bound for Europe. With Wiggett, Wilkinson sent along his drawings of Karnak for Sir William Gell. Wiggett must have regained his health on the voyage, for he traveled for more than a year in Sicily and other places before reaching Naples. When he finally arrived, Gell wrote to Wilkinson, "I like your friend Wiggett but I conclude the flesh pots of Egypt have quite changed him for the better."[45] Wiggett's departure would have been an opportune moment for Wilkinson to return to England and pursue his military ambitions, but he now firmly and finally decided against the army, choosing to remain in Egypt instead.[46]

After seeing Wiggett off, Wilkinson returned to Cairo and plunged into Egyptological studies. As we will see, he worked hard on the ancient language and soon began to achieve results. He also intensified his work as a copyist of monuments and inscriptions. These copies are probably his most enduring Egyptological accomplishment for, besides being minor works of art, they are often the best and sometimes the only surviving evidence for objects that have since been damaged or destroyed. Indeed, some were lost even while he was in Egypt. When his friend Robert Hay visited Hermopolis

Magna, the Ptolemaic cult center for the worship of Hermes Trismegistus, he found that the temple had been wantonly wrecked
since Wilkinson had been there only a short time before.[47] Although
Wilkinson's copies from his first year or two in Egypt are not especially good, he soon achieved a high standard of accuracy. He was
largely immune to the gross subjectivity of the artists of the eighteenth century and those who had prepared the *Description de
l'Egypte*. Sir·William Gell, who had concluded that many of the details in the *Description* were "quite imaginary," noted Wilkinson's
objectivity in a letter to Thomas Young: "I think you will find them
[Wilkinson's sketches of hieroglyphs] quite well drawn enough for
the purpose; and that the hand of a man like Wilkinson now long
practised in hieroglyphs is more likely to give the real character of
the objects, than if they were all drawn over again to make the birds
and beasts more like the animals they are intended for."[48] Young was
indeed impressed when he saw them, and he later wrote, "Wilkinson's copies appear to be as accurately copied as they are beautifully
executed."[49]

Wilkinson's copies have stood up well to professional scrutiny
over the years. Present-day Egyptologists find that they are accurate
and that they can be used as reliable evidence—at least up to a point,
and with experience one learns where that point is. The fact that
there is a limit to their usefulness does not mean carelessness or
dishonesty on Wilkinson's part but is merely a funcion of the subjectivity that no copyist can escape entirely. Wilkinson's level of understanding conditioned what he saw. Modern copyists see many details that Wilkinson missed because they better understand what
ought to be there and know to look for it; however, the very knowledge that aids those copyists can blind them to details that Wilkinson, working with fewer preconceptions, saw. Wilkinson himself
sometimes saw things differently. In at least one case in which he
copied the same inscription on two separate occasions, he copied it
differently each time.[50] His limitations do not detract from his accomplishment. His copies, in the judgment of one authority, "have
never been surpassed and hardly equalled by other copyists."[51]

As Wilkinson completed his first year in Egypt, he was justified if
he felt some sense of accomplishment. He was hard at work on notebooks, sketches, and linguistic studies; already he had ambitions for
publication. He had ascended the Nile into Nubia, doing an astonishingly large amount of work along the way and gaining a sense
of the lay of the land, making places he had hitherto only read about
become real to him. Now he wanted to experience it more. Sir

William Gell, sensing that he might tarry indefinitely there, wrote, "Pray when you have done a good deal, don't stay there all your life but come here & deposit & publish & then return again. You will find great advantages in so doing."[52] But many years were to pass before Wilkinson could bring himself to leave Egypt.

CHAPTER FOUR

Life in Cairo and a Trip into the Eastern Desert

WHEN WILKINSON RETURNED to Cairo after his adventures with Wiggett, he encountered James Burton, who had arrived in Egypt while he was upriver. As intended, Burton participated in Muhammad Ali's geological survey, but soon tiring of it, he resigned, choosing instead to explore independently. As they renewed their acquaintance, Wilkinson and Burton seemed to have much in common: love of travel, literary ambition, and artistic talent. Like Wilkinson, Burton corresponded with Gell.[1] Burton invited Wilkinson to take a spare room in his house in the area known as the Hasanain. Located in the northern part of the town a short distance north of al-Azhar, the Hasanain was primarily inhabited by Turkish merchants.[2] Later Wilkinson and Burton took houses close together in the elite Turkish neighborhood of Ezbekiah.[3]

Their decision to locate among the Turks was a deliberate rejection of the company and life-style of the majority of Cairo's Europeans, most of whom lived in the Frankish Quarter. For those people, whom he called "Franks" and "Pseudofranks," Wilkinson developed a deep aversion. Many of them, he felt, were not honest scholars or businessmen, but charlatans and misfits who exploited Muhammad Ali's occasionally naïve attempts to modernize Egypt. Wilkinson wrote,

A man unable to remain at home in France Italy or Malta escapes from the land of question & seeks a refuge at Cairo—arrived here he immediately applies to the Basha for employment stating that having no longer any occupation at home he is come to offer his assistance to his Highness & is sure that his knowledge in such & such an art will be of infinite service to Egt. The Basha though he has done much good for the country & acted most wisely in many points is in this no longer the same man—instead of applying to some one in Europe to select good artists & workmen who w^d be sure of succeeding in establishment of manufacturing here—listens to the vague assertions of these men the refuse of France & Italy.[4]

Burton, as it turned out, came perilously close to fitting that description, but Wilkinson was not thinking of him. Besides, Burton was English.

More than aversion to these Europeans, however, impelled Wilkinson and Burton to locate in Turkish neighborhoods, for they both wanted to adopt Turkish life-styles. Having been introduced to the intricacies of Turkish attire by Osman, they now dressed in none other. This contrasted sharply to most Europeans who wore European clothes, though some dressed in a mixture of European and Turkish garments. "They look a most disreputable set of vagabonds," Wilkinson's friend Edward William Lane wrote of the latter group.[5] Much to the astonishment of Europeans who visited him, Wilkinson even ate with Turkish table manners.[6] So complete was his transformation that his friend Robert Hay had this first impression of Wilkinson: "He is dressed as a Turk and looks much like one, and avoids the Franks as much as possible."[7] Burton also passed muster, for Hay wrote of him: "He is a pleasant and well educated man and takes great pains to dress well in the costume of the country, and wears a most magnificent shawl turban. His face is rather thin, his nose aquiline and on the whole he makes a very good Turk, wears no beard, only mustaches."[8] So good was their disguise that they passed themselves off as Muslims to servants and neighbors.[9]

Burton's and Wilkinson's household was quite numerous. There was a third disguised European named Charles Humphreys, who served as Burton's secretary. Apparently a man of no financial means, Humphreys was making his way in the East, occasionally collecting and selling antiquities. He was described as "an Englishman, dressed a la mode," that is, as a Turk.[10] Then there was Wilkinson's sais, or groom, Haji Musa, with whom he shared many adventures.[11] Completing the household were female servants and companions of whom we shall hear more later. When the traveler Henry Westcar visited them after they moved to Ezbekiah, he wrote in his diary, "I also joined company with Mess W & B who lived in houses in the Cesbakia, the Turkish quarter near the palace of the Pasha, they lived in real Turkish fashion & we passed the time very merrily."[12]

Comfortably settled into Turkish life, Wilkinson and Burton were rudely shocked when Henry Salt issued a proclamation stating that the British Consulate could take no responsibility for or extend protection to British subjects who wore oriental dress.[13] Being so notable for wearing Turkish clothing, Wilkinson and Burton felt that the proclamation was aimed specifically at them. They angrily went to the consulate and demanded to know what it all meant. Were they to be denied the protection of the consulate? Salt was in Alexandria at that moment, but when the protest reached his ears, he tried to soothe their wrath with an equivocal letter. "In answer to your inquiries made at the consulate in Cairo," Salt wrote, "I have to inform you that the fullest protection as British subjects will always be accorded to you, as by right, during your stay in Egypt; at the same time I cannot help strongly recommending to you to wear the European dress so long as you may stay in Egypt, or, otherwise, any unpleasant consequences, that may arise from your wearing the oriental dress, must rest with yourself."[14] He mentioned an Ionian subject in oriental dress who had been sentenced to a beating and asserted that his object was to prevent "similar outrages." Salt closed by inviting their opinions, which they lost no time sending to him.

Wilkinson and Burton replied immediately. "We are at loss," they wrote, "to comprehend the reasons of your strong recommendation to wear the European dress, when at the same time we almost daily witness in Cairo insults offered to individuals (as well under British as other protection) owing entirely to their wearing that dress."[15] Examples followed: a Maltese had been knocked off his donkey and insulted for not dismounting to salute a passing dignitary, something that was unheard of to anyone in oriental dress, with the possible exception of a "miserable Fellah"; and someone in Frankish dress had been nearly killed by a mob because he stepped on a black slave's foot while his companion, who happened to be wearing Turkish dress, was not molested. "We at present," they continued, "merely extend our researches to the deserts of Egypt, in which we know by experience that the Oriental costume is indispensible." In the desert, someone in European clothes would be a temptation to any passing Arab. Again they demanded to know what practical protection the consulate could offer. That posed a dilemma for Salt, because a reply that their protection was limited might have provoked a career-damaging complaint to London. He decided to blame everything on his subordinate, Charles Sloane, the chancellor of the consulate. Sloane, Salt claimed, had misunderstood his instructions, for the proclamation had been intended to apply only to British subjects employed by the pasha, not to travelers like Wilkinson and Burton.[16] There the exchanges ended, but the resentment lingered.

In playing out this little scene, Wilkinson and Burton demonstrated their belief that British citizenship should protect them, however far from British soil they might be. Assured of such protection, British travelers like Wilkinson moved more quickly and deeply into Egyptian society than they otherwise would have done. On the other hand, their insistence upon the necessity of wearing Eastern dress shows a limit to European influence in Egypt in the early nineteenth century. As Europeans Wilkinson and Burton were still part of a vulnerable minority that had to exercise some discretion. Only recently had Europeans gotten the right to do such things as use both harbors at Alexandria or to walk in front of the principal mosques of Cairo. During the second half of the nineteenth century this would change as Europeans became a privileged minority. Even then someone like Sir Richard Burton or Edward William Lane during his last visit to Cairo might occasionally adopt Eastern manners and dress, but merely as disguise to facilitate study of Eastern society, not for safety. During Wilkinson's first years in Egypt, Europeans had not yet gained such status that they could move through Egyptian society with impunity. Therefore Wilkinson and James Burton wanted not only the safety that oriental clothing afforded but also the assurance of British protection as they wore it.[17]

In assessing their life-style, it is important to understand that Wilkinson and his friends lived not as native Egyptians but as Turks. That kept a distance between them and most Egyptians. The Turks were the aristocracy of Egypt. They filled the choice places in the army and government, and they were the great landowners—in short, they were the local equivalent of the English class to which Wilkinson and Burton belonged or aspired to belong. But Wilkinson's adoption of a Turkish life-style should not be interpreted to mean that he totally approved of the Turks, for he often ridiculed their pretensions,[18] and he was especially deprecating of the Turkish soldiers who went about almost literally armed to the teeth. He wrote to Gell,

It is really amusing to see the extensive gallery erected round the bodies of these men. Every part bristles with deadly weapons, & the exterior is set round with ball cartridges, which, independent of the several cartouch boxes they carry, might suffice for defence during a moderate siege. A leather case buckled round their waist, & swathed in the folds of an ample shawl, holds in its different compartments a brace of huge pistols, an enormous ataghan, or knife, (placed transversely, with the handles projecting on one side & the points on the other,) an iron ramrod, &

another of wood, containing a pair of tongs, for applying fire to the pipe, whose tobacco bag hangs at the right side as a pendant to the sabre on the left. A handkerchief, a tindercase, & various other things are thrust in here & there to complete this assemblage of incongruities, & a string of beads hangs from the ramrod, or the handle of the ataghan. Though in this state the conscious bearer of a small powder magazine, the Turkish soldier has no scruples about the free use of his pipe, & the fire intended for lighting tobacco is never suspected of the guilt of igniting gunpowder. It sometimes however occurs (though certainly more rarely than we might expect) that inattention compromises this state of security, & a report is heard that a Turk has *gone off,* & killed or wounded several of the unfortunate bystanders.[19]

For the native Egyptians, though he insisted that they should not be measured by the standards of western Europe, Wilkinson nevertheless felt little sympathy. Nor did he show any, considering it to be unwise. In hiring a *dahabiyah,* he advised, "By all means the ry'is and boatmen must be made obedient to orders, [or the traveler] will otherwise find them insufferably unruly and continually troublesome, kind words being always considered by them the result of fear or inexperience."[20] Some aspects of their obedience to authority, such as the bastinado, seemed positively exotic to him. A bastinado was a rod with which corporal punishment was administered, usually by beating the soles of bare feet. Wilkinson later published an account of an incident in which he said he saw a government agent use the bastinado literally to beat money from a taxpayer; however, in an earlier unpublished manuscript he described it as an incident that he had heard about.[21] It does have the flavor of an oft-told tale, but it also conveys some useful information:

In the year 1822, a Copt Christian, residing at Cairo, was arrested by the Turkish authorities for the non-payment of his taxes, and taken before the Kehia, or deputy of the Pasha. "Why," inquired the angry Turk, "have you not paid your taxes?"—"Because," replied the Copt, with a pitiable expression, perfectly according with his tattered appearance, "I have not the means." He was instantly ordered to be thrown upon the floor, and bastinadoed. He prayed to be released, but in vain: the stick continued without intermission, and he was scarcely able to bear the increasing pain. Again and again he pleaded his inability to pay, and prayed for mercy: the Turk was inexorable; and the torments he felt at length overcame his resolution: they were no longer to be borne. "Release me," he cried, "and I will pay directly."—"Ah, you Giower! go." He was released, and taken home, accompanied by a soldier, and the money being paid, he imparted to his wife the sad tidings. "You coward, you fool," she exclaimed; "what, give them the money on the very first demand! I suppose, after five or six blows, you cried, 'I will pay, only release me;' next year our taxes will be doubled, through your weakness; shame!"—"No, my dear," interrupted the suffering man, "I assure you I resisted as long as it was possible: look at the state I am in, before you upbraid me. I paid the money, but they had trouble enough for it; for I obliged them to give me at least a hundred blows before they could get it." She was pacified; and the pity and commendation of his wife, added to his own satisfaction in having shown so much obstinacy and courage, consoled him for the pain, and, perhaps, in some measure, for the money thus forced from him.[22]

Recalling descriptions and depictions of the bastinado from ancient sources, Wilkinson imagined that when he saw such incidents he was seeing something from the distant past.[23] The somewhat kindly if patronizing tone in Wilkinson's account of the bastinado incident is probably typical of his attitude toward Egypt's Coptic minority. These Christians were primarily identified as a bureaucratic and therefore somewhat privileged class.

No such tolerance, however, mitigated the contempt with which he looked upon the *fellahin* (Arabic for rural dwellers), the poor peasants who made up the vast majority of Egypt's population. "The fellah," he wrote, "born in slavery, is consequently the most degraded of human beings, devoid of gratitude, & every kind of virtue, he sees none in those around him; tyranny is to him a mark of superiority, & this alone he respects."[24] And to Sir William Gell he observed, "The Egyptian peasant boasts neither honesty, modesty, nor self command."[25] These people were impenetrable to Wilkinson, just as they have been to many travelers from the time of Herodotus until the twentieth century.[26] Perhaps it was difficult to sympathize with people who seemed to be and indeed were often described more as a feature of the landscape than a society of human beings. Only the extraordinary misery of the corvée, the forced assembly of labor for the pasha's projects, moved Wilkinson to anything approaching sympathy for the lot of the *fellahin*. He wrote to Gell,

A number of peasants are levied from the villages, & forcibly driven to the spot, where they are kept till the work is completed. Those who have families are provided by them with daily provisions, & if their labor is gratuitous they suffer merely from the toil they are obliged to undergo; but the unfortunate being who has no one to bring him food during his detention sinks from exhaustion without the means of averting the death of hunger. The government does not feed them; if they were allowed to go home for provisions they would never return to their work, and no one can afford to bestow a share of his scanty provisions to a suffering comrade. Generally speaking they were better provided for than usual on the present occasion; the levy being systematic, & not suddenly made; and the loss of life will probably be very small in proportion to that which occurred at the opening of the canal of Alexandria.[27]

Wilkinson's attitude may have been intensified by the fact that when he looked at the native Egyptians, he saw them not just as an Englishman, but as an Englishman looking through a Turkish lens. Both perspectives looked downward.

Wilkinson's observations on these subjects bear on a controversial question: How did Muhammad Ali's reforms affect the condition of the Egyptian people as he sought to bring Egypt into step with the world economy? That the pasha was conducting a big program of economic reorganization was obvious to Wilkinson. One of the first things he saw as his ship approached Egypt was Muhammad Ali's granaries in Alexandria from which the pasha exported grain to earn foreign exchange for financing his development programs. Wilkinson's initial trip within Egypt was on the Mahmoudiah Canal, Muhammad Ali's first big engineering project. As he traveled he, like R. R. Madden, could not help but notice the pasha's suppression of brigandage which, Wilkinson later noted, made travel safer in Egypt than in any part of Europe.[28] Heavy taxation, corvée labor, and military conscription were evident every place he visited. He also was impressed by the number of manufacturing establishments that he saw springing up, though he was several times annoyed to find that temples had been dismantled to get building stones for a sugar factory. There was no doubt in his mind that internal conditions in Egypt had been completely transformed by Muhammad Ali.[29] Wilkinson did note, however, that though Muhammad Ali was a talented man of vision, the composition of his government was such that it lacked wisdom, vigor, and humanity.[30]

This lack of humanity worried Wilkinson and other observers. For example, Henry Salt attributed the "general misery" of the Egyptian people to the fact that Muhammad Ali's government took one third of their produce for taxes.[31] Wilkinson was moved to ask rhetorically,

> Mohammed Ali has done much for Egypt, but has he done any thing for the people! They live in security; they dread no robber who can defy justice, no lawless aggression of the soldier; & indeed this last is a great step towards raising them from their former state of slavery; but they justly complain that the taxes are more than they can afford to pay; taxes in their nature too the most oppressive & impolitic. The climax of their misfortunes is that the Pásha has taken 20 000 of their youth for soldiers whom he is training in the European discipline.[32]

But Wilkinson also noted general conditions such as the obvious underpopulation of the land, Egypt containing only a few million inhabitants, though it clearly could support many more. The land, he wrote, was so rich that it would be "the most fertile; & most opulent country in the universe" if the government were more vigorous and wise.[33] Just as he blamed the government, he also considered the Egyptian people to be lazy, conditioned by what he called "the enervating habits of the East."[34] He believed they would respond energetically only to strong discipline imposed from above. As we will see later, this is how he accounted for the glories of ancient Egypt. Consequently, he thought the short-run sacrifice of the peoples' well-being and happiness would be worth it in the long run: "Time will show, & it is to be hoped, that if the present Pasha continues to govern here the condition of the people may be considerably improved."[35]

Wilkinson's low opinion of the *fellahin* contrasted sharply with his esteem for the Ababda Arabs of the Eastern Desert whom he considered noble and trustworthy. James Burton, however, did not share Wilkinson's relatively high opinion of them. "They are," Burton wrote, "vindictive, ungrateful and avaricious, not susceptible of any good feeling—full of low cunning, which is seen through immediately, dishonorable even among themselves, bigots without being religious at all, calling upon the name of God constantly without ever keeping their word, when either interest or fear is concerned." He did, however, find some redeeming qualities in the desert folk. "They are not pilferers we never lost any little things or indeed large ones from our caravans and they if they found anything of no great value belonging to another if it was of no great value would restore it though he would try to cheat him or defraud him in the next dealing he might have with him." Burton went on to add that they were not immoral in language or actions, only using the abusive language of the *fellahin* when they were enraged. Also, he noted, they were much more conjugally faithful than the inhabitants of Cairo.[36]

Although Wilkinson was insensitive to the general plight of the Egyptians, he was shocked by the treatment of Egyptian women. "There is," he wrote to Gell, "indeed a great want of heart as well as refinement in the peasantry of this country, & woman is degraded to the level of household servant."[37] Their condition did appear deplorable. Another traveler at about the same time as Wilkinson wrote, "The women here are born in a prison, and they die in a prison, if they escape being tied in a sack and drowned."[38] Nilotic phenomena such as the excision of the clitoris, an operation intended to render women faithful by destroying their sexual desire, were subjects of fascinated horror for Wilkinson and his friends.[39] Even so, Wilkinson did not consider the Egyptian situation beyond a class-conscious comparison with England. He wrote to Gell, "Everyone inveighs, with reason, against the condition of women in the East, but I should feel sorry if obliged to institute a comparison between oriental imperiousness, & the drunken brutality of many among our labouring classes, who too often add to cruel treatment the injustice of squandering upon the indulgence of their vicious excesses, the pittance they owe to their wives & families, whose earnings are too often sacrificed to the same unworthy object."[40] With this interest in ancient Egypt, he took some pride in asserting that Egyptians in the distant past had treated women better, apparently basing this conjecture upon evidence from the tomb paintings. He noted that laws for women in ancient Egypt were just as oppressive as in the nineteenth century, but he maintained that they were interpreted more liberally.[41]

It is difficult, however, to see how Wilkinson's lofty sentiments toward Egyptian women translated into practice, for Wilkinson and Burton each acquired female sexual companions whom they used as they saw fit and later discarded. Wilkinson was very discreet about his companion, and we know little about her.[42] Burton's companion, however, was not one to remain in the background. A formidable woman quite capable of intimidating poor Burton, we shall hear more of her later; for the moment we catch just a glimpse of her in the pages of Robert Hay's diary: "On coming near Mr B.'s house I saw one of his ladies looking out of the window, for he lives like the turks in that respect, but he is not singular[.] The head was instantly withdrawn & we entered."[43] Though Wilkinson was quite discreet and Burton at least somewhat so, Charles Humphreys was not discreet at all, and it is from him that we learn much of what we know about this aspect of their lives. Humphreys, incidentally, had a companion named Achmet, whom he referred to in his correspondence as "Adriana Copigliani."[44]

These women were probably what were called the "lost women" of Cairo, women who were not harlots but were of unstable family or uncertain social prospects and therefore compelled to take such opportunities as came to them. Some of the companions, however, were slaves, purchased in the Cairo slave market. Again we find little information in the papers of Wilkinson, whose slave girl appears briefly in a passage in Henry Westcar's diary: "Dined with Wilkinson who has got his female slave with him dressed as a Mameluke."[45] An acquaintance of Burton's, a mining engineer named Charles Sheffield who came to Egypt a few months after Burton, provides a few more details, including the fact that Wilkinson's slave initially refused to have anything to do with him, it being unlawful for an infidel to own a Muslim slave. One is reminded of Gérard de Nerval's hilarious and ultimately unsuccessful attempts to control his slave.[46] Wilkinson finally convinced her that he was a devout Muslim, albeit an English one. His circumcision probably made him more convincing. This may indeed have been the primary reason he and Burton pretended to be Muslims, a pretense that gave them pause at times because the penalty for reconversion was death. On this point, Sheffield wrote, "Wilkinson has also a slave but having undergone circumcision is competent to save his life if accused by denying himself a christian—he is in fact none but a confirmed Deist."[47]

Charles Humphreys left a distressingly vivid account of the acquisition of one of these slaves when he and the indispensable Osman went to arrange a purchase for Burton who conveniently managed to be busy that morning.

This morning was ushered in by a new scene. Osmyn [Osman] came about 9'o'clock to go with Mr. B. to complete the purchase of a female slave (from the country of the Gallas a province of Abyssinia) but he being obliged to go to the Citadel to fuse some metals I was ordered to go. We went to the slave market and when arrived there a most horrible sight presented itself. The slave market is a large square, surrounded by ruinous buildings. In the square sat a number of blacks male & female for sale several children of 4 or 5 years old were to be sold they came round me for money and Osmyn said these young slaves sold for more than those who had arrived at a greater age as it was in the power of the purchaser most probably to form their minds to his wish.

There were but a few light coloured ones and these were all from
Abyssinia (a kind of copper colour) one of which was selected for
our fellow traveller and companion and the more necessary companion of Mr. B. I seated myself on the ground with Osmyn and
the slave merchant and we counted out 12,00 Egyptian piastres[48]
the sum agreed upon for the buying & selling of a fellow crea-
ture. My blood crawled in my veins. When the purchase was
completed the poor girl was called from her miserable companions who all seemed callous to every feeling of friendship for
their companion whom they were now about to lose she was
measured for clothes as she was to appear as a boy We then left
the slave market and went to the Bazaar where we purchased the
necessary clothing to the amount of 176 piastres. We returned
and she was stripped of her clothing which consisted of nothing
more than a shift & a handkerchief (India? where did she get
this) and we took her home. A duty of four piastres is paid for
every slave bought at the market besides a certain sum paid to
the government when the slaves are brought into the country
The slave purchased was not more than 12 years old at most and
she was not sold as a virgin Qy [?]. at what age do the people of
this part arrive at puberty certainly much younger than in Europe. The poor girl. . . ."[49]

The next page of the unhappy narrative is missing.

Conditioned by the antislavery sentiment of early nineteenth-
century England, Wilkinson and his friends initially recoiled with
horror from the institution. Over time, however, they become comfortable enough with it and acquired slaves of their own. They
rationalized that slavery in the East was not so bad after all, especially compared with American slavery.[50] Wilkinson's friend,
Edward William Lane, left an upbeat account of the Cairo slave market. He wrote that the slaves there were generally very happy, knowing that the worst of their experiences were over and that a Muslim
slave usually fared better than a free servant.[51]

Although Wilkinson, like most Europeans, adopted a condescending and contemptuous attitude toward the Egyptians, the fact that
they heartily returned the same attitude was not lost upon him. He
noted the "absurd notion of superiority over the Christians" that
was especially evident in the conduct of beggars: "The *Faithful* beg-
gar, barely covered with scanty rags, unclean with filth, thinks himself polluted by the contact of a Christian, whose charity he seldom
condescends to ask in the same terms as from a *True Believer*; and
'*bakshish* ya Hawágee' ('A present, shopkeeper') is substituted for

'Sowáb lilláh, ya Sídi' ('Charity, honored sir.')." The term *shop-keeper* applied to all Europeans; it carried an element of contempt similar to Napoleon's deprecation of the English as "a nation of shopkeepers." "Moslims," Wilkinson continued, "however degraded their condition, treat all Europeans as shopkeepers, unworthy of aspiring to their own innate excellence. The minuteness of religious prejudice has added another distinction; for they do not even give the Christian shopkeeper the same name as their own; the infidel being called *Hawágee*, while the *True Believer* has the more honourable distinction of *Khawágee*."[52]

Such attitudes toward Turks and Egyptians kept Wilkinson apart from Egyptian society. There is no record of his becoming close friends with a Turk, though he might be cordial with an oddity like Hekekyan Bey, an Armenian engineer who was a Catholic and a Freemason.[53] And there certainly is no indication that he ever became well acquainted with an Egyptian family, was accepted into it, and shared its inner secrets. There were, of course, Egyptians whom he knew well, such as Haji Musa—but that relationship was master and servant; nor could the woman or women he lived with have helped him much, even had he wished them to. Not that Wilkinson avoided Egyptians, for he frequently fell into conversation with them at inns and such places, but he took little opportunity to explore their thoughts and motivations. Instead, he merely found them quaint and chuckled in his letters to Gell at their outlandish notions. Between him and the people about him was a great gulf of miscomprehension that he was uninterested in crossing. His attitude, which transformed his observations into caricatures, even lampoons, limits his value as an ethnographer, though a close reader may nevertheless infer many significant details from his notebooks.

Comfortably situated, Wilkinson and Burton enjoyed themselves and got along well in Cairo. Two young men, Wilkinson in his early twenties and Burton in his early thirties, they were living a luxurious, exotic life that they could only have dreamed of in England. Each aspired to write about Egypt and was accumulating a large collection of miscellaneous notes to that end. Wilkinson's ideas were still tentative; Burton's were more developed: already he had collected material for a geological study of the Eastern Desert and a chronological history of ancient Egypt, either of which would have been important had it been completed. He also did a series of sketches of architecture and topography, occasionally employing other artists to help him, besides making copies of hieroglyphs. Burton was, indeed, the first to publish when he brought out his *Excerpta Hieroglyphica* of 1825–28. That, incidentally, was the first appearance of Wilkinson's name in print, because Burton mentioned a tomb that Wilkinson had opened.[54] But *Excerpta Hieroglyphica* marked both the beginning and the end of Burton's publishing career. Full of ambitions, too many perhaps, he could seldom finish anything, a debility that increasingly was compounded by periods of depression. Wilkinson, in contrast, could see a project through. Thomas Young, who dealt with both Wilkinson and Burton, took their relative measure. After waiting years for Burton to copy an important inscription, Young finally wrote angrily, "It is quite melancholy to think that Mr. Burton may possibly be knocked in the head without sending over a line of the Inscription in the mosque, which is well worth the life of any moderate travellers: Mr. W. would have had it all on paper in an hour or two!"[55] Wilkinson and Burton eventually drifted apart as Burton became more moody and Wilkinson went his bright, sometimes overly-optimistic way, but for the moment they were the best of friends. When Burton invited Wilkinson to accompany an expedition that he was conducting into the Eastern Desert in 1823, Wilkinson eagerly accepted.

Their primary objective was the chain of mountains that runs most of the length of the Eastern Desert. Burton had been there the year before hunting coal for Muhammad Ali. He found no coal, but gained a good knowledge of the area, hitherto only slightly explored.[56] His tales of mysterious ruins had especially excited Wilkinson's curiosity, so Wilkinson decided to accompany Burton for a distance and then strike out on his own. This is one of the best-documented periods of Wilkinson's stay in Egypt, so we will follow his little expedition in some detail.[57]

Wilkinson and Burton first passed upstream some seventy miles to the town of Beni Suef, a provincial capital and the starting point for the important caravan route west to the Fayyum. Despite the administrative and commercial importance of the town, Wilkinson found it too crude for his taste, complaining that, unlike other large towns in Egypt, it did not have a bath. When his friend Robert Hay first saw the town a year or two later, he found it so filthy and squalid that he refused to land his boat there. But in many ways the town was typical of those along the river. Wilkinson wrote, "The bank at Benisooéf presents the ordinary scenes common to all the large towns of the Nile; the most striking of which are, numerous boats tied to the shore,—buffaloes standing or lying in the water,— women at their usual morning and evening occupation of filling water-jars and washing clothes,—dogs lying in holes they have scratched in the cool earth,—and beggars importuning each newly-arrived European stranger with the odious word 'bakshish.'"[58] As for antiquities, there were only a few nearby, the most notable being the pyramid of Sesostris II, some twelve miles away. At Beni Suef, for some reason, they tarried several weeks before turning east. Perhaps they were hiring Arabs and buying camels, for Burton knew from experience that it was better to travel with one's own animals.[59] Wilkinson and Burton whiled away the hours by the river, catching crabs that, they noted, were similar to those in British waters.

They finally started east on 28 February 1823 in a caravan of sixty-six camels and twenty dromedaries.[60] Wilkinson may have imagined that he was mounted much as an ancient Egyptian traveler might have been. We know now that the camel was unknown to ancient Egypt. Even in Wilkinson's time this fact was suspected, but he never fully accepted it.[61] They followed the Wadi Araba, which provides a passage through the mountains to the Red Sea. At first the trip was dull, the monotonous landscape being broken only by occasional trees and shrubs growing in dry stream beds. After traveling seventy-six miles, they reached the Monastery of Saint Anthony, surrounded by its high walls.[62] Like many desert monasteries, Saint Anthony's had no gate: a rope was lowered from a trap door high overhead and they were pulled inside the walls. There they found a pleasant jumble of buildings interspersed with gardens full of fruit and vegetables. But Wilkinson was disappointed when the monks would not allow him to examine their library: "They were very unwilling to show us even their worn-out bibles, which they said were all they had. This is the conduct of all monks in the East, though it is well known that in some of the convents are to be found rare and valuable manuscripts." Wilkinson's suspicions were justified, for many monasteries did indeed have treasures in their libraries, though sometimes unknown to the monks. It was from one of these monastries that the Codex Sinaiticus, the famous fourth-century biblical manuscript, was discovered in 1859; and Robert Baron Curzon amassed a fine collection of manuscripts during his tour of monastic libraries in Egypt and the Near East during 1833–34. Also, Wilkinson's friend, Lord Prudhoe, discovered a Coptic word list in a monastery, a find that greatly assisted Wilkinson's linguistic efforts.

When Wilkinson and Burton left Saint Anthony's on 12 March they went to investigate stories they had heard of ancient copper mines at a place that Wilkinson called Réigatameréëh, a short day's journey to the north. They had read that this part of the desert was especially horrible, so they were pleasantly surprised to find it not so bad after all: "So far from its being for the most part destitute of every trace of animals and vegetation,—so far from its being the Avernus of the winged tribe, and a mere parched sand abandoned by all reptiles but the ant, we had the pleasure of seeing, every now and then, gazelles and taytals browsing under the shadow of the seyále, or brought in by the Arab chasseur;—vultures and kites soaring above us; and, at evening, were visited by a strolling party of scorpions, and a wandering snake." The next day, they confirmed the existence of the copper mines and inspected the remains of miners' houses and the abundant piles of potsherds. Regular shafts showed where veins of ore had been followed.

The Red Sea was quite close by, but Wilkinson was not impressed with it, noting the flatness of the beach and complaining that "the damp vapour which rises from the marshy soil must be exceedingly hurtful, and even dangerous in the hot season." His attention was characteristically drawn to seashells along the shore. One of the Arabs found in the sand some beads, European bullets, stained glass, and cloth, evidently the burying place of Europeans. As the party moved south they found nothing to interest them until they reached a ruined town that soon became something of a mystery to them. At first they thought it had been built by the ancient Egyptians, but they searched in vain for inscriptions to confirm their guess. Their perplexity only increased when they found evidence that the inhabitants had cremated their dead, something the ancient Egyptians did not do. Wilkinson, on the doubtful basis of a toponymic consideration, decided that the town probably had been Greek, not Egyptian.

Returning a few miles inland, they reached the Monastery of Saint Paul, a Coptic institution like Saint Anthony's. Since they had been roughing it for several days, they probably looked forward to rest and hospitality, but if that was indeed their expectation, then they were disappointed. The monastery was more attractive than Saint Anthony's—located in a much more spectacular place—and the monks cleaner and better dressed, but the desert-weary travelers were met with silence. Wilkinson was annoyed with this reception and concluded that the monks were ignorant, uncouth, and inhospitable. He may not have known that the rules of their order demanded silence and reserve.[63]

When he left Cairo with Burton, Wilkinson had intended to pass quickly through the Eastern Desert and then proceed to the western oases, "but alarmed at the intelligence of a fever in the wadi, & contented with the enjoyment of the pleasant society of the friend whom I had accompanied," he decided to remain with Burton on a longer trip to the southeast through the mountain chain.[64] Now, in contrast to the first portion of the journey, they entered a region of breathtaking beauty. Composed of strata of upthrusted rock, the peaks of the Red Sea Mountains have been molded by the erosion and sheering of millennia into fantastic, jagged shapes. Moving through this unforgettable terrain with its spectacular sunrises and sunsets, they came at length to the most impressive ruins that Wilkinson saw on this expedition, Mons Porphyrites, the Roman quarries near Gebel (Mount) Dokhan.[65] Such was the Roman Empire's demand for porphyry that a large fortified settlement, a castellum, had been established there as a base for extracting the stone. The most notable remains in the town were an Ionic temple of Serapis that bore an inscription dating to the reign of Hadrian and a large, pillared house, perhaps the praefect's residence. As Wilkinson wandered through the deserted site, he felt a sense of the past: "We had the satisfaction of seeing ruins of some extent; of viewing those vast quarries, from which Rome took so many superb pieces of porphyry to adorn her baths and porticos; of contemplating the labour and expense incurred in making so many fine roads, which cross the mountains in all directions; of walking in the streets and houses of the old inhabitants of an ancient town; and, above all, of finding a temple in the midst of a now deserted and uninhabitable valley."

They next returned to the Red Sea, to Abu Shaar, which Wilkinson and Burton believed to be Myos Hormos, an ancient Greek port town on the Red Sea.[66] Wilkinson thought the ruins there were somewhat disappointing after Mons Porphyrites, heavily obscured by sand as they were. He gave them less attention, though he managed to make a surprisingly accurate survey of the site in a very short time. As was his custom, he went down to the shore to look for marine life, and while wading he was attacked by some especially aggressive crabs. He stayed only one night at Abu Shaar, but contracted so serious a case of dysentery that he eventually had to cut short his trip. His sickness moved him to write, "No place can be more unhealthy. During the summer months the atmosphere is charged with damp vapour, exceedingly oppressive, and resembling that of a Turkish bath. In the time of the prosperity of Myos Hormos, many were, doubtless, the victims of its unwholesome air."

Wilkinson found the strength to return to the mountains and visit the important white granite (not marble, as Wilkinson identified the stone) quarry at Mons Claudianus. Despite the place name, Wilkinson concluded, probably incorrectly, that the quarries had been worked only during the reigns of the emperors Trajan (A.D. 98–117) and Hadrian (117–138), not Claudius (41–54). Wilkinson and Burton examined the extensive complex, which consisted of outlying villages and stations, a main town, a fort for a detachment of the twenty-fifth legion, and the quarries themselves. As always, Wilkinson carefully copied all the inscriptions that he saw, in this instance

Greek and Latin dedications dating from the time of Trajan and Hadrian.

The immediacy of the past is probably more poignant at Mons Claudianus than at Mons Porphyrites. The walls and buildings, largely composed of piled stone, are so well preserved that one gets the feeling that the inhabitants left only the week before, intending to return and resume their lives.[67] But Wilkinson was ill-inclined to experience such feelings now. Dysentery was getting the best of him. Though he had intended to travel farther, he now, in his words, "was obliged, by indisposition, to return as speedily as possible towards Cairo." When the party turned north toward Gebel Dokhan, Wilkinson took his leave of Burton, setting out for the Nile, a little more than fifty miles away in a straight line.

As they wound their way around in the longer route dictated by the terrain, the jagged mountains gave way to lower rounded hills and wastes of sand and stone swept by hot winds. It was now June; as temperatures rose, Wilkinson must have thought longingly of the cool weather when the journey had begun in the winter. They discovered that their water skins were defective, leaving them barely enough water for themselves and nothing for the dromedaries. With his dysentery Wilkinson suffered acutely. Two light camels were sent ahead to bring water back from the Nile. Two days later, they met the returning water party and were able to give their animals just enough to maintain their strength. Later that day, 10 June 1823, they sighted the palm trees and town of Qena on the Nile. "After so long an abode in the desert, everything appeared new and agreeable. Ripe water-melons were in abundance, and an universal verdure surrounded us; but nothing was so striking as the profusion and negligence with which water seemed to be lavished, an article which we had been in the habit of guarding as the most precious of our provisions. The Nile had already begun to rise, and promised another rich harvest, which it only requires a more energetic people, and a better government, to render doubly profitable."

Wilkinson floated down to Cairo on the rising Nile in late June 1823. Soon thereafter he completed his first full-length manuscript, "Journey in Nubia, the Eastern Desert, & to Báhneséh."[68] This was a rather conventional traveler's account, and it included maps, plates, and various lists, such as thermometer readings on successive days. When he finished it, he sent it to a publisher in Italy. In the preface Wilkinson equivocated about his intentions, writing that he regarded himself "as a traveller & not as an author," but he clearly hoped to see this work published.

As it turned out, "Journey in Nubia" never appeared in print, and for good reasons. Its elements lay uneasily together, with little connection between the excursions. Indeed, when the Committee of the Royal Society of Literature later considered it, they found it "not sufficiently arranged in proper form for publication."[69] Also, the quality of Wilkinson's prose, though careful and fairly clear, was not yet up to the mark. Frequently consisting of little more than bare itinerary and summary description, it conveyed little of the sense of having been there that makes a travel book succeed. Even so, it was good experience for Wilkinson to write it. For the first time he wrestled with the problems of organizing and presenting material, and the diligence he displayed in finishing and mailing his manuscript augured well for future work.

More Explorations: Geographic, Antiquarian, and Hieroglyphic

WILKINSON IS PRIMARILY REMEMBERED today for his antiquarian activities, but when he was in Egypt he devoted much of his time and energy to geographic explorations: to cartography, topographical sketches, and descriptions of people and terrain. He shared the aspirations of those nineteenth-century travelers and explorers who sought to fill in the blank spaces on the map and to document the life-styles—or the manners and customs, as they would have said—of people different from themselves. His initial trip up the Nile with Wiggett in 1822 and his tour of the Eastern Desert with Burton the following year were only the prelude to years of travel during which he covered the length and breadth of Egypt.

For his next major expedition he planned another ascent of the Nile and accordingly left Cairo on 28 February 1824 bound for Aswan, but a series of setbacks ruined his plans.[1] His first misfortune was to fall ill at Minya, some 150 miles upriver from Cairo, where he was compelled to remain for eight weeks.[2] Then came a much more serious problem when the *fellahin* of Upper Egypt revolted in one of the several such uprisings that disturbed, without seriously threatening, the reign of Muhammad Ali. Though soon suppressed, the rebellion was, while it lasted, a source of anxiety for those British travelers who happened to be on the river.[3] From their boats they witnessed scenes of violence and saw dead bodies eaten by dogs along the river banks. Wilkinson was confronted by a band of rebels at one point, but he had fallen in with some boats carrying government troops. He passed in safety. The hardships he suffered should not be exaggerated, because he was aboard a comfortable *dahabiyah* and accompanied by his female slave.[4] He eventually reached Qena where one by one the British travelers arrived, laying to rest the rumors of their demise that had been circulating. John Madox, who sailed up to Qena on 26 April 1824, recorded that he found there "all the English who had lately been in Upper Egypt, viz. Captain Pringle, and Messrs. Wilkinson, Parke, Scoles, Westcar, and Catherwood. We were all delighted at meeting, and congratulated each other on our fortunate escape."[5] Even then, Wilkinson's difficulties were not finished, for a devastating epidemic broke out downstream and compelled him to linger several weeks before he could safely return to Cairo.

Undeterred by this setback, however, Wilkinson subsequently made repeated forays on camel trail and river. He went to the Fayyum for the first time in 1824, not long after the revolt of the *fellahin.* The Fayyum is a lakeside oasis some fifty miles south-southwest of Cairo. Because of its extreme fertility, it was one of the most prosperous and densely populated parts of the country during ancient times and was the site of many monuments, including the once-magnificent Labyrinth. Wilkinson made a detailed map of the area, thereby putting his newly acquired mapmaking skills to good use.[6] During his years in Egypt he frequently indulged in cartographic exercises.

The following year he explored the western oases of Egypt. These oases are scattered through the western desert, relics of times long past when the region was much wetter than it is now. The best-known of the oases is Siwa, famous for a visit by Alexander the Great who came to consult the oracle of the god Amon. Besides temples, there were remains of fortifications, for the oases were outposts against Libyan intruders. They had been visited a few times by Europeans in modern times, all of whom ran some risk by traveling in European dress.[7] Wilkinson, of course, did not have that problem since he traveled as a Turk. He still spoke Arabic imperfectly, but so did many Turks; therefore, the deficiency completed his disguise.[8] The oases were rather unruly, and Muhammad Ali had found it necessary to send an army to subdue them in 1820.[9] To reach them was no easy undertaking, requiring a journey of nine to ten days along a waterless route. Just as he was beginning this expedition Wilkinson suffered a misadventure that he recounted in detail to Sir William Gell.

He and Haji Musa were caught on the road by a heavy rainstorm and compelled to seek shelter in a village. They could not find the *shaykh al-balad,* or village chief, whose duty it was to entertain travelers, but someone directed them to an inn where they could escape the storm. The inn, however, was crowded, so they went instead to a dry, vacant portico that they had spotted further down the street. No sooner had they reached their destination than a passing boy cried, "Ye people, the Turk has gone into the hareem." Too late Wilkinson realized that the portico was indeed connected to a harem and that he and Haji Musa were in a dangerous situation. They tried to silence the boy, but he cried out louder; then the women inside became alarmed and added their voices to the din. An angry crowd quickly gathered.

> I was on the verge of being struck to the ground by one of those formidable sticks the Egyptian peasants wield so adroitly, when I drew my pistols, & exchanged my excuses with determined threats. At the same time I commenced my retreat toward the *mándara* (receiving room), which with considerable difficulty I reached, flanked by my servant, who displayed a pistol in one hand, & a very efficient knife in the other, & followed by a dense crowd. On reaching that room the uproar increased, by the influx of a considerable reinforcement from the opposite side of the village, & great deeds were threatened; but fear fortunately prevented the striking of the first blow, & a certain respect for firearms forbade anyone from setting the example of courage & devotion to the cause.

At that moment the shaykh and the *kaimakam*, the Turkish governor, fortunately arrived. With great difficulty they calmed the crowd, and then only after someone, probably hoping for a reward, came forward as a favorable witness. The shaykh took Wilkinson home with him and gave him supper. Together they talked late into the night.[10] Writing about it to Gell, Wilkinson doubtless recalled a similar incident that Gell had experienced and described some years earlier in his book *The Topography of Troy.*[11]

Wilkinson did at length reach the western oases where he took notes about their inhabitants, their physical aspects, and their ruins.[12] But the oases left no fond impression upon him, for later, when he wrote to his friend Robert Hay who had just returned from them, he said, "At all events I wish you joy on your return for of all places on earth I do think the oases the most miserable. People used to talk of fortunate & blessed islands & other similar nonsense—it was a pity that they were not forced to live there. The people of the wadis are the most stupid beings on earth full of religious prejudice—a sure sign of ignorance. You lost nothing by not going to the little oasis."[13]

Wilkinson punctuated his years in Egypt with frequent withdrawals into the Eastern Desert. There he would remain for long periods of time, sending Haji Musa to the Nile for replenishment when provisions ran low.[14] In late 1825 and early 1826 he made two more trips into the Eastern Desert. In the first of these he mainly followed the itinerary of the 1823 trip: Saint Anthony's Monastery, Mons Porphyrites, Mons Claudianus, then back to Qena; in the second he reached much farther south along the coast to Kosseir and Bereniké before returning to Qena.[15] Other such trips into the Eastern Desert followed as he came to love the peace and solitude of the wastes and the unexpected beauty of an area that has remained little known to travelers until fairly recently. Coming to the area at that time of year, he found it even more striking than before, for the precious light of the Egyptian winter revealed delicate hues that had been washed out by the bright sunlight of late spring on his first trip.

During these travels he had to endure many hardships, for sandstorms, hunger, and thirst were recurring conditions. In 1826 when he was among the Ababda Arabs of the Eastern Desert, he shared his food with them to relieve their suffering from an especially bad famine. Consequently, he ran out of food himself and had to subsist for a time upon crude bread that he made from the camels' feed. The Ababda remembered his generosity and later repaid him by visiting him in Cairo and Thebes and telling him about antiquities they had found.[16]

From 1824 onward Wilkinson's travels began to have a sharper antiquarian focus, a sharpening that coincided with the granting of his *firman* for research that Henry Salt obtained for him that year.[17] This *firman* was essential because the pasha controlled, at least in theory, all rights to any kind of archaeological undertaking in Egypt. Before anyone could be assured of even being allowed to look at some monuments, a *firman* was required. It might be supposed that Muhammad Ali would have been sparing of *firman*s, especially to people like Salt whose primary intention was to ship away valuable antiquities, but that was not the case. Muhammad Ali's attitude was that if it pleased the Europeans to collect those objects, then let them take what they wanted. Salt was therefore able to obtain *firman*s for himself and others, and he was always willing to help British travelers in that capacity. The *firman*, however, did not solve all problems—indeed, one traveler wrote that a *firman* meant little more than permission to make the best terms possible with the local authorities—but in Wilkinson's case his *firman* was supplemented by some extraordinary grants from Muhammad Ali who, Wilkinson later wrote, was "invariably" kind to him.

Mohammad Ali not only gave me every facility for excavating & for preventing the Turks from injuring the monuments which

last I protected on every occasion when required (as in preventing the sappers & miners from continuing their havoc in the
tombs of the Assas'eef at Thebes, in stopping the destruction of
the small temple at the N. end of Gebel E'Tayr, & so many other
occasions) but gave me a private letter to the governors of the
provinces & even an unlimited order to draw upon any of them
any sums of money I might require throughout Egypt & Nubia &
in Ethiopia to Sennár.—This was indeed a gratifying compliment
to the English & one which was given to no one (except to the
Duke of Northumberland when he traveled in Egypt) & as
Mʳ——— observed to me was never accorded to any of the
French or others in Egypt though they were supposed to be such
political friends of Mohammad Ali.[18]

Obviously Wilkinson's initial opinion of Muhammad Ali had changed
for the better, and Muhammad Ali may have decided that Wilkinson
was someone worth cultivating.

When Wilkinson explored the antiquities of Egypt, he knew few of
the things that we take for granted, for ancient Egypt, unlike classical Greece or Rome, communicated no narrative history of itself to
succeeding civilizations. The coherent picture of ancient Egypt that
we enjoy today, sketchy and incomplete though it is in places, is
a fairly recent accomplishment, less than a century old. When Wilkinson and his colleagues began to assemble their framework of ancient Egyptian history, they had to build upon rudimentary, often
unsound foundations. To them, the provenance of the most important monuments was unclear. Even the origins of the Pyramids at
Giza, the very symbols of the orderly achievement of the Old Kingdom, were debated by Wilkinson and his friends. Much was made of
the fact that no hieroglyphic writing had been found on or in them,
leading some to speculate that they must have been constructed at
some dim date before the development of ancient Egyptian writing,
though a cursory reading of Herodotus should have dispelled that
notion.[19] Wilkinson rightly disagreed, correctly assigning the Pyramids to the Fourth Dynasty, a period that was, however, mostly unknown to him. His guess was confirmed some years later when
Colonel Richard Vyse, working with Giovanni Battista Caviglia and
J. S. Perring, discovered a cartouche on one of the pyramids.[20] Even
after all of his years in Egypt Wilkinson was still uncertain of the
names of the kings who had ordered them built and the circumstances of their construction, though his speculation was quite
astute.

From all that can be collected on this head, it appears that Suphis and his brother Sensuphis erected them about the year 2120 B.C.; and the tombs in their vicinity may have been built, or cut in the rock, shortly after their completion. These present the names of very ancient kings, whom we are still unable to refer to any certain epoch, or to place in the series of dynasties; but whether they were contemporary with the immediate predecessors of Osirtasen, or ruled the whole of Egypt, is a question that I do not as yet pretend to answer.[21]

Another pyramid that attracted Wilkinson's interest was the Bent, or Rhomboidal, Pyramid at Dashur, south of Giza. This pyramid slopes upward at an unusually steep angle until halfway to the top where it turns in suddenly. It presents a peculiar sight, and it aroused various conjectures about how it came to be as it was. Wilkinson guessed that the intended height of the pyramid had been reduced midway through construction for more rapid completion. This supposition received some support from Perring who examined the pyramid's superstructure in 1839 and noticed that the stones of the upper portion were laid less carefully than those below.[22] From that it followed that the king might have died before the pyramid was finished and that his successor rushed the job in order to begin his own pyramid and thereby avoid the same predicament for himself. A more likely explanation is that the height and slope of the pyramid had to be reduced to prevent collapse.

The limitations of Wilkinson's knowledge of ancient Egypt are perhaps best illustrated by his experiences at Tell el-Amarna. Amarna is located on the east bank some three hundred miles downstream from Thebes in a small plain surrounded by ridges. Today we know it well as the capital of the heretical pharaoh Akh-en-Aton who turned against Amon and the other gods of Egypt and attempted to supplant them with a new religion centered upon the worship of the solar disk, Aton. Because Thebes, the capital of Egypt, was inextricably identified with the hated Amon, Akh-en-Aton moved the capital to Amarna where he built anew, laying out a spacious, well-ordered city with royal palaces for himself and his family, estates for his nobles, and shops and quarters for the workmen. In the hills above he ordered tombs to be hewn for himself and his most exalted followers. Accompanying the religious revolution was a revolution in art, as a new and more natural style developed. Even Akh-en-Aton's deformed body was portrayed realistically. Also new was the iconography that depicted Aton as the sun with his rays reaching down as

arms and terminating in hands holding out *ankh*s, or life, to his wor-
shipers. Akh-en-Aton's revolution eventually ran into difficulties;
after his death the priests of Amon reasserted the authority of the
old gods and relentlessly attempted to expunge every memory of the
heretical interlude. Amarna was abandoned, and so successful was
the priests' work of oblivion that travelers of the eighteenth and
nineteenth centuries passed it quite ignorant of its significance or
the fact that such a king as Akh-en-Aton had ever reigned there.
Napoleon's expedition took brief note of the ruined town in the
plain, but other visitors tended to avoid it, deterred perhaps by
the evil reputation of the local people. Apparently no one visited the
tombs until 1824 when Wilkinson came.

Wilkinson's explorations apparently were confined to the northern group of tombs and primarily to the tomb of Meryra. Of the
tombs in the southern hills he was probably unaware, though he
mentions a "natural grotto" to the south with "several workings" in
it.[23] The frescoes he saw in the tombs mystified him. "The sculptures are singular & nearly in plain style as those of Gebel Toóna,
tho' not quite so much out of proportion. They are all of the same
king as that Tablet, who may possibly be some Persian, since the
arms & drapes are not common in Egt sculptures. They were not all
completed."[24] His puzzlement shows in a letter he wrote to an acquaintance shortly after he returned to Cairo: "I have discovered
some grottoes a short distance from the Nile which I believe no travellers had visited before me, in the sculptures of which (though the
work of Egyptians) the sun itself is represented with rays terminating in hands thus which is never seen in other parts of Egypt; In addition to this the name of the King (written in hieroglyphics) has
been purposely effaced, tho I have managed to get a copy of it."[25] He
included a drawing and asked his correspondent if he had seen anything like it in Persian art.

When he returned to Amarna two years later, he brought James
Burton with him. Burton also was confused by what he saw in the
tombs, noting, "No other deity but the sun is any where to be found,
either sculptures, or I believe, written."[26] The unusual artwork left
him unmoved: "I should think the style of sculpture is very peculiar
& very bad."[27] Few would agree now with Burton's judgment, but it
is understandable how the uncanonical representations at Amarna,
especially that of Akh-en-Aton's distended body, bewildered the artistic sensibilities of the first explorers. When Sir William Gell examined the copy that Wilkinson sent him of the now famous mural
depicting Akh-en-Aton and his queen Nefertiti raising their arms to

Aton, he interpreted it as a representation of two pregnant females offering sacrifice.[28]

Wilkinson and Burton found an alabaster quarry nearby and decided on that basis that they had discovered the site of Alabastron, a name known to them from classical sources. The correct identification of the area would not be established until after 1887 when the famous Amarna Tablets were discovered and systematic investigation of the town in the plain began. The mystery of the place caused Wilkinson to swear Burton to secrecy about the existence of the tombs, an unusual step among men who were accustomed to sharing information with their colleagues. He wanted Amarna all to himself, much to the annoyance of their friend Robert Hay when he found out about it.[29]

A final note about this site is the strange bit of toponymic mischief that Wilkinson played by calling it Tell el-Amarna. In fact, that was not the name by which it was known. El-Amarna, derived from the name of a local tribe, was the name of the entire district, and el-Till was one of several villages in it. From these names, Wilkinson composed Tell el-Amarna. That gives one the erroneous impression that the site is a tell, a man-made mound that is the accumulation of centuries or millennia of habitation, which Amarna assuredly is not. One might reasonably suppose Wilkinson mistakenly heard "Tell" when the natives said "Till," were it not for the fact that he himself also referred to the place as Til el Amarna in his early work.[30] For whatever reasons, Wilkinson subsequently altered the name to Tell el-Amarna and applied it to the entire site, not just the village of el-Till. The name was subsequently adopted by scholars and travelers, resulting, one historian notes, in "a name as familiar to the visitor as it is strange to the inhabitants."[31]

A few miles north of Amarna and also on the east bank is Beni Hasan. The most important Middle Kingdom necropolis, Beni Hasan contains thirty-nine rock-cut tombs. Of particular value are the sketches that Wilkinson made of the well-known pictures of birds and bats in the tomb of Bakt III. These are evidence for establishing the variety of ancient Egyptian wildfowl. Wilkinson saw and copied the pictures when they were in an almost perfect state of preservation; when Ippolito Rosellini sketched them only a few years later, they already had sustained some damage; by the century's end they had greatly deteriorated.[32] Wilkinson's sketches are, therefore, an important source, as indeed are Rosellini's, though Wilkinson found fault with Rosellini's work and noted such inaccuracies in color and detail as the addition of a spur to a bird's foot that did not have one in the original.³³ Making a deeper impression upon Wilkinson at Beni Hasan were the sculptures that showed people engaged in daily pursuits, working and playing. From these he began to form his conception of the manners and customs of the ancient Egyptians.³⁴ Wilkinson was one of the first modern explorers at Beni Hasan. His well-documented visit in 1824, which was not his first, puts him well before Champollion and Rosellini who were there in 1828 on their sketching expedition.³⁵

Wilkinson's most frequent stopping place, apart from Cairo, was Luxor, the site of ancient Thebes. Though he eventually settled down to extensive work in the tombs of the nobles at Gurna, in his earlier forays he was drawn to the more spectacular monuments, of which Thebes has many. A notable project during this stage of his research at Thebes was his investigation of the vocal statue of Memnon, described in an earlier chapter, that had been renowned in antiquity for making musical sounds at dawn. Wilkinson, well versed in the classics, was puzzled by the phenomenon and sought a plausible explanation for it.³⁶

The two so-called Colossi of Memnon stand in the plain on the west bank. According to Edward William Lane, the natives of Luxor called them Sh'mikh and Ta'mikh (both words mean "lofty") and believed that they conversed with each other at night.³⁷ The vocal statue is the one on the right, or to the north. Like the Roman geographer Strabo, Wilkinson suspected that its sounds might have been made by priestly trickery, and he set about confirming his suspicions, a task he undertook better informed than many of his predecessors. He understood that the colossi were not associated with the Homeric hero Memnon who, he wrote, "was neither an Egyptian, nor the person the colossus represented," knowing instead that they had been part of the temple complex of Amen-hotep III. Also, he carefully studied the inscriptions on the vocal statue, many of which he copied, and concluded that it had not made its sounds "at a remote period." He was wrong, however, when he assigned the restoration of the statue to the principate of Hadrian.

Wilkinson ascended to the lap of the statue and discovered "the sonorous quality of a block of fine gritstone placed immediately over the girdle." Having noted that one of the inscriptions compared the statue's sound to the striking of brass, he posted some *fellahin* around the base and struck the sonorous gritstone block with a hammer. When he asked the people below if they had heard anything, they shouted back, "You are striking brass." From this experiment Wilkinson concluded that he had reproduced the very sound that the ancients had heard. He also found a small recess where a deceiving priest could have hidden while striking the block. In his report some years later, Wilkinson concluded, "Such was the credulity of the ancients, that no inquiry was made when once the belief of a miracle was established; and superstition pronounced it dangerous to doubt the interposition of the gods." A more likely explanation is the consensus of modern scholars that the sound was triggered by expansion of the stones caused by heat from the morning sun. Septimius Severus' restoration somehow disrupted that mechanism and silenced the statue. Even so, Wilkinson's efforts were noteworthy. He wrote to Gell about his research on the colossus, and Gell in turn wrote about it to William Hamilton, the secretary of the Society of Dilettanti in London, who passed the letter on to the Royal Society of Literature. Gell, though impressed by Wilkinson's work, did not find it quite up to his own finely detailed standards. He told Hamilton, "Whether there were several pieces or only one stone I cannot tell You as my account is from a person neither very observant [n]or very musical."[38]

Of course, Gell knew that Wilkinson could be quite observant whenever he chose to be. The fact was, however, that Wilkinson gave the great monuments less notice as his attention was drawn increasingly to those remains that could tell him about everyday life in ancient Egypt. Even so, he was alert and inquisitive. For example, the obelisks of Thebes naturally aroused his curiosity, for even the most basic questions about them remained unanswered. Were they constructed of one block of stone or several? How were they quarried and moved? How were they erected? Wilkinson saw quickly enough that they were indeed one piece of granite, and his investigations in the quarry near Aswan convinced him that they were separated from their beds by leaving supports in the native rock. The spaces between those supports were then filled with wooden beams, the supports hewn away, and the obelisks laboriously dragged to the river on rollers or skids and floated by barge to their intended locations.[39] The obelisks of Thebes impressed him by being better preserved than the two obelisks known as Cleopatra's Needles at Alexandria.

In this fashion—traveling, taking notes, sketching, and speculating on a wide range of subjects—Wilkinson passed his early years in Egypt. In 1826 he was again at the Pyramids of Giza making a survey, and 1827–28 saw him back at Thebes doing extended work. He seemed to pause at one place only long enough to rest, organize his papers, write a little, and then move on. Some idea of his state of motion may be inferred from these lines he wrote to Gell from Qena in 1826:

I now go Qáhirah [Cairo] by the breezy desert, & expect to reach it
in about 40 days: then take my boat & go up direct to E'Souan, &
take everything coming down. After that look at the [cuneiform]
of Ras el Wady & the Labyrinth of Faioom which I think I can fix
upon with certity; then Natron Lakes & to Malta, where if I find
my papers not yet gone to England I remain a short time & hope
to take a sail over to you, & return to Egypt. But the Greek affair
[the Greek War of Independence] may alter my plans.[40]

Amid all of this activity, Wilkinson worked assiduously at trying
to decipher the ancient Egyptian language. His zeal and energy were
such that by the end of the summer of 1822 Henry Salt reported to
Sir William Gell, "The interest he takes in our Egyptian antiquities
far exceeds that of ordinary travellers. I have not indeed seen any
person here who has entered with so much spirit into the study of
hieroglyphics as Mr. W. and, as he has begun at the right end in
taking Dr. Young's work, so far as it merits, for a guide, he cannot
fail making considerable progress; more especially as he works *like
a horse at it."*[41] For this task his preparation under Gell's careful tutelage had carried him about as deeply into the science of Egyptian
hieroglyphs as anyone at that time could have hoped to go. That
meant that his newly acquired hieroglyphic erudition was a mixture
of genuine insight and misleading speculation.

By using Thomas Young's phonetic system, Wilkinson was able to
achieve some marginal results. It will be recalled, however, that the
method was thought to be applicable only to certain royal names,
primarily those of the Ptolemies and the Roman emperors; as Gell
reminded Wilkinson in 1822, "These Roman hierog⁵ are Alphabetic
or puns. perhaps the Greek are puns & the Roman alphabetic."[42] Applying Young's method to the names he saw in cartouches, or
"ovals" as he called them, Wilkinson was able to make out some of
them, though he could still be mystified by a Roman imperial cartouche in 1822.[43] So helpful was Young's technique that even the
much-maligned Henry Salt managed to read Cleopatra's name at
Philae by using it.[44]

But Young's method only supplied phonetic values for some
letters. Primarily useful for reading a few proper names, it was of
little use in translating most words or determining grammatical relationships. For the key to the language, Wilkinson, like many of his
colleagues, hoped to discover a multilingual inscription, another
Rosetta Stone. When he visited Rashid he spent much of his time
looking among the chunks of basalt that litter the area, vainly
hoping to find the missing pieces of the Stone.[45] He thought he had

found a parallel Greek and hieroglyphic inscription at Kom Ombo, but it turned out to be no such thing, though Rosellini later made the same mistake and published his erroneous conclusion.[46] Wilkinson also studied Coptic, the same approach that Champollion was taking, on the assumption—correct as it turned out—that the more modern language might resemble the ancient one. Had he pursued Coptic single-mindedly, Wilkinson might have achieved notable results, but he also relied heavily upon the arcane intricacies of Neoplatonism and Hermeticism, as well as the text attributed to Horapollo, another of those mysterious hieroglyphic treatises from late antiquity. From these sources Wilkinson, like many before him, derived the view that the hieroglyphs were based upon symbolic and philosophic principles, that they represented the language of learned priests. Hermetic and Neoplatonic influences are evident in his early efforts; for example, on his first trip upriver in 1822 we find him pondering over the significance of the hieroglyphic representation of a bee: "May this not in its original meaning be 'King of the people' or 'King of Men'? for the Bee (properly hornet) is said by Hor'apollo to signify 'a people obedient to the will of a King.'"[47] His attachment to Hermes Trismegistus also shows in his first major publication, *Topography of Thebes*, which he prefaced with a quotation from Hermes. Even after being in Egypt for years and having access to more accurate material, Wilkinson used Horapollo extensively.[48] Horapollo was, in fact, an especially insidious influence, for his text contains some correct elements, just enough to encourage scholars to rely upon it and be led astray.[49] Its author apparently drew upon some authentic material but misunderstood its nature. With such guides, Wilkinson could make only limited progress toward translating the hieroglyphs.

Even so, with more time Wilkinson might yet have made a linguistic breakthrough of at least modest proportions, but in 1822 Champollion published his famous *Lettre à M. Dacier*. This was the most emphatic statement of the phonetic principle of the hieroglyphs that had yet been put forward. Gell immediately wrote to inform Wilkinson of its contents. "Here you will therefore find," he wrote from Naples in June 1823, "the whole set of M͏ͬ Champollion's discoveries which begin with Young which he does not acknowledge." Gell resented the slight to Young, but went on to say, "Young has I believe contradicted some of them but I conclude the greater part of them are true." Indeed, Gell knew the subject well enough to recognize the importance of Champollion's work, because it enabled him to read some cartouches of Roman imperial names and titles that had previously been unintelligible to him. Explaining his rendering of the hieroglyphs for the emperor Trajan, he wrote, "& then to a man of your genius most illustrious Baba Mustapha eben Wilkinson [that] would mean autocrator Kaisaros Trainos Sebastos." He continued, "It appears that some of the Roman imperial titles may be found in some part of Egypt—at Philae &c. I have thus given you the chief examples of Mr. Champollion he gives about 80 but you can make them all out yourself now you have the dictionary & perhaps add others."[50]

The following year, Gell sent further results of the "new regime" (i.e., Champollion's),

> which has now superseded the old school of Young who remains the founder while Champollion has finished all the columns & friezes of the hieroglyphical edifice. He has turned all the cats Lions zigzags owls &c into letters & when you understand Coptic you have nothing left but to go on & read on a Theban wall all the newspaper advertisements for places of those days. I cannot give you a dissertation on it but the thing is quite settled so you may put implicit confidence in what I tell you so I must now begin with such letters as you may be supposed not to know.

After listing a hieroglyphic alphabet with its English phonetic equivalents, Gell concluded, "Thus you have got as far as hieroglyphics go to read everything. It is very odd that Youngs groups are often right but the parts have changed places."[51]

Champollion's announcement set off a controversy that Wilkinson watched with a well-informed eye. Thomas Young, in his *Encyclopaedia Britannica* article a few years earlier, had published a list of some alphabetic Egyptian characters and assigned correct phonetic values to most of them. Although Champollion had since then asserted that the hieroglyphs were ideographic, he now abruptly reversed himself and described how they functioned phonetically. The problem, especially as far as the British were concerned, was that Champollion nowhere mentioned Young and ever afterward maintained that the phonetic idea was his own. It, he explained, had come to him in a burst of revelation, the force of which knocked him unconscious. That Champollion had not read Young's work is doubtful, and even if he had not, scholarly etiquette called for some acknowledgment; this he never gave. Young's friends were furious, especially Gell, who wrote angrily to Young about the matter.[52] Young attempted to remain aloof from the altercations and continued to correspond and maintain cordial relations with Champollion, but the controversy continued, carried on by others. Occasionally it arouses disagreement even today.

To understand the annoyance that Young's partisans felt, the nature of Champollion's initial work must be specified. It is an overstatement to say that Champollion translated the hieroglyphs. Not until the 1840s was anyone able to translate a running hieroglyphic text. What Champollion did was provide a strong impetus to a cumulative effort that continued long after he was dead, and for years a fierce debate raged over whether he was right or not. It was at least fifteen years after the publication of the *Lettre à M. Dacier* before the emergence of a consensus that he had indeed taken the right direction.[53] In the 1820s, only a few like Wilkinson and Gell could see where it all was leading. Champollion's thesis would have initially seemed to knowledgeable people like Gell and Wilkinson to be not so much a new idea as a refinement, and a marginal one at that, of Young's method. The extent of Champollion's understanding of the hieroglyphs did not become apparent until the publication of his *Précis du système hiéroglyphique des anciens Egyptiens* in 1824 and the posthumous appearance of his works during the following decades.

Champollion's true accomplishment, therefore, was to open the door to reading ancient Egyptian. Once the nature of the script was understood, then the accumulation of a hieroglyphic vocabulary quickly followed through comparison of hieroglyphic and Coptic words, many of which are either identical or similar. Wilkinson himself participated in this process, greatly aided by the Coptic word list that his friend, Lord Prudhoe, had discovered. Wilkinson wrote to Gell, "Having no Dictionary, I have got through from the groundwork by means of Ld. Prudhoe's MSS, & gradually ascended from the grammar, of which I am very glad, as it gives a better idea of the formation of the language than what one learns from a Dictionary."[54] As the years passed and the usefulness of Champollion's subsequent work became clear, tempers cooled, and the controversy about Young and Champollion subsided into the background. Even Sir William Gell, who once had been one of Young's greatest partisans, came to see Champollion's accomplishment in clearer perspective. He wrote to Wilkinson in 1834, "I am delighted with what you say of Champollion & in looking for your coins in my book had occasion to observe how very much more imperfect everything must have been left if only the discoveries of Dr. Young had existed, for I have set down Young's translations in 1814 & 16 & certainly they are quite vague compared to what one knows after Champollion in the year 1821 & after."[55]

Although Wilkinson did not involve himself deeply in the controversy, it left him with some bias against Champollion. That may be the reason he did not bother to meet Champollioñ when the latter visited Egypt in 1828. Englishmen like Gell and Wilkinson resented Champollion's treatment of the man whose work they had studied and used—indeed, whose very work enabled them to appreciate Champollion's accomplishment. Wilkinson was well aware that Champollion once had opposed Young's phonetic thesis, maintaining that the hieroglyphs were "signs of things, and not sounds," and he always considered that the notebooks he made in the autumn of 1821 were a proof of the primacy of Young's discovery.[56] But, like Gell, Wilkinson recognized the value of Champollion's work, though he never quite forgave the Frenchman for the slight to Young.[57]

Equipped with Champollion's discoveries, Wilkinson began making important new discoveries of his own.[58] Able to read more hieroglyphs, he established a chronology for ancient Egyptian history and assigned more precise dates to the monuments that he saw. There were, of course, limits to his ability. He tended to go astray when he moved beyond his list of kings, for he, like Young, lacked Champollion's deep philological knowledge, but in many instances he noticed and corrected mistakes in Champollion's work, something that probably no one else in the world could have done at that time.[59] In 1827 we find him writing to Gell, "Mons. Champollion has made terrible mistakes in construing né *du* seigneur du monde, —— d'Amon Osarchon. It should be 'the royal offspring,' referring to Osorkon himself."[60] Perhaps what put Wilkinson off the most about Champollion was the latter's occasionally arbitrary and high-handed manner. "Ch may read a wall of hierogˢ," he wrote to Gell. "So can I or anybody else when no Egyptians are present, but I like better proofs & a more authenticated mode of interpretation than many of his kings appear to be, & many of which are incorrect; besides he has an unfair way of changing without informing his reader of former errors."[61]

When it came to transliterating Egyptian names and words into modern languages, Wilkinson was frequently more accurate than Champollion. Wilkinson was the first to identify and transliterate the name Thebes, a significant accomplishment for men in whose minds ran the Homeric tag "hundred-gated Thebes." Champollion had noticed the name on the Lateran obelisk in Rome and incorrectly rendered it Opt or Apt, but Wilkinson, examining Champollion's work, realized that the set of hieroglyphs formed Thapa or Theba.[62] Wilkinson also improved upon Champollion's transliteration of Hat-Shepsut's throne name, Ma'at-Ka-Re. Champollion's rendering of her name was quite fantastic, but Wilkinson's Amun-neitgori is reasonably close to the mark.[63] Concerning the order of the kings, about which he probably knew more than anyone, Wilkinson was able to correct several of Champollion's mistakes. He wrote to Gell, "Mons. Champollion has a great nº of Errors in his Kings, among them is the above or Osortesen Ist, whom he makes of the 23rd Dynasty, which will never do: he comes *before* any of the 18th Dynasty & is either of the 16th or 17th."[64] But even Wilkinson went astray on some of the kings of the later dynasties.

Wilkinson, downplaying his improvements, sought discreet means to correct the Frenchman's mistakes. This attitude is clear in a reply to his cousin Captain M. Stanhope Badcock who had written to inquire about the "notions of our Egyptians":

> If you are desirous of knowing anything about these last I refer you to Mon[s] Champollion's Précis or Système hieroglyphique— but in his last work of which I have had only a slight look he has made a great confusion in the list of the kings— [   ] which I hope to have an indirect way of communicating with him through Sir W Gell to whose kindness I have been indebted for every kind of useful information—I have therefore avoided in the work I sent every appearance of disagreement on all subjects, with one who may be considered as holding forth the torch which illuminates the dark path of hieroglyphical discovery. My friend M[r] Salt has made but a poor display in his essay on hy[ic]. I am sorry for it, because the French must triumph.[65]

Gell had in fact already given some of Wilkinson's material to Champollion the year before when he met him in Rome.[66] He did, however, remember Champollion's reputation for appropriating other people's ideas, so he took care to stipulate that Wilkinson be given credit. In July 1825 he wrote to Wilkinson, "I conclude D[r] Young will act according to his promise & in the mean time, I have given to Champollion in your name & with the express proviso that he mentions that you were the discoverer & copier of, & the only person who knew how to value the inscription of the offerings."[67] In the autumn of that same year, Gell wrote again to say, "I have in the mean time introduced you to M[r] Champollion the great doctor of Hieroglyphics & he desires you will be particular in getting all that may be gleaned at Abu Keshaie near the bitter lakes near or at the Isthmus of Suez." And, "I have given him several of your notices which he is to talk of as your productions in his next work."[68] This provided Champollion, who had not yet visited Egypt, with more accurate transcriptions than he could otherwise have had. Yet Champollion was initially unappreciative of them. In one instance he commented only that they were copied "passably well" and in another complained of the distortions that he said abounded in them, though he was familiar with neither the originals nor Wilkinson's methods.[69] Champollion was in part basing his criticism upon less accurate information that he was deriving from others. Had he perceived the value of Wilkinson's work, he would have saved himself some early errors, including his mistakes in the order of the kings, which Wilkinson caught.[70] Wilkinson, incidentally, never corresponded directly with Champollion, though he did later exchange some letters with Champollion's brother, Jacques Joseph Champollion-Figeac.

Because of his hieroglyphic preparation under Gell and the exciting events that he witnessed—and, indeed, in which he participated—Wilkinson was the first Egyptologist to work in Egypt using philological techniques that were at least somewhat sound, a fact for which Gell was proud to claim his share of credit. While scholars in Europe were constrained to use selected papyri and frequently inaccurate transcriptions, Wilkinson ranged about and saw an enormous amount of material for himself. He was probably at that time one of the three leading experts on Egyptian hieroglyphics in the world, Young and Champollion being the other two. Then, with the untimely deaths of Young in 1829 and Champollion in 1832 and with Champollion's students at a loss to follow their late master's direction, there was only Wilkinson. Gell wrote to him in Egypt to say, "Nothing new has lately appeared & as Young & Champollion are both dead I fear the thing is at a stand still in London & Paris, & thus we must depend upon you for what is to be learned in the future."[71] Wilkinson might have gone far in hieroglyphics. That he chose not to do so is characteristic of him, for once he acquired a basic familiarity with one subject, he preferred to move on to another.

Through all these experiences, Wilkinson's most important link with Europe was his correspondence with Sir William Gell. Letters were long in reaching their destinations and frequently went astray but were nevertheless eagerly awaited. The style of these letters quickly became friendly and informal, with Gell, as was his custom, signing his letters with playful names or facetious hieroglyphs. Wilkinson, in turn, addressed Gell with names like Most Powerful Amonrasonther, Great King of Kings, or Great Image of Re. Behind the bantering tone was an earnest, extensive exchange of information. Gell appreciated Wilkinson's letters, but he was appalled at Wilkinson's "outrageous" handwriting, a sentiment which present-day readers of Wilkinson's papers can easily understand. "For all three [letters] I thank you," he wrote to Wilkinson, "observing at the same time that it required a whole jury of matrons to decypher them which however was at last effected. Pray remember to date at least the month when you next write."[72] And in one of his notebooks Gell also wrote that one of Wilkinson's letters was "so confused & illegible that little is certain."[73] For his part, Wilkinson admitted that his handwriting was bad, so bad that he sometimes could not read it himself, but blamed faulty writing materials and the hot climate.[74] It is strange how he drew with skill and clarity, yet wrote with near, and occasionally complete, illegibility.

The correspondence benefited both men. Gell, as we have seen, kept Wilkinson fully informed of the progress toward hieroglyphic translation in Europe. He also advised Wilkinson where to go and what to look for; for example: "Abydus was so famous a burying place that I have little doubt a great deal might be done by excavating the sands which have filled it up."[75] He urged Wilkinson to examine the Fayyum, and passed along Champollion's suggestions about what Wilkinson should look for. Through it all, he was careful to keep up Wilkinson's spirits and self-esteem. Informing Wilkinson of an inscription he saw in another source, Gell wrote, "I should have been glad of an authentic copy from anyone who understands the business which you now do better than any one who has yet been in Egypt."[76] Gell, for his part, savored the information that Wilkinson sent him. This, combined with his correspondence with Young, Champollion, and others, made him perhaps the most knowledgeable outside observer of the progress of Egyptological research. He kept careful notebooks in which he made his own speculations about transliteration, order of kings, art, and so on. While there is little that is original in them, they show a high degree of awareness.[77] Wilkinson's letters also provided Gell with material for conversation, the medium in which he excelled. In the diary of one of Gell's close friends, Lady Blessington, is this comment about a dinner party: "Gell brought us some extremely interesting letters from his enterprising and learned friend, Mr. Wilkinson, the Egyptian traveller, to whom he is much attached."[78]

While Wilkinson was writing to Gell, Gell began mentioning Wilkinson more frequently in his letters to Thomas Young and praising the energy of his young protégé: "As Wilkinson says that after copying sixty large sheets he has as yet done nothing, I expect we shall have more, and still more valuable, materials before the year is past."[79] Young at first took little notice, but Gell was undeterred and thought Young might be able to realize Wilkinson's dream of having some of his better copies lithographed and published. He informed Wilkinson in March of 1824, "I shall write to Dr. Young & am quite certain he will be much interested in the proper exposition of your wonders & do his best for you. There is newly set up a Royal Literary Society which having no very clearly defined object seems as if it would lend itself to your labours. If it does it would be of advantage to you & save you a good deal of trouble & give your things the sort of eclat worth purchasing by the total."[80] Gell had indeed already written to Young about Wilkinson's copies:

I think that if I examine them myself, and put them into your hands, all the objects of Mr. Wilkinson will be much more effectually obtained with your comments than in any other possible way, as his collection will be at once introduced to all the Philo-Egyptians. He has, I believe, copied all the hieroglyphics wherever he has been in Egypt; and as the French hieroglyphics, even in the great work [the *Description de l'Egypte*], are notoriously false, he could not have done a more useful thing for all the purposes of hieroglyphical inquiry. . . . Please to let me know whether the idea of this gives you pleasure or not.[81]

It was reasonable of Gell to suppose that Young would be interested, for Young had once written of establishing an organization for collecting and publishing existing hieroglyphs "and perhaps for employing some poor Italian or Maltese to scramble over Egypt in search of more."[82] Wilkinson, it would seem, was ideal for his purposes. But during the intervening years Young's mind turned to some of his many other interests. Also, he was discouraged that the British reading public had lost interest in ancient Egypt after the frenzy aroused by Belzoni's book and popular exhibit in the early 1820s. He therefore rebuffed any suggestion that he take a strong personal role in publishing Wilkinson's copies—"I *cannot* at present attend to them"—but he did offer to arrange for the Royal Society of Literature to do it: "I believe [the R.S.L.] would be very ready to undertake the pecuniary cost of the thing if I would undertake to direct the work as I have hitherto done . . . I think it probable that I may offer to do enough to induce them to take up the work, and in this case Wilkinson's collection would afford us some valuable materials in addition to those which are in the British Museum and elsewhere."[83] Gell accordingly persisted in urging Young to help. In March 1824 he wrote to tell him that Wilkinson had copied an inscription at Karnak and hoped to have some lithographs made.[84] Three months later he sent a copy of Wilkinson's description of Roman works and quarries near the Red Sea. "The author desires no profit," Gell noted, "and only wishes to see his things lithographed." Again he praised Wilkinson's accuracy.[85] Young, however, was not to be hurried, replying to Gell, "As you wish me to acknowledge the receipt of Mr. Wilkinson's packet, I see no reason for any further delay in complying with your request, though it will be a month or two before I shall be able to look at it."[86]

The publication process finally began to move in 1826. Young seems to have found it necessary to write to Gell and inquire about Wilkinson's exact name, for Gell replied, "Wilkinson's name is J. G. Wilkinson. I long to see his things in print and to send some of them to him—they are worth all the hieroglyphics in the French work."[87] Wilkinson had entertained the notion of publishing anonymously, but Gell firmly rejected that: "As to concealing your name it is quite out of the question when a thing is supposed authentic. Without a voucher nothing can go down."[88] After some additional delays, the volume finally appeared. It is, in fact, a collection of various lithographs of which Wilkinson's are only a portion, though his is the best and largest portion. Thus Wilkinson at last achieved his ambition of having some of his work published.

There was a revealing epilogue to the event. When Young wrote to Gell to inform him of publication, he added that he had reserved six copies of the book for Wilkinson. Gell replied, "I will write to Wilkinson and tell him of the six copies you have in store for him. I cannot help thinking that as I am (although not one of the triumvirate) purveyor-general to the hieroglyphics, I might have had one copy also, for without me the things would never have come to light, my talent at betraying literary secrets being the only thing I value myself upon in the way of hieroglyphics, and if you read Wilkinson's notes he tells you that without me he should never have attended to them."[89] Young mentioned the matter only briefly in his response: "I thought Wilkinson had already expressed a wish that you should have one of *his* copies; my general rule has been to allow six for the author, and I have not now an unlimited command; but I should suppose from what has passed before that five would be amply sufficient for his wishes; he certainly deserves five hundred if he wanted them."[90] Gell was, as always, eager to acquire another book for his personal library, but there was more behind his protest than that. He craved some recognition for his role as cultural intermediary, in this instance as "purveyor-general to the hieroglyphics."

CHAPTER SIX

British Colleagues in Egypt

WILKINSON WAS BUT ONE of several like-minded British travelers, artists, and antiquarians who lived and worked in Egypt during the 1820s and 1830s. Unlike the many other British travelers who came and went during those decades, these men sought and attained more than a superficial acquaintance with Egypt. By 1825 most of Wilkinson's British friends were in the country with him. Their association was voluntary and unofficial, but they always enjoyed meeting each other on the river, visiting, exchanging information, and occasionally sharing a house, as Wilkinson did with James Burton in Cairo and with Robert Hay at Thebes. Their work, because so little of it was published, has been overshadowed by some of the better-remembered Egyptological events of the nineteenth century, but for a time Wilkinson and his friends were in the very forefront of Egyptology. Burton, Osman, Humphreys, and Salt we have met already, though of those four, only Burton was one of the inner circle. The others must be introduced, collectively as well as individually, because they formed a coherent group.

Robert Hay was twenty-five years old in 1824 when he came to Wilkinson's house in Ezbekiah carrying a letter from Sir William Gell.[1] His appearance in Egypt was the result of an unexpected turn of fortune. A younger son of a Scottish landed family, Hay initially had no prospects, being, his biographer writes, "not destined even for the church but for idle pursuits."[2] He embarked upon a naval career during which a memorable cruise in the eastern Mediterranean left him with an abiding interest Egypt. Then an elder brother was killed at Waterloo; another died a few years later, and Robert unexpectedly inherited Linplum, the principal family estate. When he got the news, he immediately resigned from the navy and returned to Scotland to collect his inheritance and prepare to take the Grand Tour in the East like a young gentleman. He planned to travel in the style of the great dilettanti of the previous century; accordingly, he assembled a retinue of artists and architects. When he passed through Naples he called on Sir William Gell who gave him the letter requesting Wilkinson to assist Hay with "advice and counsel."[3]

Accompanying Hay was Joseph Bonomi (whose name should be pronounced to rhyme with the French word *bonhommie*), a small, almost dwarfish man.[4] The son of a well-known architect who had moved to England at the invitation of the Adam brothers, Bonomi had been a promising student at the Royal Academy and exhibited there several times. In 1823 he went to Rome to study and fell in with an artistic crowd; a profligate life-style put him deeply in debt, and he was casting about for a patron when Robert Hay appeared and offered him a place on his expedition to the East. Bonomi's friends warned him not to take it: "These hard Scotch people are not the thing for you," one of them wrote, "who are an Italian after all—I have nothing against their character, but I shall hate them if they make a sacrifice of you to their confined and selfish caprices—I talk of *them*, but I believe it is only *one* of them that is bit with the travelling mania."[5] Such advice notwithstanding, Bonomi decided, "not without deliberation," to accept.[6] But while Hay was gathering his party in the style of the Great Tourists, Bonomi was determined to be no mere retainer. He would not be the kind of self-effacing clerk that Luigi Balugani had been for James Bruce.[7]

Another member of Hay's team was Frederick Catherwood, a gifted artist who had also studied at the Royal Academy under such masters as Henry Fuseli, J. M. W. Turner, and Sir John Soane.[8] A strong Piranesi influence runs through Catherwood's work, giving his sketches a presence that is more dramatic and memorable than those of any of his colleagues in Egypt. Like Hay and many others, Catherwood initially became interested in Egypt by reading Belzoni's book. His first trip was with Henry Westcar (1823–24) when he met Wilkinson during the revolt of the *fellahin;* a few years later, he returned to the East and joined Hay's expedition. Reserved and retiring, Catherwood was probably a bit put off by Wilkinson's happy, outgoing demeanor. He never took Wilkinson entirely seriously.

For depth of commitment to Egyptian studies, none could match Edward William Lane who arrived in 1825.[9] Originally apprenticed to be an engraver, Lane instead developed an acute interest in Egypt, ancient and modern. It was therefore with a strong sense of anticipation that he made his first trip to Egypt. "As I approached the shore," he later remembered, "I felt like an Eastern bridegroom, about to lift up the veil of his bride, and to see, for the first time, the features which were to charm, or disappoint, or disgust him. I was not visiting Egypt merely as a traveller, to examine its pyramids and temples and grottoes, and, after satisfying my curiosity, to quit it for other scenes and other pleasures: but I was about to throw myself entirely among strangers; to adopt their language, their customs and their dress; and, in associating almost exclusively with the natives, to prosecute the study of their literature."[10] Lane went even further into oriental life than Wilkinson, for while Wilkinson lived as a Turk, Lane eventually passed beyond that stage and lived as a native Egyptian. Perhaps being short of money, Lane occasionally joined Hay's team, but like Wilkinson, he preferred to work alone. Although their relationship was initially more cordial than close, and though they tended to go their separate ways in Egypt, their shared experiences along the Nile laid the foundation for lasting friendship. They called each other by Arabic names in Egypt and continued to do so for the rest of their lives. Wilkinson was Isma'eel, and Lane, Mansoor, according to their spelling.

One of Wilkinson's most congenial fellows in Egypt was Major Orlando Felix.[11] A professional soldier, Felix was a veteran of the Waterloo campaign and had been wounded at Quatre Bras. Later posted to a small town in Ireland, he found Champollion's books in the public library and spent his idle hours studying hieroglyphs. He was next stationed in Malta whence he accompanied his colonel on a diplomatic mission to Egypt. Felix made the most of the opportunity, sailing upriver to study the monuments of Upper Egypt. While living among the tombs at Giza, he learned that he had been promoted to major and granted a leave of absence. He subsequently traveled extensively in Egypt, often in the company of his friend Lord Prudhoe, and made a large collection of notes and drawings.[12] Major Felix and Wilkinson were always on cordial terms, and the information that they frequently exchanged, in person and by correspondence, greatly benefited Wilkinson, especially Felix's research into the order of kings.

The purest example of the old style aristocratic traveler was Wilkinson's friend Lord Prudhoe, whose brother, the Duke of Northumberland, was an avid patron of oriental studies.[13] Taking time from a naval career that apparently put few demands upon him, Lord Prudhoe spent several years in Egypt. With Major Felix he ranged about Egypt, amassing a large personal collection of antiquities. Among his finds was the Coptic manuscript that aided Wilkinson's linguistic work. In gratitude for his help, Wilkinson later dedicated his first major book, *Topography of Thebes*, to Lord Prudhoe. He, Lane, and Wilkinson became lifelong friends.

Others came and went, such as Francis Arundale and Owen Browne Carter, both of them architects and artists. Another, though his anglicity is dubious, was Achille Prisse d'Avennes, who claimed to be of an old English family, his real name being Price of Aven. More assuredly English were the merchants A. C. Harris and Samuel Briggs, whose financial and commercial contacts were frequently useful to Wilkinson and his friends. Both of these businessmen took an interest in Egyptological explorations: Briggs had helped Salt finance Caviglia's operations at Giza, and Harris was a dealer and collector of antiquities.[14] There were also various other merchants, diplomats, visiting naval officers, and travelers. When wanted, British company could be found in Egypt, especially in Cairo and Alexandria.

To alleviate the deprivation of books and newspapers that they suffered in Egypt, they established an organization called the English Reading Society that made certain basic books available to its members, as well as periodicals of the day such as the *Edinburgh Review* and *Blackwood's Edinburgh Magazine.*[15] They also produced a quasi-serious newspaper named *The Thoth* that featured a drawing of the ibis-headed god on its masthead. The first issue (there were two altogether) of *The Thoth*, detailed the doings of various people. For example, Joseph Bonomi had just composed a Spanish air "whose soothing effect has been tried with success when opium has entirely failed." And there was the wedding anniversary party of a French admiral in Egypt, but: "We regret to say that Sir Jacob Burton and the learned Mynheer von Vilkinson could not attend on account of indisposition."[16]

Standing somewhat apart from Wilkinson and his friends was Consul-General Henry Salt. Some of the reasons for his estrangement have been mentioned already, but they do not seem sufficient in themselves to explain the thoroughly deprecating attitude that Wilkinson and his friends affected towards him. The problem certainly was not a lack of cordiality on Salt's part, for he made the travelers very welcome when they came to Egypt. Edward William Lane reported that when he arrived Salt received him like an old friend, though he was in fact a stranger.[17] Nor was Salt a recluse, for his parties were famous, even notorious, among the Frankish communities of Cairo and Alexandria. But Wilkinson and his friends seem not to have frequented them.[18] A matter of taste, perhaps. And Salt was ever ready to share his knowledge with those around him, using his offices to help them whenever possible. Wilkinson, as described earlier, became angry at Salt's consular decree about oriental dress, but even he had initially been quite well disposed toward Salt.

Salt's accomplishments as an antiquarian were indeed considerable, though they brought him little credit at the time. Before Wilkinson and his colleagues came to Egypt, Salt, assisted by William Beechey, Alessandro Ricci, and Linant de Bellefonds,[19] had accumulated an enormous collection of drawings of Egyptian antiquities. In the assessment of a modern Egyptologist, "The drawings record tomb scenes and objects some of which have been lost or damaged since they were copied. The accuracy of the artists in rendering hieroglyphs is remarkable for the time."[20] Unfortunately, few of Salt's sketches were published, and most of them are lost or little known now. Even this work was held in low esteem by Wilkinson's colleagues. After seeing Salt's copies, Robert Hay wrote, "I cannot say that I was not greatly disappointed with the meagreness of the display besides the careless manner in which they were done; and all that I could learn from them is that much is to be found along the Nile, worth giving greater pains and time to than he seems to have bestowed."[21] Hay, in fact, especially disliked Salt, his first impression of him being that he resembled "a pig wrapped up in a bournoose."[22]

Perhaps Wilkinson and his friends disdained the activities of a professional antiquity collector, which Salt definitely was, but they were better able than he to afford such an attitude. Hay was wealthy; Wilkinson was at least assured of an income; and many of the others intended either to find a patron or to succeed by their art. Salt, however, was not a rich man, and his consular salary was always in arrears.[23] Besides, Salt was by no means the first British diplomat who collected professionally. But many were doubtless prejudiced before they even met him. One cause of that was his unfavorable portrayal in Belzoni's book. He occasionally considered publishing a rebuttal, but it probably was just as well that he refrained, for he would have been hard-pressed to equal Belzoni's literary elegance. Another cause was Sir William Gell, whom most of the travelers met on the way out. Gell read them his "Saline Verses," and doubtless made many disparaging comments about the consul-general. Finally, Wilkinson, after the oriental dress incident, took care to condition new arrivals against Salt.

Perhaps Salt's greatest problem was his sometimes insufferable self-importance. Had he been content to preserve and build upon the virtues that he undoubtedly possessed, he would have made a secure, if modest, name for himself both among his contemporaries and in the history of Egyptology; instead, he sought to make his mark in other areas, areas where he could not excel. As a diplomat he was constantly outmaneuvered by the French consul-general, Drovetti; as a student of hieroglyphs he claimed a degree of originality that he never achieved; and he even aspired to be a poet: "Egypt, a Descriptive Poem, with Notes," he entitled his greatest work. It begins,

Egypt, renowned of old, demands my song.
High favor'd Land, where Nilus sweeps along . . .

And so on. Hay was surely deriding it when he wrote in his diary at Thebes: "The evening was spent in my boat where we enjoyed quotations from that *beautiful* poem from the pen of Mr. Salt on the Nile and its wonders."[24] It is a fairly bad poem, though not that bad.

During their years in Egypt, Wilkinson and his colleagues pursued an extraordinary range of activities. Almost no archaeological site known to them was neglected, and many aspects of contemporary Egypt as well were captured in their notebooks and sketchbooks. Their model was the French *Description de l'Egypte*, which they intended to surpass in both scope and accuracy. There is an astonishingly modern quality about much of their material, though they worked in a tradition quite different from that of the present. Perhaps the most notable difference is that while they occasionally excavated, they did not do as modern archaeologists who keep an eye on stratigraphy and note the relationship of objects. They merely uncovered monuments to sketch them more completely. Modern scientific excavation was not practiced until the end of the century.[25] Even so, their activities—especially those of Hay and his team—are not beyond comparison with a project like the University of Chicago's Epigraphic Survey, though the latter is, of course, vastly more sophisticated than anything they might have imagined.

Despite their limitations, they attained higher archaeological standards than had been seen before and that were not surpassed until Sir William Flinders Petrie established the techniques of professional archaeology at the end of the nineteenth century. For example, when Wilkinson, Hay, and Burton examined the tomb of Seti I—or Belzoni's Tomb, as they knew it—they found it in an almost perfect state of preservation. They carefully cleared the drainage channels that had been clogged when Belzoni broke into the tomb so that rainwater would not damage it. Once inside, they worked by the light of a few wax candles instead of torches to avoid exposing the paintings to smoke. When Champollion visited the tomb, however, he cut away the stonework that pleased him the most and carried it away. Later, the tomb suffered even more from the famous Prussian expedition of Richard Lepsius. Its members tore down an ornamented column in order to secure the part of it that they wanted and left the rest in pieces on the floor. It is no wonder that when Muhammad Ali was requested by Europeans to safeguard the antiquities of Egypt, he replied, "How can I do so, and why should you ask me, since Europeans themselves are their chief enemies?"[26] In their day, Wilkinson and his colleagues were in a class by themselves. They took great pride in damaging no monument.[27]

Wilkinson was energetic and productive, but he worked alone and could not match the organized production of Robert Hay's project. Hay carefully supervised his team of artists and gave them assignments. As they completed their work, he reviewed it, ordering it corrected or redone when it failed to meet his standards. One can almost hear his voice in his marginal comments on the folios: "This is wrong," he writes about a detail; "Draw this again as it is distorted," he notes on a drawing of the tomb of Seti I; and a view of the riverbank receives the verdict, "Draw this in careful outline—no effect—give trees to the D^r [right] a little *more room.*"[28] Joseph Bonomi's diary also provides some idea how Hay's artists worked. In it we find another artist shading an outline that Bonomi had made while Bonomi double-checks the measurements.[29]

Hay and his artists relied heavily upon the camera lucida, a device consisting of a prism and a set of interchangeable lenses that cast a picture upon a table where it could be copied by the draftsman. Bonomi had known Dr. Wollaston, the inventor of the instrument, so he was especially well qualified to use it.[30] Although Hay's enthusiasm for the camera was measured—"A most correct instrument, but not so great a favorite with me as my eye"—he used it extensively for drawing panoramas, a task he usually reserved for himself.[31] Frequently they put grids over their drawings to control scale even better. This was quite different from Wilkinson's approach, which was almost entirely freehand drawing. Because Hay's team included architects as well as artists, the elevations and floor plans of buildings are especially well drawn. Like Wilkinson's, Hay's portfolio of artwork performed the vital task of recording monuments that were disappearing before their very eyes almost.[32] Nor were his efforts confined to ancient monuments, for his drawings of Islamic architecture are exquisite. His work is also the single best documentary of villages along the Nile in the 1820s.[33]

Their interests and duties scattered them to different parts of Egypt. But Wilkinson and his friends frequently met as they sailed up and down the river, and they exchanged letters, information, and gossip. For example, we find Hay, Burton, Wilkinson, and Bonomi all having a New Year's celebration together at Medinet Habu. Hay played a memorable prank by forging an antique statue and passing it off to the others as genuine, much to their annoyance when he revealed the deception.[34] When distant from each other, they sometimes communicated by messenger, a practice that could cause difficulties. "The black courier has turned obstrepalous," Wilkinson wrote to Robert Hay in one instance, "& swears by the Prophet's whiskers he will not take the packet on, as he was only engaged to Goorneh—This was badly managed by Osman—he should never direct a letter to any particular place."[35]

The members of the group frequently shared scholarly information with each other.[36] Their openness was based upon a well-understood code of conduct that protected an individual's ideas or discoveries from encroachment by others. This gentlemen's understanding, however, was grossly violated by Champollion during his visit to Egypt in the years 1828–29. The incident concerned a stone bearing a trilingual inscription that James Burton found embedded in the wall of a Cairo mosque. Drovetti also wanted it, but it properly belonged to Burton, "who," in Burton's words, "according to the etiquette of the country, having first discovered the stone, was considered as having a right to it in bar of all others, if it was to be had."[37] Burton obtained permission to remove it, but, with his customary dilatoriness, postponed doing so, despite repeated urgings from Thomas Young. Champollion later saw the stone, fancied it, and took it for himself over Burton's protests. Wilkinson was outraged and expressed his irritation in a letter to Gell.[38] Even in later years Wilkinson and his friends usually adhered to their code and acknowledged any inadvertent transgression of it.[39]

But Wilkinson himself violated the intent of the code on at least one occasion. It will be recalled that he swore Burton to secrecy about the existence of the tombs at Tell el-Amarna, but Burton was unable to keep quiet and eventually told Robert Hay about them. When Hay learned what Wilkinson had been concealing from him, his anger bordered on incoherence. His diary entry for 17 June 1827 reads:

Two travellers have known of the existence of the Tombs of Alabastron for perhaps three years—perhaps more, and yet this piece of knowledge [h]as been kept as secret, thus been guarded with as much care as coin miser watched and fondled watched and fondled the largest treasure coin told!—This too with fellow labourers in the same country and apparently living on the most friendly terms—often meeting & of course making the country a great part of the subject of conversation. Therefore there were opportunities sufficient had *Mr. Wilkinson* felt inclined to be open & behave handsomely towards those whom he saw took an equal share of interest in the antiquities with himself—perhaps there lay his great objection?—Certainly as the discoverer of the tombs, he had a right to propose such restrictions as he thought necessary before he communicated anything about them—and what man of common sense w^d have refused to comply?—If any one did not choose the terms proposed—why then he might just set out and hunt the whole country for himself, & at the end perhaps return properly rewarded for having refused information handsomely offered to him—This sordid secrecy will not bear argument—and I am convinced that Mr. Wilkinson stands single amongst the English travellers in such a feeling towards those employed as he is himself!—He must have seen the tombs while riding along the mountains on camels and then communicated his discovery to Mr. Burton whom he bound to secrecy.[40]

Whether or not this incident resulted in a confrontation is unrecorded, but it seems to have caused no permanent damage to their relationship.

Wilkinson may also have violated the unwritten code in his relationship with James Burton. One of Burton's friends had worried as early as 1822, when Wilkinson and Burton were living together, that Wilkinson would "suck James' brains and publish before him." This prompted another friend, G. B. Greenough, to write to Burton from London and ask, "Does Mr Wilkinson mean to publish? if so had you not better come to an understanding with him?"[41] Despite this warning, Burton sought no understanding. Seven years later, he was shocked when Greenough informed him that Wilkinson had made a map of the Eastern Desert and sent it to Europe for publication. Because of his early explorations, Burton considered that he had a prior claim to that area. What was worse, Wilkinson had done it secretly, without a word to Burton. Trying to sort out his feelings, Burton wrote to Greenough from the Eastern Desert,

I am sorry to find that he sent his map of this desert to Col Leake without informing me that he had done so. You first gave me the news. I say I am sorry, because the mode seems to have been adopted for the purpose of keeping me in ignorance of his intention of as rapidly appearing before the public in this new character. I was perfectly aware that he was making a map of the desert, though . . . he gave me no hint that he was sending it off to be published. But you will say, if he even did wish to anticipate you thus, he had a right. I do not question the right as an individual but as a friend. In 1822 these deserts had not been travelled or examined except in one or two small spots by any one. The French with an armed force had visited some spots. In 1823 I made a second journey through them, with a view of forming a map and I invited my friend Mr Wilkinson to accompany me. I was then the chief of a large caravan under the special protection of the Pasha. Without this protection he would not at that time have ventured into these deserts. He was aware that my great aim was to make a map and I consider that having been invited by me for the pleasure of his company, he then having no fixed pursuit other than the antiquities of Thebes, that having lived with me two or three months in my caravan (I do not mean to say at my expense) and knowing that my especial subject was the geology and geography of that desert, he had no right as a friend to act as he has done. This is betwixt ourselves.[42]

Burton went on to say, "I take to myself therefore, a priority of design and originality of plans and accuse myself of too great dilatoriness in their execution." That indeed was the problem as much as anything else, because Burton just could not bring himself to get on with the job, though given his mental sensitivity, Wilkinson's action may have made him even more reluctant to begin work. Burton undoubtedly knew more than anyone else in his day about the Eastern Desert; had he published even a portion of his work, he would be remembered today as one of the leading experts on the region. Despite his disappointment with Wilkinson, Burton did not break with him, telling Greenough, "But Wilkinson is a man of genius, well informed, and of good classical learning—has a constitution that enables him to be active. An excellent memory, an excellent pencil and is one excellent good companion. Except in this instance I have nothing to quarrel with him about."[43]

Of greater immediate concern to Wilkinson and his friends were the many dangers and hardships that they faced. Looming on the horizon was a volatile international situation. The Greek War of Independence was raging, a conflict that culminated in British intervention and the sinking of the Egyptian fleet at Navarino in 1826. Wilkinson and his colleagues were not Philhellenes, but as British subjects they worried about their position in Egypt as European involvement increased. Robert Hay found things so tense in Cairo in

1824 that he was glad to leave it to sail upstream to Thebes.[44] Writing from Cairo to tell Hay the news, Wilkinson said that he and his compatriots were awaiting events "with some anxiety but without fear" and observed that Hay was "in a good safe place."[45] Wilkinson was sufficiently disturbed that he seriously considered traveling to India to continue his Arabic studies there and to undertake a comparative study of Egyptian and Indian temple sculpture. The stability of Muhammad Ali's regime reassured him, however, and he wrote the following year, 1825: "At present all appears tranquil here. the disturbances of last year were soon checked and I believe as long as the Pasha rules here all will be perfectly safe; In this case I intend remaining three years to learn the literal Arabic I shall not look towards India unless something unpleasant occurs."[46] But when Lord Cochrane blockaded Alexandria, Wilkinson's worries suddenly returned. "What is Lord Cochrane doing?" Wilkinson asked Gell in a letter, "All are [   ] alarmed."[47] Yet the British in Egypt were never seriously threatened. Despite the loss of his fleet, Muhammad Ali remained friendly, as he reassured the British consul-general.[48] He was too firmly fixed upon his long-range goals to succumb to the temptation to vent his resentment at the British government upon those British subjects who happened to be in Egypt at that moment. Muhammad Ali was a thoroughly professional ruler who indulged in anger only when it served a purpose.

Closer to home, problems were presented by creatures such as snakes and scorpions. The scorpions of Egypt were capable of inflicting dangerous, painful stings. Bonomi made a long entry in his diary telling about being stung by one and the suffering that ensued. He carefully noted that the scorpion was caught—and, one supposes, summarily executed.[49] The danger of these insects is illustrated by the example of Dr. Alessandro Ricci, who died of a scorpion sting. Also to be avoided were the snakes. Because the serpents often shared houses with people, there was a thriving business for native snake charmers who offered their services to the European population. These men, dressed in long, flowing robes and carrying wands, uttered chants like, "Come out, come out, in the name of Abraham, if you do not come out you shall die."[50] The charmers were a great source of amusement to the British travelers who considered them charlatans. Bonomi and Catherwood tricked one by hiding a big snake in an open box and then inviting the charmer to come and perform his services. They watched him closely so he could not use an old trick and pull a snake from his robes to plant there. Unable to produce one, he declared that the house was snake free. But, they told him, they had seen one run into a hole only the day before. He tried another incantation, but in vain. They then borrowed his wand and hooked out their snake. The charmer was unruffled, saying he had no influence over that kind.[51]

Disease posed the greatest danger. Being healthy young men, full of vitality, they bore illness well and recovered from it quickly, but as they aged they became increasingly vulnerable. The most universal problem was afflictions of the eye, from which all suffered at one time or another. Blindness was, in fact, common in Egypt. Robert Hay estimated that one of every ten men he saw had either one or both eyes bandaged.[52] The specific disease was ophthalmia, or conjunctivitis, a bacterial infection that causes intense irritation and even blindness if left untreated. Wilkinson thought it came from something in the river valley and always sought the desert when it afflicted him. Hence we find him writing to Gell in 1828, "I have since I last wrote been as usual suffering from opthalmia from which the desert air has at last relieved me. It is the only place where I am free from it. I am therefore in a valley living in the gypsy style & writing & preparing my papers.[53] His experience would seem to be supported by Sir Richard Burton who wrote, "Every one knows that ophthalmia is unknown in the desert."[54] Such was its agony that had Moses afflicted Pharaoh with it, one sufferer said, that alone would have compelled him to let the Children of Israel go.[55]

The most deadly disease was the plague. Wilkinson and his friends regulated their movements by it, either fleeing at its onset or withdrawing into seclusion. Occasionally they found the river blocked by soldiers trying to contain the pestilence.[56] Although none of Wilkinson's colleagues died of the plague, it sometimes struck close by them. Henry Salt's wife died of it in 1824.[57] During that same year Dr. Cimba, one of Salt's medical attendants, and all of his family, save his wife, were killed by it. Wilkinson witnessed several epidemics during his years in Egypt, though he was fortunate enough to miss an especially bad one two years after he left. Osman wrote to him in England to say that no one remembered an outbreak of such severity and duration. Over seven hundred people a day died of it in Cairo, and that was counting only Muslims. His own wife, Osman reported, had died.[58]

What they called plague, however, was often cholera, which they occasionally called by its correct name. For example, Wilkinson once wrote to Hay that there had been eighteen cases of cholera in Gurna, four of them fatal, but that one hundred people had died across the river in Luxor.[59] Joseph Bonomi also reported a bad outbreak of cholera when he and Linant de Bellefonds were traveling upriver. Linant became anxious about the safety of his family, so they returned to

Cairo. Bonomi's diary reads, "Early before sunrise we walked to Cairo. Mr. Linant at the door of his house heard of the death of his wife. I found all well in my house."[60]

Dysentery attacked them all at one time or another. An acutely miserable affliction, especially in the Egyptian climate, dysentery could cause death, especially if the sufferer was already in a weakened condition. It killed Henry Salt and, later, Osman. In the case of Salt, his health seems to have been deteriorating for some time. Finally, he left Alexandria to go upstream to recover, a common practice in those days. He only reached the village of Disuq, some twenty-five miles south of Rashid, when he began to decline even more rapidly and died there on 29 October 1827.[61] His body was returned downstream to Alexandria where he was buried in his beautiful garden, a spot that later became a cemetery for Europeans. Osman's end in 1835 was much the same, a steady weakening followed by despair, then death.[62]

Sometimes the travelers never knew what hit them. We find Wilkinson writing to Hay in 1831 that he is suffering from "God knows what but something that has laid me up & made me perfectly helpless."[63] Medical treatment was rudimentary, sometimes worse than the disease. Bonomi was once bled from behind the ear when he was taken ill; Hay, suffering from the same affliction, took calomel instead.[64] On another occasion when Hay suffered from a pain in his side, his physician applied leeches—unsuccessfully, Hay reported.[65] Aggravating all of these medical dangers was the climate. As they became older, Wilkinson and his friends had to ask themselves each year if they could withstand another Egyptian summer.

There were, however, ample compensations for their hardships, for they usually lived at ease in their homes and *dahabiyah*s, waited on by their women and servants. There is a drawing in Hay's portfolio that shows some of them seated on a carpet in a comfortably furnished temple or tomb, smoking their water pipes while servants attentively wait on them.[66] Like Wilkinson and Burton, they wore Turkish dress, and some, though not all, used Turkish table manners. Hay wrote with some distaste of Lane: "He like most travellers at present in Egypt, wears the Turkish costume, and even eats as they do w^h only a few do—Mr. Wilkinson & Mr. Linant the french man who travels for Mr. Banks follow this custom but no one else I believe." Hay explained,

I must confess I think it a proper thing for all Eastern travellers to learn to do like the natives to avoid being thought awkward when perhaps they are obliged to dine or eat in their company, but, to do so when there is no real necessity seems to me little short of ridiculous as no one but a Turk which has been accustomed to eat with his fingers all his life & to see those round him do the same can possibly prefer it to the less clumsy way of feeding oneself with the fork, Knife & Spoon—in the first place by this useful invention we get all we want out of the dish instead of half falling back again,—in the second, we get the leavings of no one—on the contrary with the turkish—if the Dish be of a soft Nature it breaks in our fingers & while in search for another piece the gravy is dripping from our finger ends! If the pieces are large they must be torn—The shifts one is put to are equally absurd as the laying aside the knife and fork is ridiculous.[67]

Like Wilkinson and Burton, their friends soon acquired female companions. Again much of the information comes from Humphreys, who was prone to boast of his own rather sordid sexual escapades and to comment upon those of his colleagues. But, in some ways, Robert Hay was the most lasciviously inclined of them all. He liked to lurk in the bushes by the river and watch women bathe, and he enjoyed looking at pubescent girls. These young women, only just learning modesty after running about naked as children, would react to the sight of a stranger by concealing their faces, even when their bodies were uncovered, much to his amusement.[68] Early in his Egyptian travels we find him interested in the public dancing girls, the *ghawazi:* "On the evening of the 14th we saw the Dancing Ladies of Cairo, so often spoken of by travellers—We hired three of these Damsels & their band for five dollars—tho' it is certainly not an exibition [sic] one w d choose in England yet, I by no means think it devoid of grace, tho' the general attitude has not that character."[69] Lane wrote of them, "I need scarcely add that these women are the most abandoned of the courtesans of Egypt."[70] Lane in fact considered Egyptian women generally inclined toward sexual promiscuity, an opinion that was probably based upon limited experience.

Hay found his companion, the woman he eventually married, in the Cairo slave market. This institution attracted his attention from the first because of the large number of Greek Christian girls who were captured and sold into slavery by the Turks during the Greek War of Independence. These white women were prized above all others, selling, Lane noted, for three to ten times the price of Abyssinians, the next favored category of slave.[71] Because of their great value, they were rarely taken to the public market but housed in private quarters and viewed by arrangement.[72] Hay was moved by their plight. His first impulse was to buy them and set them free, but he was restrained by the advice of an elder acquaintance who pointed out that it was doing them little favor to turn them loose penniless. He accordingly attempted to set up a fund for the purpose of buying them and placing them in a viable environment.[73] While that effort met with small success, he took it upon himself to buy some women, educate them, and find a home for them. That was the case with Kalitza, whom he later married, and Nefeeseh, whom he placed with Lane. It is important, however, that the sufferings of these women should be neither under- nor overestimated. Although concubinage might be their initial lot, they were much too expensive to be used for the most menial tasks, and they often rose to higher status. Wealthy members of the European community frequently bought them to be their wives and bear their children; even in Turkish households they enjoyed a privileged position. It was quite common for them to become permanent members of the harem or to be married to relatives and retainers of their master's family. So thoroughly were some of them assimilated into Egyptian society that when a sustained effort was made to free them and return them to their homes after the conclusion of the Greek War of Independence many were unwilling to be repatriated. They preferred the comfort and security that they enjoyed in Egypt to the poverty they had left behind in their homeland.[74]

Among these women was Kalitza Psaraki, the daughter of the chief magistrate of Apodhulo, a small town on Crete. Her life was an adventure. She was first captured by Turks, then liberated by Greek sea rovers from Kassos who took her to their island. Mustapha Bey subsequently captured Kassos, killed the men, and took nine hundred women and children prisoners, Kalitza among them. She was then taken to Egypt where Hay bought her in 1824.[75] The details of the following years are unknown, but a relationship developed. Hay married her in 1828, though they toured together as man and wife before that date.

Joseph Bonomi's woman was named Fatima, and by her he had two sons, one of whom survived. Humphreys called them "the Holy Trinity." Bonomi later abandoned her and ignored her subsequent demands for recognition and money.[76] We glimpse the activities of another of Hay's artists, Francis Arundale, in this letter he wrote to Bonomi in 1833: "I have got possession of a very comfortable room close to the Mosque which is desirable as I know the hour of prayer, but although so near the Church I have a view of the 'Tents of wick-edness' the flesh is weak!—and I have found it so. I hope no strong *dose* will follow.''[77] It was much the same with Humphreys who, though he had his Achmet, or Adriana Copigliani as he called her, was also willing to buy sex: "I discovered yesterday a very pretty little girl who is content to do business (not a commoner) she is very willing but her principal holds out and makes many objections in order to gain more money but with the assistance of Venus and Plutus I seize my prize tomorrow night it will be very expensive work, but 'hunger will break down stone walls.'''[78]

After he married Kalitza, Hay became concerned about the moral condition of his colleagues and began urging them to marry their women. From some he received positive assurances. Lane agreed to marry Nefeeseh, though he postponed doing so for years, and Wilkinson apparently returned a favorable answer, though nothing came of it.[79] With others he was less successful. That he had been urging Burton to marry his woman Blackey is clear from these lines from Humphreys to Bonomi: "I do not think that he [Burton] will be foolish enough ever to marry her she is neither handsome or clever and as she cannot be introduced in those circles which he frequents or indeed in any other there is little chance of her ever improving, she will never learn a European language, she will never be a conversable being, she has no mind . . . I cannot imagine what he will do with her she is a terrible clog."[80] Hay must have persisted, for Humphreys wrote that Hay had approached Burton about the matter and received "rather a sharp answer. It is too bad that he should pretend now a days that when he purchased Calitza he did it with the intention of making her his wife—he may tell this story to the marines the sailors won't believe it."[81]

At least Burton did not merely abandon Blackey, for Humphreys wrote to tell Bonomi in 1826, "Mr B, is behaving very well to Blackey, has bought a house for her furnished it found her a husband and given her a sum of money very expensive work this, paying very dear for his pleasures, but it does him much credit."[82] Yet a few years later after Burton left Egypt, Humphreys wrote from Bordeaux to tell Bonomi, "We form here just the same household as in Egypt . . . and I think I may say that we are all pretty miserable. . . . I suspect that Mr B. regrets that he did not do as Mr Wilkinson did with his lady he would have been more free and she more happy."[83] So exactly what was happening with Burton and his companion is unclear, but Humphreys' letter suggests that Wilkinson made some kind of financial settlement with his companion and parted from her in

Egypt.[84] Two years later, she—perhaps they—died in the great pestilence of 1835. Yet another way to cast off a companion was demonstrated by Henry Salt. He, when he impregnated one of his slave girls, "made her over to a Musselman thus abandoning his progeny," an observer noted with disapproval.[85] Whether "made over" meant that he married her to the Muslim or that he gave or sold her to him as a slave is unclear.[86] Much indeed is unclear about this aspect of their lives, poorly documented as it is.

It would have pleased Wilkinson immensely if he could have numbered Sir William Gell among his colleagues in Egypt, if only for the space of a short visit. Gell was always wanting to go to Egypt. When Thomas Young passed through Naples in 1822, he found Gell contemplating a trip. A bad attack of Gell's crippling gout must have ensued, for the trip did not materialize. The following year, however, Gell wrote to tell Wilkinson, "I am much better in health & much inclined to take a trip to the pyramids & if I go on improving shall be more so next year indeed I think I shall accomplish it. If you do what I so strongly recommend return into Italy to put your acquisitions in order & then go out again I would most certainly do so & I think I am now well enough for boats & jack asses though not for prancing steeds."[87] But Gell's intention was deterred by the deteriorating international situation associated with the Greek War of Independence, compelling him to write, "I had really settled on coming to Egypt in September but Dr Watson & I have been disappointed in a lift to Alexandria & between the Algerines & the Greeks one does not know how to proceed unless Commodore Ismael would send a ship to convey us to the Nile." He added, "Nothing is wanting but a safe ship."[88] By August conditions were no better: "I do not see myself at all advanced in my voyage to Egypt. I cannot go unless I have every convenience & that does not at present seem a probable case. . . . You had much better come here for a short time to take me back with you."[89] The story was the same the following year, 1825. "I wish you would come here for a short time & take out a party under your protection for a few months. I cannot set out alone without legs or money."[90]

Finally, in the summer of 1827, Gell wrote to Wilkinson to tell him that he was indeed coming to Egypt, apparently in company with Champollion, who was preparing his Egyptian expedition. Wilkinson replied, "I was gratefully surprised to find by your letter that you are coming out at last; & hope to be here at Thebes to welcome you & lionize you among the lists of Kings & other curiosities."[91] But this visit also failed to come to pass, perhaps because of financial difficulties that Gell was then enduring. Wilkinson wrote in September from the Eastern Desert, "Champollion is arrived, & I had expected to have the pleasure of welcoming you to the Nile, but I should think so large a party as his would not be the most agreeable addition to other travelling vexations."[92] It was reserved for Gell to know Egypt only from afar through books and through letters from friends like Wilkinson.

CHAPTER SEVEN

Life among the Tombs

WILKINSON MADE several visits to Luxor, the site of ancient Thebes, during his first years in Egypt. Thebes, the capital of Egypt during the period of the New Kingdom (ca. 1570–1075 B.C.), retained its splendor even in ruins. Napoleon's soldiers burst into applause when they first saw it, and Belzoni's initial impression was, "It appeared to me like entering a city of giants, who, after a long conflict, were all destroyed, leaving the ruins of their various temples as the only proofs of their former existence."[1] From the mid-1820s Wilkinson began spending much more time at Thebes, especially on the west bank. It was there that he did his best work and built his remarkable house.

The west bank of Thebes is the site of the Theban necropolis. A more dramatic spot for it could scarcely have been imagined. Beneath the great backdrop of the rugged Libyan Chain runs a system of hills and valleys where the people of ancient Thebes buried their dead, sometimes ostentatiously, sometimes secretly. This is the richest archaeological site in Egypt. The Egyptologist Percy E. Newberry, who spent years in Thebes around the beginning of this century, wrote of the necropolis, "Within the space of three miles it contains the ruins of a royal palace, the remains of nearly a score of temples, and more than thirty tombs of the most famous kings and queens of ancient Egypt. Here, too, are the sepulchers of state officers and generals of the Eighteenth and Nineteenth Dynasties, and the more humble graves of their clerks and tradesmen."[2]

Standing alone in front of the ridge of the western mountains and just behind the Ramesseum rises the pyramidally shaped limestone hill Shaykh Abd al-Gurna, said to be named for a Muslim holy man whose tomb is on the summit. Nowadays young women who are about to marry come and walk around his tomb and leave offerings of food for the poor and the animals. Gurna (Arabic for "promontory" or "mountain point") is thoroughly honeycombed with tombs, and on its southwest face overlooking the Nile and Luxor are the finest tombs of all, those of the nobles of the New Kingdom. The best of these tombs compare in splendor with many in the nearby Valley of the Kings. The kings had their mortuary temples near the river, so they sometimes built relatively simple tombs designed more for security than splendor; being divine, the king had less need of an elaborate tomb to secure his eternal comfort. The high officials, however, concentrated their resources on their personal tombs on Gurna which, unlike the kings' tombs, were both funerary rooms and burial places.

One of the largest and certainly the best located of these tombs was that of a powerful noble named 'Amechu, governor of Thebes and grand vizier of the kingdom in the reign of Tuthmose III (ca. 1490–1436 B.C.). 'Amechu's remains and portable treasures had been carried away long before Wilkinson arrived and decided to make the tomb his home, but the tomb's interior, cut into the living rock of the hillside, was intact. With its T-shaped design, it exemplifies the predominant type of Eighteenth Dynasty tomb on Gurna: a grand transverse portico ten feet deep by eighty feet wide stretches across the front behind eight angular pillars four feet apart; a passage five feet wide goes straight back more than fifty feet into the hillside.[3] Within the portico the walls were covered with the remains of hieroglyphs that proclaimed 'Amechu's titles and those of his son User; the shaft was decorated with scenes of religious rites performed before mummies.[4] On one of the walls was the pious, perhaps hopeful statement, "I know that at the last God returns evil to him who does it, justice to him who brings it. May justice be done to me as I have done it, and good be repaid to me in every way."[5] Outside is a marvelous view that a twentieth-century Egyptologist eloquently described.

Of all possible locations at Thebes, Wilkinson had chosen the most thrilling. Straight down, he looked upon the tawny desert, filled with the tumble rubbish of ancient tombs. Just below him was the Ramesseum, from which Belzoni had snatched the colossal head. Over there to the right were the twin statues which Westerners called the Colossi of Memnon, as well as the great sprawling temple of Medinet Habu. Farther away began the black land watered by the inundation, with its fields of grain and palm trees. Then the ever-changing, ever-interesting Nile cut its pulsing course across the land. On the far side of the river were to be seen the columns of the Luxor temple and the soaring obelisks of mighty Karnak. In the distance the desert hills reared into three marked peaks in the southeast. It was a panorama of never-ending fascination, a different color at every hour of the day.[6]

Using this tomb as the basis for his house, Wilkinson installed partitions and added rooms; of course, it was probably with the labor of the *fellahin* from the village below that the hard work of construction was done. When the rooms were finished, Egyptian furniture was distributed throughout them, and Wilkinson's working library was set up in a convenient corner.[7] The work must have proceeded quickly because when R. de Buissierre visited not long after it began, he found everything comfortable. De Buissierre wrote, "Wilkinson lives in one of the tombs of the Libyan chain; to reach it we climb for half an hour among steep tracks. Eventually we arrived at our tomb; it is arranged with taste, furnished in the Egyptian style, distributed among several chambers with frescoes; a pleasant coolness reigns here."[8] The pleasantness of the temperature, which has been commented upon by many subsequent tomb-dwelling Egyptologists, was appreciated by Wilkinson who wrote to a cousin, "I am now living in a grotto at Thebes & much inclined to give the Troglodytes my praise for their good sense in choosing these abodes which present a uniform & unvaried temperature both in summer & winter."[9]

Whenever wood was needed for cooking or for warmth against the sharp chill of an Egyptian winter's night, it was gotten from ancient coffins, for there was scarcely any other source. Edward William Lane, who lived at Wilkinson's house for a time, wrote that his servant sometimes brought in cooking wood that was so beautifully ornamented that he was reluctant to allow his cook to use it.[10] Another visitor reported, "Being in want of wood, the Arabs supplied us with a considerable quantity, consisting of the remains of mummy cases, among which were some very valuable pieces which my husband saved from the *auto de fe*. The grave inhabitants of ancient Egypt certainly never suspected the use which would be made of their last abode."[11] Fires made from this wood emitted an offensive, bituminous odor.[12]

Wilkinson's British colleagues all were favorably impressed with his new house. Robert Hay wrote in his diary on 30 July 1827, "After breakfast we rode up to see Mr. Wilkinson, who has taken up his abode in the tombs. We found him in a most excellent house that he had made by adding a few brick walls, and doors to a long tomb near the more modern one of Sheikh Abd el Qoorneh. It has a capital terrace before it and commands a fine view of the plain of Thebes below."[13] And Lane, who also visited the house in 1827, wrote, "Just above [another tomb] is the tomb which has a gallery with nine entrances. It has, doubtless, been magnificent; but its paintings are almost entirely destroyed, & the plaster upon which they were executed broken down. Besides the gallery, there is only a passage, behind the central entrance, in which are several mummy-pits. In 1827, I found Mr Wilkinson residing in this tomb; which, with the help of some crude bricks from ancient ruins in the vicinity, he had made a very comfortable habitation."[14] It became a favorite stopping place for all of Wilkinson's friends, and for many others as well. As soon as they arrived at Thebes they tied up their *dahabiyah*s at a special landing located a short distance downstream from where the tourist ferry landing is now. It was marked by an ancient, spreading sycamore tree that became a landmark for all British travelers who came to Gurna and that Wilkinson, Lane, and others took care to include in their maps of the area. From there, they made their way across the wide plain and up to the house. Passing references to "Abu Wilkinson's tomb" occur frequently in diaries and letters: "Went up to Wilkinson's"; "Remained idle all day with Wilkinson"; "Went to W's—Did no work"; and "We returned to the boat intending next day to remove up to Mr. Wilkinson's house for a day or two as he had been so kind as to invite us to do so."[15] Hard-working Hay was astonished at Wilkinson's schedule. "Wilkinson's hours are so late," he wrote in his diary, "that one loses half the day before anything can be done. He breakfasts at half past 10 o'clock, takes luncheon at 3 o'clock, and dines about 1/2 8 o'clock!"[16] But Wilkinson could work much harder than Hay imagined, otherwise he would never have accomplished all that he did. He often worked without seeming to do so by using little bits of time here and there, working amid distractions that anyone else might have found intolerable. He could sketch on horseback or camelback, and he scribbled in his notebooks and prepared manuscripts in the oddest times and places. Anyone who has tried can appreciate the diligence necessary to maintain detailed notebooks, to use the many idle but not always comfortable moments that come to travelers to get it down on paper before memories fade, day in and day out, whether one feels like doing it or not. Despite his dismay at Wilkinson's working habits, Hay eventually became a partner in the house and moved his artists into the tomb just below.

In its final form, which probably took several years to evolve, Wilkinson's house was an elaborate structure. Sketches and floor plans in Hay's portfolio show how the transverse hall behind the pillars was partitioned into sleeping quarters and a dressing room. A large wall enclosed a garden and courtyard in front. Into the wall were built a pigeon house and a tower. On the left by the way that wound up from the plain were located the anteroom, the wash house, and a place for the donkeys; the servants' quarters were on the right. One lovely wash drawing shows a covered wooden porch extending out into the courtyard. Kalitza Hay stands in one of the great rock apertures where a wooden door has been attached. A servant waits in the background. Geese mill about; vines twine up the columns; sunlight streams in.[17]

Wilkinson and Hay made welcome all European gentlemen who came to Luxor, and occasionally visitors sought them out uninvited, as did Sir Hudson Lowe, Napoleon's keeper at St. Helena, who made his way up to the house and surprised Joseph Bonomi asleep in his hammock.[18] Another visitor, Benjamin Disraeli, passing through in 1831 on his Grand Tour, wrote home to his sister, "We were a week at Thebes with the advantage of the society of Mr. Wilkinson, an Englishman of vast learning, who has devoted ten years to the study of Hieroglyphics and Egyptian antiquity, and who can read you the side of an obelisk or the front of a pylon as we would the last number of the *Quarterly*."[19] Such visits were festive occasions. George Alexander Hoskins, who was entertained at the house, described the experience: "On Thursday evenings also the artists and travellers at Thebes used to assemble in his house, or rather tomb I should call it; but never was the habitation of death witness to gayer scenes. Though we wore the costume, we did not always preserve the gravity of the Turks; and the saloon, although formerly a sepulchre, threw no gloom over our mirth. The still remaining beautiful fragments of the painted roof were illuminated by the blaze of waxlights; and the odour of the mummies had long ago been dispelled by the more congenial perfume of savory viands."[20] Though that dinner party occurred in 1833, a few months after Wilkinson left Thebes to return to England, it was probably typical of many that had gone before; indeed, Hoskins came to Thebes with a letter of recommendation from Wilkinson to Hay.

Wilkinson had several other Europeans for neighbors. There was Henry Salt's employee Giovanni d'Athanasi, known as Yanni, who had worked in Thebes on and off since 1817. He lived down the hill from Wilkinson in a large, walled structure that served as Henry Salt's headquarters in Thebes.[21] Lane and Hay both stayed there during their first visits. Yanni's house was, Lane wrote, neatly built, of sunburnt brick. On entering this house for the first time, I was surprised to see doors, shutters, shelves, &c formed of the materials of mummy-chests, covered with paintings. In the principal sitting-room was, at one end, a deewa'n, & at the other end, some chairs. My servant sat down on one of these, & it fell to pieces under him: it had been found, a few days before, in an ancient tomb. The servant was not to blame; for the chair appeared perfectly strong: the seat was of thick leather; tightly stretched. Upon a table lay a small blanket full of round cakes of bread, also taken from an ancient tomb; & appearing quite fresh. Many other antiquities were in the room.[22]

Thomas Triantaphyllos, a Greek merchant, also lived in the consular building. Known as Hawagi Werda, Triantaphyllos supervised Salt's operation when Yanni was away.[23] The rival camp was represented on the nearby hill of Dra Abu el-Naga by an Italian excavator named Piccinini who lived near tomb number 161 and looked after Drovetti's interests. Piccinini is a shadowy figure in the history of Egyptian archaeology; even his first name is unrecorded, but he was well-known to his colleagues in Egypt.[24] His name, along with many others, including Belzoni's, may be seen today where he carved it in the Ramesseum. George Hoskins visited Piccinini's house and described it: "A single compartment consisted of his whole house; his windows, shutters, steps and floor were all composed of wooden coffins."[25]

Some of Wilkinson's most interesting neighbors were the *gurnawi*, the local inhabitants of the village of Gurna, some few hundred in number. To be precise, the original village of Gurna, which was located near the river by the landing that Wilkinson and his friends used, had fallen into ruin, and it had not one inhabitant, for the people had moved away from the river into the tombs of Shaykh Abd al-Gurna.[26] These tombs they built onto and subdivided with mud partitions to make quarters for themselves and their animals. The *gurnawi* had not reached nearly so high as Wilkinson's level, and indeed they tended to avoid his house because it was so unusual that they thought it was haunted, a belief that Wilkinson encouraged.[27]

Descended from a nomadic tribe that had settled at Gurna in medieval times, the *gurnawi* retained many singular characteristics, as all European travelers who became acquainted with them agreed. Belzoni visited them shortly before Wilkinson came to live at Gurna and wrote, "The people of Gournou are superior to any other Arabs in cunning and deceit, and the most independent of any in Egypt." He went on to say, "They are the most unruly people in Egypt. At various times many of them have been destroyed, so that they are reduced from three thousand, the number they formerly reckoned, to three hundred."[28] Whenever the government tried to bring them under firmer control, they hid in the tombs or in the hills, never submitting, no matter how much they suffered for their defiance. These *gurnawi* not only lived in the tombs, but also made their living from them, for the high prices that Europeans would pay for ancient Egyptian artifacts were a good source of income. Though they had recently been poor farmers—some accounts say bandits—scratching a meager living from the soil, they forsook the plow with alacrity. Belzoni reported that they were still occasionally compelled to work on the land, but "if left to their own will, they would never take a spade in their hands, except when they go to dig for mummies."[29] Bones and bands of cloth lay about the entrances of some tombs where mummies had been brought out and stripped of their valuables. Even today the people of Gurna continue to ply their ancestral trade, albeit on a somewhat reduced scale.

European writers were also impressed by the surpassing deceitfulness of the *gurnawi*. A. H. Rhind wrote, "Especially at Goorneh, no statement made by a *fellah* on the simplest question of fact is likely to be correct; and no attestation of it, however, solemn, is necessarily accurate, if he has the slightest interest in misleading, conceives any of the extravagant suspicions to which he has too good reason to be prone, or imagines, according to his most tortuous judgement, that giving wrong information might benefit him in any way what ever."[30] Their untruthfulness naturally resulted from their means of livelihood, which demanded that they either conceal the source of their artifacts or lie to increase their value. The influence of Islam had done little to soften their way of life because, Belzoni noted, the *gurnawi* "have no mosque, nor do they care for one."[31] Despite their unruliness and untruthfulness, the *gurnawi* could be useful to the Europeans. Rhind wrote, "As a body of workmen they are not very difficult to manage beyond the necessity of constant watchfulness, since their petty schemes of deception may for the most part be detected."[32] From them Wilkinson recruited household servants and workers for his excavations.

The people of Gurna did have to endure hardships. If they went to the river, some distance away, they had to bear in mind that crocodiles still lived in that stretch of it, endangering the women and children. Not long after Robert Hay arrived at Thebes a crocodile carried away a child who was drawing water. This was, he noted, a rare occurrence, though he went on to say that dogs, sheep, and goats were often carried away. But when another crocodile carried off a woman a few days later, Hay concluded, "Therefore the instances are not so very rare as I had once supposed."[33] None of the Theban crocodiles, however, equaled in notoriety the one in the neighborhood of Girga whose tail had been shot off by a cannon ball some years before. Bonomi wrote that it "still continues to commit depredations in the same place devouring every year sheep buffali women and children."[34] The men of Gurna, though less endangered by crocodiles, lived in fear of the corvée. Robert Hay witnessed the raising of one.

> This forenoon the *Kaymakan* and Sheikhs were busily employed seizing on all the wives of the men who had run away from their work on the Tura, or canal which is now in progress on the opposite side of the river above Luxor—These good dames are carried off to work as hostages in hopes that their loving help mates w^d return from the mountains and resume their work. . . . When these enslaved Arabs are called to work for the Pasha all who can effect it make their escape and hide themselves in the tombs & mountains all day and by night are supplyd [*sic*] with provisions by their wives.[35]

Wilkinson occasionally interceded to help the people and the local governors in their relations with the central government. In gratitude they maintained his house long after he had gone from among them.[36]

Wilkinson seems to have worked at Thebes without impediment, protected by the good offices of Muhammad Ali and Henry Salt. Around him, collecting proceeded on a grand scale. The ongoing rivalry of Salt and Drovetti was mirrored in their agents, Piccinini and Yanni, who continually argued over the division of the ground, one always suspecting the other of encroachment. Hot letters were exchanged and circulated, with *backshish* liberally distributed to win the loyalty of local officials. "Such has been the case ever since the time of Belzoni—One fight following another," Hay observed.[37] Acquisitive activities like that interested Wilkinson little, for his primary interests were not those of a large-scale collector.

One of his first major objectives was to make a topographical survey of the west bank, a labor similar to the pioneering surveys that his friend Gell had done elsewhere and whose work he doubtless used as a model. It was a basic job, one that many of Wilkinson's colleagues would have had neither the patience nor the ability to do, but something that had to be done if serious scholars were to have a perspective of the entire site. He carefully mapped the area, identified the monuments, and numbered the tombs of Gurna. This provided more precise identification for the tombs than the descriptive names by which they previously had been known, such as the "military tomb" (Rekhmire), the "small catacomb" (?), "the large Tomb" (?), and the "tomb by Yanni's house" (Nakht).[38] When Amelia Edwards visited the hill years later, she could still see his numbers painted above the tomb portals.[39] Wilkinson's house provided an excellent perspective for much of his topographical work, and when he climbed to the ancient path running along the ridge behind Gurna, as he often did, he got an even better view.

Wilkinson's topographical efforts eventually crystallized into the first comprehensive plan of western Thebes. Other maps had been made of the area, but none had the scope and detail of Wilkinson's.[40] "I have been of late hard at work finishing my plan of Goorneh," he wrote to Hay late in 1830, "to which [I] have added the Western Valley [i.e., the Valley of the Kings], where Amunoph 3d's tomb is—& will soon set about adding Karnak & Luxor."[41] Among the details he chose to include was the sycamore tree by the landing, drawn prominently and clearly. It is a valuable document of what was on the surface when Wilkinson was there. For some reason of his own, he inset a plan of the Pyramids of Giza in this map of Thebes—"I should think it very ill judged," Frederick Catherwood wrote of that addition when he saw it.[42] Wilkinson entitled his map "Topographical Survey of Thebes, Tápé, Thaba or Diospolis Magna by G. Wilkinson Esq.," and by the time he returned to England it was ready for publication. James Burton also began a map of Thebes, but soon abandoned the project.[43]

Most of Wilkinson's work at Thebes was careful copying during the course of which he filled some of the best of his notebooks. This was supplemented by other techniques. He made many rubbings and squeezes, some 5,500 of them altogether.[44] He also collected selectively. Never a collector in the sense of Salt or Drovetti, he did accumulate some objects that were illustrative of daily life. Furthermore, he realized that the tomb paintings provided the only reliable evidence for how these objects were used.[45] He even used chemical analysis on one occasion. Taking care not to damage the tomb murals, he sampled the pigment in them. When he returned to England he gave the samples to a chemist friend who determined the composition of the paint used by the ancient artists.[46]

As was by now customary for him, Wilkinson also worked at his writing while he was at Thebes. He completed the manuscript for *Extracts from Several Hieroglyphical Subjects*, a follow-up to his

Materia Hieroglyphica, both of which will be described in more detail in the next chapter. He also began work on another book, *Topography of Thebes, and General View of Egypt,* hoping to have it published by a printer in Alexandria. All of these books contained seeds of ideas that later flowered in his most important book, *Manners and Customs of the Ancient Egyptians.* Writing while working at topography and archaeology gave all of those activities a mutually reinforcing strength that they would have lacked had they been pursued sequentially.

Within easy reach of Wilkinson's house lay many of the most important monuments of ancient Egypt. Just over the ridge behind Gurna is the Valley of the Kings. He spent much time there, being especially interested in the Tomb of Seti I, or Belzoni's Tomb. Its rich murals became an important element in his vision of ancient Egyptian life. He surveyed the valley as part of his mapping project for the west bank and assigned numbers to the twenty-one tombs then known to him; during his 1827 visit he painted these numbers over the doors of the tombs.[47] His numbering system is still in use, numbers higher than twenty-one belonging to tombs discovered since he worked there. Some of his painted numbers are still visible. Unlike Belzoni, who believed that all of the important tombs had been discovered, Wilkinson believed more might be found. "It is perhaps in this valley [the Valley of the Kings] that other of the oldest royal catacombs may some day be discovered, and it certainly is singular that none have been yet met with of the first kings of the eighteenth dynasty."[48] In fact, the tomb of the most famous, if not the most significant, king of the Eighteenth Dynasty, Tut-ankh-Amon, lay undiscovered only a short distance from Belzoni's tomb. Wilkinson walked past it and most likely over it many times. But he made no real attempt to uncover additional tombs, his primary interests lying elsewhere. And he was in any case much less interested in excavating than in surveying and recording.[49]

A short walk down the northwest slope of Gurna took Wilkinson to Deir el-Bahri, the imposing mortuary temple of Hat-Shepsut, who was then unknown to scholars but whose cartouches Wilkinson had noticed. Directly below him was the Ramesseum, and not so far south lay the large temple of Medinet Habu. Near Medinet Habu was the village of Deir el-Medina where the artists and craftsmen who built the royal tombs had lived. This is to mention only some of the more important Theban sites, almost all of which Wilkinson examined, some more than others. At Deir el-Medina he opened and copied some of the tombs on the hillside just above the village; he also sketched objects from the village that were circulating on the

Theban antiquities market, objects that have since disappeared, but his resources and techniques did not permit him to devote much attention to the village itself.[50] The work of later scholars in excavating the village made Deir el-Medina one of the most important sites for understanding the daily life of the ancient Egyptians. This development would have especially pleased Wilkinson.

His most important work at Thebes was closer to home, in the Tombs of the Nobles, most of which are on Gurna. While others concentrated on more imposing monuments, Wilkinson became interested in the murals in these tombs. Though highly appreciated now, they were not the sort of thing that would have interested Salt or Drovetti. It has been suggested that Wilkinson became interested in them because he lacked the means to excavate the larger temples. That may well have been part of the reason at first, but it is assuredly not the entire reason. An examination of his subsequent work indicates that he was drawn to the tombs for their own sake, because he understood that they revealed much more about how the ancient Egyptians lived than did the greater monuments.[51]

The tomb paintings of the New Kingdom period at Thebes are an important chapter in the history of art. They are, in fact, by far the majority of all surviving Egyptian paintings. After the disastrous humiliation of the Hyksos occupation, Egypt recovered and became more powerful than ever as it expanded far beyond its accustomed borders and acquired an empire. The center of this new activity was Thebes, where the business of government was conducted by a powerful group of officials, the nobility of the New Kingdom. These exalted scribes used their power and wealth to establish grand tombs for themselves at Gurna, as did 'Amechu, the vizier whose tomb became Wilkinson's house. Whereas the king had been the primary patron of funerary art in previous periods in Egyptian history, the nobles now became the most important. By having the things they enjoyed the most painted on the walls of their tombs, they intended to enjoy them forever. Hence they made portrayals not only of their suitable interment, but also of the manifold exercise of their duties, and especially their pleasures—hunting, dining, drinking, music, and dance. The portrayal of these natural scenes led to naturalism in technique, for though New Kingdom art began by adhering to the centuries-old canon, it soon evolved into something new. This provided new freedom of expression for the artists who experimented with motion and profile and who had a vastly increased supply of subjects upon which to practice their techniques.

The quality of naturalism was what interested Wilkinson the most about the tomb paintings, because it made them useful evidence for detailed inferences about everyday life in ancient Egypt. Others had noticed that the Gurna paintings portrayed everyday life, but Wilkinson, who considered them an "epitome of human life," was the first to use them systematically as historical evidence. "Here," he wrote, "manners and customs, historical events and religious ceremonies, carry us back, as it were, to the society of those to whom they refer; and we are enabled to study the amusements and occupations of the ancient Egyptians, almost as though we were spectators of the scenes represented."[52] It was a great opportunity for an imaginative person, and this experience more than any other provided the material for his greatest book, *Manners and Customs of the Ancient Egyptians.*

Not far from Wilkinson's house was the tomb of Rekhmire, one of the grandest of the tombs of Gurna. The *fellahin* called it *"al bab khamsa wa talathin,"* or "tomb (door) number thirty-five," thirty-five being the number that Wilkinson assigned to it.[53] Rekhmire was the paternal grandson of 'Amechu, and like 'Amechu was governor of Thebes and vizier of the kingdom. He was also the last of his family to hold those exalted offices because he was dismissed by a king who probably decided that Rekhmire's family had become too powerful. While he lasted, however, Rekhmire was a powerful man with a high opinion of himself, for inscribed upon his tomb walls is the declaration that he knew everything in heaven, on earth, or in the world below.[54] Wilkinson wrote that Rekhmire's tomb was "by far the most curious, I may say, of all the tombs in Thebes since it throws more light on the manners and customs of the ancient Egyptians than any hitherto discovered."[55] Wilkinson was, in fact, one of the first Europeans to study the tomb which had been initially explored only a few years before when Frédéric Caillaud examined it during his visit to Egypt from 1819 to 1822.[56]

As he walked through Rekhmire's tomb, Wilkinson could see a broad range of Egyptian life. He saw the vizier receiving tribute from peoples of various lands, though he mistook the vizier for a king. Each group of people was portrayed in its peculiar way. On the opposite wall was a servant pouring wine for a lady at a party where the guests are entertained by musicians. Wilkinson noted the natural posture of the figures and the fact that one of them was shown in perspective, an important innovation.[57] He was perhaps the first to notice this departure from the canon. He sent Gell a drawing of the mural and commented, "You will observe the maid is drawn 3/4 figure & not as a stiff Eg^n—which shows they knew something more of perspective than people fancy, & I have many specimens of things done in what we should now call & allow to be perspective."[58] Elsewhere in the tomb Wilkinson saw the vizier judging tax evaders, examining the work of various craftsmen, supervising the construction of a temple, inspecting the divine offerings, receiving the petitions of the poor, and enjoying the company of his family.[59]

Another important tomb was the one that had belonged to Nakht, Scribe of the Granaries under Thutmose IV. Located near Yanni's house, Nakht's tomb was not large, consisting of just two irregularly shaped chambers, only one of which was decorated. "But in this single room," a historian of Thebes writes, "are such detailed activities, executed with such infinite charm and in such a good state of repair that the tomb of Nakht will always rank as one of the finest."[60] In the depictions in Nakht's tomb Wilkinson saw such detailed aspects of ancient Egyptian life as the structure of Egyptians' furniture, the shape of their musical instruments, and Nakht's activities, including his hunting wildfowl among papyrus reeds. Details such as a cat eating a fish beneath a chair added poignance to the scene. On another wall, Wilkinson saw laborers in the fields. Teams of cattle pull ploughs through a landscape still dotted with puddles left from the inundation. Sowers follow behind. Water and food are set out to feed the hungry men. Yet another wall depicts harvest time. Men gather grapes from abundantly bearing vines and trample out their juice in great vats. The treaders hold to straps hanging from the ceiling to keep them from slipping and sinking; juice pours into jars to be fermented into wine. Nakht and his family look on, content with the good things they enjoy.[61]

Wilkinson and his colleagues did an enormous service to Egyptology with their patient work in the tombs at Thebes, for within a few years many of the paintings were damaged or destroyed. Also, some of the tombs known to Wilkinson and his friends have since been lost.[62] In many cases his copies are the only guide we have to the way the paintings used to appear. Though the ancient artists sometimes applied their paint to a smoothed stone surface, they usually coated unfinished stone with plaster, or occasionally mud, and painted on that. Toward the bottom of the hill, where the stone was better, reliefs were sometimes sculptured, but even these were usually painted. The result was paintings that were fragile, easily damaged when the tombs were open, and especially vulnerable if the tombs became human habitations, as many at Gurna did.[63] When G. A. Hoskins visited the tomb of Rekhmire during the winter of 1860–61 he found that an Arab family had moved into one chamber and had installed their cow in another. The mural depicting Rekhmire receiving the tribute of the foreigners was already much more damaged than it had been when Wilkinson and his friends first copied it.[64]

From our standpoint today, some minor faults might appear in Wilkinson's work. For example, he was so intent upon clearing out tombs and observing the artwork that he took little interest in what might be found in the rubble. Much important contextual information was thereby lost. But it was not until the time of Sir Flinders Petrie at the end of the nineteenth century that scholars began to understand that everything was important.[65] Wilkinson also neglected to exercise adequate supervision over his workmen who consequently stole from the tombs and sold to collectors. Occasionally his disdain for objects went too far, as when some *fellahin* opened a tomb and found its floor covered with thousands of scarabs bearing the names of Eighteenth Dynasty kings. A *dragoman* brought Wilkinson a basketful and offered them to him at a token price, but he declined, saying that they were "useless things, like beads."[66] Wilkinson's thoughts were fixed upon the paintings and sculptures on the walls. By the standards of his time, he was scrupulously careful.

Thus Wilkinson happily spent his days at Thebes, working among the antiquities and living in his unique house. Even after he left Egypt in 1833, the house rendered useful service to other scholars and travelers. Robert Hay and his wife continued to live there for some time; Edward Hogg visited them not long after Wilkinson had gone and commented how they resided in a "capacious, excavated tomb, commodiously and comfortably arranged."[67] When Edward William Lane and a friend came to stay there in 1833, they found a traveler already in residence.

> It was our intention to take up our quarters in a tomb, which had been converted into a convenient dwelling by M[r] Wilkinson & M[r] Hay. We found M[r] Gosset occupying one compartment of it: I have taken possession of another apartment, separated from the former by a low wall with a door; & M[r] Fresnel has settled in a tomb just below, which was occupied by M[r] Bonomi & other artists in the employ of M[r] Hay. Our abode is in the Hill of the Sheykh, overlooking the whole plain of Thebes. A man named 'Ow'ads [Auad] has the charge of it; & M[r] Gosset & I pay him each 15 piastres a month, for his services.[68]

Lepsius stayed at the house, still in the keeping of Auad, on his famous expedition of 1842–45 and commented how "Wilkinson and

Hay have rendered an essential service to later travelers by building up the habitable rooms, which, from our being desirous of spending a long time at Thebes, we have profited by."[69]

'Amechu's tomb today is much as it was before Wilkinson came. Of Wilkinson's additions, all that remains is a small portion of wall from one of the northern towers, the rest of the mud brick no doubt recycled by the *gurnawi*, just as Wilkinson took it from other sources. That remnant is a monument to a productive generation of scholars and travelers in Egypt.

CHAPTER EIGHT

"One Seems Tied Down to It for Life"

SIR WILLIAM GELL REPEATEDLY urged Wilkinson to come to Europe, organize and publish his materials, and then return to Egypt. Wilkinson occasionally considered taking Gell's advice and in 1826 even sent all his papers to England, intending to follow them soon. He told his cousin Captain M. Stanhope Badcock to look out for the shipment, "as the papers it contains are too valuable to me to be lost."[1] But the climax of the Greek War of Independence prevented his departure, and once thwarted, he pursued the matter no further. Instead he settled down to more work, though he sorely missed his papers.[2] Despite his reluctance to return to Europe, he was eager to publish, and in the face of great odds, he achieved some marginal success.

The appearance of Champollion's work spurred him on. Previously he had assumed that his presence in Egypt put him far ahead of any competition.[3] Now he feared that if he did not hurry, he might be anticipated in other areas besides the decipherment of hieroglyphs. Besides Sir William Gell, Wilkinson also had Captain Badcock helping him with his efforts to publish. "As I told you in my last," he wrote to Badcock, "I am very desirous of getting these papers published before the French can arrive at the same train of materials."[4] Like Gell, Captain Badcock approached Thomas Young, and he received the same discouraging answers that Gell had. But Young took a more indulgent tone with Badcock, indicating that some of the impatience he occasionally displayed with Gell may have been due to the importunance and repetitiousness of Gell's requests. Young wrote to Badcock on 17 June 1828,

I am on the point of setting out for Paris, but I have looked over Mr. Wilkinson's papers and I can only repeat what I said before, that I know of no bookseller who would undertake to publish them: though the conciseness of the work and the multitude of Royal Personages contained in it ought certainly to be great inducements to the adventure. After my return, which I hope will be in two months, I may possibly be able to make further inquiries: and I shall be happy if any channel should be open: it is not impossible that the R.S.L. [Royal Society of Literature] might at a future time undertake to print the memoir: which would certainly do this country more credit than those of Mess. Yorke, Leake, Champollion and Co in their transactions. At any rate the manuscript is safe in my hands—and if I should happen to return a mummy it will be found in my upper drawer with the 6 copies of the Hieroglyphics marked for Mr. Wilkinson: that is of Plate 4 to 80.[5]

Wilkinson was understandably downcast when Badcock relayed the disappointing news to him, and he expressed his feelings to Gell. "My papers of last year or year before last are in Dr Young's hands, who says the booksellers in London will have nothing to do with hieroglyphics, & that consequently they cannot be published. Champollion I believe was too much mentioned in them. However, I can do it here when I have finished those of 1828."[6] Wilkinson was unjust, and indeed unworthy of the attention that Young had given him, if he was implying that resentment of Champollion had prevented Young from doing more. All things considered, Young acted quite handsomely toward Wilkinson, someone whom, after all, he had never even met. A memorandum of Young's dated Park Square, 13 March 1828, shows his high opinion of Wilkinson's work and the efforts he had made for him.

Mr. W. has been collecting an immense treasure of drawings which do equal credit to his zeal as an antiquary and his talent as an artist; it is time that he should return and arrange his collection for the benefit of the public: if the public has good sense enough to profit by them.

Dr. Y. made many attempts to persuade some booksellers to undertake at least a popular selection of the drawings, but none of them had courage to do it—and Dr Y has only been able to introduce about 20 plates from the drawings sent by Mr Cook from Sir W. Gell, into the 3rd and 4th numbers of the Hieroglyphics: but this work goes on very slowly: the R.S.L is afraid of venturing too much expense into the undertaking: and even the work of the artists has been very tedious.

The drawings in natural history might possibly be published by the Linnean Society: but their volumes have lately contained few coloured plates.[7]

Young did not return from Paris as a mummy, but his health was failing, and he died in London on 10 May 1829.

Thwarted in England, Wilkinson decided to publish in Egypt. Some of his friends had done so, Burton and Bonomi having lithographed Burton's *Excerpta Hieroglyphica,* and Major Felix did the lithography for his own *Notes on Hieroglyphs,*[8] which he subsequently printed on the pasha's press. Wilkinson therefore set to work, assisted only by Haji Musa, and lithographed the plates for *Materia Hieroglyphica.*[9] A. C. Harris arranged for the government press in Malta to do the printing. In that way, *Materia Hieroglyphica,* with its preface dated at the Pyramids, was published in 1828, followed by *Extracts from Several Hieroglyphic Subjects* in 1830, dedicated to Sir William Gell.

Materia Hieroglyphica, supplemented by the *Extracts,* primarily addressed itself to ancient Egyptian religion and chronology, though attention was also given to art. In addition, the book contained some important material about hieroglyphic translation, but Wilkinson avoided an explanatory account of it, wishing to make no claims to primacy in that area. His pantheon was an important advance beyond previous treatments of Egyptian religion, despite the inclusion of such unsound Neoplatonic and Hermetic elements as numbering Hermes Trismegistus among the gods of ancient Egypt. Also, as he admitted, "Several deities are still wanting, but I trust, at some future period, to be enabled to introduce them."[10] His chronology was the best that had ever been published, though its defects are readily apparent to our eyes today. He did not, for example, list the kings between Menes, the first king of the First Dynasty (ca. 3100 B.C.), and those of the Sixteenth Dynasty (ca. 1600 B.C.), though he offered some speculations about the Shepherd Kings of the Second Intermediate Period. These, he thought, might have been Assyrian, though that could "only be proved by the future discoveries of travellers."[11] His reason for omitting the greater part of fifteen dynasties was, "Of the intermediate kings, from Menes to Osirtesen, no monument worthy of notice now exists, if we except the great pyramids."[12]

Whatever may have been the shortcomings of these early works, they contained much that was of value. Wilkinson's treatment of chronology and theology, and even language, is superior in many respects to that contained in Champollion's books of the 1820s, the *Panthéon égyptien* and *Précis du système hiéroglyphique*. But *Materia Hieroglyphica* and *Extracts from Several Hieroglyphical Subjects* were not destined to be widely read. The press in Malta, working without Wilkinson's supervision, produced editions with so many errors that he was obliged to correct by hand as many copies as he could. Also, the printing run was too small for either book to be widely disseminated. Only one hundred or so copies of each was printed. The books did attract passing notice in British literary circles. *Fraser's Magazine*, in its review of *Materia Hieroglyphica*, commended Wilkinson for not writing "one of those frothy traveller's quartos, which, though they may increase the wealth of the author, do not add greatly to his credit."[13] But this review concentrated on his hieroglyphic work, which was but one of the book's many aspects, and not necessarily its most important. The *Edinburgh Review* decided against reviewing *Materia Hieroglyphica*, later explaining that it was "a crude and ill-digested performance, devoid of method or arrangement as far as the *matter* is concerned."[14] Even so, Wilkinson's first books were a significant accomplishment, and he must have taken some encouragement from being elected to the Royal Society of Literature in 1831 because of them.

Another, and the most important, of the book-length manuscripts that Wilkinson produced in Egypt was *Topography of Thebes, and General View of Egypt*, described below, but when he attempted to publish it he experienced his usual difficulties. Unlike *Materia Hieroglyphica* and *Extracts from Several Hieroglyphical Subjects*, Wilkinson intended to publish this book in Egypt. That plan came to naught when his intended publisher suddenly died of cholera in Alexandria.[15] The manuscript was too large to entrust to the government press in Malta, so Wilkinson was obliged to send it to London, hoping his luck there might have changed. It was no use. Egyptian books, and indeed all things Egyptian, had gone out of fashion, following the brief burst of Egyptomania inspired by Belzoni in 1821. Literary tastes had moved to other things. "Hieroglyphs," Major Felix reported from London, "are at a discount, & every thing else of taste of science, but Lady Charlotte Bury got a £1000 the other day for a novel, which writing is a much better speculation." He claimed to avoid even talking about Egypt "for fear of being blackballed in the clubs."[16] Wilkinson wrote plaintively to Gell: "I have sent my MS of a new work to England, which I mentioned to you—but the booksellers will have nothing to do with it. This is very hard. However I intend to do it myself. It is rather disheartening to have all the trouble & then the expense besides. No one cares about Egypt. It is the same with my map. In it is a large Survey of Thebes which would amuse you."[17] By doing it himself, he meant publishing by subscription, which was still quite common in those days, but even that could be difficult, as he learned: "I am sorry to hear that the work on Egypt of Champollion Figeac & Rosellini is likely to be given up for want of subscribers—this holds out poor hopes for anyone who intends publishing on Egypt, as this must necessarily be the most complete & most interesting work that anyone can make on Egyptian antiquities & it will not succeed with a subscription."[18]

One publication success in Britain during Wilkinson's sojourn in Egypt was an account of the 1823 trip in the Eastern Desert, published in the *Journal of the Royal Geographical Society* in 1832. Entitled "Notes on a Part of the Eastern Desert of Upper Egypt," it was an adaptation of his "Journey in Nubia, the Eastern Desert, & to Báhneséh" manuscript, which had apparently made its way to the society's headquarters in London. Besides making Wilkinson a leading authority on the Eastern Desert of Egypt, then little-known, it became an important part of the small but notable body of literature devoted to the region.[19] Here, as in many other instances, one regrets that Burton never published his research. He knew the area better than Wilkinson, having traveled more widely there, and could have contributed more geological information; but Wilkinson published, and Burton did not. Wilkinson must have been pleased to have his work published by the successor organization to his father's beloved African Exploration Society, but he was irritated when he learned that most of his antiquarian observations, which were deemed inappropriate for the society's journal, had been edited out.

While one sympathizes with Wilkinson's early publishing difficulties, much of the problem lay with him. His copies of antiquities were good, but his prose was less well developed. He was only beginning to master the art of literary exposition by the time he completed the manuscript for *Topography of Thebes*, his earlier efforts being part of the frustrating process of practice and preparation that aspiring writers must endure. The greatest impediment to publication, of course, was his excessive reliance upon others to take care of business, a dangerous procedure, even with people as well disposed as Sir William Gell and Thomas Young. If Wilkinson wanted his things published, and published properly, then he needed to go to England and do it himself, not impose upon others. Gell had told him so repeatedly, and even Wilkinson was beginning to get the idea; nonetheless, he could not yet bring himself to leave. "It is so difficult to tear myself away from this place & from Egypt altogether," he wrote to Robert Hay. "One seems tied down to it for life."[20]

Busily writing and preparing for publication, Wilkinson also encouraged his colleagues to do the same, especially Edward William Lane, who replied from Thebes: "I *have* thought seriously of your advice; but dare not follow it entirely. I am meditating upon trying, at least as a beginning, a small volume on Thebes, not to follow your example, but to confine myself as much as possible to the picturesque."[21] Lane was a prudent man who chose to take his time and define his subject. When he set to work he produced an excellent manuscript entitled "Description of Egypt," which promised to be one of the best travelogues of nineteenth-century Egypt.[22]

Wilkinson's most hortatory efforts were directed at Robert Hay who, having accomplished so much, began to show alarming signs of losing interest in his materials. The thought that Hay's extraordinary project might come to naught prompted Wilkinson to write to his friend and say,

> You think you have given up too much time to Egypt—we perhaps all have as far as the world is concerned or rather interested—but your work is invaluable—Your collection of drawings done with the exactitude of the camera will be Egypt itself. but to repay yourself with the eclat of the world you must publish this collection. Your labor will then not be lost either to yourself or to the world. & what are a few hundreds laid aside annually for so praiseworthy an object, even if in the end you lose the whole expense, which by the bye you might not. These are not vain words. I advise you as I would do myself. Indeed to substantiate this fact I may state that my present will not cost me less than 180 or 200 pounds.[23]

Hay went back to Scotland briefly in 1828 to handle some affairs on his estate and may have cast about for a publisher while he was there, but because of the difficulty and expense that his book would entail, none would undertake the risk. It was at about this time that Hay began to exhibit what his biographer calls "that remarkable lack of application and financial sense" that was a recurring theme in his later life.[24] Unlike Wilkinson, who intended to publish from the time he set foot in Egypt, Hay never developed a clear idea what to do with his portfolio. He later admitted as much to a friend. "But my perfect conviction from the time of my entering Egypt, that there was nothing *unknown*, after the *many learned*, and busy Travellers who had preceded me, that I looked on everything more as matters of *wonder* and *instruction* to *myself*—rather than with any idea of finding in them what was new that I might communicate it to others—This was a great error, I freely admit."[25]

One person who had required no encouragement to publish, and indeed who published despite strong discouragement, was Henry Salt. Unlike Gell, Salt was not content merely to be an active observer and helper; he wanted to be remembered as one of the pioneers in the decipherment of the hieroglyphs. Considering that he had arrived at his hieroglyphic conclusions independently of Champollion, although he knew of Champollion's work, Salt published his *Essay on Dr. Young's and M. Champollion's Phonetic System of Hieroglyphics* in 1825. Salt sent Wilkinson a copy of his new book, but Wilkinson, suffering from opthalmia at that moment, was too bleary-eyed to read it closely, so he gave it only a cursory examination. "He afterwards asked me my opinion of it," Wilkinson wrote to Gell. "One could not say otherwise than excellent. But the fact was I had not looked into it properly. I now see that his list of kings, Pharaoon, is all wrong, and I believe not one in its place." "How Champollion must laugh at Salt's work," he subsequently wrote. "I am sorry that S. himself is inclined to think there is anything in it." Wilkinson must have had another conversation with Salt in which he gave him an honest evaluation of the book, for in September 1828, after Salt was dead, he wrote to Gell, "Poor fellow, he was terribly mistaken in his book, & very mad with me for saying so."[26] Gell apparently read the book too, for he had much harsher things to say about it in a letter to Young:

As for Salt's claims to originality, they were only fit to be set up in the region of Humbugia, for I myself have sent to Egypt all the inventions of yourself and Champollion as fast as they come out, and particularly wrote four years ago or thereabouts to advise Salt not to publish a Pantheon which he talked about, because all his new knowledge had been printed long before in Europe, and moreover I doubt whether anything printed existed that I had not sent to Wilkinson. I understand from Mr. Scoles the architect, that Salt went crazy on the subject of *his own inventions*, and told them all that you and Champollion knew nothing about it, and that he was the only real discoverer. Wherever Champollion has not published Salt is generally wrong.[27]

Amid publication efforts, Wilkinson continued to pursue his many other activities, filling his notebooks and sketchbooks, copying antiquities, traveling up and down the Nile, and occasionally withdrawing into the desert. He made several extended stays at Gurna, during which he added to the material he was accumulating from that rich site. He also continued to work at the hieroglyphs, and his notebooks of the period show a growing knowledge of their significance.[28] Aided by Champollion's work and the Coptic word list from Lord Prudhoe, he began the ambitious task of enlarging the list of deciphered Egyptian words. *The Thoth* announced, "In the Press and Speedily will be published the Dictionary of Dictionaries in Egyptian & English by Von Vilkinson."[29] This, however, probably took the form of the word list that appeared in *Materia Hieroglyphica.*

Wilkinson also pursued a variety of nonantiquarian activities. Foremost among them was botany. During the course of his years in Egypt, he made a collection of four hundred Egyptian plants and filled two of his large portfolios with colored sketches of them.[30] By the time he left Egypt, he had nearly completed a book-length manuscript about the subject, entitled "Desert Plants of Egypt," but it was never published. He also dabbled in zoology, making, among other things, a collection of snakes. A large collection of minerals, probably made with the advice of James Burton, was the result of his geologic ramblings. Living on and near the Nile aroused in him an interest in hydrology, and he devoted considerable effort to answering two pressing questions of the day: (1) whether the successive alluvial deposits were raising the level of the river and (2) how much the size of the delta had increased since antiquity. He concluded that the river had indeed risen, but, contrary to popular opinion, had not significantly enlarged its delta in historical times.[31] He also worked hard at language, intending to master classical Arabic.[32]

Despite his energy, Wilkinson, as noted, could not match the productive volume of Robert Hay's team, but neither did he have to tolerate the aggravating personnel problems that Hay eventually encountered, problems that Wilkinson observed with sympathy. First came a build-up of tension between Hay and Bonomi. If Hay had cast Bonomi in the role of loyal retainer-artist, then he was disappointed, because Bonomi had no intention of playing that part. He soon resented his arrangement with Hay and wrote to a friend that he had only accepted Hay's offer because he had "got in to all sorts of trouble because careless got robbed and abandoned to all sorts of vices." Hay, he continued, was just "a *Scot* and not one of those who have a belly full of learning . . . one of the most ignorant men I ever met excessively purse proud and extremely rich." Bonomi went so far as to claim that many of the copies he had made for Hay, and even some that Hay had made, were his, but he was warned by friends that he stood upon doubtful legal ground.[33] He finally gave notice and sailed for England, leaving Hay to complain about his conduct. Fortunately for Hay, Edward William Lane arrived at about the same time and lent his hand to the project.

Dissatisfaction spread among the other artists. Hay's diary has this entry for 15 November 1830: "Wilkinson spent the day with us—gave audience to the artists who struck for wages!" Negotiations followed, and it was not until 19 November that Hay could note, "Settled matters with the artists."[34] But the problems cannot have been solved, for the next month Wilkinson was writing to Hay who was at Philae that he was "upset . . . that your artists have been of so little use to you. How unlucky you are."[35] A year later Wilkinson wrote to Hay in Nubia, "I hope you will not be again troubled this year with your artists—you are very unlucky. But your perseverance deserves better treatment from fortune or the god or folleys of artists."[36]

Wilkinson was able to help Hay in sending him Francis Arundale, who had arrived in Egypt. "I hope you will be more fortunate with Mr A. than you have been with other artists—& I wish you every success on the continuation of your endless labors."[37] And, "Mr Arundale has I suppose reached you long since—his chief fort [sic] I believe lies in architecture. I did not see his drawings. I hope at all counts you will proceed better with his labors than you have with others."[38] When Arundale joined his team, Hay took care to bind him to an elaborate contract requiring him to leave Egypt when his contract was over, or, if he stayed, to make no more drawings.[39] Hay's relations with his artists gradually improved, and the important work continued, but as late as 1832 Wilkinson thought it necessary to caution him, "At all costs take care of your health & do not allow the unhappy artists to annoy you. I mean do not be annoyed by it—take all cooly—this is of primary importance in this climate."[40]

One of the great events during Wilkinson's later years in Egypt was the tour of Egypt by Champollion and his retinue of artists and scholars during the years 1827–29. It was an event that Wilkinson missed, for when he learned that Gell was not accompanying Champollion, he withdrew for a lengthy stay in the Eastern Desert. "Champollion still at Thebes," he wrote to Gell, "doing wonders in copying. But he seems to make but few discoveries, & certainly has too many theories unfounded & contrary to experience; but in return much ingenuity. I have not met him yet."[41] Wilkinson's friends in Egypt did, however, meet Champollion and later informed Wilkinson of their impressions. Major Felix wrote on 25 January 1829, to say, "We met Champollion at Korosko on his return to Ebsamboul

[Abu Simbel] who paid us a long visit and showed us all his labors w^h are immense." The French had tried to get into Abu Simbel, Felix reported, and when that did not work, "they tried to excavate for the Greek inscription but were obliged to desist—it was too great an undertaking—and then they expressed a doubt if there *was* such an inscription tho' Ritchie one of their party had seen it—the whole party are perfectly disgusting." Felix concluded on a note of grudging admiration: "But altho' he is not to be trusted—catching eagerly at any shadow which suits his Theory on his Coptic his book will be a splendid & a valuable one." The French savants, Felix added, used facetious names for each other and the places they visited: Thebes they called Paris; and Champollion went by the name of Francis Bey.[42] Burton also claimed to have met Champollion at Korosko and likewise reported mixed feelings in a letter to Hay:

> What they have done is incredible—All the battles—All the
> Arts—All Natural History—All the portraits of all the Kings
> and Queens—All the Exercises, occupations, amusements and I
> know not what else of the Egyptians—we began looking over his
> Folios at 9am and had not finished till midnight—The colouring
> is beautiful and minute but the Figures are not like yours—some
> too lanky, some too fat, some too Muscular. The face of Sesostris
> at Ebsamboul is thin and affected and Ritchie has drawn him
> from the walls with a pair of Calves that would disgrace a coal
> heaver.[43]

Burton's opinion of Champollion probably plunged even further after the conflict over the multilingual inscription.

Champollion made an even more negative impression upon Joseph Bonomi. First there was a disagreement between the two over Champollion's rights to remove some friezes in Belzoni's (Seti I's) Tomb, a dispute that was at length resolved amicably.[44] But even more annoying to Bonomi was Champollion's exclusive self-aggrandizement, the quality that had been such an ugly element in his controversy with Young:

> He seems to want to have it all for himself and is so determined
> to be the sole proprietor that he will not allow the least credit to
> anyone else. . . . [He] told me that it is impossible for anyone to
> copy hieroglyphics or to read them till he has published his
> grammar. He is extremely out with everyone about him and he
> really says such rude things that I do not wonder. Everyone that
> has a different opinion must be a 'foutue bete', two of his em-

ployees are gone being disinclined to stop longer than they contracted for with a man of his temper. His portfolio is infinitely
less rich than Rosellini's which is another source of his dis-
pleasure. I saw an excessively outré drawing of that part of the
east wall of Karnak where the barbarian king is strangled by the
bowstring of the Egyptian hero.

Bonomi may have chuckled as he added, "I can imagine how black
he will look when he sees Wilkinson's gods."[45]

Wilkinson's most memorable notice of Champollion's visit to
Egypt took the form of a short poem in which he had Champollion
hold forth on the antiquity of the Pyramids:

> Les Pyramides, "sans aucune doute"
> (Je veux le dire coûte ce qu'il coûte),
> Ont sept mille ans, quelque chose de plus:
> Le [La] preuve est dans un papyrus.

> [The Pyramids, "without a doubt"
> (I want to say so at whatever cost),
> Are seven thousand years old, and something more:
> The proof is in a papyrus.]

At least it seems probable that Wilkinson was the author of these
lines. Burton, who sent the poem to Gell, wrote that Champollion,
"so Mr Wilkinson *says*," had composed them, but it is improbable
that Champollion would have written such self-mocking verse, and
he would in any case have had no opportunity to pass it on to
Wilkinson. It is much more likely that Wilkinson wrote it and mis-
chievously attributed it to the Frenchman. "Sans aucune doute," enclosed in quotation marks as it is, must have been a favorite phrase
of Champollion's when he expounded opinions to which he would
allow no contradictory views. In this instance it was the excessively
early date that he assigned to the Pyramids, a date that Wilkinson
correctly believed to be mistaken. Gell set the verses to music and
sent them to his friend Baron von Bunsen, who replied, "The specimen of composition of Champollion's fine verses is so promising
(particularly the dashing rise of the growing tone of the Galley), that
Mrs B. hopes you will complete it, and execute it here on the organ.
Who has made the verses?"[46]

Champollion seems not to have regretted Wilkinson's absence. At
least his published journal and letters from the expedition say nothing to that effect, though he lamented not meeting Henry Salt, who

died a few months before his arrival.[47] A meeting between Champollion and Wilkinson might not have been a success, however, if Champollion was disinclined to give Wilkinson full credit for his accomplishments. Wilkinson, for his part, besides disliking Frenchmen in general, still resented Champollion's treatment of Young, a resentment that must have deepened after Champollion's disputes with Burton and Bonomi. Even so, it would have been a memorable moment in Egyptology if they had met, and, as it turned out, they did not have another opportunity.

Although Wilkinson successfully avoided Champollion, he did meet the French expedition of 1831 that came to take one of the finest Theben obelisks to Paris. This was the western one in front of Luxor Temple. Champollion had noticed it and had arranged for it to be given to the French instead of one of the Alexandrian obelisks that originally had been promised them. The expedition sailed up the Nile in a large, rigged sailing vessel that looked decidedly out of place on the river.[48] Wilkinson wrote a letter to *John Bull* in which he ridiculed the difficulties that the French were having in maneuvering their vessel across the sandbars near the mouth of the Nile.[49] Had he been able, Wilkinson probably would have slipped away upon this occasion also, but he had important work to do at Thebes. "We expect the French daily. It has already given me a fit of the liver, but I am sorry to say I have not yet done at Thebes & cannot escape from this very great annoyance. What a lucky man you are to be out of it. But I hope to avoid some part of the nuisance of the 'foreigners,'" he wrote to Hay, using the hieroglyph for foreigners.[50] In fact, when the French obelisk team finally reached Thebes and moved into a house built for them above the sanctuary of the Luxor temple, Wilkinson found them not nearly so bad as he anticipated. "The French party are pleasant enough & no annoyance at all—very retired—one or two well informed men," he wrote to Hay a few months later.[51] He became especially cordial with Jean Baptiste Apollinaire Lebas, the French engineer who directed the expedition, and made a fine drawing of the removal of the obelisk, which later became one of the outstanding illustrations in *Topography of Thebes.*[52]

French news obtruded one more time upon Wilkinson and his friends when they learned of Champollion's sudden death in 1832. Although Wilkinson had found much to criticize in Champollion's conduct and attitude, he understood the value of the Frenchman's work. Relaying the news to Robert Hay, he wrote, "What a loss— there is an end to hieroglyphics—for say what they like no one knew any thing about the subject but himself, though wrong—as must necessarily happen in a similar study—in some instances."[53] To Sir William Gell, he went on in greater length:

> You mention Champollion's death. I have heard of it long since & a great loss indeed it is. Adieux to hieroglyphics. There is no one I believe able to go on with them. At such a time it was the greatest of losses. He had however the fault of pretending to read & understand more than he could. But he had a happy facility of making out the meaning of hierog[s] which no one else ever had. He seldom hesitated but made a dash according to probability, this was his fault, but he frequently made a happy hit where the sense was obscure & where another would have given it up. At other times he was occasionally mistaken. He had great self confidence & much ingenuity. I do not expect to see another like him for this study.[54]

Almost until the moment that Wilkinson left Egypt, Sir William Gell kept sending him questions and suggestions. In the spring of 1832 Gell was writing, "Next what have you done about the vestiges of Avaris or Abaris [   ] Are any characters or hieroglyphics found there. I wi[sh   ] would make out that the Shepherds were Greeks after [   ]er even the 600,000 Hebrews Psoai + abominations. Did the people & civilization ascend tow[d] Meroe or descend tow[d] Egypt. Memnon evidently is found quite to the south."[55] For his part, Wilkinson's ideas continued to form, change, and grow. For example, "I said in my 'Materia' that the Egyptians did not make any permanent settlements in the countries they conquered, I find I was wrong & a subsequent examination of the temples & tombs has led me to the conclusion that they not only left garrisons there but levied troops among them & disciplined them in the regular tactics of their own armies. They seem to have placed them in the centre. They wore their own arms & dress. These are the mercenary troops mentioned I believe by Strabo, & this accounts for the colony of Colchis." And in answer to one of Gell's questions, Wilkinson added, "I believe the civilization ascended rather than descended the Nile. In Ethiopia I see they scarcely knew how to arrange their hierog[ls] & sculptures."[56]

By 1831 Wilkinson was beginning to recognize the inevitability of leaving Egypt, at least for a time. "All people advise me to go to England," he wrote to Hay from Gurna in 1831. "I suppose I must soon—but [   ] must be seen."[57] He now realized that some of the things he had wanted to do would not be possible. A special ambition of his had been to travel to Mount Sinai. He had researched the area carefully, no doubt discussed it with his friends and other travelers, and prepared a map of the area that bears the note, "Prepared for my journey to Mt. Sinai which I was prevented from making." [58] Even some of the opportunities right before his eyes exceeded his endurance. In a letter to Hay sometime early in 1832 he wrote, "Nothing new at Thebes in discoveries of any kind. I hear of two written tombs, but I have not the courage to have them opened." As he was preparing to leave for Cairo, he added, "I leave the house for you with doors &—not windows but bars of wood. If I can I will leave all the former—as it is more convenient to come into a house ready to receive one than to be obliged to set a carpenter to work. I expect to start in 4 or 5 days." [59]

When he reached Cairo, he again hesitated rather than leave immediately for England. "I am still here as you see but threaten to start for Alexandria in a few days—& thence to Smyrna & Constantinople so that I shall winter here again, & then start for England [   ] next spring." His decision to linger was reinforced by news of a cholera epidemic in England. "All things considered I find it better to pass the winter here." [60] The trip to Smyrna and Constantinople never materialized, and by January 1833 it was clear that the moment of departure must come soon. "We are all ailing here," Wilkinson wrote to Hay.

> Mr Burton who was quite recovered has now a violent cold & lumbago from which he suffers this morning greatly. The winter has been unusually severe. I still feel the effects of it & am persuaded that a visit to Europe is absolutely necessary for me. So that I shall start in March or April next. I am still a great invalid & can do little or nothing—but in spite of all I have resolved on getting through a little lithography—though study is out of the question. You have been a prudent & temperate man all your life which I am sorry to say I have not been, & now I suffer for it. [61]

CHAPTER NINE

England Again

WILKINSON SAILED FROM Alexandria aboard an Austrian brig on 1 June 1833. His customary bad luck at sea stuck with him, so the crossing was rough, a fact that the superstitious crew blamed on him because he had brought aboard a box of thirteen mummy heads. Altogether it took more than a month to reach Malta whence he proceeded to Leghorn where he and his mummy heads were quarantined. He spent the idle time pleasantly enough, writing to Gell and talking to Ippolito Rosellini, who visited and brought the first volume of his new work, *I Monumenti dell'Egitto e della Nubia*. "It is very good," Wilkinson informed Gell,

> but in some things I differ very much from him. & I am surprised that he has been so confused about his Ptolemies. I suppose the Ombos inscription led him wrong, which by the bye it ought not to have done, as hierog^s were so far advanced when he saw it, but he has I see run into the usual mistake & unfortunately introduced it into his work (vol 2. p. 36) if you have the work. His colouring is very gaudy & unEgyptian (V. the plates) nor are the hierog^s of good style, considering the number of artists & the means they had. Many of the colours of animals and birds at Beni Hassan are inaccurate—tho' I must allow they are not easily made out in the original, especially by a person unacquainted with Eg^n drawing.[1]

Wilkinson also used the time to be fitted by a tailor, for, as he explained to Gell, "I cannot move from this till I get my clothes made." All of his European garments had been lost or had fallen to pieces long ago. Even after his quarantine was finished there was more delay because his mummy heads were detained ten days longer.[2] From Leghorn he sailed up to Genoa and thence traveled across Europe to England. Why did he not pause to visit Sir William Gell? Perhaps he intended to return to Egypt in a year or two and planned to stop and see Gell when he went out again.

When he reached England he found things changing. The excitement of the Reform Bill lingered in the air; railroads soon would begin binding the island together. Altogether Wilkinson liked what he saw and wrote to Robert Hay who was still in Egypt, "London I find greatly altered & greatly improved—the people are still more improved & remarkably kind & obliging—I cannot say the same for the French."[3] And Wilkinson himself had changed, just as England had. His middle and late twenties as well as his early thirties all had been spent in Egypt, important formative years, but his experience and personal connections helped him into a social milieu that was disposed to welcome people like him. "After all," Gell wrote to him, "London is the only place where a Lion lasts for any time or where there is food for a lion of every species. Perhaps in Prussia the Court has more people who admire & most willingly lends itself to reward people of merit."[4]

Wilkinson's way was considerably eased by Gell who prepared his return to England just as he had prepared the way when Wilkinson went to Egypt twelve years before. For example, he wrote to William Richard Hamilton, the secretary of the Society of Dilettanti, to herald Wilkinson's impending arrival:

> It will not be uninteresting to You to learn that Wilkins[on] who certainly except Champollion knows more of hieroglyphics than anyone is now at Leghorn in his way to England. He was 12 years in Egypt & was the first person who knew what was known of the subject who went there. I had the pleasure to instruct him in all Young had discovered, & I sent him all Champollions discoveries afterwards as they appeared. Salt profited by these also & though he might say he never saw Champollions book he had seen from me all it contained & whenever he went alone was mistaken. Wilkinsons experience and knowledge is immense & I shall send him in a letter to You that You may at once pop him into the midst of the literary world instead of letting him languish unknown for many months as he would without such introduction.[5]

Apparently Hamilton did as Gell asked, for when Gell again wrote to him the following January, he said, "I am glad You protect Wilkin-

son who must have seen more of Egypt & besides went better prepared for it than anyone since the discovery of hieroglyphs."[6] Having
already been elected to the Royal Society of Literature, Wilkinson
appeared before that body in December 1833 to read his paper, "On
the Contrivances by Which the Statue of Memnon at Thebes Was
Made Vocal," which was later published in the society's *Transactions*. Another important honor came at the end of 1834 when he
became a fellow of the Royal Society.

Wilkinson also improved his situation by becoming a member of
some clubs, first the Oriental Club, where he seems to have stayed
during his early days back in London, and later the Athenaeum.[7] A
good club was important not merely for society, but even for food; a
bachelor in London could be hard-put to fend for himself in that respect. Sir William Gell expressed the solitary dilemma in a letter to
his friend, Lady Charlotte Bury: "A London life is pleasant enough
from twenty to thirty, but not after that period—at least not the
kind of life a poor single man is able to lead—hunting for dinners,
and paying court to every stupid person who hangs out notice that
they give 'good entertainment for man and woman'; which *good* entertainment, by the way, is very often exceedingly bad, both as to
provender for body and mind."[8]

The Athenaeum was, and is, housed in a fine neoclassical building
in Pall Mall designed by James Burton's brother, Decimus Burton. In
front stood a statue of the goddess Athena, holding her shield and
spear. Among the club's founders were Sir Walter Scott, Thomas
Young, and Lord Palmerston. They created it for "persons who shall
have attained to distinguished eminence in science, literature, or the
arts."[9] In 1848 the words "or for public service" were added to the
membership criteria. The Cabinet regularly met there each Wed-
nesday to dine, and besides great politicians, there were men of science such as Charles Darwin and Sir Charles Lyell and writers such
as Charles Dickens, Robert Browning, and Anthony Trollope.[10] Many
scholars including George Rawlinson, Henry Layard, and George
Grote were members, as was Wilkinson's acquaintance from Harrow,
the photographer and cuneiform expert, Fox Talbot. Lord Macaulay
often could be found writing in the corner of one of the smaller libraries.[11] It was a good place for a seemingly confirmed bachelor like
Wilkinson. As another single member, Goldwyn Smith, wrote in his
Reminiscences, "Blessed are Clubs and above all in my memory the
Athenaeum, with its splendid library and its social opportunities.
Without Clubs what would bachelor life in London be?"[12]

Rumors went round that Wilkinson's bachelorhood might soon
end, for James Burton, who had also returned to England, wrote to

tell Robert Hay, "Wilkinson report says, is about to be married to a very pretty girl—Have you heard anything of *it*, or *him?*—I found a letter from him with his plans & work upon my arrival and wrote to him to thank him—He does not mention his health. His Hareem died with the Plague." But impending marriage may have been no more than a rumor, for later in the same letter Burton added, "Whilst writing I have rec^d another letter from Wilkinson—he is at Alnwick—and talks of being in London the beginning of Feb 9—He is not going to be married."[13]

All the while Wilkinson continued to write, though he worked at it in a way that must have been imperceptible to those who saw him making his way from club to club and party to party. Never a person who needed large blocks of time, he continued his habit of taking a few minutes here, half an hour there and working productively. He wrote most of *Manners and Customs of the Ancient Egyptians* in early morning hours after returning from parties before falling asleep.[14] But he continued to be depressed that he could not publish. Even his map of Thebes was not accepted, and he finally decided to publish it at his own expense. Sir William Gell, who had himself experienced many difficulties with publication, commiserated: "It is really too hard upon you to have to pay for the engraving of your map after having had all the trouble & expense of making it—also here where every bodys wits are at grass there exists no one likely either to subscribe or to wish for it, What do the Antiquaries Literaries Royals & Dilettantis do with themselves that they do not contend for the honor of introducing your things to the world . . . The universities will not spend a farthing in any literary enterprise."[15] Even as Wilkinson despaired, however, things began to improve. First, the Royal Geographical Society came to the rescue and paid for the publication of the map.[16] Then Wilkinson's luck with publication changed much for the better.

The agent of change was John Murray II, one of the great publishers of nineteenth-century England. Murray was himself a literary figure of considerable importance, for his house was the gathering place of many of the great writers of his day. He published Byron and Scott, and Jane Austen—"A rogue, but a very civil one," she described him. Murray also liked to publish scientific and historical books. He knew how to take good scholarly work and make money for both author and publisher. His greatest talent was an ability to spot promising writers.[17] His worst fault was a tendency to handle business inattentively—"Still no word from Murray" is a frequently recurring line in letters of writers who dealt with him.

Murray published Wilkinson's *Topography of Thebes, and General View of Egypt* in 1835. It was one of the most scholarly books about Egypt that had yet appeared, dealing with the country in both ancient and modern times. Had it appeared as originally intended in the 1820s, well before Edward William Lane's study of the modern Egyptians, which was published in 1836, it would have been even more valuable than it was.[18] Even so, it contains lots of quantitative, detailed information that Lane's book does not about such things as taxation, bribery, and prices in Cairo. It is still an important source for early nineteenth-century Egypt. Doubtless influenced by the topographical works of Sir William Gell, it resembles Gell's work more than any other book of Wilkinson's. It was a basic but extremely important work that allowed scholars who had never seen Egypt to visualize the lay of the land and the physical relationship of various antiquities. It removed the objects from the fantastic world of the imagination and assigned them to real places. But *Topography of Thebes* turned out to be much more than a mere topographical essay, for Wilkinson included some chapters about the daily life of the ancient Egyptians.

The best of these *vie quotidienne* chapters was the one he entitled "The Manners and Customs of the Ancient Egyptian." The idea behind these chapters subsequently developed into his book *Manners and Customs of the Ancient Egyptians*. Several of his fine sketches illustrated the book, though his colleague from Egypt, Frederick Catherwood, was characteristically deprecating of them. "Mr. W's plates are not very good nor can they be said to be bad," Catherwood wrote to Hay.[19] Catherwood's reservations notwithstanding, the book was well received, and Murray began negotiating with Wilkinson about a more ambitious work about the ancient Egyptians.

In contrast to Wilkinson's experience with Murray was Edward William Lane's frustrating attempt to publish with him. Lane took Murray his promising manuscript "Description of Egypt," and Murray was initially encouraging, but then delays set in, postponing publication. At first Murray blamed the delays on the general disruption of business caused by the crisis of the Reform Bill of 1832, but even after that crisis, nothing was done. Given Murray's working habits, it is entirely possible that he had not yet read the manuscript. Lane finally wrote to complain that it had been five years since Murray first accepted it. Murray replied that he was returning the manuscript and that he thought it better that Lane continue with another publisher.[20] "Description of Egypt" exists in manuscript in various British collections.[21] It has never been published, though it deserves to be, even now, not just for its intrinsic merits, but also because it displays an aspect of Lane as a talented travel writer that is not apparent in his other works.

Having lived for years among Egyptian antiquities, Wilkinson was astonished when he saw the high prices they were fetching on the British market. "I wish I had known how many trifling objects are valuable here," he wrote to Robert Hay. "I would have brought every thing I could meet with."[22] These comments were not serious, however, because he never used any of his subsequent opportunities to build a profit-making collection, and in 1834 he donated at least part of his personal collection to the British Museum along with a detailed catalogue of its contents.[23] As a collection it was not particularly outstanding, but it was useful at the time, because most of the museum's acquisitions until then had been large pieces of sculpture. Wilkinson's collection, consisting as it did of everyday things, household objects, papyri, Coptic manuscripts, and tracings, helped correct the collection's bias. He also gave the museum his collections of Egyptian rocks and plants.

Because of his expertise and growing reputation, the British Museum began to request Wilkinson's advice about acquisitions, whether to buy an object and how much to pay. When the trustees were considering the purchase of an expensive sarcophagus, Wilkinson urged them instead to spend the money on a collection that was soon to be offered for sale. "[This sarcophagus] cannot as I have always said compete with the objects that relate to the customs of the Egyptians, of which I hear many are to be met with in the above mentioned collection. For my own part I am no advocate as I have always said, for the purchase of sarcophagi when such interesting objects can be obtained."[24] Wilkinson continued to advise the museum about acquisitions throughout his life. He was involved in the purchase of many of the treasures that are now in the Department of Egyptian Antiquities.[25]

It should not be inferred that Wilkinson was always opposed to the acquisition of colossal or spectacular antiquities. Charles Sloane, the secretary of the British consulate in Egypt, wrote to inform him that the statue of Ramses II at Mit Rahina, the site of ancient Memphis, had been offered to the British if they cared to remove it. This colossal statue was considered quite desirable; long ago fallen over and damaged in a few places, it was in excellent overall condition. Wilkinson urged the trustees of the British Museum to acquire it. He described the fine quality of its workmanship and the significance of the fact that it was a portrait of the same monarch called the Young Memnon whose colossal bust was one of the museum's greatest treasures. The trustees were eventually persuaded, and various schemes for removal were considered, but the difficulties of lifting and transporting the thirty-five-foot statue were formidable. When no progress was made, Wilkinson wrote to remind the trustees.

This Statue, if you remember, was offered as a present to the Museum, provided it was removed within three years, so that if the Museum really intends to have it, some decision must be made; it is worth possessing, and it is not at all probable that if the English neglect this offer another Government will do the same, and when it is taken to Paris or elsewhere it will be needless to recollect that we had the first offer. It seems very hard that when offered as a present it should not be accepted; I shall be much obliged by a decided answer upon the subject, which indeed it is but fair for Mr Sloane, who offered to make so liberal a present.[26]

Ideas for removal continued to be offered, including one from an involved observer who suggested cutting away the bottom of the statue since "there was not any thing interesting" on the lower part of it.[27] Wilkinson later wrote of that suggestion: "I am glad to say the barbarism was not committed & we did not become the ridicule of civilized Europe."[28] All the plans came to nothing, and the colossus still lies at Mit Rahina where a museum has been built around it.

News from Egypt periodically reached Wilkinson, the saddest tidings from that quarter being those of the death of the ever-helpful Osman Effendi. Osman's end was similar to that of Henry Salt, steady weakening caused or compounded by dysentery. When he realized that the end was near, Osman drew up a will providing that his property, with the exception of his library, was to go to his children. The children were to be sent to Scotland, and his library was to be placed in the British Consulate for the use of travelers. His death belied the doubts of those who, like Hay, had cynically assumed that he was a Muslim only from expediency. The Protestant minister in Cairo, hearing that Osman was on his deathbed, rushed to his side to receive him again into the faith of his fathers, but Osman sent him away. He chose to die as a Muslim and directed that he be buried in the Muslim manner. Thus Osman Effendi, formerly Donald Thomson of Inverness, died on 8 November 1835, and was laid to rest in the tomb of his friend, the renowned explorer J.L. Burckhardt, in the Bab al-Nasr Cemetery. "Poor Osman, what a loss," Wilkinson wrote to Robert Hay.[29]

When Wilkinson left Egypt, he told Hay he intended to return within two years, and he intimated in a letter to Gell that it might be sooner, but it was not to be. For one thing, his health was not yet sufficiently recovered to make the voyage—"The Doctors have sworn by the beard of their prophet Esculapius that if I do I shall never support the climate."[30] He was also distracted by his busy social life and by the business of publishing *Topography of Thebes* and composing *Manners and Customs of the Ancient Egyptians*. Besides those projects he was preparing an edition of the letters he had written in Egypt to Sir William Gell, though nothing came of that.[31] But it seems that the urgency of his intention to work again in Egypt was fading over time. When he finally did return, and it was several years before he did, he went with reluctance.

Gell must have been disappointed that Wilkinson kept postponing returning to Egypt and thereby passing through Italy and visiting him again, but he kept himself informed of Wilkinson's work. He wrote to Wilkinson, "Your letters to me from Egypt will be doing me too much honour which I assure you I am very sensible of. I beg you will recollect that as far as I am concerned I shall be highly flattered by it. You will see that Mr Bulwer has dedicated his novel on Pompeii to me & I hear from Lady Blessington that it is done in the kindest & handsomest manner. It is enough to make one grow some inches taller & to cure one of a fit of the gout in ones old age."[32] News of Wilkinson's forthcoming book, *Manners and Customs of the Ancient Egyptians*, excited Gell very much, and, as always, he sought to encourage Wilkinson. "Col Vyse to my surprise breakfasted with me this morning & in a book showed me a sort of advertisement for your work on Egypt which promises so much that it would be quite a treasure if you could ever publish it, & nobody but you has the knowledge necessary."[33]

As he contemplated seeing Wilkinson again, Gell thought how their relative roles had changed over the years. In 1821 Wilkinson had been in awe of the great antiquarian and had hung upon his every word, but now that Wilkinson was an experienced, published traveler, Gell diffidently wondered what his "former student in Ægyptiaca" might think of him. In his last letter to Wilkinson he wrote, "You talk of coming here in the Spring. It would be a real satisfaction after so many years to me. I unluckily have had my wits at grass ever since while you have been improving & you will probably detect my dulness & ignorance at the first fire though you went away with the impression that I was a great man—among little boys—some 12 or 14 years ago."[34]

Had Wilkinson indeed gone to Italy that spring, he would have seen Gell, but as it happened he waited too long, for Gell took sick and died on 4 February 1836. Another year and he would have seen the crowning achievement of Wilkinson's Egyptological labors, *Manners and Customs of the Ancient Egyptians*. As it was, Wilkinson mentioned his debt to Gell in the preface of that book, where he expressed his "deep regret at the death of so excellent a friend as Sir W. Gell."

In him the literary world has sustained a great loss: but friendship and gratitude combine to increase my sorrow; and I can never forget that, for all the satisfaction I have derived from the prosecution of researches to which he first directed my attention,—however unimportant their results,—I am indebted to his kindness and instruction. To many has he lent his powerful assistance in those studies, whose advancement his "classic" talents so ably promoted: no distinction of nation ever prevented his generous mind from aiding others in investigating subjects of which he possessed such an extensive knowledge, and no deficiency of good feeling and liberality checked his exertions, or damped his zeal, in furthering the object of those who followed the same pursuits.[35]

"I have regretted Gell's death very much," Wilkinson wrote to Robert Hay. "I shall always remember him with gratitude and affection."[36]

Quite apart from sentimental considerations, there is another reason to regret that Wilkinson never enjoyed another extensive visit with Gell. The two months he spent studying under Gell's direction in 1821 were crucial to Wilkinson's intellectual formation—indeed, those two months were worth more than the three years he spent at Oxford. Augmented by their exchange of letters, the experience sustained him through his years of fieldwork and the publication of *Manners and Customs of the Ancient Egyptians*. After that, Wilkinson had less sense of direction. Aware that the Egyptological potential of his research was still largely untapped, he nevertheless could not find the way to develop it. Gell might have helped him maintain his momentum.

As the years in England stretched on, Wilkinson completed *Manners and Customs of the Ancient Egyptians* and continued to recover his health by his favorite English recreation, long walks, though he frequently sprained an ankle. Always one to covet an invitation, he began spending time at various peoples' houses. He also started traveling again. In 1835 he toured Ireland, Scotland, and the English

Lake District, and the following year he left London by steamer and
proceeded to Berlin and other places in Germany before wintering in
Paris. Egypt seems to have been less and less in his thoughts, and
when he contemplated returning to the East, he thought not of
Egypt but of Syria.

One by one, the others who had worked and traveled with Wilkinson in Egypt straggled back to England and Scotland. A change also
came over them as their zeal for Egypt diminished and they took
new directions. Robert Hay, who returned in 1835, got caught up in
the life of a landed gentleman, taking more pleasure in his estates
and social duties than in the dream he once had of documenting ancient and modern Egypt. Frederick Catherwood, worried about Hay's
loss of interest, wrote to say that he was "sorry to find that your
Egyptian energy is giving way."[37] Hay himself confirmed this mental
drift in a letter to Bonomi, "I am very *ill indeed*, as far as regards
Egypt. Not a drawing has been out of the case since I arrived!—I
often *think* of Egypt but do *nothing* concerning it!"[38] His great accumulation of notes, maps, casts, and—most important of all—his
portfolio of sketches were stored away.

All of the Englishmen found it difficult to readjust to the British
climate. Major Felix, one of the first to return, had written to his
friends still in Egypt that he was "convinced the Prophet w^d not
have been sober, had he been last winter in Eng^d."[39] But no one expressed his discomfort quite so eloquently or so pathetically as did
James Burton who wrote to tell Hay, "I cannot yet conquer the effect
of this drear climate—the privation of sun—this cheerless sky, these
thick *coughiferous* lung-tearing fogs—this parapluie, and flannel-
doubled-indian-rubber-great-coat-atmosphere.—Moreover I find I
have been living too long on claret and truffles, and that your English
port and sherry and muggy ale induce gastric afflictions, that add
wonderfully, I believe, to my gloomy state of mind, and magnify the
annoyances of society."[40] Burton's return to England was considerably delayed by a curious enterprise of his, a wild beast show, consisting of animals that he had collected in Egypt.[41] With his menag-
erie he intended to tour western Europe and make his fortune. Sir
William Gell had followed his progress and wrote to Wilkinson in
1834, "I should hope ere this Burton must have arrived in England
for we saw him in the papers at Marseilles with all his griffins & sala-
manders duly advertised. It would be entertaining to walk through
France with a museum of monsters & make a fortune by showing
them at all the places on the road. It would be entertaining if one
were young enough."[42] But misfortune struck. First Burton's primary

attraction, his giraffe, died; then one of the other animals mangled his Arab servant's arm, leaving him with a cripple to support. He finally gave the remainder of his animals to the Jardin des Plantes in Paris in return for the animals' transportation and keep. When he straggled into England he was entirely at loose ends. Another blow came about a year later with the death of Charles Humphreys, to whom he was much attached. All thoughts of publishing about Egypt had long since fallen by the wayside, despite the promising start he once made. He lapsed into depression and inactivity.

Impervious to culture shock and bad weather was Edward William Lane who took a more distinct but lonelier path than the others. He devoted himself to Arabic language studies with such intensity that he soon became a recluse in the home he shared with his sister and Nefeeseh, whom he still had not married, despite his promise to Hay. Wilkinson observed, "Lane is at Kensington gravel pits—he might almost be said to live buried as in a Theban pit—for he rarely goes out, & there is no getting over every moment as when at Osman's house."[43] Even so, Wilkinson visited him occasionally on Friday afternoons when Lane customarily broke off his labors and received guests. He and Wilkinson remained good friends and correspondents, still calling themselves Isma'eel and Mansoor, just as they had done in Egypt. There was trouble when Hay learned that Lane had not married Nefeeseh. Angrily, he demanded that Lane return her. Rather than do that, Lane married Nefeeseh in July 1840. The marriage seems not initially to have been ideal, at least not for Nefeeseh. Lane was always writing to his friends that Nefeeseh was "improving," prompting his biographer to comment that Nefeeseh seemed to have an infinite capacity for improvement.[44] Although he had been disappointed in his first effort at publication, Lane soon was off again to Egypt to gather material for another book, *An Account of the Manners and Customs of the Modern Egyptians,* that would establish his reputation.

Frederick Catherwood returned to England but lingered only briefly before writing to Hay that he was off to America to "practice among the Yankees as an Architect."[45] He later accompanied John Lloyd Stephens to Central America where he did important archaeological work.[46] Joseph Bonomi came back to England but soon thereafter accepted a place on Lepsius' expedition to Egypt, though he did not stay with it long. He seems never to have thrived as a team member. Major Felix was promoted to Lieutenant Colonel and soon was off again for the East, which had left an indelible impression upon him. He served with distinction, first in China and later in India. Lord Prudhoe, the young aristocrat returned from his Grand Tour, came home to the family seat in Northumberland. He became a patron of oriental studies, and it was he who supported much of Lane's work. By the mid-1830s all of Wilkinson's colleagues had returned from Egypt, thus closing a fruitful chapter in the origins of British Egyptology.

CHAPTER TEN

Manners and Customs of the Ancient Egyptians

THE IDEA for *Manners and Customs of the Ancient Egyptians* probably began to form in Wilkinson's mind when he was working at Gurna and realized how much he was learning about daily life in ancient Egypt from the paintings on the tomb walls. As we have seen, he developed the idea into several chapters in *Topography of Thebes.* By the time the latter book appeared in 1835, it contained a publisher's announcement that *Manners and Customs of the Ancient Egyptians* was preparing for press.

To organize the material for this book, Wilkinson chose a peculiar literary form, now obscure, but once very popular; this, for lack of another accepted term, might be called the "manners and customs" genre. It developed in response to the desire of nineteenth-century British readers to know and, if possible, to sympathize with the ways of people different from themselves. The words *manners and customs* appear frequently as a phrase in travel literature of the early nineteenth century. By the 1830s, manners and customs material was increasingly in demand, and several books with the words *manners and customs* in their titles had appeared.[1] Indeed, at exactly the same time that Wilkinson was writing, Edward William Lane was preparing his *An Account of the Manners and Customs of the Modern Egyptians.* An outgrowth of the travelogue, the manners and customs genre differed significantly from it by abandoning the structural limitations of travel narrative and concentrating instead upon topical description. Personal observation was still important in manners and customs writing, but the personality of the author and the first-person itinerary of travel was removed to the subtext, replaced by a more detached mode of third-person exposition. The genre represented an important step away from incidental information communicated within a travel account toward systematic ethnography and anthropology.

Most manners and customs books dealt with contemporary societies, usually those observed by the author, but Wilkinson's work in the tombs of Gurna where he saw the representations of everyday life in the Egyptian past was an experience similar to traveling in distant lands and observing exotic peoples. His innovation, therefore, was to take the manners and customs genre and apply it to the past. It was an act of imagination, one that served its author well, though not destined to be widely imitated. J. A. St. John did indeed publish *The History of the Manners and Customs of Ancient Greece* in 1842, but he drew upon narrative political sources and could not re-create the textures of ancient Greek life as Wilkinson had for ancient Egypt. Other imitators were few. Had historians of that day been inclined to draw upon the rich, though uncritically assembled, antiquarian materials that were abundantly available to them, they might have created a new kind of history of culture and society in addition to the great narrative works of political history that dominated nineteenth-century historiography. But fruitful interaction between historians and antiquarians was slight.

Unlike earlier works about ancient Egypt, most of which were organized topographically, the topical organization of the manners and customs genre enabled Wilkinson to range widely. *Manners and Customs of the Ancient Egyptians* dealt with more than fifty basic subjects: daily life, chronology, botany, astronomy, geology, funerary beliefs, historical demography, and many more.[2] The manners and customs format was excellent for what was essentially an antiquarian presentation—not that Wilkinson never raised historical questions, for he did frequently, but he did not organize his material around them. Far from seeming old-fashioned, however, some of the book's passages—a long description of a banquet with disquisitions about the music, the furniture, the food, and the guests, or a detailed description of the organization and functioning of a profession—can remind one of present-day social history. The usual sequence in the development of historical knowledge is to draw the political lineaments first and then color them with social texture, but Wilkinson reversed the process: he saw the textures of Egyptian life before he understood its political outlines. That makes his book seem rather modern in places, though it was in fact a product of its time. Another peculiarity arose from the fact that some elements of the travelogue still lingered in the manners and customs genre, just enough to give the reader of Wilkinson's book an uncanny impression of traveling through time.

Working within this versatile form, Wilkinson first presented the physical and human geography of ancient Egypt. He realized that the land had influenced the development of the civilization: "It seems as if made for Man,"[3] he had written during his early years in Egypt, echoing Herodotus' famous observation that Egypt was the gift of the Nile. Accordingly, he accepted some of the geographical determinism that Sir William Gell—or at least Gell's successors—and others had developed, but only to a point. He would not, for example, have gone as far as Edward William Lane who began his book with the sentence, "It is generally observed that many of the most remarkable peculiarities in the manners, customs, and character of a nation are attributable to the physical peculiarities of the country."[4] Wilkinson could not have maintained such a position because the glories of the ancient kingdom and what he considered the degraded condition of modern Egypt were both set against the same geographical background; yet he had to account for a fundamental change: "Nor can we judge the former state of Egypt by its degraded condition at the present day," he had written in *Topography of Thebes.*[5] His solution was to attribute the decline to changes in both the government and the people: the government had become less efficient and the people less energetic.[6]

With the geographical background established, Wilkinson next devoted several chapters to a chronological narrative of ancient Egyptian history. He knew nothing about predynastic Egypt, although he speculated, "It may also be inferred, from their great advancement in arts and sciences at this early period, that many ages of civilization had preceded the accession of their first monarch."[7] The dynasties of the Old and Middle Kingdoms were little more than numbers to him, Egyptian history being, he wrote, almost "a blank from the foundation of the monarchy to the era of Sesostris."[8] Writing of a tomb near the Pyramids, however, Wilkinson noted that its murals "show the Egyptians to have had the same customs at that early time, and to have arrived at the same state of civilization as in the subsequent ages of the 18th and later dynasties,—a fact which cannot but suggest most interesting thoughts to an inquiring mind, respecting the state of the world at that remote period."[9] This did not stop him from concluding, "During the period which elapsed from Menes to Sesostris, no monarch of note reigned in Egypt, if we except those above mentioned."[10] And those exceptions, known to him from classical sources, were more fabulous than factual. Yet, archaic and inadequate though his exposition of these centuries might seem now, in at least one detail his judgment has been vindicated. The most important single date in the chronology of ancient Egypt is the year in which Menes, the first king of the First Dynasty, began to reign. Although it is debated whether such a person as Menes really existed, his reign is the basis for the rest of ancient Egyptian chronology. Unfortunately, the date of his accession is unknown. Manetho, the most important source, merely provides the series of dynasties; he does not tell when the kings reigned. The dates suggested for Menes, therefore, varied widely. Champollion proposed 5867 B.C.; Mariette and Lepsius later estimated 5004 B.C. and 3892 B.C., respectively. The theological implications of this were enormous. Archbishop Ussher's date of 4004 B.C. for the creation of the world was accepted by many as a biblical fact almost, yet here were people placing Menes, who obviously lived long after the creation, either before or uncomfortably close to it. These chronological speculations of the Egyptologists were a factor in extending public awareness of the antiquity of man. Although it was the geologists such as Lyell who provided the most dramatic and conclusive proofs, Egyptologists also played a part in the process.

Wilkinson, however, must have reassured the devout Englishmen of the 1830s, for he proposed a date of ca. 2320 B.C. for the accession of Menes.[11] Was it merely his deeply held religious convictions that impelled him to choose that date? The outspoken Egyptologist E. A. Wallis Budge, almost always unsympathetic to Wilkinson, thought so: "The idea uppermost in [Wilkinson's book] was to make the Egyptian chronology harmonize with that given by Archbishop Ussher to ancient nations printed in our English Bibles at that period."[12] Budge believed the correct date lay somewhere around 3500 B.C. Perhaps Budge was correct about Wilkinson's motive; Wilkinson would not have been the first to be misled by mistaken religious notions. But decades of scholarship since Budge's time have steadily adjusted the date for the accession of Menes to the point where a present-day consensus might place it somewhere around 3000 B.C. Wilkinson, it turns out, was almost as close as his detractor Budge, though his reasoning may have been based upon false assumptions.[13]

Wilkinson's chronological account of ancient Egyptian history became much fuller when he reached the New Kingdom, for which he was able to draw upon his experience with the monuments, especially those at Thebes. Even so, he retained some elements more appropriate to mythology than history.[14] Relying heavily upon the Bible, he considered the stories of Joseph and the Exodus to be events of preeminent importance in the history of the land. On the other hand, he knew little or nothing about two of the most interesting events of the New Kingdom, the reigns of Hat-Shepsut and Akh-en-Aton. Of Hat-Shepsut, the woman who became king, he was in fact marginally aware, though he could only guess her significance. His guesses, however, made the most of the scanty, confusing evidence available to him. He wrote of "a queen,"

whom I have ventured to call Amun-neit-gore [i.e., Hat-Shepsut], and who has hitherto given rise to more doubts and questions than any other sovereign of this Dynasty. But whether she was only regent during the minority of Thothmes II. and III., or succeeded to the throne in right of Thothmes I., in whose honour she erected several monuments, is still uncertain, and some have doubted her being a queen. Her name has been generally erased, and those of the 2d and 3d Thothmes are placed over it; but sufficient remains to prove that the small temple of Medeenet Haboo, the elegant edifice under the Qoorneh rocks [Deir el Bahri], and the great obelisks of Karnak, with many other handsome monuments, were erected by her orders, and the attention paid to the military caste is testified by the subjects of the sculptures.[15]

To those who had doubted that the ruler in question was female, he countered, "The constant use of the female sign, and the title Daughter of the Sun, seem to require it to be so, notwithstanding the dress, which is that of a king."[16] Considering the sources available to him, Wilkinson could scarcely have done better.

When he described events for which he had sufficient source material, he worked with a much surer touch. He was thoroughly taken with the reign of Ramses II, which he described as a period of military triumph, internal security, and artistic creativity. The Augustan era of Egypt, he called it. The reigns of the subsequent kings Wilkinson correctly interpreted as a period of decline, and he broke off his chronological narrative with the accession of the Ptolemies.

The overall thinness of the narrative is readily understandable when one considers how his vision of ancient Egypt rested upon two primary bases of evidence: the monuments and the accounts of the classical writers. This approach was explicit in his book's subtitle which reads, "derived from a comparison of the paintings, sculptures, and monuments still existing, with the accounts of ancient authors." These sources were supplemented by others, including his rudimentary knowledge of hieroglyphs, his readings in Neoplatonic and Hermetic philosophy, and his knowledge of the Bible; nevertheless, the limitations were severe, causing Wilkinson himself to bemoan the "scanty means of information afforded either by the writers of antiquity, or by monumental record."[17] Most monuments being from the New Kingdom, especially at Thebes, Wilkinson's narrative was biased toward that period, leaving earlier periods to speculation. Even so, he was the first to use monumental evidence systematically.

Wilkinson's technique of using the classical writers to explain and supplement the information provided by the monuments was in the very best of the antiquarian tradition. The dichronous nature of these two major sources, however, allowed many anachronisms to slip into his interpretation, for the classical writers knew Egypt long after its decline and wrote of ancient Egypt with many distorting preconceptions. Theirs was, in fact, a doubly distorted view, for not only did their own cultural outlook differ vastly from that of ancient Egypt, but also the view of ancient Egypt that contemporary Egyptians presented to them was, at least in part, incorrect.[18] Wilkinson did, however, sometimes apply critical standards to the classics and the Hermetic and Neoplatonic philosophers by using the monuments to correct mistakes. He did not apply such a critical approach to the Bible, which he considered a valid source—indeed the best of all sources, because it was infallible. The broad inferences that he drew about Egyptian government, society, and economy from such biblical stories as Joseph's experiences in Egypt were questionable, to say the least, though very appealing to Victorian readers who saw in them a new context for and further confirmation of the Mosaic account of the early ages of mankind. The resulting mixture of evidence looks quite archaic to modern Egyptologists, one of whom noted that a random page from *Manners and Customs of the Ancient Egyptians* yielded eight biblical and seven classical references and two citations from modern Arab customs.[19] Nevertheless, by its extensive use of monumental evidence and its much more modest use of hieroglyphic inscriptions, Wilkinson's work was a substantial advance that pointed the way to a time when Egyptology could depend upon Egyptological evidence. Insufficient though his sources were for constructing chronological narrative, Wilkinson used them much more effectively when he turned his attention to ancient Egyptian society.

He believed that ancient Egyptian society had been organized within a rigid caste system, a structure that he derived from the classics and from the books about Indian society which were then much in vogue. At the apex of society he placed the sacerdotal order; next came the soldiers' caste, which also included agricultural workers; below it were the townsmen; and at the bottom was the fourth caste, the commoners. "In no country, except perhaps India, does the distinction of castes appear to have been so arbitrarily maintained as with the ancient Egyptians," he wrote.[20] This system of four castes was an anachronism, for ancient Egyptian society was not formed into rigid classes, with warriors and priests as especially privileged castes, until the late Empire, though such an organization became increasingly important from that time on.[21] Furthermore, none of Wilkinson's classical or Indian models suited his purposes: the Indian model obviously could not be applied directly to ancient Egypt, and the classical writers—principally Herodotus, Diodorus Siculus, Strabo, and Plato—differed about the number of castes that had existed there. Undaunted, he worked out a system of "four great comprehensive classes, and the principal subdivisions of each," a system that may have corresponded more to arbitrary preconceptions of his own than to any past reality.[22] Despite its shortcomings, the system provided a useful framework for describing some aspects of ancient Egyptian society.

Following Plutarch, Wilkinson believed that the king was chosen either from the first caste, the priests, or from the second, the warriors. Although he seemed inclined to place the monarch among the priestly class, his examination of the monuments convinced him that most pharaohs, "at least during the glorious era of the 18th dynasty," were of warrior origin. In that case, the first task after the accession of such a monarch was to teach him the mysteries and induct him into the college of priests.[23] To describe the monarchy, Wilkinson relied as heavily as he could upon monumental sources, but these, to the extent that he understood them, provided little insight into the nature of the institution beyond the names and titles of the kings, the order of succession, and the appearance of the court. Inevitably he was compelled to rely upon the classical writers. Although he used these with some caution, rejecting, for example, Diodorus' assertion that the kingship was elective, they nevertheless led him astray.[24] From them he derived the idea of a king so bound by minute regulations that he retained scarcely any initiative: "The hours for washing, walking, and all the amusements and occupations of the day, were settled with precision, and the quantity as well as the quality of his food were regulated by law."[25] Such a portrayal might have been reasonably accurate for the late dynastic period, but it did not describe earlier times when the king, as the incarnation of the state, wielded great power.[26] It was, however, a depiction readily comprehensible to Wilkinson's British readers who were conscious of their own monarch becoming increasingly bound by constitutional constraints.

The sacerdotal caste was, Wilkinson wrote, exclusively entrusted with keeping the mysteries of the ancient religion. As a group, he considered the priests to have been a positive force in Egyptian society and described how the "stern regulations of the priesthood, which, by scrupulously watching over the actions of the monarch, and obliging him to conform to certain rules established for his conduct both in public and private, prevented the demoralizing effect of luxurious habits, with the baneful example of a corrupt court, and by a similar attention to the conduct of all classes, exercised a salutary influence over the whole community. And the successful promotion of industry, the skill of their artisans, and the efficiency of their army, were owing to the same well-ordered system."[27] It sounds a bit like the Evangelical tenet that the conduct of the British lower classes could be improved if the superior classes would set the proper example. Yet Wilkinson identified this factor as the dynamic of ancient Egyptian society. Because of the discipline of the priests the government had been better and the people more productive than those of modern Egypt. Because of them the splendor of ancient Egypt endured so long, unlike other nations of the ancient Near East, like Assyria, which rapidly declined when "luxury and indolence invaded."[28] Inspiring the priests to maintain their discipline over the centuries, as will be shown below, was a vital secret entrusted only to them.

The military, Wilkinson's second caste, was an agricultural class that owned one-third of the land in Egypt.[29] He believed that the military, like other professions and castes, was hereditary, so every soldier's son entered the army, perhaps after a brief period of rudimentary training. Taking Herodotus for his source, Wilkinson estimated the total size of the regular army at 410,000 men, not counting the large auxiliary force. Such an enormous army, much larger than that of the Roman Empire, was plausible during extraordinary times such as the Ramesside expansion, but it was certainly much larger than the state could have afforded to maintain permanently. The soldiers were distributed in garrison towns on the Nile and along the frontiers. After the specified period of service, they retired to their lands, which were located near the garrisons. They sound a bit like Roman legionnaires. Echoes of Edward Gibbon's *Decline and Fall of the Roman Empire* resonate frequently through the pages of *Manners and Customs of the Ancient Egyptians*.

From military depictions in the tomb murals and from artifacts, Wilkinson formed a reasonably accurate idea of the appearance, armament, and even the order of battle of the ancient Egyptian army. Its primary strength lay in its archers, Wilkinson wrote, "as it did in the case of our own ancestors during the wars waged by them in France."[30] These bowmen, fighting either on foot or from chariots, were deployed on the flanks of the army. The foot soldiers were arrayed in the center. Supporting them was a large body of cavalry. Wilkinson's statements about the cavalry clearly show the extent to which his unreliable literary sources could lead him away from the authentic evidence of the monuments:

> Though we have no representation of Egyptian horsemen in the sculptures, we find them too frequently and positively noticed in sacred and profane history to allow us to question their employment; and it is reasonable to suppose them well acquainted with the proper mode of using this serviceable force. In the battle scenes of the temples in Upper Egypt, we meet with five or six instances of men fighting on horseback; but they are part of the enemy's troops, and I can therefore only account for their exclusive introduction, and the omission of every notice of Egyptian cavalry, by supposing that the artists intended to show how much more numerous the horsemen of those nations were than of their own people.[31]

The same problem appears in Wilkinson's descriptions of armament. Although he made detailed descriptions and depictions of swords, shields, chariots, and various accoutrements, he interpreted their use by the classical sources, especially the *Iliad*. Any picture of ancient Egypt viewed through the lens of Mycenaean Greece was bound to be unclear.

The third caste was primarily urban: "artificers, tradesmen or shopkeepers, musicians, builders, masons, carpenters, cabinet-makers, potters, public weighers, and an inferior class of notaries"; the fourth was rural: "pastors, poulterers, fowlers, fishermen, labourers, servants, and common people." By this point, however, Wilkinson's caste framework began to impede his narrative, so he abandoned it for a wide-ranging examination of the manifold experiences of ancient Egyptian life, both urban and rural, though his attention was primarily drawn to the towns. At Tell el-Amarna, or Alabastron as he identified it, he had made a drawing of the city, reproduced in the book, that shows the main street with many houses shaded in and some of the main buildings drawn in detail.[32] This he presented as a model for an Egyptian town. In fact, Tell el-Amarna may have been an anomalous city, but it was all that Wilkinson had to rely upon; even today the urban archaeology of ancient Egypt is a problem. To imagine the appearance of the storefronts, he drew upon contemporary experience, writing, "The shops of an Egyptian town were probably similar to those of Cairo, and other Egyptian cities."[33] He made ancient Egyptian shopkeepers seem like their modern British counterparts by speculating that they might have affixed emblems of royal patronage to their establishments.[34]

When he turned his attention to individual homes, Wilkinson did some of his best work from the standpoint of reliance upon the monuments. Although he could not resist an occasional reference to Vitruvius and other classical writers, his archaeological work served him well, as did his study of a detailed model of an ancient house that Henry Salt had found. Doubtless inspired by the format of Sir William Gell's *Pompeiana*, Wilkinson led his readers through an Egyptian house of thousands of years before, showing them the apportionment of the rooms, with thoughtful aids to the imagination such as details about the shapes of doorways and windows. In the kitchen and dining rooms he lingered over utensils, techniques for preparing and serving food, and other minutiae that was at once so exotic, yet so familiar as to convey a powerful sense of reality. This was especially the case with his descriptions of Egyptian furniture, examples of which he had seen from the tombs at Thebes where paintings showed them being used. Wilkinson was one of the first writers to address the making of Egyptian furniture, and many of his assumptions have been proved valid.[35] It was a subject that he obviously warmed to, for unlike monumental art, he found that the making of household furniture and ornamental objects was free from the restriction of established rules, therefore, "much taste was displayed."[36] From his detailed but rarely tedious descriptions the reader could easily imagine what it was like to lie on an Egyptian bed or sit in an Egyptian chair.

Drawing upon the scenes he had studied in the tombs at Gurna and upon his own Egyptian dining experiences, Wilkinson reconstructed an ancient banquet: "The guests sat on the ground, or on stools and chairs, and, having neither knives and forks, nor any substitute for them answering to the chopsticks of the Chinese, they ate with their fingers, as the modern Asiatics, and invariably with the right hand. Spoons were introduced at table when soup or other liquids required their use, and, perhaps, even a knife was employed on some occasions, to facilitate the carving of a large joint, which is sometimes done in the East at the present day."[37] He was able to take his reconstruction even further, because the "talent for caricature" in the Theban paintings was so poignant that one could even infer the topic of conversation from it.[38]

While the guests were entertained with music and the dance, dinner was prepared; but as it consisted of a considerable number of dishes, and the meat was killed for the occasion, as at the present day in Eastern and tropical climates, some time elapsed before it was put upon table. During this interval conversation was not neglected; and the chitchat of the day, public affairs, and questions of business or amusement, occupied the attention of the men. . . . A circumstance of this kind is represented in a tomb at Thebes. A party, assembled at the house of a friend, are regaled with the sound of music, and the customary introduction of refreshments; and no attention which the host could show his visitors appears to be neglected on the occasion. The wine has circulated freely . . .[39]

This was one of the most appreciated passages in the book, for it reminded Victorian readers of their own worries about keeping conversation going at dinner parties during the uncomfortable moments between the arrival of guests and the commencement of dinner.

The picture that emerges from these pages is one of a happy people, fun loving and industrious by turn, who could prosper under the guidance of a good monarch. Wilkinson knew that his evidence portrayed only a tiny portion of the Egyptian population, but he did not dwell upon that fact. The great mass of the people, he assumed, were reasonably content, much in the same way that the masses of the Roman Empire were once assumed to have been happy in the age of the Antonines.

The portion of *Manners and Customs of the Ancient Egyptians* that might seem the quaintest to us today is the lengthy exposition of ancient Egyptian religion. Although Wilkinson denied an intention to engage in comparative mythology, just such an effort is both implicit and explicit in his book. He sought correspondences between the pantheons of ancient Greece and Egypt, matching Amon with Zeus, Ptah to Hephaestus, and so on, though in several instances he could find no Greek counterpart to an Egyptian god. A case may be made for some of his correlations, but too much of it, seeking as he did to pair deities of vastly different theological systems, inevitably went astray. A further complication arose from his unconscious application of Judeo-Christian principles to his organization of the Egyptian pantheon. This led him to assign the highest place to the god Ptah, and to put the mighty god Amon second, his reason being "if Neph [Ptah] really answered to the Spirit which pervaded and presided over the creation . . . he may in justice claim a rank above Amun."[40] This is extraordinary considering how well Wilkinson knew Thebes, where the paramount position of Amon was obvious; furthermore, he was aware that Amon's title was King of the Gods and that the Greeks considered him the same as Zeus.[41]

To interpret the theory and practice of ancient Egyptian religion, Wilkinson again relied heavily upon his classical sources. This led him to some inaccurate, even disparaging conclusions, as in this example: "The animal worship of the Egyptians naturally struck all people as a ludicrous and gross superstition"; and, "nothing could be more open to censure than the folly of the Egyptians in paying divine honours to the brute creation."[42] But the ancient Egyptians did not worship animals; they merely selected a single animal, not an entire species, as a place of manifestation for a god. Only in much later times did true animal worship begin, a phenomenon that was correctly reported by the Greeks but mistakenly extended into the past.[43] Even further from the mark was his assertion, based upon a misunderstanding by classical writers, that the ancient Egyptians believed in metempsychosis, the transmigration of souls from one body to another. Wilkinson concluded that the teaching that the wicked would be reborn as "the most hateful and disgusting animals" was designed to bring the idea of punishment "to a level with their comprehension."[44] In fact, the ancient Egyptians never believed in reincarnation. They believed that the *akh,* or spirit, could take various forms at will but was not bound to them for a lifetime.

In this as in other areas, Wilkinson realized that there were problems with the classical sources and attempted to use them with some discrimination. The writings of Plato and those attributed to Pythagoras he deemed useful because they had studied Egyptian religion before "it had been encumbered with the superstructure of arbitrary fancy, which the schools of Alexandria [Neoplatonist philosphy] heaped upon it."[45] Neoplatonist sources—primarily Porphyry, Iamblichus, and Proclus—were to be used only "with considerable caution." Though their speculations were derived from an authentic Egyptian source, the distortion in their interpretation was so great that no doctrine of theirs could be accepted as illustrative unless it was "confirmed by the monuments, or expressly stated to be taken from the philosphy, of ancient Egypt." But he did not heed his own caveat, for in another passage he mentioned writers like Iamblichus "who had studied, and were initiated into, the mysteries of Egypt," stating that they could be used as evidence.[46] There were, however, limits to what he would accept. The assertions of classical writers who claimed that some of the rites of the ancient Egyptian religion featured sexual immorality were dismissed as conflicting with monumental evidence.[47] Wilkinson also doubted the accounts by Plutarch and Porphyry of human sacrifice: "If, indeed, this were ever the case, it could only have been at a very remote period, long before the Egyptians were the civilised nation we know them [to have been] from their monuments."[48]

One other source, besides the Bible, that Wilkinson admitted with little discrimination, was the *Corpus Hermeticum*, that body of literature attributed to the fictive philosopher Hermes Trismegistus. Although the unreliability and, indeed, the spuriousness of much of the *Corpus Hermeticum* had long before been exposed, Wilkinson nevertheless presented an orthodox Hermetic interpretation. He was, in fact, one of the last writers to do so, though he doubted that the Egyptians had really raised Hermes Trismegistus to the status of a deity as the classical sources asserted.[49]

Essential to Wilkinson's assessment of ancient Egyptian religion was the premise that it originally had been monotheistic.

> In the early ages of mankind, the existence of a sole and omnipotent Deity, who created all things, seems to have been the universal belief; and tradition taught men the same notions on this subject, which in later times have been adopted by all civilised people. Whether the Egyptians arrived at this conclusion from mere tradition, or from the conviction resulting from a careful consideration of the question, I will not pretend to decide; suffice it to know that such was their belief, and the same belief was entertained by many philosophers of other nations of antiquity.[50]

Indeed, he believed that monotheistic belief had persisted throughout ancient Egypt; this belief, however, eventually became the property of a few initiated priests, leaving the masses in the darkness of polytheism. Two reasons impelled him to make that assumption, the first being his readings in Neoplatonism and the *Corpus Hermeticum*, both of which had a monotheistic thrust. But even more important was his unquestioning belief in the literal truth of the Old Testament. Wilkinson accepted as historical fact that Egypt after the biblical flood had been resettled by Noah's son Ham who became the progenitor of the Egyptian people. Ham, of course, knew of the "One True God" and would have passed that knowledge along to his descendents, though at some point their monotheism degenerated into the polytheism of ancient Egypt.[51] "Thus," Wilkinson wrote, "the sole indivisible God was overlooked and became at length totally unknown, except to those who were admitted to participate in the important secret of his existence."[52] Wilkinson was somewhat uneasy at finding no vestigial monotheistic remnants, no word or name for even the concept, but he escaped this difficulty by concluding that the singular deity was, like the Hebrew god, unnameable.[53] This secret knowledge presumably moved the priests to impose the salutary discipline that accounted for the greatness of ancient Egypt.

Guiding Wilkinson's interpretation of ancient Egyptian religion was his Christian background. This is clear in may passages in *Manners and Customs of the Ancient Egyptians* and even clearer in a notebook that he kept a few years after the publication of his book. There he wrote how the Israelites were the only people suited to receive the "doctrine of the unity of the Deity." This was because of their "eminently religious frame of mind which no others among the people of antiquity ever possessed; for though many among the Egyptians were moral, virtuous, mindful of social duties, & religious as far as their peculiar belief enabled them to be, still they were wanting in real religion their views and ideas not extending beyond superstition." Inheriting ancient traditions with elements "of the Truth which was one day to enlighten the world," they corrupted them into the speculative mysteries of Osiris. "But," Wilkinson wrote, "real religion, as I have just said, was unknown to the people of antiquity; & true religious feeling was nowhere except in the mind & heart of the Israelites." He continued, "On no other stem could Christianity have been engrafted. The Egyptians, it is true, had an idea of the Unity of the Deity, but to what did it lead?"[54]

That the progression of ancient Egyptian religion was one of degeneration Wilkinson never doubted. He was well aware that Egyptian deities often appropriated one another's powers, duties, personalities, and even names. He had seen the substitution of Amon's name for others on monuments and had noted the systematic erasures of the sun at Tell el-Amarna.[55] Such changes could be and have been interpreted as a tendency toward monotheism, but Wilkinson saw them as meaningless fluctuations of idolatrous forms. He believed that the essence of Egyptian religion never changed: "Even the alteration which took place in the name of Amon, and the introduction of the worship of the Sun with rays, represented at Tel-el-Amarna, and some other places, about the time of the 18th Dynasty, cannot be looked upon as changes in the religion."[56] One reasonably wonders what conclusions he would have drawn had he known more about Tell el-Amarna.

By concentrating on the shortcomings in Wilkinson's work, the foregoing pages might be taken as deprecative of his accomplishment. In fact, the intention has been to show how, despite inadequate evidence, he achieved remarkable results. More than any other person of his time, he pierced the grand façade of ancient Egyptian culture and saw behind it the daily life of a human society. Furthermore, he succeeded in communicating that vision to the Victorian reading public. It was a rare bit of imagination, the full implications of which would not be realized for a long time, despite the enthusiasm with which his book was instantly received. *Manners and Customs of the Ancient Egyptians* made Wilkinson famous as England's foremost writer on the ancient Egyptians.

First, however, he had to get John Murray to publish the book. Murray had indeed already approved the project but had envisoned two volumes; Wilkinson brought him enough for five. After much discussion, Murray agreed to publish three volumes, but no more, leaving Wilkinson to choose between abridging the entire work or omitting whole sections of it. Wilkinson reluctantly took the latter course and removed the sections on agriculture and religion, intending to publish them intact someday.[57] This difficult decision turned out for the best, because the commercial success of the first three volumes convinced Murray to publish the other two as a second series of *Manners and Customs of the Ancient Egyptians*. In fact, all five volumes formed one work, and they were presented as such in subsequent printings where the second series distinction was dropped.[58]

Murray also compelled Wilkinson to cut out more than one hundred illustrations that he wanted to use.[59] The remaining illustrations, however, thickly interspersed among the pages and filling a supplemental volume to the second series, some of them in color, formed an integral part of the book. Without detracting from the good work that Murray's printers did with the colored illustrations, including some fine fold-out plates of Rekhmire's tomb, it should be noted that their quality does not approach that of the originals. At least one reviewer regretted that the engravings in Rosellini's *I monumenti dell'Egitto e della Nubia* were more elegantly done, but proudly asserted that Wilkinson's were nevertheless good and had been produced by private initiative, whereas Rosellini's had been lavishly subsidized by the Tuscan government.[60]

Some say that Joseph Bonomi prepared the illustrations for *Manners and Customs of the Ancient Egyptians*; others maintain that Wilkinson did them all himself. In fact, Wilkinson asked Bonomi to do the illustrations for the 1837 volumes, but Bonomi declined because of previous engagements.[61] Wilkinson therefore hired another lithographist, though there were some problems resulting from the latter's unfamiliarity with hieroglyphs, and at least one plate had to be redone with help from Francis Arundale.[62] Bonomi did, however, agree to prepare the illustrations for the second series, so we find him writing plaintively to Robert Hay in 1841, "I am working for

Wilkinson no rest nor peace he is going to press, wants a hundred things to be done at once it is always so at the last."[63]

When *Manners and Customs of the Ancient Egyptians* appeared in 1837 it became an instant success; soon a second edition was being planned, followed by many others. British readers were attracted by the sensuous, lifelike quality of the illustrations and a text that presented the ancient Egyptians as real people. Wilkinson enabled them to visualize a richly exotic society, so exotic that it contained an escapist element, even as the realistic detail of the book resonated with the tone of the 1830s when taste was moving toward social realism, away from the dreams of the Romantics. One reader, Samuel Rogers, wrote to say, "How can I thank you as I ought for your invaluable volumes! We turn over the leaves, & are at once, as it were, in another world. Three thousand years roll backward & we live familiarly with a people the most interesting & hitherto, I may say, the most unknown of any that have appeared among us—a people to whom all & every one of us now living are deeply indebted, for what may we not have derived from them through the Greeks?"[64] Other reactions were similar, prompting a modern Egyptologist to observe, "One might say that Wilkinson took the mummy wrappings off the ancient Egyptians and made them human beings who had loved and labored, fought and played, like other peoples in less remote lands."[65]

Reviews from the journals of the day were all favorable. Though dismayed at the scantiness of clothing of some of the women in the illustrations, the *Quarterly Review* wrote, "This restoration to life, as it were, of the ancient Pharaohs, and their subjects, in the nineteenth century of our aera, is the most extraordinary event in literary or antiquarian history."[66] The *Athenaeum* commented in similar terms.[67] The reviewer for the *Edinburgh Review* acutely found fault with the description of the ancient Egyptian caste system and the consequent organization of some chapters, yet pronounced Wilkinson's book a "safe guide" to its subject.[68] Unreservedly favorable was the *Gentlemen's Magazine*, which praised "the agreeable manner in which his extensive information is conveyed.[69] These opinions came entirely from popular, literary, and amateur writers, for there was no jury of peers to pass judgment upon Wilkinson's work. The men best qualified to evaluate it—Gell, Young, and Champollion—were gone, leaving no one to replace them. An establishment of professional Egyptologists with scholarly journals to express their considered opinions was many years in the future. By the time such an establishment had come into being, the science of

Egyptology had so advanced that its practitioners looked askance at Wilkinson's accomplishment.

Manners and Customs of the Ancient Egyptians retained its popularity throughout the nineteenth century. There were, in fact, few other works to which the British reader interested in Egypt could turn, because it was the first topical work in English exclusively devoted to ancient Egypt. Various writers in the eighteenth century had included Egypt in their universal histories, but as one theme among many. Also, these works were based upon the classical view, though some of them drew upon modern travelers' accounts. The great *Description de l'Egypte* was still an important work, but it was large, difficult to handle, and very expensive; so were many of the other continental productions, which were, in any case, rarely available in translation. Wilkinson's book was handily sized and moderately priced, putting it within range of more readers.

During the years after the publication of *Manners and Customs of the Ancient Egyptians*, several other Egyptological works appeared. Baron von Bunsen published *Egypt's Place in Universal History* in English and German, the first volume appearing in 1844, but it was so dull that it attracted few readers. In contrast, Samuel Sharpe's *History of Egypt* (1846) was very popular. Sharpe ambitiously tried to use hieroglyphic sources but, like Wilkinson, fell back upon the Bible and classical sources. Even more popular was John Kendrick's *Ancient Egypt under the Pharaohs* (1850), which was nearly as widely read as Wilkinson.[70] None of these, however, displaced Wilkinson's book.

In appealing to a wide readership, Wilkinson took a very different approach than his mentor, Sir William Gell, had taken. Gell was an unashamed elitist, in intellectual as well as political and social matters. He intended his work only for the select few who could afford his large, expensive volumes. To produce these he sought not royalties from sales but aristocratic patronage, and he spent much of his life seeking the right patron. During Gell's career, however, two great changes occurred in the literate world. One was the vast increase in the size of the reading public.[71] Another was the rise of the middle class, the most rapidly growing class in nineteenth-century Britain. Publishers such as John Murray realized that a new, lucrative market had appeared and moved to serve it with large runs of books. Produced in quantity and efficiently distributed, such books were much more affordable than Gell's had been. Not only did they reach more individual buyers but also circulated widely through subscription libraries like Mudie's, another nineteenth-century innovation. Such a popular appeal would have been almost inconceivable to Gell. "We shall finish by writing for the penny magazines," he once told Wilkinson, as if writing for the masses was the worst fate imaginable. Wilkinson and Murray, by contrast, sought to reach the largest possible audience. The patronage of the paying middle class had supplanted that of the aristocrat.

Popular as it was in its own time, *Manners and Customs of the Ancient Egyptians* lacked those qualities that allow a work to live on after it has become dated. One would search in vain among its pages for provocative philosophical generalizations that could catch the imagination of later generations. Nor was Wilkinson's writing style the stuff of which immortal works are made. Sometimes he was careless with rhetorical points, occasionally employing indefinite antecedents. He included repetitious passages and digressions, sometimes with chronologically jarring allusions to modern events, though he usually managed to find the way back to his subject. Another hindrance to readability was his frequent use of long quotations from the classical writers. This meant that sometimes there was too much quotation and not enough Wilkinson, though the result was a good topical sourcebook for classical references to ancient Egyptian subjects. Perhaps the most serious disqualification for long-term readability was the fact that the field of Egyptology moved so far in the nineteenth century, eventually making Wilkinson's view of ancient Egypt seem hopelessly out of date. As decades passed, one could no longer read *Manners and Customs of the Ancient Egyptians* with the same profitability that still rewarded a reading of Edward Gibbon's *Decline and Fall of the Roman Empire*. By the beginning of the twentieth century, Wilkinson's book was seldom read, in contrast to Edward William Lane's *An Account of the Manners and Customs of the Modern Egyptians*, which remains a classic in its field.

As it turned out, Wilkinson's *Ancient Egyptians* and Lane's *Modern Egyptians* became companion volumes. Lane had followed his discouraging experience with "Description of Egypt" with another research expedition and produced a scholarly survey of ancient and modern Egypt. When it became apparent that Wilkinson's book would appear at about the same time, Lane was encouraged to drop his sections about ancient Egypt and to concentrate entirely on modern Egypt. In that way, Wilkinson and Lane's books would complement and advertise each other; anyone who wanted an up-to-date library on things Egyptian would have to have both. The change of strategy may have cost Lane some unanticipated revision, but his book was better for it—better than even he may have understood at the time. Books about Egypt had hitherto been a mixture of ancient and modern elements with a hieroglyph on one page and a mosque on the next—indeed, Lane's "Description of Egypt" had been just such a work. But a book of detailed description and analysis entirely devoted to modern Egypt was something new, a fact that one of Lane's reviewers noted with surprise, "So closely, indeed, has he stuck to his subject, that we verily believe the words obelisk, pyramid, tomb, temple, never once occur . . . not a mummy crosses his path."[72] It was a turning point for Lane. Although he continued to maintain some personal interest in ancient Egypt, all of his professional energies from then on were devoted to the subjects that he had outlined in his *Modern Egyptians*.[73] Lane's book subsequently was altered in size, format, and appearance to match Wilkinson's.[74] Thus Wilkinson's and Lane's books stood side by side upon many Victorian library shelves.

CHAPTER ELEVEN

Sir Gardner Wilkinson

THE DECADE FOLLOWING the publication of *Manners and Customs of the Ancient Egyptians* was for Wilkinson a period of traveling, writing, and making new acquaintances. Late in 1837, against the advice of his physicians, he set out for Syria, intending to pass the winter there. His primary object was to survey the Holy Land, an idea that he may have inherited from Sir William Gell who had once dreamed of doing so. It was a worthy ambition, one in which the Royal Geographical Society took some interest, but Wilkinson fell ill in Paris on the way out and, as he wrote to the secretary of the society, "I take this opportunity of returning you my thanks for all your kindness & the trouble you have taken I am sorry to add without any result as far as I am concerned—for I fear I must with a heavy heart abandon my project of going to Syria."[1] As soon as he was able, he returned to England.

The following year he successfully escaped the English winter, though the Holy Land project was not revived. He sailed to Lisbon, where he saw a bullfight—"It is a very cruel sight, particularly to see the horses gored."[2] He made his way through Spain, thence to Sicily, and on to Naples—too late to see Sir William Gell. Passing through Rome he met Joseph Bonomi, and the two combined to copy the Egyptian obelisks of that city. Careful to claim an equal place, Bonomi wrote to Edward William Lane, "My agreement with Wilkinson is merely one of convenience to both of us as he is to copy those in his neighbourhood and I those in mine and we are to lend our copies to each other."[3] Another face from the past in Rome was Yanni from Thebes, who was on his way to England to try and make his fortune there.[4] After wintering in Rome, Wilkinson proceeded to Paris where he presented a copy of *Manners and Customs of the*

Ancient Egyptians to King Louis Philippe. He pleasantly passed the time conversing with the king until they were interrupted by Marshal Soult who came to discuss the formation of his new ministry. Paris, Wilkinson recorded, was "full of the fashionable world" as he made the round of embassy receptions.

When he returned to England from his European jaunt, rumors of a new honor were circulating. James Burton wrote to Robert Hay, "Wilkinson will, I fancy, at the next levee be dubbed Sir John Gardner Wilkinson."[5] This prediction was realized on 28 August 1839, when he was awarded a knighthood at the recommendation of Viscount Melbourne's government.[6] Melbourne rarely rewarded literary accomplishments, but Wilkinson's achievement clearly put him into the company of the many men of science and exploration who were knighted in the course of the nineteenth century.[7] Also important was the well-publicized fact that he had worked without government assistance, unlike certain foreign scholars such as Champollion and Rosellini.[8] This would have appealed to almost any Liberal of those days, and especially to Melbourne and his colleagues, for it was a triumph for the doctrine of laissez-faire in the realm of scholarship. Wilkinson chose to be called Sir Gardner instead of Sir John,[9] and he seems to have taken his title quite seriously all his life. Not long after the event, Burton was writing to Hay, "Sir Gardner W^i is still at Lord Prudhoe's—(You see I do not forget his title[)]."[10] Lane, by contrast, was never knighted, despite a life of solid scholarly accomplishment, but he apparently felt no slight at not being dubbed. He merely continued his hard-working ways; indeed, in the same year as Wilkinson's knighthood, Lane published his highly acclaimed translation of the *Arabian Nights.* Much more was to follow during his long, fruitful career.

The literary successes achieved by Wilkinson and Lane contrasted sharply with the misfortune of their friend Robert Hay. Over the years Wilkinson had continued to urge, even to nag Hay to publish some of his unrivaled portfolio. Before Hay returned to England, Wilkinson had written to say, "I hope you will at last come home & publish some of those valuable materials that you have copied so faithfully. I do not know that anything is to be gained, on the contrary, but much can be done gradually at little expense."[11] Two years later, Wilkinson added, "Why do you not make the Dilettanti or some other equally spirited society publish them?"[12] But there were problems from the start: first Hay equivocated between conflicting advice from various artists whom he consulted about setting up the plates, and then he recoiled from the task of writing. Lane prodded him just to sit down and do it. "Your diffidence on this point is provoking," he wrote to Hay. "If you write simply, & to the purpose," Lane urged, "you cannot fail to give satisfaction; & I think, for such an exceeding diffident person as you, the best plan would be to write as you would to a friend, in a familiar way, & then to make the necessary alterations."[13] But Hay could not face blank paper; finally, he asked Burton to do the writing. Two less productive literary collaborators can scarcely be imagined. Despite the problems, the work proceeded, albeit slowly. Recognizing that the great *Description de l'Egypte* contained many errors and that Champollion's and Rosellini's works were primarily archaeological in content, Hay intended his work to be "suited at once to the wants of the Antiquary, the Architect, & and [sic] the lover of the Picturesque, & serving to elucidate the descriptions both of ancient & modern Authors."[14] He decided to organize the material into two or more volumes, the first containing views of Cairo; architectural and antiquarian subjects would fill the others.

The first volume, entitled *Illustrations of Cairo* and dedicated to Edward William Lane, finally appeared in 1841.[15] Wilkinson, to whom Hay sent a copy, perused it eagerly and wrote to Hay that he was "delighted" with it and hoped the publishing project would extend to the sculpture.[16] This, however, was not to be. Despite the book's merits, it did not sell. Popular taste had moved away from such great, illustrated volumes, however fine they were. Hay, who spent a large sum of money producing the book, lost almost everything that he put into it. Catherwood commiserated, "I am the more sorry for this result as it evidently will be a bar to your publishing anything else."[17] It was indeed, for the rest of Hay's magnificent portfolio was never published.

Impelled by his success with *Manners and Customs of the Ancient Egyptians*, Wilkinson continued to write. Perhaps the most unusual work to come from his pen during this period was *Three Letters on the Policy of England towards the Porte and Mohammed Ali*, which John Murray published in 1840. The occasion for this short book was the latest of the several conflicts that characterized Muhammad Ali's ambiguous relationship with his nominal master, the sultan in Istanbul. In this instance, Muhammad Ali, stung by his losses on the sultan's behalf during the Greek War of Independence, decided to realize his old ambition of conquering Syria. Accordingly, he dispatched his son Ibrahim at the head of an army into Syria in 1831. Ibrahim easily overran the country and seemed poised to invade Turkey and capture Istanbul. Terrified at this prospect, the sultan quickly concluded a treaty with Russia. This development, which raised the possibility of Russian intervention and domination of the strategic passage through the Bosporus and Dardanelles, roused the Western powers into action. The British government seemed inclined to compel Muhammad Ali to withdraw from Syria or, failing that, to strike directly at him in Egypt.

Wilkinson, in *Three Letters*, argued for a more moderate, better informed approach: "We might expect that misapprehension could occur respecting the Eastern question, or the relative position of Mohammed Ali and the Porte; but many persons, as well as part of the English press, are still disposed to treat the Egyptian Pacha [pasha] as a mere rebel, directing hostilities against his sovereign."[18] The case was, in fact, quite different: "For years before the invasion of Syria Sultan Mahmood looked with jealousy on the growing power of Mohammed Ali, who had extended his victorious arms over Arabia and Ethiopia, who had acquired the admiration of the Ottoman empire, and whose love of improvement, and desire to introduce the arts and knowledge of civilized Europe, had gained for him the respect of all enlightened people."[19] Muhammad Ali's invasion was, therefore, an anticipation of the sultan's jealous wrath, a resort to defense by offense. To take arms against Muhammad Ali now would, Wilkinson further reasoned, be an act of folly. Although the British could easily defeat his navy in another battle of Navarino—an "untoward act," Wilkinson called that event, repeating the understated wording of the British apology for it—Muhammad Ali was still strong by land and would go down fighting. In the end it would take a Russian army to protect the sultan and defeat Muhammad Ali, a solution worse than the problem. The correct course, Wilkinson concluded, was to bind both sultan and pasha by treaty and to threaten them if they broke it.

British statesmen worried that dismemberment of the Ottoman Empire might bring on a general European war from which Russia stood to gain the most. Their policy, therefore, was to support the Ottoman Empire and resist any attempts to dismember it. Wilkinson, however, acutely argued that to strike Egypt was to strike at the empire's most dynamic component, a point that Muhammad Ali himself liked to make. To the argument that Muhammad Ali was aiming at Egyptian independence and thereby the dismemberment of the Ottoman Empire, Wilkinson countered that his real intention was to secure succession as pasha for his son. For their part, the diplomats were better aware than Wilkinson of the various unmistakable hints at independence that Muhammad Ali had made, especially in 1834; Wilkinson also missed the point that one of the government's essential concerns was Muhammad Ali as an economic threat to Britain. By praising the level of Muhammad Ali's accomplishments, Wilkinson failed to see that a strong Egypt was probably the last thing the foreign secretary, Lord Palmerston, wanted. Palmerston dismissed the pasha's achievements with contempt: "For my part I hate Mehemet Ali, whom I consider as nothing but an ignorant barbarian, who by cunning and boldness and mother wit has been successful in rebellion . . . I look upon his boasted civilization of Egypt as the arrantest humbug, and I believe that he is as great a tyrant and oppressor as ever made a people wretched."[20]

Besides Wilkinson's, other opinions favorable to Muhammad Ali appeared. Thomas Waghorn, a steam agent in Egypt, wrote a pamphlet entitled *Egypt As It Is* in 1838 in which he maintained that Egyptian independence would be beneficial to British commercial interests.[21] But Palmerston was not prepared to hear other views than his own. When Patrick Campbell, then the consul-general in Egypt, ventured to praise Muhammad Ali in his dispatches, he was promptly dismissed.[22] It was not, therefore, so unusual for Muhammad Ali to have defenders, but it surprised those who had known Wilkinson in Egypt to see how much his original opinions had altered. Frederick Catherwood speculated to Robert Hay: "Have you remarked in Wilkinson's book that his opinions respecting the pasha are much changed. When I last saw W. he was most bitter against his Highness and now in his book he finds much to praise. I thought this might be policy on his part intending to return to Egypt but I have heard lately that he has been soliciting the situation of custodian or keeper of the Egyptian antiquities of the British Museum. I am not however sure that this report is correct."[23] Perhaps too Wilkinson was swayed by the special favors from the pasha and by the force of his character. "His manner has a *charm*," Henry Salt wrote of Muhammad Ali, "that it is difficult to conceive without witnessing."[24]

Wilkinson's book does seem overly adulatory in places, especially when it refers to Muhammad Ali as "one of the most remarkable men the world has produced."[25] Yet just three years later, after Muhammad Ali had been compelled to leave Syria, Wilkinson was referring to him in these terms in a private letter: "He is very fond of flattery & they [the French] can do as they like with him by pretty speeches & he actually thinks himself a greater man than Napoleon. He is very much out of humor with us & says he thinks we shall find we made a mistake depriving him of Syria. I think we shall see him there again . . . I should like to see England & Russia come to an understanding and divide the country between them."[26] Wilkinson's opinion had changed again.

During these years Wilkinson was becoming a feature of the British intellectual landscape. Baron von Bunsen, preparing a trip to England, wrote to his friend Thomas Arnold, "I must see the British Museum, Westminster, the Docks, and Mr. Wilkinson, the Egyptian."[27] Honors and memberships in scholarly societies steadily came his way, more, perhaps, than any other Egyptologist has ever received.[28] In 1852 he finally got a college degree when he went up to Oxford to be created D.C.L. by the Earl of Derby who had recently become chancellor of the university. The *Daily Telegraph* reported, "The irreverent undergraduates saluted him with ringing cheers for 'Old Hieroglyphics,' coupling his reputation with that of the hippopotamus, the first specimen of which was at that time on the point of arriving on these shores."[29]

One of the honors that probably meant the most to him was an invitation to join the Council of the Royal Geographical Society. When he was first asked in 1840, he begged to defer because of an impending trip abroad, but the following year he accepted, despite his intention to travel abroad again.[30] Wilkinson's subsequent letters to the society show that he frequently missed council meetings because of illness or absence from town; he did, however, take an interest in the issues before the society and corresponded frequently with its secretary. His position permitted him to influence the society's distribution of honors and recognition, the publication of books and articles, and the support of expeditions of exploration. For example, when the society was deliberating whether to award its annual gold medal to (Sir) Richard Burton, who had recently completed his extraordinary pilgrimage to the holy cities of Arabia, or to the central African explorer Heinrich Barth, Wilkinson favored Barth, who received it.[31] Wilkinson also acted as referee for Burton's article about his pilgrimage that appeared in the society's journal.[32] His advice, which was frequently asked, was usually sound, as when the secretary requested his opinion about a new book that suggested a common origin for ancient Egyptian and pre-Columbian Mexican cultures. Wilkinson was not carried away by the book's provocative thesis:

With regard to the Mexicans & Egyptians I think that they are unlike in all those points where if they had ever had any communication, or a common origin *as a nation*, they ought to have resembled each other. As to their pyramids, they are in no way like those of Egypt either in use or construction, they are much more like tumuli, with a casing added as a subsequent improvement, & having steps to the summit in order to render the ascent of that part more commodious are very unlike the smooth inaccessible pyramid of Egypt which has a base of between 7 & 800 feet to a height of nearly 500, while some of those of the Mexicans have a base of upwards of 600 feet & height 130 or 160 feet, & sometimes a base of 2200 & height of 200 feet. It is unnecessary to remark how simple & natural the form of the tumulus & pyramid are, & even when these last are built of stone the idea is so likely to strike anyone & the durability of a monument of this shape is so obvious that any people who are desirous of erecting a building intended to last for ages are more likely to hit upon this form than any other, & indeed I am so surprised that fewer nations have adopted this style of monument but that it is ill adapted for interior use.[33]

Somewhat less sound was his decision to participate in the White River Society, an organization formed in the late 1830s by Wilkinson and some other gentlemen to investigate the source of the Nile.[34] This, of course, was one of the great geographical questions of the nineteenth century, not resolved until the explorations of Sir Richard Burton, John Speke, and others in the late 1850s and early 1860s. Wilkinson surely had pondered it as he watched the river course by in Egypt, for Gell had written about it many times. Attention centered upon the western branch of the Nile, the White Nile, which joins with the Blue Nile at Khartoum. Wilkinson realized that a major lake was somewhere upstream because the annual flood brought with it large fish and shellfish.[35] Gell wondered if Lake Chad might be involved, but by the time the White River Society was formed, that conjecture had been disproved. The source of the river was somewhere far to the south, obscured by the heavy swamps and fierce inhabitants of equatorial Africa.

Joining Wilkinson in the White River Society were such people as James Burton, Robert Hay, the Earl of Munster, and Colonel William Martin Leake. Together they issued a circular describing their purpose and soliciting donations to finance an expedition.[36] None of these worthy individuals intended to go himself, however, for the natives of the upper reaches of the Nile were known to kill white men on sight, as the recent murder of a well-known explorer in Central Africa had shown. Instead, they decided to send a black man, a native of Dongola called Kerim Effendi who had lived in Europe for several years and was at that moment in London. This Kerim, they assured potential donors, was "a person deserving of trust, likely to give every satisfaction, and one who may be expected to succeed in the undertaking, which he is evidently disposed to enter upon with zeal and interest." Unspoken, but perhaps not entirely absent from the minds of the members of the White River Committee, was the thought that Kerim Effendi was expendable.

The fund-raising effort met with only marginal success, soon reducing the White River Society to strenuous economies. Members repeatedly requested the government to allow Kerim to travel with the Queen's messenger through France and even considered having their explorer work as a servant to earn his passage over the sea. Furthermore, doubts about Kerim's abilities developed as the expedition progressed, because one of the society's friends reported from Marseilles, "I really fear very much that he does not possess sufficient energy for the arduous task he has undertaken. We however will do every thing in our power to promote your views. He has been very well behaved on the journey, but perfectly useless & was always completely knocked up at the end of each stage. But we hope that in his own country he will recover that active spirit which he certainly must have possessed when he left it."[37] Despite these and other misadventures, Kerim eventually reached Egypt and passed up the river to his home, but no conclusive results came from this odd expedition. It was probably unreasonable for the gentlemen of the White River Society to hope that any would.[38]

Wilkinson began a more realistic project when John Murray invited him to write the Egyptian volume for Murray's new series of handbooks for travelers. The origin of the handbook series lay in Murray's own experiences on the Continent a few years previously. He had noticed how much easier it was to travel through places for which he had notes from friends—where to stay, what to eat, and that sort of thing—and how much he missed these notes when he entered regions for which he had none. He began keeping his own notebooks which his father later published. They called them "handbooks," a term previously applied to manuals of ecclesiastical offices.[39] These were the first systematic guidebooks for travelers in modern times, antedating Baedeker's series by several years. Successful from the first, Murray's handbooks represented the shift away from upper-class tourists toward middle-class travelers, "to whom where to feed was a more important question than what to see," as Murray's grandson put it.[40] Murray realized that he could not continue the project single-handedly and turned to others for help. Being a fellow of the Royal Geographical Society, he approached three fellow members with excellent results. Sir Lambert Playfair wrote the volume on Algeria and the Mediterranean, Richard Ford prepared the guide to Spain, and Wilkinson wrote the handbook for Egypt.

Of these three volumes, Richard Ford's is generally considered the best; certainly it is the most sought after by book collectors today. Ford poured his intimate knowledge of Spain into his handbook, filling it with deep digressions about Spanish history, art, and culture. But it can be argued that Wilkinson's volume was a better guidebook than Ford's. Ford compiled so much contextual material that it submerged the essential traveler's information and made his manuscript so long that the printers had to use overly small type. Wilkinson was more selective, and even if he did not approach Ford's literary elegance, he better served the practical needs of travelers. Also, the comparative cultural aridity of Wilkinson's volume was not so great a disadvantage, for he had already written about Egyptian culture in other books. Many English travelers in Egypt subsequently floated up and down the Nile with *Handbook for Travellers in Egypt* in one hand and *Manners and Customs of the Ancient Egyptians* in the other.[41] The handbook sold well, appearing in several revised editions throughout the nineteenth century.

So busy with writing and committee meetings, it may have been apparent neither to Wilkinson nor to those around him that he was gradually losing focus on Egyptology. *Manners and Customs of the Ancient Egyptians* was not followed by another in-depth study of ancient Egypt. Unlike his friend Edward William Lane, whose *An Account of the Manners and Customs of the Modern Egyptians* was merely the prelude to more work in the same vein, Wilkinson scattered his energies in many directions, sampling various topics but not studying them deeply. When he published *Manners and Customs of the Ancient Egyptians*, he was one of the foremost of Egyptologists. He was experienced in fieldwork and as knowledgeable as anyone about the ancient language. Vast possibilities lay before him. Of the many topics he touched upon in *Manners and Customs of the Ancient Egyptians*, he might have pursued almost any, or he could have branched into new but related topics such as Ptolemaic or Roman Egypt. His classical education combined with his knowledge of ancient Egypt could have taken him far in those fields where he would have been a pioneer, but they did not interest him. Strange though his intellectual dislocation might seem from our standpoint, however, Wilkinson would not have perceived it so. As a man of leisure and an amateur scholar of his day, it was natural to turn to other topics to pass his time and bring him into contact with other like-minded gentlemen. Not that he forgot ancient Egypt; on the contrary, he believed that his experience still gave him something worth sharing with the public. At one point he considered preparing and publishing a set of letters, perhaps to Lord Prudhoe, about Egyptological matters. When he asked the opinion of his friend Captain Basil Hall, a successful writer, Hall dissuaded him, arguing that such a book would not "answer the public or popular purpose at all."[42] Wilkinson could not imagine how to organize the still largely untapped potential in his notebooks.

Typical of the varied but superficial interests that took increasing amounts of his time was his study of the origin of the pointed arch, a fascination that exemplifies his essentially antiquarian turn of mind. This topic had been a lively issue in the 1790s and early 1800s among English antiquarians who studied Gothic architecture, but it had grown stale long before Wilkinson took it up.[43] Wilkinson was most likely introduced to the subject by James Burton who wrote that he became interested in "tracing the origin of the pointed arch" in 1827 and had sketches made to document its use.[44] Wilkinson later noted in a communication to the Royal Institute of British Architects, "During my stay at Thebes, in 1830, the accidental discovery of a tomb I opened there enabled me to prove the use of the round arch by the Egyptians, as early as the reign of Amunoph 1ˢᵗ, about 1540 BC; & during a recent visit to Thebes I have seen other tombs of similar construction which date in the time of the Remses, or the beginning of the 13th century before our era. . . . But besides their knowledge of the *round arch*, I believe it is not altogether impossible that the ancient Egyptians were acquainted with the *pointed arch.*"[45] This interest conditioned his observations during later travels. For example, in Italy we find him writing, "At Tusculum I have been delighted to find a regular pointed arch of Pelasgian time which I have measured carefully—Tho' Murray's handbook pretends to say it is not on the principle of the arch. The writer only saw the outer one which as he says is cut into the stone."[46]

It was not until 1841 that Wilkinson finally returned to Egypt, this time by steamer, forever ending the difficulties of his journeys by sea.[47] This trip was less for the purpose of continuing his former work than gathering detailed information for the Egyptian travel guide that he was writing for Murray. Accordingly, when he arrived in Egypt, he made careful notes about travel expenses, hotels, and other such details, obviously with reference to the handbook.[48] With it in mind, he compiled a lengthy packing list: "Eau de Cologne, Syringe, pipe, gloves. Compass, Soap—Copper, Comb, indian rubber Heads, wafers . . . 1 portmanteau, 1 bag of books, 1 sword & 1 key . . . 2 black & 1 blue cravat. 1 summer trousers, & 1 velvet waistcoat . . . 1 chest of drawers, iron bedstead, 2 tables, rope ladders . . . print of Tintoretto's Crucifixion . . . Cough pills of 2/3rds Camphor & 1/3 syrup of Poppies . . . 1 large Portmanteau, 1 small do. 1 carpet bag, 1 Hat box," and much more.[49] It must have taken a fair-sized *dahabiyah* and a strong troop of porters to carry it all. Wilkinson proved a generalization of Sir William Gell's: "There are no people like the English," Gell had written. "They transport with them to every clime the luxurious habits, and appliances that administer to them, of their own."[50]

Not long after landing in Alexandria Wilkinson was laid low by a debilitating illness that reduced his intended range of travels. "I was sorry to hear, the other day, from Bonomi," Edward William Lane wrote to Robert Hay, "that Wilkinson was unwell at Alexandria, so much so that he feared he could not make the intended voyage up the Nile. This I regret also on account of his "Hand-Book for Egypt & Nubia."[51] Within a short time, however, he was recovered and in Cairo where he wrote to Hay, "Egypt's much altered for the worst & has lost much of its oriental character [and] is much dearer & not much more comfortable."[52] In a letter to another friend, he went on in much the same vein: "Egypt is much spoilt since I saw it before— it is overrun with Indians & the travellers who go up the Nile will I fear soon be like Rhine tourists. & Cheapside will pour out its Legions upon Egypt."[53] Yet just such tourists were those for whom his *Handbook for Travellers in Egypt* was being written. There were happy reunions with many old friends and acquaintances, including Major Felix who passed through briefly on the way to his new posting in India.[54] Wilkinson was well received by a literary society that Henry Abbott and Prisse d'Avennes had founded, and the French Association Littéraire d'Egypte in Cairo elected him one of its first honorary members, perhaps partly because of his gifts of books and a lithographic press.[55] It must have seemed a bit like old times, especially since, as he wrote to Hay, "I am of course à la Turque as before" (i.e., dressed in Turkish attire).[56]

Wilkinson admitted in letters to friends that he had come to Egypt reluctantly, but once on the ground he became excited about the opportunities.[57] Again he filled his notebooks with notes, sketches, barometric readings (he carried three barometers with him), and so forth. Some of the observations are of high quality, including those he made at Tell Basta, the ancient Bubastis, in the Delta.[58] As at many other archaeological sites in Egypt, Wilkinson found that the once lovely temple at Bubastis had deteriorated since his last visit. This was the temple of which Herodotus had written, "Other temples may be larger, or have cost more to build, but none is a greater pleasure to look at."[59] The pleasure of looking at it was greatly diminished by the 1840s, however, for much of it had been quarried away, and the remainder was used for storehousing.[60] It had been in relatively good condition when Napoleon's expedition recorded it but suffered heavily during subsequent decades.

"I am hard at work on my new book," Wilkinson wrote to his friend, T. J. Pettigrew, perhaps referring to the *Handbook for Travellers in Egypt:* "which I certainly could never have done had I not come to Egypt. I do not know whether I shall go to Upper Egypt or no. At all events I shall first finish what I have to do here, & probably go to the Natron Lakes the first thing when I do leave Cairo. Egypt is spoilt by the overland communication & everything is very dear comparatively. Boats which used to be 700 are now 1250 & 2200 piastres a month or from 12 1/2 to 22£."[61] He did in fact survey the Natron Lakes Valley, later publishing the results in the *Journal of the Royal Geographical Society.* "I only regret that my health would not allow me to follow the Bahr-el-Fargh to the Fyúm," he wrote in that communication.[62] Because of his health, he was soon planning his return to England, apprehensive of the approaching Egyptian summer. "I found that I could not bear the heat as formerly," he later wrote to Hay, "& I was obliged to leave the country when the thermometer was 100° in the shade." In May of 1842 Wilkinson sailed downstream to Rashid, which he considered the prettiest town in Egypt, and spent some time in the Delta sketching. After the usual leisurely trip across the Mediterranean and through the Continent, he returned to London in February 1843.[63]

He remained in England scarcely long enough to finish the *Handbook for Travellers in Egypt* and see to the initial stages of its publication, though he may also have worked on the enlarged edition of *Topography of Thebes* that Murray published in 1843 under the tile *Modern Egypt and Thebes.* He was anxious to be on his way again and fulfill an old desire to visit Greece. He sailed in September, taking with him some annoyance at John Murray, writing to a friend, "The printers I find have allowed numerous mistakes to creep into my last book on Egᵗ especially in numbers, but Murray put off the printing till the last moment & I could not wait to correct it properly as I should have remained so long that I should have fallen into the feverish season or been obliged to give up Greece. I am tired of publishing with such contrarietes."[64]

Wilkinson's first impression of Greece, which he had never visited before, was one of astonishment. He wrote to Hay, "No one can visit [Greece] without feeling the most absorbing interest & where every monument that remains is full of taste and beauty. I was never so delighted with any country."[65] At Delphi he copied an inscription that he communicated to the Royal Society of Literature where it was read on 25 January 1844. Colonel Leake, the vice-president of the society noted, "Sir Gardner must have had no small difficulty in making these transcripts, as the originals were engraved on the faces of the substractions and avenues of the temple, on a kind of stone much less hard and homogenous than those marbles which have preserved so many Greek inscriptions from the injuries of twenty centuries."[66]

From Greece he went to Alexandria and thence to Cairo. There he found Bonomi, who had left Lepsius's party, living in a tent near the Sphinx. Wilkinson moved into a nearby tomb and took a party of men into the Great Pyramid to do some excavations.[67] "One feels the pleasure of writing a letter," he wrote to Hay, "at no time so thoroughly as when revisiting scenes that bring back the recollections of an old meeting."[68] This visit to Egypt was very brief, however, for soon he was sailing around the eastern Mediterranean with his acquaintances Mr. and Mrs. Highford Burr[69] on their yacht. In this manner he visited Beirut, Damascus, and Baalbek, sketching ruins and seeing sights. Damascus he found "interesting," with houses superior to Cairo's, though the mosques were, in his opinion, not as good.[70] The sketchbooks show that he visited Troy and surrounding areas such as Mount Ida, as well as the Greek islands in the Aegean Sea. When the Burrs' yacht sailed into the Adriatic, he took the opportunity to disembark at Trieste for a tour of the Illyrian coast and interior, which he later recounted in his book *Dalmatia and Montenegro.*[71]

Sailing southward on a steamer through the coastal islands, Wilkinson reached Split, where he was particularly impressed with the vast remains of Diocletian's palace, which he knew from the writings of the architect Robert Adam (whom he repeatedly called Adams in his book). Establishing Split as his base, he traveled as far south as Ragusa and Kotor. The notebooks and sketchbooks filled more quickly as his observations sharpened. The dramatic terrain and peculiar houses of the regions caught his eye, but his strongest artistic interest was in the array of native costumes that he saw in the varied regions through which he passed. Many of these sketches, frequently colored, are of high quality.[72] This was in fact a standing interest of his, evident as early as his first trip to Italy. He accumulated sufficient material during his career to make a book on costume alone, had he so chosen.

On his most extensive excursion inland, he traveled among the Montenegrins, who deeply impressed him by their extremes of character. They displayed great personal warmth toward friends and guests, but treated enemies with fierce brutality. He was discomfited by the custom of Montenegrin men who greeted strangers with a kiss on the mouth. After a few encounters, he became adept at avoiding their lips by grasping his new acquaintance in a firm embrace until the osculatory impulse passed. He noticed, "The women only kiss a stranger's hand; and on no occasion does one feel how advantagiously the two sexes might change places, as when welcomed to a Montenegrin's house."[73] His experiences among this intense people seemed to heighten his power of social observation, for the Montenegrin passages in *Dalmatia and Montenegro* are the most vivid in the book, though his biases could lead him to convoluted descriptions, such as this one about Montenegrin women:

> In Turkey, and in Montenegro, man is equally "a despot, and woman a slave;" but the difference in the two countries is that in one she is an object of caprice, and part of the establishment, as a horse is a member of its master's stud; in the other, she is the working beast of burthen, and his substitute in all laborious tasks. But the Montenegrin woman has the advantage of being in a Christian community; and however arduous her duties, she is the helpmeet of her husband, and is not degraded to the condition of a mere component part of the harem. She is still his companion, his only partner, the only mother of his children; and she sees not the reproach of her position in the splendor of her dress, or the show of kindness lavished upon her by her lord and master, from motives of self-gratification. At the same time, however degraded the condition of women in the East, they have one great consolation, in the affection of their children; who are more attached to their mothers, than in many more civilized communities; and no oriental youth is deluded, by a false idea of manliness, into disrespect towards either of his parents.[74]

It is difficult from this to see exactly how the Christian women of Montenegro were better off than their Turkish counterparts.

Generations of fierce warfare with the Turks had instilled in the Montenegrins a deep hatred of their ancestral enemies. Although at the time of Wilkinson's visit there was a truce, raiding across the border with Turkish Herzegovina was common. Wilkinson was appalled at the brutality of the conflict, especially at the Montenegrins' custom of decapitating Turks, whether taken alive or found dead. He became convinced that it was this custom, more than anything else, that perpetuated the conflict between the Montenegrins and the Turks, for while both could accept death in battle with fatalism, decapitation and the display of the trophy head was an insult requiring revenge. When he was granted an interview with the vladika, the leader of the Montenegrins, he took the opportunity to protest against decapitation and the evil results that he thought proceeded from it. The vladika seemed to agree, but added that if he were the first to propose that decapitation cease, then the Turks would surely interpret it as a sign of fear. "Our making any propositions of the kind," the vladika concluded, "would almost be tantamount to an invitation to invade our territory; and I must continue to regret, what I cannot venture, for our own security, to discontinue." Wilkinson was impressed by this reply: "I could not but confess that he was perfectly right in his estimation of the Turkish character, which long and painful experience has taught his countrymen to understand; I acknowledged the impossibility of doing this, unaided by some intermediary advocate; and I determined within myself, if I ever went into any of the Osmanli provinces, to leave no means untried, to make the Turks sensible of the injurious tendency of this odious practice."[75]

Such an opportunity soon presented itself, for after returning to Split, Wilkinson was again sailing to Kotor when he happened to meet General Turzsky, the governor of Dalmatia, aboard the same vessel. He explained his desire to pass into the Turkish land of Herzegovina, and the governor readily gave him permission. The necessary approval of the vizier of Herzegovina also was obtained, and Wilkinson set out for Mostar, the Herzegovinan capital. Traveling through the countryside, he noticed that most of the peasants were Christians, though the landlords all were Turks. He also saw many signs of agricultural neglect and concluded that the decline of Turkish power in Europe was evident. At Mostar he found much of interest, especially the famous arched bridge over the Neretva for which the town is named (mostar means "old bridge" in Serbo-Croatian). The vizier granted him an audience and Wilkinson quickly touched upon his favorite topic by urging him to discontinue the atrocity of decapitation. "And can you not distinguish men, who are brave in war," Wilkinson argued, "without requiring from them a human head, to prove their valour in battle? We had, in past times, many a battle with the French; but neither people found it necessary to make their heroes bring back a head, as proof of courage; and yet we rewarded those who were brave, quite as effectually as the Montenegrins, or the Turks; and the truly brave are always the most humane."[76] If the vizier was insulted by this rather condescending speech, he gave no sign. Quite likely he, as well as the vladika, was aware that Wilkinson, though a person of no diplomatic significance, was a well-known travel writer who might be induced to write favorably about him and his land. It cost the vizier little to humor Wilkinson, and some good might come of doing so. Accordingly, he made a general assurance of his willingness to make a pacific effort, despite the Montenegrins' outrageous behavior in the past. Wilkinson departed Mostar convinced that he was really going to accomplish something in this regard.

Despite his naïveté in the matter of decapitation, some of Wilkinson's other experiences in Dalmatia, Montenegro, and Herzegovina show that he had attained at least a limited ability to transcend his own cultural limitations. For example, at Mostar he met a Turk from Baghdad with whom he could talk in Arabic. Together they had long conversations about the East. Wilkinson later reflected,

This is one of the many instances I have known, of the advantage of some Eastern language, in making friends with, or at least overcoming the prejudices of, Moslems; and much may often be done to conciliate them, by attending to some of those peculiarities, to which they attach great importance. On the other hand, very little suffices to have a contrary effect; to take, or offer, any thing with the left hand would offend one, who had the kindest intentions; and their customs, and their life, are made up of trifles, as with other people; who are often less ready to admit it than Orientals.

One of the great reasons for their dislike of Franks is the difference of our habits; and the prejudices they have fostered against us, for imaginary faults, of which we are not guilty, often arise from want of inquiry, or from perversion of facts. Idle tales are repeated from one to another, and implicitly believed; and the sight of the Frank calls up a bitterness against him, which they indulge, by relating to each other his supposed odious customs; among which, the most common is his total disregard of all cleanly habits. I was therefore much amused by their embarrassment at Mostar, where an Englishman had never before been seen, respecting the quantity of water I required for my ablutions. I was asked if I was not in reality a Moslem; and on my assuring them, that I merely followed a custom common to my compatriots, I was evidently thought to be availing myself of a traveller's privilege; and they seemed rather inclined to suppose I had acquired those habits, from a long sojourn on the Nile, than that any race of Europeans could have adopted them, without being indebted to the precepts of Islám.[77]

But Wilkinson's transcendence had its limits, limits that are perhaps clearest in his attitude toward the Turks. At one point he reflected,

That the Turks have not at heart the real feelings of civilisation is possible; they never had any inclination toward them; they came into Europe as a horde, they became great as a horde, they remained as a horde; and they are the only instance of a nation that has reached the zenith of its power, and fallen again, without ever having become civilised. But now they are imitating our habits, and we ought therefore to avail ourselves of their readiness to adopt them, whenever the objects of humanity can be advanced; and even though the Vizier may be *naturally* cruel, "as in the time of Osman and Bajazet," a desirable result will be obtained, if he is persuaded to *conform* to the customs of civilisation.[78]

The most improvement that he expected from the Turks, therefore, was that they might be induced to imitate, without really incorporating, the ways of the West.

After his visit to Herzegovina, Wilkinson passed back through Montenegro to Split and resumed his Mediterranean travels. Still thinking his intervention between the Turks and the Montenegrins might be effective, he tried to use his contacts to obtain diplomatic assistance for his efforts. By the time he reached Malta in the spring of 1845, however, he had fewer illusions about his prospects. He wrote to a friend,

I expect to be in England—June—unless they want me to go again to Montenegro to arrange matters between the Montenegrins & Turks which if necessary I have promised to do. When I wrote to you about it I wanted to excite an interest about it in England in order that the Government might be induced to assist me with its sanction & enable me to talk to the parties with more authority—but I am happy to say I do not require it now & hope to have it from another quarter, & that too quickly without exciting the observation or suspicions of other people. So instead of saying anything about it—I wish rather on the contrary now that it should not be mentioned.[79]

Before returning to England he sailed to Sicily, where he saw all the ruins he could find, covering some five hundred miles on horseback during his stay there. "They [the ruins of Sicily] fully confirm all I have said & thought of the early use of the pointed arch. I only hope to find something more about it in the Dominions of the Fatemites of Africa," Wilkinson wrote.[80] That opportunity came shortly afterward on Malta, where he met the master of HMS *Beacon*, who offered Wilkinson passage on his vessel to Tunis, near the site of ancient Carthage.

Wilkinson did not tarry in Tunis, but made his way some seventy miles south to the town of Kairouan. Kairouan, then little more than an isolated market town, had once been the base for the Muslim conquest of the Magreb and later became the capital of the Aghlabid, Fatimid, and Zirid dynasties. It developed into one of the great cultural centers of Islam, and just outside of town was a *zawiyah*, or religious college, where a Companion of the Prophet was buried. The most splendid building of Kairouan was the Great Mosque, dating from the eighth century, one of the best-preserved examples of an Arab hypostyle mosque. Wilkinson's visit to the town, therefore, was an extraordinary opportunity. According to his calculations, he was only the third Christian to "lodge within its precincts." Unfortunately, he was primarily interested in pursuing his ideas about the pointed arch.

Wilkinson called upon the regional governor, but soon went out to see the sights and make sketches. "On leaving the governor's house, I was warned to be very prudent, and not to excite attention by attempting to draw or write while any one was in sight, particularly while going near the mosques. I took care, therefore, whenever I ventured to make any memoranda, to do so under the cover of my capacious *bornoos*."[81] Wilkinson should not have needed the warning to be careful. He had frequently sketched in mosques in Cairo while pretending to pray, hiding his sketchbook in his robe,[82] and he undoubtedly knew how Frederick Catherwood had nearly been killed when he was caught sketching in the Dome of the Rock at Jerusalem. Experienced travelers know that note taking and sketching were regarded with deep suspicion in the Islamic world. Wilkinson accordingly proceeded cautiously, making occasional surreptitious notes inside the folds of his garment. Soon he came to the Great Mosque where the eastern gateway was spanned by a particularly interesting pointed arch. Looking around and seeing no one, Wilkinson began to sketch it. Several men who were standing just inside the gateway saw him thus impiously engaged and angrily came out to confront him. The situation was dangerous, potentially fatal, but Wilkinson saved himself by a quick thought.

It was too late to stop and affect innocence; my offense was too evident; therefore, without waiting for the outburst of their indignation, I advanced to meet them, and, after the usual salutations, told them I had come from Cairo, where the learned declared that the Egyptians had invented the pointed arch, but that as the

Foátem princes went from Kairawán to Musr-el-Káhirah (Cairo), and used the pointed arch at that time in their buildings, there was a possibility of it having been employed long before at Kairawán, and I was anxious to know if they could produce any proofs of a prior claim. This so disarmed their prejudices that, with a view of maintaining the claims of their city, they took me to every pointed arch in the place, except, of course, in the interior of the mosques; and, though disappointed in my hopes of meeting with some of great or well defined antiquity, I was enabled to see the one already mentioned, and to copy the Cufic inscription at the city gate, as well as to make other observations, and even hasty sketches of the buildings themselves.[83]

He wanted to spend more time at Kairouan and visit its suburbs, but his time was short, for he had to return to the *Beacon* before it sailed. His infatuation with the pointed arch had at least saved him from harm.[84]

When Wilkinson returned to England toward the end of 1845, he remained for three years. He was not sedentary, however, spending his time visiting first one friend or acquaintance and then another. The first edition of the *Handbook for Travellers in Egypt* appeared in 1847, and another edition of *Manners and Customs of the Ancient Egyptians* was published that same year. His primary literary task, which must have been a difficult one, was to write up his experiences in Dalmatia, Montenegro, and Herzegovina. The result, however, was a good travelogue, equal to some of the best of that popular nineteenth-century genre. He took a wealth of supplemental information and skillfully wove it onto the narrative warp of his journey. He also attached numerous historical digressions without losing his narrative thread. Some of these are quite good, especially the one about the Paulician heresy. A negative aspect is the fact that the book's visual imagery is flat; for example, "the ruins of Salona; and the first view of Clissa, backed by the sea and the Isle of Brazza, is very imposing."[85] This difficulty is, however, remedied to some degree by the illustrations. Commercial and political information abounds, including some observations of a specifically strategic nature. The finished product, entitled *Dalmatia and Montenegro: With a Journey to Mostar in Herzegovina*, was, therefore, an important contribution to understanding a part of Europe that was being viewed with increasing speculation and apprehension. That is clear from the fact that the book was promptly translated into German.[86] Because of its rich social and historical detail, it has been an important source for succeeding generations of scholars of that little-studied region. *Dalmatia and Montenegro* came out in 1848. Late that September Wilkinson was on his way to Egypt again.

Though he spent only the winter of 1848–49 in Egypt and Nubia, Wilkinson kept quite busy during that time. There was also much more Egyptological activity on this occasion than on the two previous trips. He filled the pages of his notebooks with hieroglyphic transcription and architectural sketches. He now took the opportunity that he had been denied on the 1841–42 visit to sail far upstream, which he did in the company of Mr. and Mrs. Burr. In a letter to the Royal Society of Literature he called the trip "a short & hurried journey," but his notes show the astonishing amount of observation that he could record within a limited time.[87] He sailed past Abu Simbel to the Second Cataract and stopped at Semna, which he had visited with Wiggett seventeen years earlier. With a much more informed eye he now examined the frontier fortifications of ancient Egypt, an essential task for the book on Egyptian architecture that he had been considering for some time. His inspection of the fortifications convinced him that they had been intended as defenses against the Ethiopians, not as a refuge from the Shepherd People as some had hypothesized.

He continued south through Dongola on his farthest penetration into Africa, reaching Gebel Berkel, with its extensive ruins of temple complexes and pyramidal tombs of the ancient Kings of Kush. This place, which he considered part of Ethiopia, is located in the present-day Sudan, some miles downstream from Khartoum in the great bend of the Nile. Only a half dozen Europeans had visited and documented it in modern times. Wilkinson's notebooks from the trip are a good mixture of illustrations and text, with some attention to antiquities but most to contemporary observation. At one point he noted, "The girls here have the same broad hips as of old in Eg^n paintings," and included a piquant illustrative sketch.[88] On the return trip he stopped for a fortnight at Thebes and opened some chambers with his traveling companions at the temple of Medinet Habu.[89]

He subsequently published an article based on this journey in the *Journal of the Royal Geographical Society.*[90] In this case, however, as in so many others, the article drew upon only a fraction of his material. He had enough to fill a volume of travel memoirs, had he wished. In fact, he made a promising draft, clearly written with high-quality illustrations to accompany it.[91] Perhaps the area failed to impress him enough to edit the manuscript into publishable condition. He wrote to a friend, "I . . . told you of my journey in Ethiopia which on the whole pleased me though I advise no one to take the trouble of going into that country. Dongola is monotonous in the extreme."⁹² Whatever may have been the reason for not making more use of his material, this is another example of the untapped richness that lies in the Wilkinson manuscripts.

On his way back to England, Wilkinson spent a year in Italy and Switzerland, writing, traveling, and doing an occasional piece of scholarly work. Of the last, the most notable project was his examination of the Turin Papyrus. This important papyrus, which had deteriorated into many fragments, had been examined and published several times, but never adequately. Champollion had repeatedly examined the fragments, but Gustavus Seyffarth, an adversary of Champollion's, later came and found some fragments that Champollion had missed and then joined them all together in a haphazard way. Richard Lepsius thereafter made yet another survey of the papyrus, but ignored the inscriptions on the reverse side and failed to indicate where the breaks were.⁹³ Wilkinson's task was clear: "The great point," he wrote,

> was to ascertain, for certain, which of the fragments had been properly joined; and in order to facilitate this, it was necessary that a fac-simile should be made of all of them, with their exact outlines, which was accordingly done by Dr. Lepsius, and published in his *Auswahl;* but as both sides of the papyrus bore an inscription, it was equally important for the arrangement of the parts that both sides should be copied and made public; and it is in order to supply the omission of the inscription at the back that the present copy of the papyrus has been made.⁹⁴

Wilkinson's worst fear was that the keepers of the papyrus in the museum at Turin might deny him access to it, and he accordingly sought letters of introduction from every influential quarter.⁹⁵ His apprehension was based on charges that the museum had withheld from Champollion the fragments of the papyrus that he had missed. These charges the director of the museum denied, and the assistance that he and his assistant provided convinced Wilkinson that he was telling the truth.⁹⁶ He made a thorough examination of the Turin Papyrus and published his results two years later, aided by consultation with the Reverend Edward Hincks.

After finishing with the Turin Papyrus, Wilkinson spent the winter of 1849–50 meandering through northern Italy, studying Etruscan inscriptions and ruins and making a vain effort to decipher the Etruscan alphabet.⁹⁷ Before settling in Lucerne the following summer, he had completed and mailed several manuscripts, including an account of ancient Egyptian fortifications to the Royal Society of Literature, some notes on architecture to the Royal Institute of British Architects, and the brief account of the geology of Ethiopia to the Royal Geographical Society.[98] "I wished to find out some thing for the Arch[l] Association, but I knew of nothing that would do—Egyptian antiquities are rather out of the way. I am now going to set hard at work on my Eg[n] architecture."[99]

Before the end of 1850 Wilkinson was in England again. That return marked the end of a phase of his life. Although he continued to move about frequently, especially within England, he never again traveled as relentlessly as he did during the 1840s.

CHAPTER TWELVE

A Gentleman Scholar

A CALLER at Sir Gardner's London residence in the 1850s would have been ushered by his housekeeper into the presence of a slender gentleman of medium height and weight, for despite frequent illnesses, Wilkinson kept himself physically fit with his long walks. Now in his mid-fifties, he was quite bald on top, though he wore thick muttonchop whiskers down his cheeks and sported a drooping mustache, a relic, perhaps, of bygone Egyptian days. The caller also would have found Sir Gardner fastidiously dressed, for his sartorial elegance was legendary. A few years before, when Joseph Bonomi encountered Wilkinson abroad, he wrote home, "We have got Wilkinson down here with an immense variety of waistcoats, some of them very distinguished ones too."[1] And when Samuel Sharpe was beginning his career in Egyptology and worrying if he could succeed, his uncle told him, "Why! Surely you can do it if Wilkinson can; his only thought is where to buy his kid gloves!"[2]

But quite possibly the caller would not have found Wilkinson at home, for now more than ever, his life had become a succession of lengthy visits at one country house after another. The names and pictures of many of them are preserved on the headings of his letters or in the pages of his sketchbooks—Maple Durham, Aldermaston, Brooklands, Kiplin Hall, Wiltersley Towers, and especially Calke Abbey, the seat of his cousins the Harpur-Crewes, a magnificent estate set in a remote corner of Derbyshire.[3] Occasionally he journeyed up to the isolated majesty of Alnwick Castle in Northumberland where he could recall old times with his former companion in Egypt, Lord Prudhoe. He spent so much time in the castle's museum that Lord and Lady Prudhoe began calling him "the curator of the Alnwick Museum."[4] Whenever he had no invitation, he pined for one: "It is dreadfully dull being alone, except in the Desert & there I enjoy solitude," he wrote to his friend Augusta Ada Lovelace, Lord Byron's daughter.[5] Indeed, he actively, sometimes shamelessly, solicited invitations. In another letter to Lady Lovelace, he said he had had no reply to a letter to her husband, the Earl of Lovelace, and added, "As I leave this [place] today & cannot remain in Town— where the pavement lames me—I am under the necessity of accepting some other invitations in the country. . . . Had you been at Ashley Combe I would have put off Yorkshire notwithstanding the cold—but that not being the case & as I am obliged to send answers to the invitations I have received & cannot stop in Town I have accepted them."[6] His tone leaves little doubt that had Lady Lovelace even then condescended to invite him, he would have accepted, regardless of other commitments.

Lady Lovelace was one of his favorite friends. He must have been flattered to be associated with the daughter of the poet he had most admired in his youth. For her part, Lady Lovelace seems not quite to have accepted him as an equal. This shows in an incident when her mother, Lady Byron, a great believer in phrenology, persuaded her to consult a practitioner. She, Lord Lovelace, and Wilkinson went to see one, but without revealing their identities. Ada later wrote, "It was very clear that he thought *much* the most highly of Sir G. Wilkinson, amongst the three." Her tone suggested that placing a mere scholar like Wilkinson above her and her husband was in itself enough to discredit phrenology.[7] Her affection for him was genuine, however. When she lay dying of cancer of the womb in 1852, one of her desires was to see him again.[8] Her mother cruelly denied her painkillers that would have alleviated her suffering, but Wilkinson told her to try cannabis, which at least helped her sleep.[9]

Another of Wilkinson's social outlets was correspondence. Even by Victorian standards he wrote many letters, so many that they must have taken a large portion of his day. He corresponded with a wide variety of people. The topics were sometimes scholarly matters, but also everyday things—health, who was doing what, and so on. Among his most frequent scholarly correspondents were the antiquarian Anthony Cumby; the Italian professor Francesco Carrara, with whom he discussed excavations in Dalmatia; and Count Valerian Krasinski. Much of his correspondence about Egyptological matters was with Thomas Joseph Pettigrew and Reginald Stuart Poole. Pettigrew was a physician and an accomplished amateur Egyptologist. Poole, who was Edward William Lane's nephew, was keeper of coins and medals at the British Museum. He was also an enthusiastic Egyptologist who did such services for Wilkinson as keeping him abreast of Lepsius's work.

One of his most colorful correspondents was Charles Babbage, Lucasian Professor of Mathematics at Cambridge, one of the notable eccentric geniuses of Victorian England. Babbage, who had been acquainted with Sir William Gell,[10] was also the author of an influential book, *Réflections on the Decline of Science in England, and Some of Its Causes.* A gifted mathematician, he devoted much of his life to the creation of a programmable calculating machine that could store data, a precursor of the modern computer. It never quite worked, though his idea was sound, and his friend Lady Lovelace devised a way to program it. It was most likely Babbage who introduced Lady Lovelace to Wilkinson. Wilkinson enjoyed keeping abreast of what he called Babbage's "numerous & interesting occupations."[11]

To most of his old friends from the 1820s and 1830s Wilkinson wrote only occasionally. There were a few exchanges with Bonomi, and Wilkinson and Lord Prudhoe kept in touch by mail between Wilkinson's periodic visits to Alnwick Castle. With Edward William Lane, however, he corresponded fairly frequently. The two men continued to call each other Mansoor and Isma'eel as they had done in Egypt. Their friendship seemed to grow and ripen with time. Wilkinson's handwriting was as bad as ever, perhaps worse. Hekekyan Bey struggled with one of his letters and wrote of the experience to a friend, "I think I have deciphered it—at least that part of it which concerns the arch in question."[12]

The 1850s were a period of varied and productive literary activity for Wilkinson. His first book of the decade was *The Architecture of the Ancient Egyptians,* a book he had considered writing for years. When it became clear that Robert Hay would never publish his book on the subject, Wilkinson was prompted by anxiety that some Frenchman or German might do it first, thereby robbing the English of the credit for their extensive labors in Egypt in the 1820s and 1830s.[13] He accordingly hurried his pace, completing the manuscript and plates in 1850. But when he went to John Murray, he received a skeptical reception, for the publisher considered the book a bad risk. It would be big and heavily illustrated, expensive to produce, but without the general appeal of Wilkinson's earlier books. Despite what Wilkinson described as "a very liberal offer to Murray respecting it," Murray was not interested.[14] Other publishers also rejected it. Wilkinson decided to publish it by subscription. Developed in the last half of the eighteenth century, publication by subscription was in some ways a throwback to patronage, relying as it did upon prior commitments by interested parties. "My object," he wrote to Lady Lovelace, "is to do this before it is brought out by some foreigner & I want it to be done in England—if I can get back the money it costs me I shall be pleased, if not I hope not to be a great loser & shall be satisfied with the recovery of a portion of it."[15] He told Lady Lovelace to urge all of her friends to subscribe. The partial list of subscribers in the prospectus included Wilkinson's friends, relatives, his colleagues from Egypt—and even John Murray who, though unwilling to bear the financial risk of publishing the book, at least subscribed for a copy of it.[16]

Wilkinson's approach to ancient Egyptian architecture was both utilitarian and antiquarian. He performed a function for Victorian architecture similar to what his mentor, Sir William Gell (whom he remembered in his Introduction) had done for the classical style: he supplied detailed information that architects and builders could use with confidence. Of course, the range of Wilkinson's influence was not nearly so great as Gell's, for Victorian architecture was not so pure a revival of any one architectural ideal as neoclassicism had been. Instead, the Victorians reacted deliberately against the architecture of Georgian England, which they considered dull and unimaginative. Once the Battle of Styles had been fought, eclecticism prevailed, though some specialization was permitted. Occasionally a purely Egyptian edifice might be constructed, such as John Marshall's flax mill in Leeds. Its façade was a replica of the temple of Edfu, and even its smokestack was disguised as an obelisk.[17] More frequently, however, Egyptian motifs were used to ornament buildings predominantly composed of other styles. Hence one may walk about London and glimpse a hieroglyph or sphinx on a corner of one building and fluted Egyptian column pretending to support the façade of another. This mixture of styles, incidentally, was not something of which Wilkinson necessarily approved. He also worried about accurate reproduction of Egyptian architectural forms, a concern that surfaced some years later when Joseph Bonomi wrote to ask his advice about an obelisk-shaped design that was being considered for Prince Albert's memorial.[18] Wilkinson replied that his worst fear was "that they will make a pistachio of the obelisk."[19] As will be seen, Wilkinson had even stronger ideas about obelisks. His goal in The Architecture of the Ancient Egyptians was to present the architectural ideas of ancient Egypt tastefully and accurately.

Ancient Egyptian architecture would have been the subject of Robert Hay's second book had he persevered with his publishing ambitions, but when Bonomi approached him with the idea, Hay rebuffed it. "With regard to Publishing Egyptian Architecture: having burnt my fingers in the first attempt I by no means feel disposed to 'try again'.—if there was a fair prospect of such a Work succeeding— wh. I very much doubt—I might be induced to find the drawings if some one else would find the money!"[20] Later, when Bonomi informed Hay of the impending publication of Wilkinson's book, Hay replied even more bitterly:

> I am *rather* entertained with yr. saying, Wilkinson is abt. to do that wh *I* ought to have accomplished; having all the materials in my portfolio for years.—The latter part is but too true!—But, who's fault is it?—Certainly not mine!
>   I tried the public with what I thought wd. please most,—the Picturesque—intending, if they *paid* to proceed and make them Masters of the *whole* subject, to the best of my abilities. —In the attempt to *enlighten* their dark understandings I let *slip* more than £2,000, and if £400 found its way *back*, it is *abt.* the utmost!—After that, no great wonder that my 'materials' should feel somewhat drowsy?[21]

Although Wilkinson did a careful job, it is much to be regretted that Hay never published, for the drawings in his portfolio are magnificent.

In 1854 Wilkinson published an abridged edition of *Manners and Customs of the Ancient Egyptians* entitled *A Popular Account of the Ancient Egyptians.* That was followed by *The Egyptians in the Time of the Pharaohs; Being a Companion to the Crystal Palace Egyptian Collections.* Although he emphasized that it contained new material, this book was mostly made up of items left over from the composition of *Manners and Customs of the Ancient Egyptians.* It did, however, apply some new research, such as that from his explorations of European museums. The occasion of the book, the Great Exposition of 1851 and the subsequent establishment of the Crystal Palace at Sydenham, brought Wilkinson's cautious approval. "The exposition will probably do some good," he wrote to Lady Lovelace, "though I confess it would have been more prudent to have had an exposition for home-made things first."[22] Despite his reservations, he actively participated as a juror, an exhibitor, and a frequent spectator.[23] Even more deeply involved were his former colleagues in Egypt, Owen Jones and Joseph Bonomi, who designed the popular Egyptian Court.[24]

Wilkinson's next major book of the 1850s was *On Colour.*[25] This work might be best classified among the many artists' treatises and manuals that appeared in Britain in the nineteenth century; indeed, in no nation were these so popular as in Britain, where widespread popularity of watercolor provided a ready market for artist-writers.[26] This gave him an opportunity to present and develop some of Charles Babbage's ideas on color, a subject to which Babbage had devoted much time and interest. But the predominant theme of his book was the conviction, shared by many of his countrymen in the mid-nineteenth century, that the English were sadly lacking in taste. Wilkinson even suspended his usual disparagement of all things French to conclude that the French were more advanced in taste than the English, though he thought the English condition was changing for the better.[27] Returning to England from a trip abroad in 1850, he wrote to Lady Lovelace, "I find a great change & I am glad to say an improvement in England in matters relating to taste. I hope the English will succeed at last in understanding the three things they want so much, form proportion & color."[28] This book was a conscious effort to remedy the deficiency.

On Colour is somewhat diffuse and contains some sweeping generalizations, such as, "The introduction of large quantities of green is one of the mistakes which always creeps in when society becomes artificial, and is one of the signs of a want or of a decline of taste."[29] Much of the book is hortatory, telling the British that they lacked taste and needed to acquire it. His primary argument was for a natural approach to color theory. What pleased the eye was good; all else was pedantry. Because he thought the tastes of the English were atrophied, he turned to what he considered simpler, but more genuine sources. He remembered how Henry Salt used to buy children's playthings in the streets of Cairo because he was charmed by their unsophisticated yet harmonious beauty. "Among these I remember an orange, into the surface of which they had cut a mosaic pattern, leaving the orange rind as a ground, and filling in all the triangular and other hollows with various brilliant colours; than which (comparing small things with great) nothing could be found more harmonious in the mosaics of Italy, or of Damascus, or on the walls of the Alhambra."[30]

On Colour received favorable reviews, including one by Sir David Brewster, the inventor of the kaleidoscope.[31] The most searching criticism of the book came not in public reviews but in a series of private letters to Wilkinson from John Ruskin, who had just completed some of his most productive years and had not yet begun the sad decline of the later decades of his life. He knew Wilkinson's Egyptological work well, having become interested in ancient Egyptian art and antiquities by reading *Manners and Customs of the An-*

cient Egyptians.[32] For his part, Wilkinson had previously affected a disparaging opinion of the eminent art critic, noting in his commonplace book that Ruskin had "no appreciation of Greek & other architecture," but he was clearly flattered to receive Ruskin's attention and anxious to present himself in the best light possible.

Ruskin began amiably enough, writing, "I have been much interested by your book on colour in my first glance at it. It seems to me the first statement of colour-law which has been founded on any real knowledge of the subject." From that favorable preamble, however, Ruskin proceeded to take Wilkinson to task on several points. For one thing, he was concerned about Wilkinson's imprecise and inaccurate use of some terms, especially *drawing* and *outline.* This was authoritative criticism from the man who had published *The Elements of Drawing* only the year before. Also, Ruskin was miffed that Wilkinson had cited a lesser authority on a question about Venetian art, while ignoring *The Stones of Venice.* "It is not my custom," he chided Wilkinson, "to vindicate claims of my own to priorities of statement. I am always happy to see the truth stated—by whomsoever first discovered. But you will perhaps pardon my expressing at least some surprise at your having supposed Mr. Street's blunders respecting the Doge's palace—the three-days conjecture of a person generally ignorant of archaeology—could be quoted as of any weight or value, after my investigation of the complete subject in all the accessible chronicles relating to the subject."[33]

Wilkinson agreed with Ruskin about *drawing* and *outline* and claimed that he merely "did not recall" Ruskin's work when he was writing. Other objections of Ruskin's he argued against. In his next letter, however, Ruskin probed the fundamental weakness of Wilkinson's work by writing that he could not find the principle for Wilkinson's statement that certain colors were discords: "I quite admit that the instances you have given in the plates *are* discords;— and you are the first writer on the subject who has appeared to me to know what really good and bad colour was. But you seem to me merely to declare that such and such colours are discordant without assigning a reason: and among your stated (though not among your represented) discords, are several of the associations of colour which nature most delights in—and painters also—Purple and green for instance—as in Highland heather with pine—and shadows on green sea."[34]

Wilkinson defended himself as best he could: "In stating what colours are discords I do not propose to lay down any rules[.] I prefer that we should be guided by the eye like the Arabs & others who have true perception of the harmony of color. Our ear in like manner judges of a discord in music & enables us to perceive (without any rules) whenever a false note is played. Indeed I think it better not to pretend to give the reason why some combinations are concords or discords."[35] Ruskin pressed him no further on the matter, perhaps recognizing and not wanting to disturb the amateurish delusion that analysis somehow diminishes appreciation. He did, however, firmly correct Wilkinson when the latter indicated that he thought Ruskin was going to write a review of *On Colour*: "I surely did not say I was going to write a review of your book? I never do such things now, thinking it much too saucy: But I hope some time this season to give a lecture at Kensington on conventional ornament—in which I mean to allude largely to your present work as well as to your Egypt."[36]

It was probably best for Wilkinson that Ruskin did not review the book, because some of Ruskin's incisive criticisms could have hurt. As it was, the correspondence concluded on a friendly note with Ruskin inviting Wilkinson to visit him and see a thirteenth-century psalter that was notable for its solemn purples. "And with this—and a Turner and a Sir Joshua—side by side—I think we might come to some *modus vivendi* which would prevent our puzzling the public by making statements in different senses."[37]

Another work, one that does not bear Wilkinson's name but to which he contributed much effort and expertise, was a new English edition of Herodotus by George Rawlinson. Rawlinson relied heavily upon Wilkinson for the preparation of the Egyptian sections, just as he relied upon his brother Sir Henry Rawlinson to help with the Persian passages. All of the copious notes for the Egyptian references were written by Wilkinson, and he helped in other ways. The opportunity to return to Herodotus, and through Herodotus to Egypt, must have been pleasant for Wilkinson. Herodotus and Wilkinson were similar in that both were curious about the past, fond of travel, and interested in the manners and customs of people different from themselves.

Wilkinson's name has also been linked peripherally to Sir Richard Burton's *Personal Narrative of a Pilgrimage to Al-Madinah and Meccah*. In the introduction to the third edition of this classic, published after Wilkinson and Burton both were dead, Edward William Lane's grand-nephew Stanley Lane-Poole wrote how the inclusion of "anthropological"—by which he meant sexual—data in Burton's translation of the *Arabian Nights* restricted the circulation of that work. Lane-Poole went on to say, "It seems that the Pilgrimage to Mekka itself was only saved from the top shelf by the absence of its author from England; for Sir Gardner Wilkinson, to whom the manuscript was entrusted, remarked that the amount of unpleasant garbage which he took upon himself to reject would have rendered the book unfit for publication."[38] The assertion that Wilkinson took it upon himself to delete such material from Burton's manuscript has been repeated in biographies of Burton published in this century.[39] Although it probably would have been in character for Wilkinson to have exercised such a censorial function, positive evidence that he did does not appear in his papers. Though Burton did not edit his manuscript himself, choosing to make an expedition to Harar rather than return to London and attend to publication, he sent the manuscript not to Wilkinson but to the Rev. L. Wolley, whose name appears at the bottom of the introduction to the first edition. Wilkinson did edit the article that Burton wrote about his expedition for the *Journal of the Royal Geographical Society*, but this was a separate work.[40] In other correspondence where he mentions Burton's *Personal Narrative* Wilkinson seems detached and only marginally involved. To the secretary of the Royal Geographical Society he wrote, "You know I suppose that Lt. Burton is publishing his 'Pilgrimage to Medina & Mecca'—It is in the press—Longman the publisher. A friend of his a clergyman is correcting the proofs. He is staying at Torquay & has sent me some of the proof sheets to look at."[41] And in another letter he also mentioned Burton's book: "I cannot get you a copy of the Burton proofs as one only is sent me from the Editor & I have to return it immediately by post."[42] It is possible, however, that Lane-Poole had access to information that does not appear in Wilkinson's correspondence or that Wilkinson suggested deletions that Rev. Wolley incorporated.

Expurgation of material was quite common during these years when books that now seem above reproach were deemed in need of tasteful excisions. Even Herodotus had felt the scissors, for in Rawlinson's edition of the historian, Rawlinson explained, "Occasional passages offensive to modern delicacy have been retrenched, and others have been modified by the alteration of a few phrases."[43] And Edward William Lane, in his translation of the *Arabian Nights*, had omitted explicit sexual passages. Burton, of course, took care to leave them in his translation of the Arabic classic, and may indeed have used material that was expurgated from his *Personal Narrative*. Stanley Lane-Poole, who heartily approved of the excisions from Burton's *Personal Narrative*, even felt compelled to edit out passages in a new edition of Jonathan Swift that he prepared. Lane-Poole wrote, "For often his [Swift's] best writings are defaced by a coarse mess of illustration, which though it may find its parallel in the literature of the age can hardly be excused, and certainly not be tolerated in a book for general reading."[44] This sensibility helps to explain, if not excuse, such actions as Lady Burton's burning of most of her husband's papers after his death—and, on a smaller scale, the heavy marks that someone, perhaps Lady Wilkinson, inflicted upon passages in Wilkinson's notebooks.

Because of his status as a well-known figure in scholarly society, Wilkinson's opinion was much sought after on issues of the day. One such instance was the Rawlinson-Hincks translation controversy. This arose from the progress that was being made in the translation of cuneiform, the wedge-shaped script of ancient Mesopotamia. By the 1850s, scholars like Sir Henry Rawlinson, Fox Talbot, Edward Hincks, and Jules Oppert were able to read running cuneiform texts. This accomplishment, however, was doubted by many, so it was resolved to put the matter to a test under the auspices of the Royal Asiatic Society. Oppert, Talbot, Rawlinson, and Hincks would separately be given a cuneiform text to translate as best they could. The committee appointed to judge the results consisted of the dean of St. Paul's, Dr. Henry Hart Milman, who served as chairman; Dr. William Whewell, master of Trinity College, Cambridge; William Cureton, a Syriac scholar from the British Museum; George Grote, the renowned Greek historian; Professor Horace Hayman Wilson; and Wilkinson.[45]

The insight that Wilkinson had gained from observing the controversy about Champollion and Young in the decipherment of Egyptian hieroglyphs made him well qualified to serve on such a committee. He knew little about cuneiform, though he had copied some "arrow-headed" inscriptions during his travels. But the committee members needed no such knowledge. They had only to examine the participants' efforts and see if they agreed sufficiently to establish that translations were in fact being made. A text from a prism of Tiglath Pileser I was chosen for the test. When the results were compared, Wilkinson and his colleagues found no significant difference between them and announced their favorable opinion. In his individual report Wilkinson wrote that the translations were often "word for word" the same and that even the areas of uncertainty were similar. He concluded, "The similarity in the different translations is quite equal to what it would be in the translation of an ordinary historical inscription written in Egyptian hieroglyphics made by the same number of persons who, as in this case, gave it quite independently of & without any communication with each other,—And this comparison I am disposed to make as it is the most analogous case that I can suggest."[46]

Wilkinson also was drawn into the debate over Cleopatra's Needle, the popular name for the hieroglyph-covered obelisk in Alexandria that was described in an earlier chapter. It and a companion obelisk had been transported by the emperor Augustus from Luxor to Alexandria where they were erected, though one of them subsequently fell on its side. The obelisks were objects of interest to travelers over the centuries, and they were one of the first sights that Wilkinson saw in Egypt. Shortly after expelling the French from Egypt, the British commander obtained permission from the Turkish authorities to remove the fallen obelisk to London as a memento of the expedition; but the government was unenthusiastic about the idea, so nothing was done. The matter later came to the attention of King George IV who ordered the Foreign Office to consider it, but Parliament never voted funds for removal. Occasionally Muhammad Ali, and, later, Khedive Ismail, reminded the British government that the obelisk was there for the taking, but it was difficult and expensive to transport an obelisk. The government did not want it anyway.

As time passed, however, public interest in the obelisk grew. The prince consort became concerned when he heard that the French might carry the obelisk to Paris. He wrote to Lord John Russell and asked him to take action to have the obelisk brought to London. It would be, he said, a national disgrace if the French got it first. At about the same time, questions about the obelisk began to be asked in Parliament, particularly by such radical members as Joseph Hume, whose repeated urgings at last moved the government to action. An estimate was prepared in 1849, concluding that the cost of transporting the obelisk from Alexandria to London would be £15,000. Hume was then informed that the government had decided positively to bring the obelisk over. But at that moment, Wilkinson and a small group of classical scholars intervened and argued against bringing it to England. The obelisk was, they claimed, a poor specimen and not worth the trouble or expense. As one historian of the matter comments, "this was a rebuff indeed, from an unexpected quarter." Governments of those days listened readily to expert opinion, and no one's opinion in matters Egyptological carried more weight with the public than Wilkinson's. His opposition was sufficient to kill the enterprise. He later wrote with satisfaction, "The project has been wisely abandoned; and cooler deliberation has pronounced that, from its mutilated state, and the obliteration of many of the hieroglyphs by exposure to the sea air, it is unworthy the expense of removal."[47]

It is difficult today to see how the monument's condition could arouse such opposition. Though somewhat worn, especially near the base, almost all of the hieroglyphs are legible, and most are quite clear, except the ones near the top where pigeon droppings, not permanent wear, obscure them. Perhaps the obelisk was not as sharp as some that Wilkinson had seen at Thebes, and indeed Robert Hay considered it so inferior to the one that the French had taken from Luxor Temple that it would be a national disgrace to acquire it.[48] But it seems that Wilkinson's feelings about obelisks were based upon even deeper convictions. A few years later in answer to an inquiry from Samuel Birch, an Egyptologist at the British Museum, Wilkinson declared, "I do think it is a great mistake bringing obelisks to this country. We have no idea of the meaning of an obelisk [and] we have no association of ideas connected with it. & we (& other Europeans) always place them in a position ill suited to them. The two standing at the end of an avenue leading to a temple were very effective, contrasted with the long horizontal line of the cornice, but a simple obelisk is without meaning & out of place."[49] The obelisk remained on its side in Alexandria until a few years after Wilkinson's death when it was learned that a Greek landowner intended to cut it up for building stone. Under the leadership of a wealthy businessman named Erasmus Wilson, the obelisk was finally brought to London by private initiative and placed upon the Victoria Embankment, where it now stands.[50]

Among the possible reasons for Wilkinson's opposition to the removal should not be included a general aversion to taking Egyptian monuments from their native soil, for he had lobbied extensively in the 1830s for the removal of the Mit Rahina colossus. Nor had his opinion changed over the years, for he wrote to Samuel Birch in 1865 that he still considered the colossus worth having.[51] It is ironic how things worked out. In the one instance, Wilkinson urged that the obelisk not be brought to England, but it was; and in the other, despite all his efforts to have the colossus moved to England, it was not. Each case probably worked out for the best. The obelisk was definitely endangered in Egypt, prey to vandals and souvenir seekers.[52] The statue of Ramses, on the other hand, is quite well off in its museum in Egypt.

Wilkinson's renown could occasionally take a turn for the ridiculous, as it did in 1852 when he found himself involved, without his permission, in the promotion of some fraudulent Egyptian peas that were alleged to have superior qualities.[53] Annoyed as he was by that episode, he was much more disturbed when he read a passage in Harriet Martineau's new book, *Eastern Life*, an account of her trip to Egypt and the East. A convert to atheism who had the zeal that converts often do, Miss Martineau thought she had found a target in Wilkinson. At Beni Hasan she had seen a mural that many had speculated was a procession of Israelites, perhaps even Joseph's brothers, bearing offerings. She detected a detail that she thought disproved that notion. She wrote,

> The offerings brought are not like what the sons of Jacob would have to give. After a wild goat and gazelle, come a handsome present of ostriches;—quite a flock of them, and the procession closes with a red man who carries an ibis.—Now it is curious that no account that I have met with of this celebrated procession has mentioned the ostriches; which are precisely the gift of the whole set which Joseph's brethren could not have brought [ostriches, she believed, not being found in Syria]. And there is no pretence that we could see for stopping short at the ostriches, which join on to the rest of the procession without any interval, and, with the man carrying the ibis, finish the subject. What shall we say to this omission? [54]

The answer to Martineau's rhetorical question was that writers had suppressed the ostriches in order to accord with the biblical account. Although she did not mention him by name, Wilkinson was convinced that she especially meant him because of her many other references to his work. Martineau's accusations stung because they impugned his scholarly integrity, suggesting that he had knowingly omitted pertinent facts. He wrote to his friend Pettigrew to complain, "She severely censures me (at least I suppose so) for an intentional omission of the ostriches in the representation of the 'strangers' at Beni Hasan. . . . For my own part I can only say that the omission was quite accidental & that it matters not at all. As to the 'strangers' being Israelites (which by the bye I do not maintain they were) my remark was only if they proved to be so that they could be looked upon with additional interest." Furthermore, he continued, ostriches used to live in Syria, and only recently had been driven south by firearms. [55]

Examining Martineau's book closely, Wilkinson found several faults with it. He was repelled by her credulous treatment of mesmerism, then much in vogue, and did not believe her story about how her hearing—she was almost entirely deaf—had mysteriously improved atop the Great Pyramid: "How curious it is that those who are great skeptics are sure to believe something ten times more extravagant than what they reject." [56] Even so, Wilkinson liked much of the book, perhaps because of the lavish compliment she paid him in its introduction, and he wanted to persuade instead of confront.

To that end he sought Pettigrew's aid. Pettigrew accordingly supplied Wilkinson with her address and wrote to her himself. In a letter that was subsequently forwarded to Wilkinson, Martineau replied that she had had no intention to cast doubt upon his honesty and that she would change the wording in the next edition so that no negative inferences could be drawn. On the bottom of this letter in Wilkinson's (or Lady Wilkinson's) hand is the note: "When Sir Gardner Wilkinson returned to Egypt after reading Miss Martineau's reproaches against Egyptologists who had not observed the 'ostriches' which she supposed she had seen in a temple he examined the painting in question & found they were *cranes*."[57] Wilkinson also sent some tracings from Beni Hasan to Miss Martineau "to show that they [were] not ostriches but wading birds."[58] Wilkinson's letter was conciliatory, because Martineau's reply was friendly. She was glad, she wrote, "to find that you acquit me of any charge against you in the matter—I will look well to the wording of the passage in the next edition & I will then avail myself of your remarks about the ostriches in such a way as may do you most justice. I have to apologize for delay, & for haste now—in answering your note. My mother is dying, & I have little thought or time at my own command."[59]

Amid his many other activities, Wilkinson always found time to direct a steady stream of letters to newspapers and friends expressing his opinions on the issues of the day, both political and intellectual. Like many others, he criticized the government's conduct of the Crimean War (1853–56) and, drawing upon his own experiences, urged that soldiers sick with diarrhea be given rice.[60] Toward Ireland he took a hard line, writing to Pettigrew in an undated letter that the island was in a "state" and that conflict was inevitable there: "It must come some day sooner or later & better now."[61] But he was at least moved to mild compassion by the sufferings of the Irish during the famine caused by the potato blight.

One of his favorite subjects was the Suez Canal, to which he was strongly opposed. To Pettigrew he wrote, "If you hear anyone speak in favor of the canal from the Red Sea to the Mediterranean mind & expose the folly of our wishing it as it could obviously destroy our Indian trade & throw it into the hands of the Austrians Greeks French, Russians and all petty traders who can carry cheaper than the English. I need use no arguments as it is sufficiently evident."[62] Even a railway line from the Nile to the Red Sea was undesirable, he told the secretary of the Royal Geographical Society. He believed it was impossible for both political and physical reasons and that it was undesirable in any case.[63] But when the Suez Canal was completed, he was deeply flattered to receive an invitation from Khedive Ismail to the opening.[64]

Wilkinson also threw himself enthusiastically into the debate over the antiquity of man. This important intellectual discussion was provoked by a series of discoveries in caves where human remains and artifacts were found mixed with those of extinct animals. The origin of man was, at that time, thought to be quite recent, no more than a few thousand years in the past. How then could human remains be found among those of animals whose extinction preceded the presumed creation of man? At first the mixture was explained by accidents of deposit, intrusive burials, and great disturbances such as the biblical flood. The leading geologists of the first half of the nineteenth century—even Sir Charles Lyell in his earlier writings—generally agreed with the prevailing view of the recent appearance of man and did little to disturb it in their writings. By the 1850s, however, several more sites had been discovered where human and extinct animal remains were deposited together under circumstances that precluded accidental or intrusive mixture. Confronted with this evidence, many geologists, Lyell among them, altered their positions and concluded that man was much older than previously believed, so old as to ill accord with the account in Genesis.[65]

Wilkinson followed this latest development with disapproval. *"The geologists are becoming crazy,"* he wrote to his friend Babbage, who also doubted such antiquity for the human race.[66] He even addressed some letters to Lyell, the most eminent of the crazy geologists.[67] To the editor of the *Athenaeum* Wilkinson reiterated his views: "The conclusion that, because the [human] bones are deposited together in the same cave, the men & extinct animals must have lived at the same period, is as unnecessary as it is unreasonable." Accidents of deposit, he insisted, were what made them seem contemporaneous.[68] A reader of the *Athenaeum*, the Reverend Thomas D. Allan, wrote to Wilkinson and marshaled the weighty arguments that the geologists were accumulating.[69] Wilkinson's ideas, however, remained unshaken. "I have no preconceived opinion on the matter," he replied to the Reverend Allan, convinced that his mind was truly open, and he went on to doubt that the case for contemporaneity had been proved. But by this time the case had indeed been proved, and Wilkinson and others who thought like him were increasingly hard-pressed to argue against it.[70]

Not always, however, did Wilkinson take the conservative side of controversies, for he was in the forefront of the fight against Sabbatarianism. Sabbatarianism was an old idea, but one that had been resurgent during the 1820s and 1830s. By mid-century, under the leadership of a voluntary association known as the Lord's Day Observance Society, the Sabbatarians were waging a powerful offensive against what they considered transgressions of the Sabbath. They especially opposed Sunday train service and the opening of the British Museum and the National Gallery on Sunday. Other targets were the free Sunday concerts performed by military bands and educational activities such as Robert Owen's Sunday lectures, part of that reformer's program for improving the masses. Sunday newspapers were opposed, as was the teaching of writing in Sunday School. It was a great Sabbatarian victory when the Crystal Palace was kept closed on Sundays.[71]

Some rather unpleasant class attitudes were involved in the Sabbatarian stance, because it distinguished between public and private behavior. A property owner could use his servants, animals, and grounds on Sunday as he pleased, but the public use of post offices and railways on that same day could be prohibited. Masters might require their servants to keep the Sabbath, but servants could not use the Sabbath as a reason to avoid work. Wilkinson noted that the public debate over the issue gave the impression "that it is the Aristocracy who are opposed to the recreations of the working classes on Sunday," but he believed the problem was not one of class: "The opposition to the Sunday recreations of the people really proceeds from certain narrow sectarian views (no doubt well meaning in themselves but mistaken). The real cause of the impediment will be found to arise from the customs allowed to creep in through the influence of the Puritanical element & from our usual reluctance to change what has been long established."[72]

Wilkinson indeed had a condescending attitude toward the lower classes, though he considered them capable of improvement. But how, he reasoned, were they to be improved if all the agencies of improvement were closed to them on Sundays, their one day of leisure, leaving them only trivial amusements and gin? This issue was one of Wilkinson's favorite themes in *On Colour*, whose subtitle in part had been, "On the Necessity for a General Diffusion of Taste among All Classes." "Nowhere is wholesome recreation so much required as in England," he wrote in that book,

> where the frequent occurrence of wet weather so often prevents the working man from seeking it in the country, and so often drives him to idle amusements and to drink. For it is folly to pretend that men who have been working six days will not seek,

and do not require, some kind of recreation; and if a good one is not provided for them they will too frequently be tempted to what is bad. So far from tending to irreligion, it will make them less animal and more intellectual, consequently, more soberminded and religious; and we shall do better to provide a remedy for ignorance and drunkenness, than persist in their encouragement.

To counter the argument that Sunday openings might interfere with church services, he suggested that no gallery or museum be allowed to open before two o'clock. He concluded, "The time will come when a more practical generation will wonder at our blindness, which might be an innocent one if it did not commit an injustice."[73]

Many of Wilkinson's own generation, however, were unpersuaded. Sir David Brewster, in his otherwise favorable review of *On Colour*, strongly disagreed with Wilkinson's advocacy of Sunday openings for museums. It was, Sir David wrote, an idea of "doubtful propriety, and which might bring evils in its train that would be poorly compensated by the amount of diffused taste which it might produce."[74] Others dismissed the idea out of hand. Sir Henry Ellis, the principal librarian at the British Museum, opposed extending the hours of opening to hours when the working classes might attend, because, he said, "the most mischievous portion of the population is abroad and about at such a time . . . the more vulgar class would crowd into the Museum . . . the mere gazing at our curiosities is not one of the . . . objects of the museum."[75] This point of view seemed justified when a spectator, in a shocking incident, wantonly attacked the Portland Vase in the British Museum. Sir Frederick Madden, the museum's keeper of manuscripts, observed, "This is the result of exhibiting such valuable and unique specimens of art to the mob."[76]

To counter the Sabbatarian point of view, Wilkinson and some like-minded people associated themselves into the National Sunday League, of which Wilkinson became a vice-president. The prospectus issued by the NSL began: "This society was established for the improvement of the industrious classes, socially, morally, and intellectually." It argued that museums, libraries, and galleries built by public money were intended not just for the social and intellectual elite, but for the "industrious classes" as well: "it being found that in proportion as the intellect is enlightened, morals are improved."[77] Yet, for all the efforts of Wilkinson and the National Sunday League, it was a losing battle, at least in the short run, as one Sunday diversion after another was closed.

Busy with his many interests, Wilkinson traveled abroad little during the 1850s, except for an occasional, brief jaunt to the Continent, and mostly confined himself to his customary wanderings about England. In mid-1855 he found himself becoming increasingly sickly; he moved about more urgently, seeking a healthy place. Finally, on 6 October, he wrote in his notebook, "Returned to Town & became gradually worse. At last resolved to go to Egypt to try change of climate—having become very nervous and ill."[78] So bad did he feel that he wrote to the P & O Company to inquire if the steamship journey could be broken with a stop at Gibraltar.[79] Eventually he completed arrangements and sailed for Egypt aboard the *Indus* on 18 October 1855.[80]

The following month he was welcomed to Cairo by many European travelers there, including his friend Alexander Henry Rhind, a promising young scholar. Soon he was busy copying hieroglyphs.[81] As with his earlier copies, these are useful to modern Egyptologists. For example, his sketches in Giza of tomb G 7948 are the latest portrayals of the tomb that were made before it was damaged and partially dismantled; not only does his sketch show how scattered pieces fitted together, but his copies of the hieroglyphic inscriptions also help to resolve at least one doubtful area.[82]

His primary scholarly purpose on this trip was to study Christian remains in Egypt, an original and worthy project had he completed it. Sailing upstream in a *dahabiyah*, he stopped at Thebes where he visited his house at Gurna, still in good repair and often used by European travelers. Then, one day while sketching, he was felled by a severe sunstroke that, he wrote, left him "very weak and ill." Even his handwriting was altered, and he was confined to his *dahabiyah* for most of his remaining stay in Egypt. By the time he returned to France he was once again sketching with enthusiasm, and the handwriting returned to normal. In Paris he filled up a notebook with sketches of Egyptian objects in the Louvre.[83] But he never returned to Thebes again.

Wilkinson had, by mid-century, drifted far from the mainstream of Egyptology. He was aware of this, writing, "Though I have given up Egyptian matters for many years I should return to them with great pleasure."[84] Among the general public he was still one of the leading scholars of ancient Egypt, often receiving letters such as this one from George Wilson, a professor of technology at the University of Edinburgh: "I confess to having a great admiration of the Old Egyptians," Professor Wilson wrote. "I have read & re-read all your books & dreamed of the wondrous genius & skill of the dwellers by the Nile, since I was a schoolboy."[85] But among the growing numbers of more or less professional Egyptologists his reputation stood not nearly so tall. For example, George Cecil Renouard wrote to

Edward Hincks in 1851: "The little I have seen and heard of Sir G. W. had not inspired me with a favorable notion of his ability." [86] Wilkinson's knowledge of Egyptology, once among the best, had become far out of date; meanwhile, others were finding fault with the detail, if not the outline, of his picture of ancient Egyptian life.

The most valuable thing that Wilkinson could offer the next generation of Egyptologists was his experience in the field. Whenever he was asked, he was generous with his old Egyptian material; on one occasion he wrote about such a request: "I should feel great pleasure in giving him any materials I may have that would assist him in the completion of a work by which I shall not fail to profit in common with everyone who takes up the study of hieroglyphics." [87] But the wealth of information in his notebooks was tapped less often than one might suppose. Wilkinson's positive attitude toward fieldwork was, in fact, one of the very qualities that put him out of touch with the current mood of Egyptology. Whereas Wilkinson and his colleagues had gone to Egypt, examined the ground, and recorded their observations in situ, the succeeding generation of British and Irish Egyptologists did not. Men like Samuel Birch and Edward Hincks, neither of whom ever visited Egypt, were more content in their libraries at home than in tombs by the Nile. Perhaps it was necessary that the large amount of data that had been gathered in the early decades of the century be organized and assimilated, but Wilkinson considered it a serious mistake for an Egyptologist not to go to Egypt. The Egyptologist Sir E. A. Wallis Budge, who as a young man was present at some meetings between Wilkinson and Birch, later remembered this of Wilkinson: "On more than one occasion he advised me to get to Egypt as soon as I could, saying that no man who had not seen that country could ever hope to understand its history. With a laugh he often told Birch that if he had had a knowledge of Egypt at first hand, he would have been the 'perfect Egyptologist,' and year by year he urged him to take if it were only a holiday in that country before he became too old." [88] One of Birch's dying regrets was that he never took Wilkinson's advice. [89]

After the 1830s, leadership in Egyptian fieldwork, an area in which the British had once reigned supreme, was assumed by others. The 1840s were highlighted by the Prussian expedition led by Lepsius, and then the French moved ahead when Auguste Mariette became the director-general of the Service of Antiquities in Egypt. Wilkinson witnessed this development with annoyance: "There is a pedantry in it," he wrote, referring to Lepsius's *Letters from Egypt, Ethiopia, and the Peninsula of Sinai*. "They omit the mention of what others have done & try to make it appear that every discovery

was Prussian one would think that nobody ever studied the tombs at
the Pyramids before the Prussians (in p. 24 trans) with the exception
of one or two."[90] When the great British archaeologists of the late
nineteenth and early twentieth centuries followed the lead of Sir
Flinders Petrie and returned to Egypt to begin scientific excavations,
they began not with a sense of starting where Wilkinson and his colleagues left off but as a new point of departure.

Wilkinson frequently corresponded with many of the new leaders
in Egyptology, and his letters were answered promptly and deferen-
tially; but it was usually he who asked them for information, not the
other way around. When his opinion was requested, it was frequently about a question of ownership that his memory might elucidate.[91] Wilkinson's advice was still occasionally requested by the
British Museum, though his advice was not always taken, as was the
case with Henry Abbott's collection. Henry Abbott, whom Wilkinson had met on one of his later trips to Egypt, had assembled a large
and important collection of Egyptian antiquities that he offered to
the British Museum. In 1849 Samuel Birch requested Wilkinson to
examine the collection and report. "You are however so conversant
with our collection and the whole subject," Birch wrote, "that I
think our Board would be much guided by your opinion."[92] But time,
or perhaps money, must have diluted the force of that opinion, for
though Wilkinson repeatedly relayed Abbott's offer to sell his collection for £10,000, the trustees rejected it.[93] The museum did, however, accept a subsequent recommendation from Wilkinson that it
buy a particularly fine papyrus that Abbott wanted to sell. The papyrus, now famous as the Henry Abbott Papyrus, is one of the treasures of the museum's Department of Egyptian Antiquities.

The one man who might have served as a transitional figure between Wilkinson and his colleagues, on the one hand, and Sir Flinders Petrie and his, on the other, was Wilkinson's young friend Alexander Henry Rhind, whose criticisms of artifact collecting were
quoted in an earlier chapter. This talented young Scot, originally
trained as a lawyer, shared Wilkinson's interest in antiquities, and,
probably inspired by Wilkinson's example and encouragement, traveled to Egypt where he excavated at Thebes. Though his intellectual
roots were in the British antiquarian tradition, he showed signs of
transcending the limitations of his fellow antiquarians. For one
thing, he looked more deeply than they into the archaeological possibilities of a site. In his careful excavations he meticulously recorded the location of each object that he found and its relationship
to everything else. This provided data for determining successive
layers of occupation. Rhind also wrote better than most anti-

quarians. Elegant and clear, his entertaining *Thebes: Its Tombs and Their Tenants* is of high scholarly quality. But he became gravely ill during a second trip to Egypt (1862–63) and died in Italy on the return trip. His death at age twenty-nine was a loss to Egyptology.

There is, therefore, a lack of continuity between Wilkinson and his successors in Egyptology, a gap that, though probably imperceptible at the time, is obvious from our standpoint today. Part of the reason was Wilkinson's disinclination to pursue the promising start that he had made. A reader of *Manners and Customs of the Ancient Egyptians* senses a mastery of the field. When he wrote it he was a leader in hieroglyphic research, well-versed in the secondary literature, and full of explanations and conjectures that represented the limits of knowledge about ancient Egypt. But then came his relative neglect of the field, and as time passed he had less and less in common with those who were active in it. Wilkinson had surprisingly little direct influence upon his immediate successors, despite his relations with men like Pettigrew and Birch. They regarded him more as an inspiration than a master or mentor.

When Wilkinson finally roused himself to a determined effort, he turned not to Egyptology, but to Greek vases. He had for some years been accumulating a collection of these, probably intending to use them for research. One of his objectives was to describe their daily use in ancient Greece. He also wanted to develop a standard system of nomenclature as a basis for future study. His method was to divide vases into a number of classes by use and by styles and then to derive a chronological framework from the classifications. Nothing of that kind then existed apart from an inadequate work by Jean Antoine Letronne. Wilkinson's manuscripts show him working hard gathering material for the project. He corresponded with Birch about it and wrote several manuscript drafts.[94] As he worked, however, it must have become increasingly obvious to him that the subject was deeper and required broader expertise than he possessed. He found himself obliged to work long hours on a daily basis. This was a project that Sir William Gell might have enjoyed, though it would have taxed even his classic abilities; for Wilkinson it was an undertaking that carried him far beyond his depth. The strain was too much, and his health broke. The Greek vases project was abandoned; never again did he attempt any sustained work. We might wonder if this was a nervous as well as a physical collapse, something similar to what befell him at Harrow forty years earlier.

With Wilkinson's mind moving away from Egyptian thoughts, we might pause to compare the subsequent careers of his colleagues in Egypt with whom he had formed such a coherent and congenial group. Robert Hay, who once had done so much, had drifted even further from Egypt than Wilkinson. In 1826, at the height of his infatuation with Egypt, convinced of the worthiness of what he was doing, Hay had written, "To those accustomed to the quiet repose of Egypt—to days spent amongst the silent tombs of Thebes—there is a certain something that is indescribable in the enjoyment to visit them in the company with those who can appreciate their merits, or by oneself, there is something so intensely interesting that I left them in the evening but to return in the morning with increased pleasure."[95] But a quarter of a century later, the magic of Egypt was quite faded from Hay's imagination. When he wrote to Bonomi upon learning that his subscription to the Syro-Egyptian Society[96] was past due, he said,

> I am shocked at being proclaimed a defaulter to the Syro-Egyptian Society: but it is too true!!—It is equally true, that I am a most unworthy Member of that honorable Society; but there is no great wonder, living as I do, in the most unhealthsome atmosphere of the Lammermoor hills!—My head being *now* only full of Hunting, Fencing, Draining, etc etc. We are all the creatures of habit: and if we happen to fall into *bad* company, we are too apt to get out of the good track and follow the bad!—That is my case; no *Egyptians* or *Syro-Egyptians* live about the Lammermoors, so that my spirit is *dried up* within me!—and I go the way of all flesh, & do just as others do about me![97]

As for his *Illustrations of Cairo*, he bitterly regretted ever publishing it and wished he had again the money it cost him so he could "rebuild and improve my poor tumble-down house."[98]

Hay's mention of his house referred to the collapse of his financial situation. Some heavy investments in land went bad; debts mounted; and, although he was not reduced to penury, he could no longer afford to live in Scotland in the style to which he aspired. He chose instead to wander about Europe, spending one season in Germany, another in Italy, wherever prices were lower. Hay and Wilkinson did not keep in regular contact with each other, but in 1851 when Hay was making one of his brief visits to Britain he passed through London and called at Wilkinson's house. No one was home, so after ringing and knocking for a long time he left his card and went away, sad at not seeing his old friend again.[99] Occasionally he would reminisce wistfully about the old days in Egypt in long letters to Bonomi with whom he had long since been reconciled.[100] Even in adversity he retained his accustomed generosity, for when James Burton died and Hay was appointed one of the executors of his estate, he found that Burton had borrowed a large amount from Bonomi over thirty years earlier that he had never repaid. This sum Hay immediately paid Bonomi from his own funds.[101] One fall when he returned to Scotland in another attempt to mend his fortunes and to attend a daughter's wedding, he contracted pneumonia and died on 8 November 1863.

James Burton's last years were probably the least happy of the old group. Having failed at his various schemes and being unable to do anything with his Egyptian material, he became obsessed with his genealogy. The energies he once had poured into Egyptian research now went into studying his family history. His family name having once been Haliburton, he changed his accordingly. Unable to make a future for himself, he sought meaning for his life in his family's past. His emotional condition continued to decline. As early as 1842, Wilkinson had written to Hay, "Haliburton is unhealthy and depressed & won't go out into society."[102] Quite likely Hay knew more about Burton's problems than Wilkinson did, as may be inferred from this letter of Burton's: "My affairs continue as yet in an unsettled state, but my friend Hay with whom I have been staying *incog* has vigorously taken part with me."[103] Burton died on 22 February 1862 and was buried in West Dean Cemetery, Edinburgh. Upon his tombstone is written, "A zealous investigator in Egypt of its language and antiquities." His brother, the architect Decimus Burton, gathered James's papers and donated them to the British Museum, where they are today, a rich source for scholars of both ancient and modern Egypt.[104] Though little credited for it, his research contributed to the published work of Wilkinson, Lane, and others.

In contrast to the intellectual aimlessness of Hay and Burton—and indeed of Wilkinson—were the persistent, almost compulsive labors of Edward William Lane. In 1850 he wrote to Wilkinson to announce his return from several years of research in Egypt: "What do you think of my being able to boast of not having allowed myself quite half a week of holidays during all that time? At this quiet place [Hastings] I am going on with my work like a steam engine." He went on to speak of himself, "buried as I am here, out of the world." As for Cairo, he wrote, "[I] hope I shall not be obliged to go there again. I am quite tired of Cairo."[105] He became even more reclusive than before, never calling upon anyone and keeping no society, except on Friday afternoon, when certain callers, Wilkinson among them, were admitted.[106] Otherwise, he gave himself over entirely to his work, following his translation of the *Arabian Nights* with a highly acclaimed one of the Quran. Then he began compiling his *Arabic-English Lexicon*, a work that to this day remains supreme in its field. Although Lane's grand-nephew, Stanley Lane-Poole, took pains to emphasize that his grand-uncle was a good, Christian gentleman, there was more than a hint of heterodoxy about Lane's later years, especially in his scrupulous Friday observances. Writers differ about whether his marriage with Nefeeseh was truly companionate. At first it seems not to have been, but a miscarriage and serious illness in 1844 brought him to a deeper appreciation of her. "For never . . . has there existed a more affectionate wife," he wrote to Robert Hay.[107]

Frederick Catherwood continued his various adventures, occasionally buffeted by misfortune. A bad fire in 1842 destroyed most of his artwork as well as his collection of antiquities. Then a grand project that he had conceived to publish American archaeological materials failed for lack of financial support, though he did manage to publish his book *Views of Ancient Monuments in Central America, Chiapas and Yucatán* in 1844. In it he rejected the view, then prevailing, that the great pre-Columbian monuments of America were the work of errant Egyptians, Greeks, or anyone other than the native peoples. He endured an unpleasant experience when he accused his wife of adultery and brought suit against her lover. He won the case, but his reputation was damaged by hints from his wife of a homosexual relationship between him and Joseph Bonomi.[108] He was sailing to America in 1854 when his ship, the SS *Arctic*, sank with the loss of almost all of the passengers. A few days later, the *New York Herald* reported, almost as an afterthought, "Mr. Catherwood Also is Missing."[109] Catherwood is best remembered today for his excellent work in the Yucatán jungle, but had Hay's portfolio been published, Catherwood would be better remembered as a pioneer of Egyptology.

Joseph Bonomi kept busy at contract jobs for Hay, Wilkinson, and others until he was appointed to a position at the British Museum. He was there in 1848 anxiously helping to barricade the museum against an anticipated attack by Chartists, an attack that never came.[110] Not long after and perhaps because of the scandal associated with Catherwood's divorce, Bonomi married. This action, which surprised his friends, was probably intended to allay any suspicions resulting from Mrs. Catherwood's accusations. Fatima and his child in Egypt presumably were long ago forgotten. He eventually became curator at the Sir John Soane Museum and continued to perform various services to Egyptology, including designing the first hieroglyphic printing font in England. Because of these activities his notice in *Who Was Who in Egyptology* reads, "Although not an Egyptologist he yet made greater contributions than most."[111]

The others also went their various ways.[112] Major Felix continued his successful army career, eventually becoming deputy quarter-master-general in India and attaining the rank of major-general before he retired. He died at Genoa in 1860. Most of his Egyptological papers were deposited at Alnwick Castle with his longtime friend, Lord Prudhoe. Lord Prudhoe had meanwhile become the Fourth Duke of Northumberland in 1847 and continued his brother's practice of generous patronage to oriental studies. He also devoted much of his attention to restoring Alnwick Castle. Wilkinson frequently visited there where they indulged their shared love of long walks. Though no longer a coherent group, Wilkinson and his former colleagues in Egypt maintained at least loose contact and kept themselves informed of each others' fortunes as the years passed. "Alas, alas!—We are all getting *very* old!!!" Robert Hay had written to Joseph Bonomi.[113]

CHAPTER THIRTEEN

Brynfield

AFTER HIS BREAKDOWN during the Greek vases project, Wilkinson turned his remaining energies almost exclusively to British antiquities. This in turn drew him to Wales, rich with Celtic heritage, where he spent most of his last years. Seeking to get out of doors, just as he had when he took up horseback riding after his breakdown at Harrow, he happily pursued his new pastime with long walks over early British sites. Liveliness and clarity, sometimes missing in the previous decade, returned to the pages of his sketchbooks.[1] He took up the antiquarian issues of the day, such as the debate over whether cromlechs, the prehistoric stone slabs, had originally been covered with earth and stones or not, at first doubting that they had been and then reconsidering.[2] In 1869 he became a vice-president of the Cambrian Archaeological Association, and he made several contributions to the association's journal.[3] Another attraction of Wales was its climate. Repelled by London fog and English winters, Wilkinson found the warmth and sunshine of South Wales much to his liking. Wales also satisfied his appetite for the beautiful and picturesque. The Gower peninsula, where he eventually settled, is now designated an Area of Outstanding Beauty.

Wilkinson soon formed a social network in Wales and spent much of his time there on extended visits to one friend or another. One of his favorite stops was Llanover, the seat of Lady Llanover. This eccentric woman, a minor literary figure for editing *The Autobiography and Correspondence of Mary Granville, Mrs. Delany,* was the wife of Benjamin Hall, Baron Llanover, first commissioner of works in the government, who rebuilt the houses of Parliament after the fire of 1834. Big Ben is named for him. Though not Welsh, Lady Llanover had been one of the leading figures of the Welsh revival of the 1840s. She enthusiastically embraced all things Welsh, and even her dinners featured the music of a richly dressed harpist. But it soon became clear that the primary attraction for Wilkinson at Lady Llanover's was her younger companion, Caroline Lucas. A romance developed, and in September 1856 Lady Llanover had occasion to write to Miss Lucas's younger brother, Reverend Ponsonby Lucas:

> Reverend Sir,
>   Although we have never met I am sure the announcement I have to make will not be considered out of place from my hand—Your excellent sister has accepted the proposal of that eminent man Sir Gardner Wilkinson, who has been here on a visit for some time. She will of course write herself—but as this has taken place under my roof I cannot refrain from saying that I think her *most fortunate.* Sir Gardner is *not a rich* man and therefore his attachment is more disinterested. He is, as you know, of *more* than *European* celebrity and is as much esteemed in private life as he is admired for his literary talents and his Antiquarian knowledge. He begs me to say that all is proper on his part.[4]

How astonished Wilkinson's friends must have been to learn that he was getting married at last. It does seem quite an alteration in his life-style, though we know little of his relations, if any, with women over the years. There were, of course, the slave girls and companions in Egypt, but that had been long ago. His personal life in England is largely hidden, and speculation about what inclinations the aging bachelor had toward women must be based upon slight evidence. There was, for example, his interest in the question of whether the sculptures of classical goddesses, especially Venus, were displayed nude or draped in antiquity, his conclusion being that they were nude. A stuffy discussion on the surface, it indicates a deep vein of sensuous imagination among classically aware Englishmen of the last century.[5] As to specific relationships, again there is little basis for conclusion. His friendship with Lady Lovelace was particularly warm, and we find her asking him "Could you take a Mutton Chop with me tomorrow evening at 7 o'clock in a *very homely* way?" on one occasion and on another urging that the duration of his next visit be "indefinite."[6] Such requests from Lady Lovelace resulted in his immediate compliance and if necessary a change of plans.[7] Lord Lovelace, by comparison, never seemed particularly taken with Wilkinson, their relationship remaining formal, though they ex-changed a few polite notes. Wilkinson's friendship with Lady Lovelace took place during a difficult time in her life. She had been a fairly reclusive woman during her earlier years, but she eventually became impatient with her kind but unromantic husband. Lord Byron's daughter would not tolerate such a condition indefinitely, and she turned to other men.[8] But it is assuming quite a bit to posit any intimate relationship between Lady Lovelace and Wilkinson.

Of his ideal in womanhood, Wilkinson seems to have been of two minds. Among his papers is a poem, apparently composed by Wilkinson, entitled "Miss Hanum, the Learned Lady." It is an attack upon the intellectual pretensions of a certain Miss Hanum and, one suspects, of women in general.[9] But Lady Lovelace and Miss Lucas, both admired by Wilkinson, were much the kind of woman derided in the poem. As for marriage, his papers also include some verses entitled, "Parody on Hamlet's 'To Be, or Not To Be,'" perhaps written by Wilkinson, perhaps by someone else, but quite bad by whomever. They read in part,

> For in that union what jars may come,
> After we have shuffled on the fatal yoke
> Must give us pause,—there's the respect
> That makes our celibacy last so long.[10]

But these lines were probably nothing more than facetious nonsense.

The object of his affections, Caroline Catherine Lucas, was thirty-four years of age. Her father was Henry Lucas, heir of a gentry family in Gower, who ran through most of his fortune by breeding and racing horses. He did, however, give his daughter a good education, and she developed special interests in literature and natural history. She liked to sketch fossils, flowers, and butterflies. A regular contributor to the *Chambers Journal*, she also wrote *Weeds and Wild-flowers*, which was published in 1858. One reviewer wrote that her book was "particularly suitable for ladies. . . . No intellectual pursuit is more innocent in itself or better fitted to preserve a healthful tone in the youthful mind and guard against the frivolities of gay society. We wish such refreshing and elevating studies were introduced also amongst the working classes as a safeguard against the low tastes and pursuits which beset a town life."[11] Caroline lost her mother at age twelve or thirteen, and her father's second wife was not to her liking. Alienated by an unpleasant situation at home, she went to live with Lady Llanover, probably as a paid companion, though the two soon became fast friends. The remaining link with her family was her brother, to whom she was deeply devoted. Wilkinson was characteristically proud of Caroline's genealogy and took care to note her distinguished ancestors, including those who did notable service for the Royalist cause during the English Civil War.[12] Wilkinson's sketch of her, entitled "Catty," shows her dressed in black, adorned with blue ribbons and white lace.[13] The wedding was on 16 October 1856 at the church at Llandovery, of which Wilkinson also made a charming sketch.[14] Their wedding trip seems to have been a tour of Welsh antiquities. Despite twenty-four years' difference in age, the couple was quite happy. Caroline wrote that Wilkinson was "of a bright and joyous nature, full of fun, and full of tenderness and affection."[15]

The couple settled temporarily at Tenby but began to search for a permanent home. His correspondence shows him intensively house hunting, collecting and studying floor plans and elevations. He nearly closed the deal on one house before backing out when he learned that the mining rights were reserved; another was rejected on the advice of his solicitors. None was quite right. In a letter to a friend, he set forth his requirements: besides being in South Wales, it had to be "*by the Sea* and as well sheltered from the north and east and sunny and open to the sea and in a mild climate and on *dry* land."[16] After some years and what must have been a frustrating search, Brynfield House at Reynoldston, a property that had been associated with Caroline's family since the Middle Ages, became vacant, and they decided to lease it. At about that time, Wilkinson sold his family home at Hardendale, Westmorland, thereby losing his steady income but gaining the means to take the lease and renovate Brynfield House.

Brynfield was an appropriate home for an antiquarian. A new house had been built near the end of the 1700s within the ruins of an older one. It stood on the site of a British camp that had been designed to guard the road that ran under Cefn Bryn, a long hill behind the house. The agger and ditch of the camp were still visible. It was inconveniently far from the nearest railway and post office at Swansea, but Sir Gardner and Lady Wilkinson were happy with their home. Set among pleasant gardens and fields, with Oxwich Bay visible in the distance, it was (and still is) a lovely place, as Wilkinson's many sketches of it show. He wrote to Babbage, "We have two excellent gardens one full of fruit which to one (like me) who spent a great part of his life in eating fruit is a comfort & a luxury."[17]

Loving long walks as he did, Wilkinson could indulge his favorite pastime in a glorious setting rich with Celtic remains. This he frequently did, ranging all over Gower with his beloved dog Harb at his side. Just over Cefn Bryn and commanding the salt marshes of the Llanrhidian Sands that fill the inlet to the north of the peninsula, stands the large Celtic cairn called Arthur's Stone, which he often visited and wrote about for the Cambrian Archaeological Association.[18] A bit farther away and to the west is Gower's land's end, a high cliff looking out to sea along the southern coast of Wales. Sitting at the highest point, the Beacon, Wilkinson sketched the bay, the rocky outcrop known as Worm's Head, and lonely Rhossili Rectory where lived Caroline's much-loved brother Ponsonby Lucas and his growing family.[19] Such Gower scenes fill many pages of his sketchbooks.

Brynfield had one serious deficiency, however, for it did not have room for Wilkinson's library. Accordingly, he set to work, telling Babbage, "I could not do without a good library so that I am obliged to build and am half worn out by the tiresome occupation of superintending masons & carpenters being my own architect and clerk of the works also. Added to which the rain has set in."[20] When it was completed, the library was the largest room in the house. He fitted it out with bookshelves and cabinets for his collections of fossils, artifacts, seashells, and such. Now he could organize his notebooks, sketchbooks, and correspondence, which he did repeatedly, arranging and rearranging them, stirring old memories as he turned their pages. He had suitable shelf space for treasures such as his copy of Lepsius's *Denkmäler aus Aegypten und Aethiopien,* a gift from the emperor of Germany, as well as his other books, which now numbered many thousands. He prepared several catalogs of his collections, papers, and books, culminating in "Catalogue of Library Belonging to Sir Gardner Wilkinson, Brynfield House, Gower, Glamorgan, 1866."[21] It has lists of books borrowed and loaned with the persons' names beside; a list of books wanted; and a sketch of his cabinets and shelves. The index of books lists each book according to number of volumes, size, case, shelf, and date. It is an elaborate— and astonishingly legible—manuscript catalog. The processes of preparing and revising all of the catalogs must have taken months, or longer, but it was a task that gave him pleasure, spending long hours working at his papers with Harb, now getting rather old himself, asleep on the rug at his feet.

While he was busy organizing and cataloging, Wilkinson also put his collections of antiquities in order and donated them to Harrow School in 1864 along with a detailed catalog of their contents.[22] As he later explained, he was thinking of his own youth when he made the gift.

It is now many years since I determined to present my collection of antiquities to Harrow; & to this I was prompted by the recollection of the interest which I, in common with some other men of my own standing, felt in the Arundel, & other collections, when at Oxford, and subsequent experience confirmed me in the belief that many advantages are to be gained by having in our youth an opportunity of examining objects illustrative of classical authors, as well as those connected with science and art. At that period of life our minds are more open to receive impressions, & a strong interest is often awakened when we are predisposed to such inquiries.[23]

In arranging the bequest, Wilkinson conducted an intensive correspondence with the headmaster of Harrow that shows minute attention to the placement and display of the collection.

Though never a commercial collector as Salt or Drovetti had been, Wilkinson made several specialized collections throughout his life, from his snakes and stones in Egypt to the seashells from Tenby Bay, in addition to antiquities. Most of these collections were further focused by their being accumulated to aid particular research and writing projects. The collections of antiquities were always characterized by his desire to illuminate the daily lives of the ancients. What Wilkinson called "my collection" was therefore actually several collections that fell into four categories: Egyptian antiquities, classical antiquities, coins and medals, and fossils and stones from Derbyshire. The Egyptian collection was acquired primarily at Thebes during his first trip to Egypt, though some items were added during other Egyptian travels, and a few were bought at auction. Consisting of everyday things, the Egyptian collection is undistinguished, though it is interesting to see among it some of the objects depicted in *Manners and Customs of the Ancient Egyptians*. The collections of Greek, Roman, and Etruscan antiquities, almost a thousand objects altogether, are mostly unremarkable as collections, though interesting to view. The engraved gemstones from Dalmatia are an outstanding part of them.

Wilkinson was not fully aware of it, but his collection of Greek vases was by far the most significant portion of his bequest.[24] This collection is now the finest private collection of Greek vases in the country, and of all collections both public and private, only those at the British Museum, the Ashmolean, and the Fitzwilliam are better. Even for its time, it was exceptional, especially since it was assembled by a man of limited means. By applying his discerning taste to opportunities afforded by his travels and public sales, he made a collection of vases that a much wealthier connoisseur might well have envied. *Harrow Painter* and *Harrow Class* are now internationally accepted terms based upon vases in the collection.[25]

In addition to these, Wilkinson bequeathed his collection of Derbyshire fossils, mostly accumulated during visits to Calke Abbey, and his coin collection. The numismatic bequest came later than the rest, in 1873. By then his health was declining and he had to regret in a letter to the headmaster that he could not catalog them. The headmaster replied, "I then arranged with my old pupil, Arthur John Evans—a remarkably able young man—that he should take the coins to his father's house during the Christmas holidays, and there draw up a catalogue."[26] This was the first academic work of the future Sir Arthur Evans, who became famous as the archaeologist of ancient Crete.

Wilkinson's collections created quite a stir of interest among the boys at Harrow School when they arrived. His hope that they would inspire the young men was amply realized. Besides (Sir) Arthur Evans, other future scholars who were very interested in Wilkinson's collections and perhaps influenced by them were Sinclair Hood (Bronze Age), William Taylor (Mycenae), and Gerald Cadogan (ancient Cyprus), in addition to many other Harrovians who benefited in various ways from the proximity of the collections. Wilkinson made other benefactions to the school, including such books as his copies of Lepsius and Rosellini and an album of Islamic sketches that he made during his Egyptian days. In his will he frequently mentioned Harrow regarding a number of details and objects he had not sent in the larger donations.[27] His affection for Harrow had remained constant throughout his life.

As the Brynfield years passed, much of the delight that Wilkinson found with his wife and their home was blighted by increasing ill health. In his notebooks he began to refer to himself as an invalid. Each bout of illness was worse than the one before. In 1871, a notice in the *Athenaeum* reads, "Sir Gardner Wilkinson is slowly, but we trust surely, recovering from the dangerous illness from which he has been suffering from some weeks past."[28] The decline in his activity is evident in his last notebook, where archaeological notes diminish after 1864.[29] Local excursions were sometimes impossible, and he mentioned in one of his articles on Welsh antiquities that he had not been able to visit the site in question. Reminders of advancing age came in the news of the passing of old friends. Entries appear in his notebook such as one that reads, "The dear good Duke of Northumberland died at Alnwick Castle—a great grief to me."[30] Even the task of making the catalog for Harrow was difficult for him.

He wrote to Babbage, "I have given my collection of antiquities to Harrow & have been occupied in making a catalogue of the same but am every now & then stopped by my health which begins to give way the moment I begin to work at any thing requiring thought & application."[31]

Several opportunities for remunerative work came to Wilkinson, but he turned them all away. John Murray sent him a copy of a new edition of the Bible that he was intending to publish and requested from Wilkinson "all your notes relating to Biblical subjects," for which he offered to pay 100 guineas. Wilkinson, however, declined the project on grounds of ill health. Murray also asked him to write his account of Christianity in Egypt and was also rebuffed. Yet another request from Murray to write articles for the *Dictionary of the Bible* that Sir William Smith was preparing received the same answer.[32] He did do some writing during his years at Brynfield, a few miscellaneous essays, culminating in his last paper, "The Listening Slave and the Flaying of Marsyas," prepared for the Royal Society of Literature. But these were matters of no great depth or preparation. New hobbies probably took more of his attention. He began music lessons, and he engaged someone from Tenby to teach him wood carving, in which he attained a sufficiently high degree of skill to carve a fine chimney piece for the library. In a letter to Babbage, he reflected on his life-style, "Only fancy my having taken to carving ornamental designs in wood & learning the violin! But these will be recreations in the country—& I cannot work now at books having overdone myself & lost time by too many hours work while I thought I was gaining time & strong enough to do any labor of the kind."[33]

There was, however, one project which he took up with some interest, and that was the revision of *Manners and Customs of the Ancient Egyptians*. As the years had passed, Wilkinson's greatest book had remained popular but had become increasingly dated, so John Murray decided to publish a revised edition. Wilkinson was no longer sufficiently involved in Egyptology to make the necessary revisions, but he was assisted by his younger friend Samuel Birch from the British Museum. Indeed, the task of revision fell most heavily upon Birch, with Wilkinson agreeing to almost all changes he suggested. This was mostly a matter of inserting new material; little of Wilkinson's original text was altered, only those portions that were no longer correct or pertinent. The revised edition, which did not appear until after Wilkinson's death, brought the book sufficiently up-to-date for it to be read into the twentieth century, when it was supplanted by the works of Hall, Breasted, Meyer, and Petrie.

Ill health limited his ability to travel, though he still made excursions into the countryside and visited friends from time to time. His last trip abroad was in December 1863 when he and Lady Wilkinson sailed for Spain, where they spent most of their time at Cadiz, Seville, and Coruña. Although he visited museums and sketched coins, his primary interest was the seashells at Cadiz. He noted that these were frequently the same as were to be found in England, though the Spanish ones seemed smaller.[34] This interest he continued, in company with Lady Wilkinson, after returning to Britain. In 1865 he published an account of a new oyster he discovered at Tenby. There are among the Wilkinson Manuscripts three bound volumes of organized notes and sketches of seashells. Lady Wilkinson compiled an album of sketches of. crabs.[35] They also shared an interest in wildflowers. Besides her book *Weeds and Wild-flowers*, she also prepared an unpublished work entitled "Distribution of Plants."[36] This botanical activity was probably what revived his interest in publishing his "Desert Plants of Egypt," which he was hoping to do during his last years.

In late January of 1867, Wilkinson received the disturbing news that the corporation of the town of Tenby had voted to destroy the town's five-arched medieval gateway for the ostensible purpose of providing greater access to the town. This gateway, a remnant of the old town walls, was an extraordinary piece of military architecture, one of the few remaining structures like it in Britain. The move was bitterly opposed by the mayor of Tenby and many of its citizens. Angry public meetings were held, but it seemed likely that the corporation would prevail. The desperation of those who opposed the demolition was expressed in these lines of "original poetry" that appeared in the *Tenby Observer* in which the arches plead for aid.

> Listen—pity—help us stranger,
> We are doomed by some to fall;
> If thou can'st avert the danger,
> Plead for us!—plead for us all.
>
> Is it that we're old and dingy
> That these Goths would seal our fate?
> Archaeologists, where are ye?
> Rouse ye e're it be too late.[37]

Wilkinson indeed roused himself and wrote to everyone he knew who might be able to help. Carefully stating that he acted not as a blind opponent of progress and improvement, he complained to his antiquarian friend Albert Way that the gate was condemned to be pulled down "without excuse or good reason." After pointing out the historical importance of the gate, he continued:

> I feel sure that you will be able to prevent this piece of unneces-
> sary vandalism—for unnecessary it certainly is since it is not in
> a situation that will prevent the town being benefitted by the
> erection of new houses. . . . Indeed I can only imagine that the
> idea emanated from the mere love of change as it is distant from
> every street where new accommodation is required for visitors to
> Tenby or for public buildings of any kind. Its removal is therefore
> not required for public or general purposes & it would only be a
> wanton destruction of the most curious & interesting part of the
> old walls.[38]

Albert Way reacted indignantly to the proposed destruction. "Who are the aggressors?" he asked Wilkinson, wanting only to know to whom a suitable remonstrance should be addressed. Together Wilkinson and Way coordinated a protest by an influential group of scholars and politicians. The effect of Wilkinson's influence was quickly felt when the Royal Archaeological Institute addressed a strong remonstrance to the Corporation of Tenby.[39] Likewise was the Society of Antiquaries moved to action as the Secretary of that body wrote to Wilkinson on February 4: "At our last meeting a protest was read from the chair by the Pres., Earl Stanhope. It received the unanimous consent of the Society and has been forwarded to the mayor & corporation of Tenby."[40] This protest, to which was added the objections of many national politicians and scholars, overwhelmed the corporation of Tenby which reluctantly shelved the demolition plan. A few days later, Way wrote to Wilkinson, "The gateway I hope is really rescued—there seem to be some determined levelers amongst the municipals of Tenby."[41]

As things turned out, Way's cautious tone was justified, for the very next year the corporation revived the demolition plan. Again Wilkinson and Way organized a protest, and again the corporation reluctantly acquiesced. But such was the corporation's determination to destroy the gate that the demolition plan was brought forward for the third time in 1873. This time the corporation moved quickly, perhaps aided by a more sympathetic mayor. Although fifty-two of the town's sixty freeholders protested the move, the corporation was about to let a contract for the demolition when a private citizen, one George Chater, took the matter to the vice-chancellor's court. The corporation failed to appear, and the vice-chancellor issued an injunction prohibiting the destruction. The matter was settled before the court early the following year when the corporation agreed to drop the demolition plan once and for all.[42] Had it not been for the efforts of Wilkinson and Way, and later of Chater, the gate would have been destroyed.

During the winter of 1874–75, Wilkinson fell ill again. As he lay bedridden, he thought of his old friend Edward William Lane, who had also been confined to bed, and wrote to inquire about his condition. Lane suffered much from chronic bronchitis caused by his life-long use of the narghile, or water pipe, that he had become addicted to in Egypt. Despite bad health, Lane continued to work at his Arabic-English lexicon in the vain hope that he could complete it. His reply to Wilkinson's letter, which came promptly, has the tone of a valedictory from an old friend who still has some hope of keeping body and soul together but recognizes that the end may be near.

Worthing
March 19, 1875

My dear Isma'eel,

I had just put before me this sheet of paper to write to you when your kind letter of yesterday's date was put into my hand. Very many thanks for it; & particularly for the gratifying terms in which you mention my Lexicon. I do indeed earnestly hope that we may both live to see its completion, & as much longer as may be good for us. We have now been friends for nearly half a century, the events of which, connected with yourself, often afford me matter for very pleasing recollections & reflections. I should have written to you many days ago, but for two reasons: first: I wanted to receive, before my doing so, some account of your state of health; & secondly, a severe attack of illness, which confined me to my bed for nearly a fortnight, obliged me during that period, & for some time after, to pass my days in unaccustomed idleness, imposing upon Stuart & others all affairs that I should otherwise have taken upon myself. This morning only I received from him an account of you not as good as I had hoped for, & therefore held back from me for about a couple of weeks. I find that you had been again forbidden to write; but this I can scarcely wonder at after so trying a winter. Your letter to me looks as if written with a vigorous hand, which makes me hope that the prohibition was only for a short time.

We are very sorry that Lady Wilkinson has been suffering from Erysipelas. I suppose she knows that Tincture of Steel is a

specific for that complaint. Some years ago I had an attack of
Erysipelas of the scalp, & my Physician cured me in a few days
by means of ten drops of that Tincture in a wineglass of water
taken immediately after dinner. It is a most innocent medicine;
& I often take it, with perfect success, for Erythema, which, if
suffered to continue long, frequently becomes Erysipelas.

My Wife & Sister unite with me in kindest regards to her.
Pray accept the same yourself, from them & from me, & believe
me

Ever most truly yours
Mansoor.[43]

The vigorous hand to which Lane referred may have been that of
Lady Wilkinson who had taken over much of Wilkinson's correspondence as well as the entries in his journal.

Wilkinson's condition improved slightly in the spring, and he decided to prepare a series of illustrations for Horace based upon the
1608 edition of Torrentius of Antwerp. His intention was to present
the work to the queen who graciously assented to accept the gift
from him. Then, in May, he felt well enough to visit Calke Abbey,
but after his arrival suffered a severe relapse and was compelled to
remain with the Harpur-Crewes for some time. From his bed there
he made a long list of things he wanted sent to him from Brynfield,
including the sketchbook for the Horace illustrations. He continued
to work at them when he was able, but at length he despaired of
finishing them. In August he dictated a letter to General Sir Thomas
Biddulph, a member of the queen's household, to say that he had
been dangerously ill and quite unable to write for the past three
months.

Before my illness I added some more illustrations to the Horace
but was not able to complete the work—& as I fear it will be
some time before I can continue it I will beg you to do me the
favor to ask Her Majesty if she will be graciously pleased to allow me to send the whole work to Her Majesty at Balmoral in
its present state? I ask this favor of Her Majesty lest my health
might never allow me to complete the rest of the illustrations
while I shall have before me the hope at least of being sufficiently recovered to continue the most welcome duty & pleasure
of copying the remaining ones from my sketch books which I
have destined for the Horace & of sending them to Her Majesty.[44]

He left Calke Abbey in mid-September in an ambulance carriage. Had he momentarily improved, or did he feel that his welcome at Calke Abbey was wearing thin? Perhaps he longed to see Brynfield House again. If the last motive was the true one, then he was disappointed, for he had to pause in Llandovery at the house of Caroline's sister Maria, the wife of the rector of Llandovery College. There his condition worsened, until 29 October 1875, when Lady Wilkinson wrote in his journal, "I lost the light of my life."[45] Five days later he was buried in the churchyard of Llandovery at a sunny spot that he had chosen himself. A local newspaper, in its account of the event, contained an interesting error: "The sun, which he had loved so well and feared so much, blazed out in all the brightness of its summer glory as his body was lowered into the ground." A couple of days later, the newspaper corrected "feared" to "prized."[46] His grave is marked by a monument of his own design, an obelisk atop a pedestal.

Lady Wilkinson was in a precarious financial situation, for Sir Gardner left her little money. One might wonder if he had ever considered selling some of his antiquities to provide for her rather than donating them all to Harrow. Samuel Birch brought her plight to the attention of the prime minister, Benjamin Disraeli, who persuaded the queen to grant her a civil list pension of £150 per annum in recognition of her husband's services to science and archaeological literature.[47] Wilkinson quite possibly was thinking along these lines when he prepared the Horace illustrations as a gift for the queen. His scholarly achievements alone might have merited the pension, but it is unlikely that Disraeli had forgotten the man who, half a century earlier, had shown him around Thebes.

In accordance with her husband's last wishes, Lady Wilkinson attempted to put some of his unpublished manuscripts into print. The project that she took the farthest was his illustrated study of the desert plants of Egypt, a finished work that Wilkinson had long wanted to publish. She enlisted the help of William Carruthers, F.R.S., and together they prepared a prospectus stating, "The work is sufficiently advanced to justify the Publishers to announce its appearance by the beginning of next year [1881]."[48] But something went amiss, delays set in, and the project was abandoned. Despite a request to do so, Carruthers seems never to have returned the manuscript to Lady Wilkinson, a fact that occasioned some heated correspondence. The result is that the two volumes of Wilkinson's sketches of the desert plants of Egypt are missing from the Wilkinson manuscripts.

Meanwhile, Samuel Birch completed the work for the revised edition of *Manners and Customs of the Ancient Egyptians,* which he and Wilkinson had begun. This was published in three volumes in 1878, three years after Wilkinson's death.[49] In gratitude for the assistance that she had received from Disraeli, Lady Wilkinson placed a handsome dedication to him at the front of the book. She also sent a set to the queen, who responded with a copy of Sir Theodore Martin's *Life of the Prince Consort,* autographed by herself.[50] Royalties from the new edition provided a pleasant addition to her pension.

Lady Wilkinson moved away from Brynfield after her husband died and spent the rest of her days with her relatives at Llandovery. She attempted to find a publisher for her husband's Greek vases manuscript, but met with no success, for that work had never been developed to an acceptable level of completion. She also began a biography of Wilkinson, but soon faltered in the attempt.[51] She died at Llandovery on 2 October 1881 at the age of 59 and is buried beside her husband in the churchyard there.

Wilkinson's papers were sent to Calke Abbey, where he had willed that they be kept in perpetuity. Accompanying them were other things such as his large personal library, his Ethiopian shields and spears, his Turkish sword, and the carved mantlepiece from Brynfield. Though the shipment was quite large, it hardly made an impression at Calke Abbey, stuffed with collections and curiosities as it was. There the manuscripts lay, some for more than a century, safe but almost forgotten.

Epilogue

SAMUEL BIRCH'S REVISIONS brought *Manners and Customs of the Ancient Egyptians* abreast with current scholarship, and it continued to be read frequently until the early years of the twentieth century. Thereafter, scholars and general public alike turned to other works about ancient Egypt. This was a natural process. As knowledge of Egyptian texts grew, it became possible to use Egyptian sources to describe ancient Egypt and to assign the classical sources an ancillary role. Adolf Erman first pointed the way in this regard in 1885;[1] then, in 1905 James Breasted published an English-language history of ancient Egypt based upon a firsthand translation of all available historical texts.[2] Meanwhile the new archaeological methods developed by Sir Flinders Petrie were bringing in a wealth of material from the field. The general public was able to turn to books like Breasted's for readable, up-to-date substitutes for Wilkinson's book. By the second decade of the twentieth century, *Manners and Customs of the Ancient Egyptians* was largely supplanted.

That Wilkinson's published work should pass out of date was inevitable, but it is strange that he should then have dropped out of sight as much as he did. Why was he not better remembered as a significant figure in the intellectual history of Victorian England? One reason was that so much of the awareness of his work rested upon *Manners and Customs of the Ancient Egyptians*. Significant work like his map of Thebes had little circulation and was therefore little appreciated. Most of his best work was unpublished. The value of his iconographic work was not readily evident, especially since his Egyptological notebooks were unavailable for consultation. *Manners and Customs* began to drop out of the footnotes of works by scholars who distrusted his methodology, his use of classical sources and the Bible, and his rudimentary understanding of hieroglyphics. As the readership of *Manners and Customs* diminished, so did public awareness of Wilkinson.

Part of the responsibility for this was Wilkinson's. By moving out of the mainstream of Egyptology during the second half of his life he failed to ensure his place as the discipline was taking shape. By not staying with any one subject longer than he did, he failed to reap the benefits of a sustained line of inquiry. His working habits made it even more difficult for him, for while he had the talent of taking splinters of time and using them well, he was less successful at applying himself in a continuing effort. He could not see how to utilize more of the possibilities that he had developed in his research. In vain he tried to think of new ways to organize his material and present it to the public. Quite likely he never fully analyzed the reasons for the success of *Manners and Customs of the Ancient Egyptians*, just as he did not visualize new ways to build upon it.

But one should not judge Wilkinson as if he were a professor of Egyptology. His very limitations were characteristic of a scholarly milieu of which he was one of the best representatives. Wilkinson is best understood as a Victorian man of letters, a person who relied upon his pen to make his name and who was expected to have wide-ranging interests.[3] Wilkinson did his best work at a time when most significant contributions in virtually all fields of literature and scholarship were made by amateurs and men of letters. The universities had little to offer. After mid-century, however, this situation was changing as the universities and other institutions began to develop as bases for professional scholars. The boundaries of the intellectual disciplines became clearly defined, and Wilkinson fit poorly into the initial definition. As a man of letters Wilkinson had achieved some intellectual authority, but the establishment of the disciplines undermined it. People like the professional Egyptologists of the late nineteenth and early twentieth centuries who relied not upon the publishing marketplace but upon salaried positions tended not to take someone like Wilkinson seriously.

Of course, people from Wilkinson's background could make impressions both immediate and lasting. Darwin, Lyell, and Huxley resembled Wilkinson closely. They were men of independent means—Huxley less so than the others—and classical educations who drew their primary material from travels and observations. They largely supported themselves by their books. But they were also men of sustained application. Like Edward William Lane with his lexicography project, they established long-term goals and structured their lives around them. Wilkinson did not. His was a life-style that required dispersal rather than concentration of energies; lines of inquiry were abandoned before being fully developed. Wilkinson and the many others like him in Victorian England could contribute up to a point, but then the limits of amateur scholars were reached. Specialists and professional scholars took their place.

An assessment of the limitations of Wilkinson's work should not be overdone. Looking at his overall publication record, one sees a half dozen substantial books and as many articles, a significant accomplishment for anyone—this in addition to the notebooks and sketchbooks, arguably his most important achievement. One should also note that Wilkinson, while having no academic position, used his memberships in voluntary scholarly associations, especially during the 1840s, to their full extent, sending a steady stream of articles and letters to them. Just because Wilkinson's research material was so rich that he could not find ways to use it all fully is not to say that he lacked imagination. His development of the technique of making accurate copies and using them to understand ancient Egyptian life was an utterly original innovation in the development of scientific Egyptology.[4] So too was his application of the manners and customs genre to portray the variety of daily life in ancient Egypt. At least he could see that his fieldwork had untapped possibilities, while others tended to dismiss it.

The lack of exploitation of Wilkinson's work was as much a failure of imagination on the part of the nascent scholarly establishment as it was of Wilkinson. Wilkinson was willing to make his work available, but the establishment, which should have had the critical techniques to develop it, never dialogued effectively with him. The gap between amateur and professional scholars was too wide. Wilkinson could not imagine how to bridge it; the first generation of professional scholars, busy constructing the edifice of professional Egyptology, was uninterested in doing so. Such things as the reluctance of the first generation of Egyptologists to go to Egypt kept them apart. Wilkinson urged them to go, but they were more comfortable in their libraries, preferring the Egypt of their imaginations to the one that really existed. This was the "armchair scholarship" that Sir Flinders Petrie contemptuously dismissed.[5]

In his inaugural address at University College London in 1892, Petrie urged that British Egyptology take up the approaches that Wilkinson had begun and focus upon the artistic and material civilization of the ancient Egyptians.[6] It was Petrie who put British Egyptology back into the field again, half a century after Wilkinson had left it. Petrie's pupil, Norman de Garis Davies, was Wilkinson's successor in the particular method of making accurate copies and using them to reconstruct ancient Egyptian life.[7] But Davies began his work in 1898, some sixty years after Wilkinson's most active years. The gap between Wilkinson on one side and Petrie and Davies on the other was too wide for any strong sense of continuity. As Petrie, Davies, and their successors took the field, it seemed much more urgent to confront the tasks before them than to reassess Wilkinson's work.

Wilkinson's most enduring legacy was his large collection of manuscripts: his notebooks, sketchbooks, letters, and documents of all kinds. He realized that much of the richness that lay in them was untapped; occasionally he expressed the hope that they might be published. For a time, however, it seemed that they might be forgotten entirely. Calke Abbey is a remote place; the Harpur-Crewes were a reclusive family. In 1925, however, Professor F. Ll. Griffith heard of their existence and borrowed fifty-six volumes of them, less than half of the total, to aid the preparation of the *Topographical Bibliography of Ancient Egyptian Hieroglyphic Texts, Reliefs, and Paintings* by Bertha Porter and Rosalind Moss. Because of the great Egyptological importance of these manuscripts they were, with permission from Calke Abbey, subsequently kept in the Archives of the Griffith Institute at Oxford.[8] Over the following decades, Egyptologists occasionally examined and cited them in their published works as they came to appreciate Wilkinson's accuracy and the value of his copies as evidence for detail that had vanished from the monuments.

The manuscripts were reunited in 1981. The occasion was an inheritance crisis at Calke Abbey. In order to escape an intolerable burden of capital transfer taxes, Calke Abbey was donated to the National Trust.[9] The Wilkinson manuscripts were moved to Oxford; the manuscripts on loan to the Griffith Institute were reclaimed; and, after some years of negotiation, all of them were deposited in the Department of Western Manuscripts of the Bodleian Library. Since they became available there in 1985, the manuscripts have been much consulted, not only by Egyptologists, but also by others, as scholars from different disciplines began to notice that the manuscript material pertains to much more than Egyptology. The letter of Wilkinson's will that his papers be kept at Calke Abbey has not been kept, but its spirit has been fulfilled.

The scholar of Wilkinson's life notes with particular interest the recovery of Wilkinson's reputation. Always known to Egyptologists, his work has received more space and analysis in their recent work. Even more interesting is the attention that he is receiving from the general public. Fifteen years ago scarcely any educated person, apart from an Egyptologist, knew his name. Since then, several popular works have devoted space, sometimes of chapter length, to his life and work. Wilkinson, fond of people as he was, would have been delighted at this. Perhaps it required the appearance of a later generation of scholars and interested readers to realize the measure of his greatness.

Wilkinson's accomplishments were extraordinary. The limitations of his time and place make them all the more so. He took a jumble of uninterpreted evidence and constructed a coherent picture of life in ancient Egypt. He then communicated that vision in so compelling a way as to capture the imaginations of generations of readers. Wilkinson was more than a momentary literary fashion of the nineteenth century. His impact on the understanding of ancient Egypt was permanent and profound. The full possibilities of his work are yet to be realized. When the definitive history of Egyptology is written, Wilkinson should be accorded a firm place within it.

APPENDIX

A Note on the
Wilkinson Manuscripts

THE PRINCIPAL ARCHIVAL SOURCE for this work was Sir Gardner Wilkinson's large collection of papers. The movements of the collection after Wilkinson's death is described in the Epilogue. I initially examined the Wilkinson manuscripts when they were in temporary keeping at St. John's College, Oxford, and subsequently consulted them in the Bodleian Library, which became their permanent repository. As of this writing, however, they have not been shelf marked by the Bodleian Library, and the sharp reduction in funding inflicted upon the library in recent years makes it impossible to predict when they will be, because the task will be extraordinarily difficult and expensive. Consequently, it is important to explain the present condition of the manuscripts and the method of citing them that I have adopted, for none of the existing systems of cataloging them was suitable for comprehensive use.

Sir Gardner Wilkinson, probably with some posthumous assistance from Lady Wilkinson, organized, labeled, and numbered his manuscripts and prepared an index to them. In many instances they were gathered and bound into volumes with titles such as "Letters &c" or "Portraits of Kings & Other Rubbings from the Monum ts Thebes." The journals were usually, though not invariably, labeled according to their content (e.g., "Journal 1821 Egypt" or "Journal in England in 1845 to 48").

The sketchbooks were likewise titled and numbered. They were further divided into two series with roman numbers assigned to the large sketchbooks and Arabic numbers to the small ones. Sketchbook X, therefore, is not the same as sketchbook 10. There are also two portfolios of sketches labelled A and B. Wilkinson made the first of these in Italy and Malta on his way to Egypt in 1820 and 1821 and the second in those same places on his return trip in 1833.

Although Wilkinson devoted extensive effort to his organizational system, it has shortcomings. For one, his numbered index does not include all of his manuscripts; also, in a few instances it is unclear to which manuscripts his index entries refer. Another difficulty arises from the fact that not all of the manuscripts were bound and labeled. Many important papers are in a large leather satchel, while others are in loose, unindexed folders or collected in similar makeshift arrangements. Finally, one frequently finds various papers and letters placed unbound between the pages of volumes to which they have no apparent relevance. Will they remain so when the manuscripts are finally shelf marked? One can only conjecture.

Those manuscripts that were loaned to the Griffith Institute between 1925 and 1981 were cataloged entirely differently by the institute, being assigned roman numerals I-LVI. Publications of the past several decades refer to them in that manner. The Griffith Institute's system, however, was inadequate for the purposes of this biography because it covers less than half of the manuscripts, and it is uncertain if that system or any element of it will be retained in future organizational schemes.

The Bodleian Library has applied a provisional cataloging system to the manuscripts to permit readers to access them until some other arrangement can be made, but it too is unusable here. The system was not developed until I had done the bulk of my research, and then it was revised at least once. Nor does it include all of the manuscripts. In any event, it is a temporary system that is intended to be replaced by a permanent one at some date.

The solution adopted in this book was to refer to each volume or portfolio by the name that Sir Gardner or Lady Wilkinson assigned to it, with that name enclosed in quotation marks. The citations in my notes thus appear: "Wilkinson MSS, 'Letters &c'" or "Wilkinson MSS, 'Journal 1821 Egypt.'" Untitled manuscripts are referred to according to their container: "Wilkinson MSS, leather satchel." A document loosely inserted in a volume or container is referred to according to the volume or container. In many, indeed in most, cases I do not refer to page or folio numbers. Wilkinson's duplication of numbers, and occasionally his application of more than one numbering system within a single volume, frequently makes such specificity of marginal value.

It is likely that the Bodleian Library will impose an entirely different organizational scheme upon the Wilkinson manuscripts. My goal in the meantime is to identify each item as completely as possible and minimize confusion to researchers who consult the manuscripts after reading this work.

Notes

Works and depositories frequently cited have been identified by the
following abbreviations:

BL   British Library, Department of Manuscripts.

DNB   *The Dictionary of National Biography.* Ed. Sir
Leslie Stephen and Sir Sidney Lee. Oxford: Oxford University Press, 1921–1922.

GIA   Archives, Griffith Institute, Ashmolean Museum, Oxford.

MCAE   Sir Gardner Wilkinson. *Manners and Customs
of the Ancient Egyptians.* 6 vols. London: John
Murray, 1836.

RGS   Royal Geographical Society, Archives.

Wilkinson MSS   Wilkinson Manuscripts. The personal papers of
Sir Gardner Wilkinson, Bodleian Library, Department of Western Manuscripts.

WWW   Warren R. Dawson and Eric H. Uphill. *Who Was
Who in Egyptology.* 2d ed. London: Egypt Exploration Society, 1972.

Introduction

1. Warren R. Dawson and Eric H. Uphill, *Who Was Who in Egyptology,*
s.v. "(Sir) John Gardner Wilkinson" (*Who Was Who* hereafter cited as *WWW*).

2. The earliest citation for *Egyptology* in the *Oxford English Dictionary*
is 1859. Not until the 1870s was the word used consistently to refer to the
systematic study of ancient Egypt. *Oxford English Dictionary,* 2d ed., s.v.

"Egyptology." From that standpoint it is, strictly speaking, anachronistic to write of Egyptology in the early nineteenth century, but in this book the term *Egyptology* is applied to the study of ancient Egypt both before and after the term itself came into use and the formal discipline of Egyptology was established.

3. I frequently use the term Thebes to refer to the town of Luxor and its environs, both the east and the west banks of the Nile, as Wilkinson and his colleagues did.

4. This is stated most forcefully in *WWW*, s.v. "(Sir) John Gardner Wilkinson": "Curiously no full-length biography of Wilkinson has ever been published, yet he took a prominent part in all archaeological movements in his day and occupied a position in Egyptology analogous to Rawlinson in Assyrian archaeology."

5. Leslie Greener, *The Discovery of Egypt*.

6. John A. Wilson, *Signs and Wonders upon Pharaoh*.

7. John David Wortham, *British Egyptology 1549–1906*.

8. Brian M. Fagan, *The Rape of the Nile: Tomb Robbers, Tourists, and Archaeologists in Egypt*.

9. Peter A. Clayton, *The Rediscovery of Ancient Egypt: Artists and Travellers in the 19th Century*.

10. John Romer, *Valley of the Kings*.

11. M. L. Bierbrier, *The Tomb-Builders of the Pharaohs*.

12. Lise Manniche, *The Tombs of the Nobles at Luxor*, and *Lost Tombs: A Study of Certain Eighteenth Dynasty Monuments in the Theban Necropolis*.

13. John Baines and Jaromír Málek, *Atlas of Ancient Egypt*.

14. Leila Ahmed, *Edward W. Lane*.

15. Selwyn Tillett, *Egypt Itself: The .Career of Robert Hay, Esquire of Linplum and Nunraw, 1799–1863*.

16. Victor W. von Hagen, *Frederick Catherwood Arch^t*, and *F. Catherwood: Architect-Explorer of Two Worlds*.

17. By Bestseller Publications Ltd., 1988. His *Dalmatia and Montenegro* also was reprinted in 1971 by Arno Press, New York.

18. Edward Said, *Orientalism*.

19. For an overview of this transformation see T. W. Heyck, *The Transformation of Intellectual Life in Victorian England*. For an analysis of how the transformation particularly affected the study of the past see P. J. A. Levine, *The Amateur and the Professional: Historians, Antiquarians and Archaeologists in Nineteenth-Century England, 1838–1886*.

1. The Origins of an Egyptologist

1. *The Dictionary of National Biography*, ed. Sir Leslie Stephen and Sir Sidney Lee s.v. "Sir Salathiel Lovell" (*The Dictionary of National Biography* hereafter cited as *DNB*).

2. John Robert Moore, *Daniel Defoe: Citizen of the Modern World* (Chicago: University of Chicago Press, 1958), 130–141.

3. The principal published accounts of Wilkinson's life are the entries for him in *DNB* and *WWW*. Among the contemporary notices is one by Lovell Reeve, *Men of Eminence in Literature, Science, and Art*, 1:73–80, which includes a photograph. The brief "Memoir of Sir Gardner Wilkinson, F. R. S.," an address of the Council of the Royal Society of Literature in April 1876 was written by W. S. W. Vaux with material supplied by Lady Wilkinson. Her copy of it, now in my possession, has the penned note, "Though this is but a very slight sketch it is correct as far as it goes[.] C. C. W."

4. Wilkinson seems not to have known or at least not to have recorded his birthplace. Because of his parents' early deaths and his long sojourn in Egypt, he may never have learned it. Lady Wilkinson wrote that he was "in all probability" born at Little Missenden Abbey. The Wilkinson Manuscripts (hereafter cited as Wilkinson MSS), "Heads of a Subject," Lady Wilkinson's incomplete manuscript of a biography of her husband. For conventions in citing the Wilkinson MSS and background information about them see the Appendix.

5. Greater London Record Office, parish registers of St. Luke, Chelsea, ref. P74/LUK.

6. The African Exploration Society was the precursor of the Royal Geographical Society. It sponsored the travels of several explorers, including J. L. Burckhardt, most of whom perished on their journeys. See Robin Hallett, ed., *Records of the African Association 1788–1831*. Hallett identifies the John Wilkinson on the rolls of the African Society as the famous Staffordshire ironmaster of the same name, but this seems to be an error.

7. James Grey Jackson was the author of *An Account of the Empire of Marocco etc.* (London: W. Bulmer and Co., 1809) and also of *Letters Descriptive of Travels through West and South Barbary, and across the Mountains of Atlas* (London: Longman, Hurst, Rees, Orme, and Brown, 1820).

8. British Library, Department of Manuscripts, Additional Manuscripts (hereafter cited as BL, Add MSS) 28512:255. Folios 255–258 of this manuscript are a biographical essay of Wilkinson and corrected by Wilkinson for Charles Griffin's *Handbook of Contemporary Biography*, perhaps published in London, 1861.

9. Lady Wilkinson's biographical manuscript in "Heads of a Subject," part of the Wilkinson MSS, mentions another guardian, someone named Wilkinson, but not a relative.

10. Wilkinson MSS, "Heads of a Subject," Lady Wilkinson's biographical manuscript.

11. Ibid.

12. Bodleian Library, Department of Western Manuscripts, MS Autogr. d. 43, fol. 47.

13. John Fischer Williams, *Harrow*, 82.

14. Anthony Trollope, *An Autobiography* (London: Blackwood and Sons, 1883).

15. Wilkinson was well aware of this controversy, which he mentioned in Wilkinson MSS, "Poetry."

16. Philip H. M. Bryant, *Harrow*, 37.

17. Williams, *Harrow*, 83.
18. Ibid.
19. Wilkinson MSS, "Catalogue of Library Belonging to Sir Gardner Wilkinson Brynfield House, Gower, Glamorgan, 1866."
20. Williams, *Harrow*, 83.
21. H. Montagu Butler, "Harrow Benefactors and Benefactions," in *Harrow School*, ed. Edmund W. Howson and George Townsend Warner, 145.
22. *WWW*, s.v. "George Butler."
23. Wilkinson MSS, "Poetry," and information from the archivist of Harrow School.
24. Reeve, *Men of Eminence*, 1:74–75.
25. Sir Astley Paston Cooper, F.R.S. (1768–1841). A renowned surgeon, Sir Astley was a lecturer at the Royal College of Surgeons when Wilkinson knew him. He became Surgeon to the King in 1828.
26. W. S. W. Vaux, "Memoir of Sir Gardner Wilkinson, F.R.S."
27. E. A. Wallis Budge, *Catalogue of the Egyptian Antiquities from the Collection of the Late Sir Gardner Wilkinson*, 3.
28. Joseph Foster, *Alumni Oxonienses 1715–1886*, 4:1556. Lady Wilkinson later wrote that Wilkinson was "placed under the tutelage of the Revd T. Higgett at Chelsea by whom he was prepared for Oxford" in 1816 and that he did not enter Exeter College until 1817 (Wilkinson MSS, "Heads of a Subject," Lady Wilkinson's biographical manuscript). Allowing for her handwriting, we could read "Higgett" as "Wiggett," who might be a relative of the Wiggett mentioned below or even the same person.
29. Sir Charles Oman, *On the Writing of History* (London: Methuen, 1939), 221–229.
30. Wilkinson MSS, Sketchbooks 1 and 2.
31. Wilkinson MSS, "Heads of a Subject," Lady Wilkinson's biographical manuscript; also Reeve, *Men of Eminence*, 1:74.
32. Wilkinson MSS, "Oxford CP Book," "Poetry Selections," and "Poetry."
33. Wilkinson MSS, "Heads of a Subject," Lady Wilkinson's biographical manuscript; also BL, Add MSS 28512:255–256.
34. E.g., *DNB*, s.v. "Sir John Gardner Wilkinson."
35. Wilkinson MSS, "Heads of a Subject," Lady Wilkinson's biographical manuscript.
36. BL, Add MSS, 28517:258.
37. Wilkinson MSS, "Heads of a Subject," Lady Wilkinson's biographical manuscript.
38. James Burton to G. B. Greenough, 12 August 1821, University College London Library, Manuscript Room, UCL35/2.
39. Wilkinson MSS, "Journal 1819."
40. Wilkinson MSS, "Journal 1819."
41. Wilkinson MSS, "Heads of a Subject," Lady Wilkinson's biographical manuscript; also BL, Add MSS 28512:255.
42. "They have pretty faces, neat figures, good feet and ankles, dress in

the short French style." Wilkinson MSS, "Journal 1819."

43. Wilkinson MSS, "Journal 1819."

44. Ibid.

45. Ibid.

46. For Gell, see *DNB*, s.v. "Sir William Gell"; also, the introduction of Edith Clay, ed., *Sir William Gell in Italy: Letters to the Society of Dilettanti 1831–1835*; there is, however, no full-length biography of Gell.

47. Sir William Gell, *The Topography of Troy and Its Vicinity.*

48. Byron wrote "coxcomb Gell" in his manuscript of "English Bards," but changed it to "classic Gell" when he sent it to the printer; in the fifth edition he made yet another change, this time to "furious Gell." *DNB*, s.v. "Sir William Gell."

49. Sir William Gell, *The Geography and Antiquities of Ithaca.*

50. Sir William Gell, *Pompeiana.*

51. Sir William Gell and Antonio Nibby, *Le mura di Roma disegnate da Sir W. Gell: Illustrate con testo e note da A. Nibby.*

52. Clay, *Sir William Gell in Italy*, 11–12.

53. Richard Robert Madden, *The Literary Life of the Countess of Blessington*, 1:331–332.

54. Edith Clay, ed., *Lady Blessington at Naples*, 50.

55. *DNB*, s.v. "Sir William Gell."

56. Madden, *Countess of Blessington*, 1:331.

57. Lady Charlotte Bury, *The Diary of a Lady-in-Waiting*, 1:57. Lady Charlotte wrote, "I think I never knew a man of a more kind and gentle turn of mind, nor one so humanized by literature and the particular pursuits to which he devoted himself as Mr. Gell. He was affectionate in the highest degree and willing to impart all he knew, (no common stock of information,) in the least pedantic and most agreeable manner."

58. Wilkinson MSS, "Heads of a Subject," Lady Wilkinson's biographical manuscript.

59. Wilkinson MSS, "June 1820."

60. Wilkinson's sketches of the Austrian soldiers are in Wilkinson MSS, Sketchbook IV.

61. The vase he saw in Naples would have been the kalpis by the Kleophrades Painter. Jasper Gaunt and D. C. Kurtz, "Corpus Vasorum Antiquorum: Harrow," unpublished manuscript.

62. Wilkinson MSS, Sketchbook 4.

63. Samuel Birch, the introduction to *Manners and Customs of the Ancient Egyptians*, by Sir Gardner Wilkinson, ix n.

64. Wilkinson MSS, "Heads of a Subject," Lady Wilkinson's biographical manuscript.

65. Ibid.; also see Wilkinson MSS, the two notebooks entitled "Green Extracts."

66. Sir William Gell to Thomas Young, Rome, 25 May 1821, National Library of Scotland, Department of Manuscripts, 584, no. 789, fols. 168–169; also see Madden, *Countess of Blessington*, 2:492.

2. The Origins of Egyptology

1. The preparation of this chapter has relied upon several histories of Egyptology. Two have been especially useful: Leslie Greener's *The Discovery of Egypt* for the period to the eighteenth century and John A. Wilson's *Signs and Wonders upon Pharaoh* for the eighteenth and nineteenth centuries.

2. Diodorus Siculus 1.45.6 (Loeb series).

3. Ibid., 1.69.

4. Ibid., 1.96.

5. Herodotus 2.143; cf. Solon's experience as recounted in Plato's *Timaeus* (23B [Loeb series]) when the priests at Saïs told him that the genealogies that he had related to them were "little better than children's tales."

6. Herodotus 2.35 (trans. George Rawlinson, *The History of Herodotus*); Wilkinson edited the Egyptian passages in this edition.

7. *Phaedrus* 274D (trans. Harold North Taylor, Loeb series). Thoth is also mentioned in the *Philebus*.

8. Diodorus Siculus 9.98. Plutarch (*On Isis and Osiris* 10) gives a similar list.

9. Erik Iversen, *The Myth of Egypt and Its Hieroglyphs in European Tradition*, 38.

10. R. E. Witt, *Isis in the Graeco-Roman World* (London: Thames and Hudson, 1971), 203.

11. Erik Iversen, *Obelisks in Exile*, vol. 1, *The Obelisks of Rome*, 56–64; the erection of the obelisk in Rome is described by Ammianus Marcellinus (17.4).

12. Aelius Aristides, *Roman Oration*, 101 (trans. James O. Oliver in *The Ruling Power* [Philadelphia: American Philosophical Society, 1953]).

13. J. G. (Sir Gardner) Wilkinson, "On the Contrivances by Means of Which the Statue of Memnon at Thebes Was Made Vocal," *Transactions of the Royal Society of Literature of the United Kingdom* 2 (1834):451–456.

14. André and Etienne Bernard, *Les inscriptions Greques et Latines du Colosse de Memnon* (Paris: Institut Français d'Archéologie Orientale, 1960), 68 (my translation).

15. H. J. Rose, *The Roman Questions of Plutarch* (Oxford: Clarendon Press, 1924), 53.

16. Thomas Whittaker, *The Neo-Platonists*, 26–27.

17. For Hermeticism see A. J. Festugière, *La révélation d'Hermès Trismégiste*.

18. Lactantius, *Divinae institutiones*, 1.6; 4.6; 8.18.

19. Augustine, *De civitate Dei*, 8.23.

20. Sir John Maundeville [pseud.], *The Voiage and Travaile of Sir John Maundevile, K*ᵗ, 63–64.

21. Greener, *Discovery of Egypt*, 32.

22. The Tyger is mentioned in Shakespeare's *Macbeth* by the First Witch: "Her husband's to Aleppo gone, master of the Tyger" (1.3.7).

23. Greener, *Discovery of Egypt*, 44.

24. Ibid., 43.

25. Ibid.

26. Francis A. Yates, *Giordano Bruno and the Hermetic Tradition*, 12–14.

27. From *Oedipus Aegyptiacus*, quoted in Yates, *Giordano Bruno*, 417–418.

28. (Sir) John Gardner Wilkinson, *Manners and Customs of the Ancient Egyptians*, 4:12 (hereafter cited as *MCAE*). In these notes, volumes 1 and 2 of the second series are numbered 4 and 5 as they were in later editions.

29. Greener, *Discovery of Egypt*, 54–55.

30. Frederick Lewis Norden, *Travels in Egypt and Nubia*, and (a volume of plates) *The Antiquities, Natural History, Ruins and Other Curiosities of Egypt, Nubia, and Thebes;* Richard Pococke, *A Description of the East and Some Other Countries*.

31. James Bruce, *Travels to Discover the Source of the Nile, in the Years 1768, 1769, 1770, 1771, 1772, and 1773*. For the reception of Bruce's book, see Patrick Conner, *The Inspiration of Egypt*.

32. Warren R. Dawson, "The First Egyptian Society," *Journal of Egyptian Archaeology* 23 (1937):259–260; M. Anis, "The First Egyptian Society in London (1741–1743)," *Bulletin de l'Institut Français d'Archéologie Orientale* 50 (1952):95–105.

33. BL, Add MSS 52362.

34. J. Christopher Herold, *Bonaparte in Egypt* (New York: Harper & Row, 1962), 151.

35. *The Edinburgh Review* 1 (January 1803):330.

36. The twenty-four volumes of the *Description de l'Egypte* were published between 1809 and 1813 in Paris by Imprimerie de C. L. F. Panckoucke.

37. R. R. Madden, *Egypt and Mohammed Ali*, 25–26.

38. For Salt, see *DNB* and *WWW;* J. J. Halls, *The Life and Correspondence of Henry Salt;* C. E. Bosworth, "Henry Salt, Consul in Egypt 1816–1827 and Pioneer Egyptologist," *Bulletin of the John Rylands University Library of Manchester* 57, no. 1 (Autumn 1974):69–91; and Lewis McNaught, "Henry Salt: His Contribution to the Collections of Egyptian Sculpture in the British Museum," *Apollo* 108 (October 1978):224–231.

39. Johan David Akerblad to Thomas Young, Rome, 19 April 1816, BL, Add MSS 21026:29–30. It would have been at Naples that Salt became acquainted with Sir William Gell, if they had not already met. Akerblad (1763–1819) was a Swedish diplomat and orientalist. He and his teacher, Silvestre de Sacy (1758–1838), made marginal progress in reading some demotic names on the Rosetta Stone.

40. Jaromír Málek and Mark Smith, "Henry Salt's Egyptian Copies and Drawings," *Göttinger Miszellen* 64 (1983):35–52; also M. L. Bierbrier, "The Salt Watercolours," *Göttinger Miszellen* 61 (1983):9–12.

41. Giovanni Battista Belzoni, *Narrative of the Operations and Recent*

Discoveries within the Pyramids, Temples, Tombs, and Excavations in Egypt and Nubia. The sarcophagus of Seti I is now in the Sir John Soane Museum, London.

42. Some of the correspondence pertaining to this transaction is in BL, Add MSS 19347:350 et seq.

43. Sir Richard F. Burton, "Giovanni Battista Belzoni," *Cornhill Magazine* 42 (July 1880): 39–40.

44. M. Saulnier, Fils, *Notice sur le voyage de M. Lelorrain en Egypte; et observations sur le zodiaque circulaire de Denderah,* 16.

45. Sir Frederick Henniker, Bart., *Notes during a Visit to Egypt, Nubia, the Oasis, Mount Sinai, and Jerusalem,* 139.

46. John A. Wilson, *The Culture of Ancient Egypt,* 284.

47. Ibid., 287.

48. Alexander Henry Rhind, *Thebes, Its Tombs and Their Tenants,* 69. The agent was probably Giovanni d'Athanasi.

49. Ibid., 62–63.

50. Ammianus 17.4.10–11.

51. A summary of the writers on hieroglyphics until the time of Champollion is in Henri Gautier, "Un précurseur de Champollion au XVIᵉ siècle," *Bulletin de l'Institut Français d'Archéologie Orientale* 5 (1906): 65–86.

52. For Warburton, see John David Wortham's *British Egyptology 1549–1906,* 42–43.

53. Wilson, *Signs and Wonders,* 11.

54. It has been said that demotic is a shorthand for hieroglyphic script, but that is inaccurate. Demotic was used to write the Egyptian language as it was spoken long after the spoken language of the hieroglyphic script had become archaic. The two scripts therefore not only employed different orthography, but also represented substantially different languages.

55. Greener, *Discovery of Egypt,* 146.

56. Alexander Wood and Frank Oldham, *Thomas Young, Natural Philosopher 1773–1829.*

57. It is ironic that Thomas Young has no entry in the current edition of the *Encyclopaedia Britannica,* despite his contributions to Egyptology and many other fields of knowledge.

3. Egypt

1. Wilkinson MSS, "1821 Green Extracts Naples."

2. Wilkinson MSS, "Turkish History. Voltaire. Diodors. etc." Some of this may have been done at Malta.

3. Giuseppe Campanile, *Storia della regione del Kurdistan e delle sette di religione ivi esistenti* (Naples: Fratelli Fernandes, 1818).

4. James Burton to G. B. Greenough, Naples, 12 August 1821, University College London Library, Manuscript Room, UCL35/2.

5. Examples of Gell's hieroglyphics are on a page in Wilkinson MSS, "Letters &c," and in Gell's three Egyptological notebooks, Archives, Griffith Institute, Ashmolean Museum, Oxford, England (hereafter cited as GIA).

Someone who saw Gell sketch wrote, "His hands were as big as a leg of mutton and covered with chalkstones, and yet he could handle a pencil or a reed-pen with the greatest delicacy and precision" (Charles Dickens, ed., *Life of Charles J. Matthews*, 95).

6. Sir Gardner Wilkinson, *The Architecture of the Ancient Egyptians*, xii.

7. Wilkinson MSS, Sketchbook 4.

8. Wilkinson MSS, "Journey in Nubia, the Eastern Desert, & to Báhneséh by J. G. W., 1821–23" (hereafter cited as "Journey in Nubia").

9. Wilkinson MSS, "Heads of a Subject," Lady Wilkinson's biographical manuscript.

10. Wilkinson MSS, "Journal 1821 Egypt," 3.

11. J. G. (Sir Gardner) Wilkinson, *Topography of Thebes and General View of Egypt*, 287–288.

12. For this distinction, see Edward William Lane, manuscript draft "Notes and Views in Egypt and Nubia, Made During the Years 1825, —26, —27, & —28," BL, Add MSS 34080:4.

13. Wilkinson translated *shemálak*, your left; *riglak*, your leg; *dahrak*, your back.

14. Wilkinson MSS, "Letters to Sir William Gell," 7–8. The first moments in Alexandria always left a powerful impression on European travelers, even on Robert Hay, who had been there before. Hay wrote in 1824, "The scene that at once broke upon me was truly curious & strikingly interesting, and cannot fail to have the same effect on all Europeans & create the same feelings as it did on me, & as [I] could see it also did on Bonomi." Hay diary, BL Add MSS 31054:50. Depictions of Alexandria are numerous in the sketchbooks of James Burton, Robert Hay, and Edward William Lane, as well as in those of Wilkinson.

15. Wilkinson MSS, "Journal 1821 Egypt," 5, and Wilkinson MSS, "Letters to Sir William Gell," 5.

16. Wilkinson MSS, "Letters to Sir William Gell," 4.

17. Sir Richard Burton, *Personal Narrative of a Pilgrimage to Al-Madinah and Meccah*, 1:29.

18. There were three primary kinds of river craft. The *canjah*, which Edward William Lane described as the most common, was long and narrow with twin masts and sails and a low cabin. The *dahabiyah* was larger than most *canjah*s and wider in proportion to its length, though similar in other respects. The *maash* was even larger, large enough to transport not only passengers but also bulky cargo such as grain. Apart from its extra carrying space near the front, however, the *maash* closely resembled the *canjah* and *dahabiyah* (Edward William Lane, manuscript draft "Notes and Views in Egypt and Nubia, Made During the Years 1825, —26, —27, & —28," BL Add MSS 34080:40–41).

19. Wilkinson MSS, leather satchel, has a detailed scale drawing of a *dahabiyah*, and Wilkinson MSS, Sketchbook V, shows his *dahabiyah* on the river.

20. Wilkinson, *Topography of Thebes*, 565.

21. Wilkinson MSS, "Letters to Sir William Gell," 12.

22. Ibid., 11.

23. Wilkinson MSS, "Letters to Sir William Gell," 10v, and Wilkinson MSS, "Journal 1821 Egypt." His sketch of the dancing crew is in Wilkinson MSS, Sketchbook V.

24. Wilkinson, *Topography of Thebes*, 297.

25. Wilkinson MSS, "Letters to Sir William Gell," 7–8.

26. In his text to Robert Hay's *Illustrations of Cairo*, 13.

27. For Cairo see Janet Abu-Lughod, *Cairo: 1001 Years of the City Victorious* (Princeton: Princeton University Press, 1971); also see Robert Hay's description in the typescript of his diary, 10, GIA.

28. This is taken from Gell's autograph version that he wrote circa 1820 and gave to James Burton (BL Add MSS 25661:33); Wilkinson's copy is in Wilkinson MSS, "Poetry," 43. By Tentyra Gell meant Dendera.

29. Salt still occasionally made notable portraits, such as the one he did of J. L. Burckhardt and his provocative depiction of R. R. Madden in the beginning of Madden's *Travels in Turkey, Egypt, Nubia, and Palestine in 1824–7.*

30. Wilkinson MSS, "Journey in Nubia," 159.

31. Wilkinson MSS, "Journal 1821 Egypt," 9. Wilkinson recorded little about this visit. Details of an audience with Muhammad Ali are taken from the account of Sir Frederick Henniker, Bart., whom the vice-consul took on a visit to the pasha not long before Wilkinson's. Henniker, *Notes*, 62–63.

32. Wilkinson MSS, "Letters to Sir William Gell," 12.

33. Where Henry Westcar saw it. The manuscript diary of Henry Westcar, entitled "A Journal of a Tour Made through Egypt Upper and Lower Nubia on the Nile," 1 June 1824, fol. 248, Library of the German Institute of Archaeology, Cairo.

Although Wilkinson carved his name on places such as the rock at Abusir and atop the Second Pyramid at Giza, he was not one to deface monuments by carving it conspicuously on temple walls and so forth. For example, Warren Dawson does not record it as being carved on the temple at Abu Simbel (Notebook no. 3, BL, Add MSS 56319). Wilkinson had only ridicule for Richard Lepsius's Prussian expedition and its graffito: "You have of course read Dr Lepsius' letters from Egypt & I dare say have wondered as I have how people could be so silly as to put up that inscription in hieroglyphs on the great Pyramid about the King of Prussia & the rest. The English have been laughed at for scribbling their names but this far exceeds in folly any thing done by them" (Wilkinson to an unidentified correspondent, illegible date, National Library of Scotland, Department of Manuscripts, 583, no. 873, fols. 326–327).

34. Westcar diary, fols. 258–260.

35. Hay diary typescript, 37, GIA. In his first major published work, Wilkinson recommended Osman to his readers: "For further information . . . I refer the traveller who visits the capital of Egypt to Osman Effendee, dragoman of the Consulate, who combines with the greatest readiness to assist his compatriots, a perfect acquaintance with the customs of the country, in which he has lived so long, and to judge from my own opin-

ion as well as that of other travellers, I feel persuaded he will have reason to acknowledge the value of his services in the British Consulate" (Wilkinson, *Topography of Thebes*, 568). References to Osman may be found in many of the books, journals, and letters of travelers of the day.

36. Wilkinson MSS, "Journal 1821 Egypt."

37. This description is taken primarily from the account of Robert Hay whom Osman assisted into Turkish attire in 1824 (Hay diary typescript, 31–33, GIA).

38. Westcar diary, 25 June 1824, fols. 253–254.

39. William Martin Leake (1777–1860), a classical topographer and numismatist. He traveled extensively in the East during the first decade of the nineteenth century. A prominent member of many scholarly societies, he became well acquainted with Wilkinson after the latter returned to England.

40. This is inside the Eighteenth Dynasty temple near the Great Gate. It is dated 12 March 1822. Apparently a relative subsequently made the trip, for just under Wiggett's name is chisled "E. H. Wiggett" with the date December 1844.

41. Wilkinson MSS, "Journey in Nubia," chapter 1.

42. James Augustus St. John, *Egypt and Mohammed Ali; or Travels in the Valley of the Nile*, 1:499. Warren Dawson supplied other names that St. John failed to include (Notebook no. 155, BL, Add MSS 56326).

43. Wilkinson MSS, "Heads of a Subject," Lady Wilkinson's biographical manuscript.

44. Alessandro Ricci, who died in 1832, was an Italian explorer, collector, and physician, though his medical status seems to have been more a matter of experience and courtesy than university degree. He served as physician on Champollion's expedition to Egypt.

45. Sir William Gell to Wilkinson, Naples, 5 March 1824, in Wilkinson MSS, "Letters &c." Wiggett's name and address appear in Wilkinson's address book in later life, suggesting that Wilkinson maintained at least loose contact with him.

46. Wilkinson MSS, "Heads of a Subject," Lady Wilkinson's biographical manuscript.

47. Hay diary, BL, Add MSS 31054:117v–119.

48. Sir William Gell to Thomas Young, Terracina, 10 March 1824, in John Leitch, ed., *Miscellaneous Works of the Late Thomas Young*, 3:374.

49. Ibid., 3:461n.

50. Jaromír Málek, "A Graffito of Year 17 of Amenemhet II at el-Hôsh," *Göttinger Miszellen* 24 (1977):51.

51. *WWW*, s.v. "(Sir) John Gardner Wilkinson."

52. Sir William Gell to Wilkinson, July 1822, Wilkinson MSS, "Letters &c."

4. Life in Cairo and a Trip into the Eastern Desert

1. BL, Add MSS 25653 passim.

2. Wilkinson MSS, "Letters to Sir W. Gell 1825," 1. The Hasanain should

not be confused with the Husayniya, Cairo's medieval suburb just beyond the northern wall. The Hasanain was so called because of the Mosque of the Hasanain, named for the grandsons of the Prophet, which occupied the same site as the present-day Mosque of Sayyidna al-Husayn.

Burton's friend Charles Sheffield reported that Wiggett also shared Burton's extra room for a few months before leaving Egypt. He and Wilkinson each paid Burton two piastres per day, which Sheffield considered very mean. Sheffield also thought it tight of Wilkinson to give the servants a tip of only ten piastres or so when he left. All he gave Burton was a present of two cocks. Charles Sheffield's account (notes taken by G. B. Greenough) roughly dated September 1824 and related to events in 1822 (University College London Library, Manuscript Room, UCL35/4).

3. Westcar diary, 25 June 1824, fol. 254.

4. Wilkinson MSS, "Arabic Words &c."

5. Bodleian Library, Department of Western Manuscripts, Ms. Eng. misc. d. 234, fol. 74. Note also this observation by the traveler Joseph Moyle Sherer:

> The Franks, I am sorry to say, are by far the most disreputable-looking class in Cairo. No pencil, but such a one as the late Mr. Scott's, could at all convey to the reader's mind the portraits of these people. The lively fidelity of one late traveller [Belzoni?] might have done something for it, and I am surprised that he omitted the mention of them. I can only beg you to image to yourself a set of needy, indolent, adventurous, dissipated, sharp-visaged men, whose offences, or fortunes, or hopes have driven them from Trieste or Venice, Genoa or Marseilles.

And, "On Sunday all, however, are to be seen in something looking new. How they live is a matter of wonder, as many are without employ" (*Scenes and Impressions in Egypt and in Italy*, 163–164, 164n).

6. Hay diary, BL, Add MSS 31054:109.

7. Hay diary typescript, 12 December 1824, GIA.

8. Ibid., 11–12.

9. Charles Sheffield's account (notes taken by G. B. Greenough), roughly dated September 1824 and relating to events in 1822 (University College London Library, Manuscript Room, UCL35/4).

10. Hay diary, BL, Add MSS 31054:83.

11. Wilkinson MSS, Sketchbooks 3 and 4; there are two, perhaps three, sketches of Haji Musa there.

12. Westcar diary, 25 June 1824, fol. 254.

13. BL Add MSS 25658: 7, 9.

14. Ibid., fol. 8.

15. Ibid., fols. 11–12.

16. Hay diary typescript, 30, GIA.

17. Some change in the situation may be evident in Wilkinson's considered opinion about the usefulness of oriental dress in his *Topography of Thebes*, 562. Also see the opinion of James Silk Buckingham, who traveled

in Egypt at the same time Wilkinson was there, about the necessity of wearing oriental clothing ("Excursions on the Banks of the Nile," *The Oriental Herald* 13, no. 4 [June 1827]: 465).

18. As when he derided a Turk's shooting party. Westcar diary, 22 April 1824, fols. 200–201.

19. Wilkinson MSS, "Letters to Sir W. Gell 1825," 3–4.

20. *Topography of Thebes*, 563.

21. "I remember the story," he wrote in the manuscript version in Wilkinson MSS, "Journey in Nubia," 157v.

22. Wilkinson, *MCAE* 2:43–44. Cf. Edward William Lane, *An Account of the Manners and Customs of the Modern Egyptians*, 135.

23. *MCAE* 2:41–42.

24. Wilkinson MSS, "Journey in Nubia," 149.

25. Wilkinson MSS, "Letters to Sir W. Gell," 22.

26. For example, "They are as impervious and enduring as the granite of their temples, and once the form is fixed, they are as slow to change as were the forms of that art. The glances of their daily life which we get from Pharaonic tombs or from Coptic legends, from the Arab historians or the Napoleonic expeditions, from the earlier English explorers or the travelers of our own day, seem to form one single sequence. One has the impression that all these scenes, separated by centuries, only repeat and confirm each other" (Henry Habib Ayrout, *The Egyptian Peasant*, trans. John Alden Williams [1938; reprint, Boston: Beacon Press, 1963], 2).

27. Wilkinson MSS, "Letters to Sir W. Gell 1825," 23. Wilkinson's knowledge of the *fellahin* was not close enough for him to be absolutely correct in detail. Like most observers of that day, he exaggerated the horrors of the corvée, asserting that the workers were unpaid and that as many as tens of thousands of lives were lost on big projects such as the Maḥmoudiah Canal, the "canal of Alexandria" that he mentioned. Wilkinson was not present when that canal was constructed and relied upon heresay evidence for his assessment of it. It has been shown that corvée workers were paid wages and given rations, though some abuses probably occurred during the construction of the Mahmoudiah Canal, which may have involved a quarter million workers. The main reason the *fellahin* hated corvée labor was because it took them away from their homes and families. Families frequently followed the workers because the families had no means of support without them. See Afaf Lutfi al-Sayyid Marsot, *Egypt in the Reign of Muhammad Ali*, 151.

28. Sir Gardner Wilkinson, *Three Letters on the Policy of England towards the Porte and Mohammed Ali*, 30.

29. Ibid., 27.

30. Wilkinson MSS, "Journey in Nubia," 149.

31. Marsot, *Egypt in the Reign of Muhammad Ali*, 102.

32. Wilkinson MSS, "Journey in Nubia," 149–151.

33. Ibid., 149.

34. Wilkinson, *Topography of Thebes*, xix.

35. Wilkinson MSS, "Journey in Nubia," 151.

36. BL, Add MSS 25630:33.

37. Wilkinson MSS, "Letters to Sir William Gell," 13.

38. Henniker, *Notes*, 5.

39. Wilkinson's friend Joseph Bonomi reported, "The people of Der after having performed the operation of the excision of the clitoris, they boil butter dates and henna leaves together and whilst the decoction is extremely hot, they pour it into the parts newly operated. This they say is to render the women faithful by destroying in them the desire of coition" (Bonomi diary typescript, GIA); Burton also briefly mentioned this (BL Add MSS 25662:11).

40. Wilkinson MSS, "Letters to Sir. W. Gell," 22–23.

41. *Topography of Thebes*, 252.

42. See below. Possibly Wilkinson was less discreet than his papers indicate, and the censorship of Lady Wilkinson may explain the lack of information. She may also have removed some papers when she examined his manuscripts after his death.

43. Hay diary, BL, Add MSS 31054:82v.

44. Tillet, *Egypt Itself*, 38.

45. Westcar diary, 22 April 1824, fol. 200.

46. Recounted in his *Voyage en Orient*, the definitive edition of which was published in 1851.

47. Charles Sheffield's account (notes taken by G. B. Greenough), roughly dated September 1824 and related to events in 1822 (University College London Library, Manuscript Room, UCL35/4).

48. The comma is the decimal point. Twelve hundred piastres, or twelve pounds, was about the normal price for such a slave according to the price range that Wilkinson lists in his *Topography of Thebes* (p. 286).

49. BL, Add MSS 25662:12–13. An illustration of the slave market is in Robert Hay's *Illustrations of Cairo*, plate 25.

50. *Topography of Thebes*, 302–303. Also see Robert Hay's comments in regard to his illustration, cited above.

51. Edward William Lane, manuscript draft "Notes and Views in Egypt and Nubia, Made During the Years 1825, —26, —27, & —28," BL, Add MSS 34080:165–166.

52. Wilkinson, *Modern Egypt and Thebes*, 2:18–19.

53. Joseph Hekekyan Bey (1807–1875) was an Armenian civil engineer. Educated in England, he served the Egyptian government in various capacities until 1850 when he, along with other Christians, was dismissed (*WWW*, s.v. "Joseph Hekekyan Bey").

54. *Excerpta Hieroglyphica*, which consists of sixty-four plates without letterpress, was published 1825–28 in Cairo. Wilkinson is mentioned in connection with plate 35. Even in later years Wilkinson considered Burton's *Excerpta Hieroglyphica* to be "a very useful collection containing as it does copies of the monuments relating to the succession of the Kings of the most interesting period of Egyptian history & many other important subjects" (Wilkinson to Bernard Quaritch, 31 May, year illegible but between 1857

and 1859, Bodleian Library, Department of Western Manuscript, MS. Eng. lett. e. 147, fol. 21).

55. Thomas Young's manuscript memorandum, Wilkinson MSS, "Letters &c II."

56. Burton's diary of his Eastern Desert trip of 1822 is in BL, Add MSS 25622; his notes from the trip are in BL Add MSS 25624.

57. J. G. (Sir Gardner) Wilkinson, "Notes on a Part of the Eastern Desert of Upper Egypt," *Journal of the Royal Geographical Society* 2 (1832):28–60. There are several drafts of Wilkinson's account of the trip among the Wilkinson MSS. Burton's diary of this trip is in BL, Add MSS 25623; BL, Add MSS 25628 is some of his Eastern Desert plans and drawings.

58. Wilkinson, *Modern Egypt and Thebes*, 2:18.

59. BL, Add MSS 25626:1.

60. Wilkinson MSS, "Eastern Desert & [   ] 1823 J.G.W." Although the animals that they distinguished as camels and dromedaries all were camels, travelers of that day were careful to maintain a distinction; for example: "A dromedary differs from a camel in its make, its uses, and its *master*, as a hunter differs from a pack-horse" (Henniker, *Notes*, 258n. 1).

61. Wilkinson, *Modern Egypt and Thebes*, 2:229n.

62. For the monastic institutions see Otto F. A. Meinardus, *Monks and Monasteries of the Egyptian Deserts.*

63. As the editor of the *Journal of the Royal Geographical Society* noted. See Wilkinson, "Notes on the Eastern Desert," 34n.

64. Wilkinson MSS, "Journey in Nubia," chapter 2.

65. For an assessment of Wilkinson's work at Mons Porphyrites and at some of the way stations, see C. H. O. Scaife, "Two Inscriptions at Mons Porphyrites (Gebel Dokhan). Also a Description with Plans, of the Stations: Between Kainopolis & Myos Hormos Together with Some Other Ruins in the Neighborhood of Gebel Dokhan," *Bulletin of the Faculty of Arts Fouad I University* 3, no. 2 (1935):58–104.

66. Wilkinson and Burton were mistaken about Abu Shaar being the site of Myos Hormos. For an assessment of Wilkinson's work at Abu Shaar, see Steven E. Sidebotham et al., "Fieldwork on the Red Sea Coast: The 1987 Season," *Journal of the American Research Center in Egypt* 26 (1989):131–132. Abu Shaar is located less than ten miles north of Hurghada (more properly, Ghardaka).

67. For an evocative description of this quality see A. E. P. Weigall, *Travels in the Upper Egyptian Deserts*, 122–130. The nearly pristine state of the ruins lasted until the 1980s when the site began to be visited by increasing numbers of tourists. It is now being destroyed rapidly, making it difficult to capture that sensation of the past that moved earlier visitors.

68. The manuscript "Journey in Nubia" is in the Wilkinson MSS. Bahnasah is the site of the ancient Greek town of Oxyrhhynchus, a fact that Wilkinson considered likely ("Journey in Nubia," 153), though it was as yet unconfirmed. At the end of the nineteenth century Oxyrhhynchus was discovered to be the most important source of papyri in all of Egypt.

69. Thomas Young's memorandum, Wilkinson MSS, "Letters &c II."

5. More Explorations

1. Wilkinson MSS, "Cairo to Asouan & Fyoom & Oases to Thebes 1824–5."
2. Westcar diary, 21 April 1824, fols. 199–200.
3. The Westcar diary provides a vivid account of their worries.
4. Westcar diary, 23 April 1824, fol. 200.
5. John Madox, *Excursions in the Holy Land, Egypt, Nubia, Syria, &c,* 2:28.
6. His map of the "Feioom" was later published by Arrowsmith. A copy is in the Wilkinson MSS.
7. Ahmed Fakhry, *The Oases of Egypt,* 2 vols. (Cairo: American University in Cairo Press, 1974), 2:52–53.
8. Wilkinson MSS, "Letters to Sir W. Gell 1825," 8–10.
9. Fakhry, *The Oases of Egypt,* 2:53–54. Apparently the pasha's efforts were inconclusive, for the natives of Siwa Oasis revolted in 1829 (Sir Gardner Wilkinson, *Handbook for Travellers in Egypt,* 234).
10. Wilkinson MSS, "Letters to Sir W. Gell 1825," 4–7.
11. Gell, *Topography of Troy,* 8–10.
12. Ahmed Fahkry criticized Wilkinson for not saying more about the antiquities of the oases (*The Oases of Egypt,* 2:74). Wilkinson's notebooks contain information about them, but he never treated them extensively in print. One should always bear in mind that Wilkinson's published material incorporates only a fraction of his research.
13. Wilkinson to Robert Hay, 15 January 1833, BL, Add MSS 38094: 56–57.
14. BL, Add MSS 29858:65.
15. Wilkinson MSS, "1825" and an envelope labeled "'Ababda Desert, 1826." Several other volumes of notebooks and loose notes in the Wilkinson MSS are devoted to the Eastern Desert.
16. Reeve, *Men of Eminence* 1:77.
17. Henry Salt to James Burton, Cairo, 30 March 1824, BL, Add MSS 25658:3–4.
18. Wilkinson MSS, "1863 = 1875 to the End."
19. Herodotus mentioned seeing Egyptian writing on the Great Pyramid; it was inscribed on the casing stones which were removed during the interval between Herodotus and the nineteenth-century travelers. Herodotus wrote, "An inscription is cut upon it [the Great Pyramid] in Egyptian characters recording the amount spent on radishes, onions, and leeks for the labourers, and I remember distinctly that the interpreter who read me the inscription said the sum was 1600 talents of silver" (Herodotus 2.124, trans. Aubrey de Selincourt). Egyptologists today, however, doubt that such an inscription existed. Herodotus may have been deceived by his interpreter.
20. "I have the impression that this confirms W's notion," Anthony Charles Harris wrote on 28 May 1837, when he announced the discovery to Edward William Lane (BL, Add MSS 56273:50); also, Letter no. 31, Lane collection, GIA.

21. *MCAE* 1:19. By Suphis, Wilkinson means Cheops; by Sensuphis, Cephren.

22. I. E. S. Edwards, *The Pyramids of Egypt*, 97.

23. Wilkinson MSS, "Cairo to Asouan & Fyoom to Thebes 1824–5," fol. d verso.

24. Ibid. Also see Wilkinson's description of Amarna in his *Extracts from Several Hieroglyphical Subjects, Found at Thebes, and Other Parts of Egypt: With Remarks on the Same*, 21–22. Wilkinson refers to Tuna el-Gebel on the west bank where two of Akh-en-Aton's stelae marked the boundary of the territory attached to Tell el-Amarna.

25. Wilkinson to Major General J. Nicolls, Cairo, 13 August 1825, private collection of Robert Lucas.

26. BL, Add MSS 25653:24.

27. Ibid. Some of Burton's sketches of Amarna are in BL, Add MSS 25634.

28. Sir William Gell, notebook no. 1, 11, GIA.

29. See chapter 6, pp. 89–90.

30. Wilkinson MSS, "Cairo to Asouan & Fyoom to Thebes 1824–5," fol. d verso; also in his *Extracts from Several Hieroglyphical Subjects*, 21–22.

31. Norman de Garis Davies, *The Rock Tombs of El Amarna: Part I. The Tomb of Meryra*, 1.

32. Nina M. Davies, "Birds and Bats at Beni Hasan," *Journal of Egyptian Archaeology* 35 (1949): 13–14. For the use that Wilkinson made of this information see his detailed list and description of fowl known in ancient Egypt (*MCAE*, 3:48–53).

33. Nina M. Davies, "Birds and Bats at Beni Hasan," 13, and a fragment of a letter from Wilkinson to Sir William Gell, undated but 1833, in Wilkinson MSS, "Letters &c."

34. *MCAE*, 2:44.

35. In 1824 Wilkinson mentioned a "3rd visit to Beni Hasan." Nina M. Davies, "Birds and Bats at Beni Hasan," 13.

36. For Wilkinson's account of his investigation of the colossus, see J. G. (Sir Gardner) Wilkinson, "On the Contrivances by Means of Which the Statue of Memnon at Thebes Was Made Vocal"; also, Wilkinson, *Topography of Thebes*, 37.

37. Lane notebooks, Notebook no. 14, 19 November 1827, 8, Lane collection, GIA. The natives called the plain "Salama't," or "Salutations," Lane noted.

38. Sir William Gell to William Hamilton, Naples, 29 July 1833, in Clay, *Sir William Gell in Italy*, 131.

39. E. A. Wallis Budge, *Cleopatra's Needles*, 27. Wilkinson omitted a step in the process: the wooded supports were soaked in water; when they swelled the obelisk was exploded from its matrix.

40. Wilkinson to Sir William Gell, Qena, 4 December 1826, in H. R. Hall, "Letters to Sir William Gell from Henry Salt, (Sir) J. G. Wilkinson, and Baron von Bunsen," *Journal of Egyptian Archaeology* 2 (1915): 144.

41. Henry Salt to Sir William Gell, Alexandria, 16 September 1822, in Hall, "Letters to Sir William Gell," 138.

42. Sir William Gell to Wilkinson, July 1822, Wilkinson MSS, "Letters &c."

43. Wilkinson MSS, "Journey in Nubia," 52v.

44. E. A. Wallis Budge, *The Rosetta Stone in the British Museum*, 12.

45. Wilkinson, *Handbook for Travellers in Egypt*, 104.

46. Wilkinson to Sir William Gell, Cairo, 3 October 1832, Wilkinson MSS, "Letters &c"; and Wilkinson to Sir William Gell, Leghorn, undated but 1833, Wilkinson MSS, "Letters &c."

47. Wilkinson MSS, "Journey in Nubia," 52v; cf. the quotation from Ammianus Marcellinus in chapter 2, p. 28.

48. Wilkinson to Sir William Gell, undated but probably 1828, in Hall, "Letters to Sir William Gell," 163.

49. See Henry Salt's observations on Horapollo in Hall, "Letters to Sir William Gell," 139.

50. Sir William Gell to Wilkinson, Naples, 25 June 1823, Wilkinson MSS, "Letters &c."

51. Sir William Gell to Wilkinson, Naples, 10 August 1824, Wilkinson MSS, "Letters &c."

52. Leitch, *Thomas Young*, 3:363–366.

53. Dawson and Uphill call Lepsius's letter to Rosellini in 1837 the turning point in hieroglyphic studies (*WWW*, s.v. "Karl Richard Lepsius"). They assign the achievement of being the first to read a running text to Vicomte de Rougé (*WWW*, s.v. "[Vicomte] Olivier Charles Camille Emmanuel de Rogué").

54. Wilkinson to Sir William Gell, undated but probably 1828, in Hall, "Letters to Sir William Gell," 161. The manuscript that Lord Prudhoe gave him is among the Wilkinson MSS: "Bound Paper Volume: *Coptic Manuscript* from One of the Natron Lakes. Gift of Lord Prudhoe."

55. Sir William Gell to Wilkinson, "Napsholes" [Naples], 4 November 1834, Wilkinson MSS, "Letters &c."

56. Wilkinson MSS, Lady Wilkinson's biographical manuscript, fol. 8; also see Leitch, *Thomas Young*, 3:465n.

57. For Wilkinson's considered opinion of the matter see *MCAE*, 3:192–194.

58. For an assessment of Wilkinson's work at this stage see Hall, "Letters to Sir William Gell," 134–135.

59. As Dawson and Uphill point out in *WWW*, s.v. "(Sir) John Gardner Wilkinson." Wilkinson wrote in 1835, "I have arrived at the same general results, with some few immaterial exceptions, as the savant I have just mentioned [i.e., Champollion], without having had the least communication with him, either in Europe or during his stay in Egypt, and the *same* conclusions have sometimes been formed previously, sometimes subsequently, to his" (*Topography of Thebes*, 56).

60. Wilkinson to Sir William Gell, Thebes, 2 July 1827, in Hall, "Letters to Sir William Gell," 154.

61. Wilkinson to Sir William Gell, Eastern Desert, September 1828, in

Hall, "Letters to Sir William Gell," 158. Also see Wilkinson, *Topography of Thebes*, 57.

62. See BL, Add MSS 25663:60. Wilkinson and Champollion were not the first to realize that Luxor was the site of ancient Thebes. That fact had been established early in the eighteenth century by the Jesuit Father Claude Sicard who detected the correspondences in Strabo and Diodorus.

63. James Baikie, *A Century of Excavation in the Land of the Pharaohs*, 92; but Baikie fails to see the superiority of Wilkinson's transliteration. For Wilkinson's thoughts on "the Pharaoh Amunneitgori," see *Topography of Thebes* (pp. 90–91).

64. Wilkinson to Sir William Gell, Thebes, 2 July 1827, in Hall, "Letters to Sir William Gell," 148; also see Hall's observation on p. 136.

65. Wilkinson to M. Stanhope Badcock, Thebes, 28 June 1827, Wilkinson MSS, "Eastern Desert to Thebes 1826." For Salt's "essay" see chapter 8, p. 121.

66. Hermine Hartleben, ed., *Lettres de Champollion le Jeune*, 1:204, 208, 213–214, 376; for Gell's and Wilkinson's influence on Champollion, also see Hartleben's *Champollion: Sein Leben und sein Werk*, 2:52, 547.

67. Sir William Gell to Wilkinson, Naples, 5 July 1825, Wilkinson MSS, "Letters &c."

68. Sir William Gell to Wilkinson, 2 November 1825, Wilkinson MSS, "Letters &c." Gell also sent some of James Burton's material to Champollion. BL, Add MSS 25653:9.

69. Hartleben, *Lettres de Champollion*, 1:213–214, 220, 376, 382, and 2:141 (my translation).

70. Hartleben, *Champollion*, 2:501.

71. Sir William Gell to Wilkinson, Naples, 10 April 1832, Wilkinson MSS, "Letters &c."

72. Sir William Gell to Wilkinson, Naples, 5 March 1824, Wilkinson MSS, "Letters &c."

73. Gell notebooks, Notebook no. 3, GIA.

74. Wilkinson to Captain M. Stanhope Badcock, Thebes, 28 June 1827, Wilkinson MSS, "Eastern Desert to Thebes 1826"; and Wilkinson to Sir William Gell, Thebes, 2 July 1827, in Hall, "Letters to Sir William Gell," 151.

75. Sir William Gell to Wilkinson, July 1822, Wilkinson MSS, "Letters &c."

76. Sir William Gell to Wilkinson, Naples, 25 June 1823, Wilkinson MSS, "Letters &c."

77. See Gell's three Egyptological notebooks in the GIA.

78. Clay, *Lady Blessington*, 110.

79. Sir William Gell to Thomas Young, 10 March 1824, in Leitch, *Thomas Young*, 3:374.

80. Sir William Gell to Wilkinson, Naples, 5 March 1824, Wilkinson MSS, "Letters &c."

81. Sir William Gell to Thomas Young, Naples, 22 July 1823, in Leitch, *Thomas Young*, 3:363–364.

82. George Peacock, *Life of Thomas Young, M.D., F.R.S., &c., and One of the Eight Foreign Associates of the National Institute of France,* 440–441.
83. Thomas Young to Sir William Gell, 13 September 1823, in Leitch, *Thomas Young,* 3:370.
84. Sir William Gell to Thomas Young, Terracina, 10 March 1824, ibid., 3:374.
85. Sir William Gell to Thomas Young, Rome, 6 June 1824, ibid., 3:377.
86. Thomas Young to Sir William Gell, Spa, 13 August 1825, ibid., 3:382–383.
87. Sir William Gell to Thomas Young, Naples, 5 August 1826, ibid., 3:395.
88. Sir William Gell to Wilkinson, Naples, 5 March 1824, Wilkinson MSS, "Letters &c."
89. Sir William Gell to Thomas Young, Naples, 18 March 1827, in Leitch, *Thomas Young,* 3:408. The "triumvirate" to which Gell refers was composed of Young, Champollion, and Gustavus Seyffarth; see H. R. Hall, "Letters of Champollion le Jeune and of Seyffarth to Sir William Gell," *Journal of Egyptian Archaeology* 2 (1915):80.
90. Thomas Young to Sir William Gell, London, 10 April 1827, in Leitch, *Thomas Young,* 3:415.

6. British Colleagues in Egypt

1. For Robert Hay, see Tillett's *Egypt Itself;* also *DNB* and *WWW.* Hay's autograph diary is in the British Library (BL, Add MSS 31054), but there is a typescript in the GIA that contains material from another version of the diary that apparently is no longer extant.
2. Tillett, *Egypt Itself,* 11.
3. Sir William Gell to Wilkinson, Naples, 10 August 1824, Wilkinson MSS, "Letters &c."
4. For Joseph Bonomi, see *DNB* and *WWW,* as well as relevant passages in Tillett. The typescript of his diary is in the GIA; the preface to the typescript also contains some biographical data.
5. Tillett, *Egypt Itself,* 16.
6. Ibid., 14.
7. See chapter 2, p. 20.
8. For Frederick Catherwood, see von Hagen's *Frederick Catherwood Arch^t;* some additional material is in von Hagen's *F. Catherwood: Architect-Explorer of Two Worlds;* also *WWW.*
9. For Edward William Lane, see Ahmed, *Edward W. Lane* and Stanley Lane-Poole, *Life of Edward William Lane;* also *DNB* and *WWW.*
10. Bodleian Library, Department of Western Manuscripts, MS. Eng. misc. d. 234, fol. 5.
11. Biographical information about Major Felix is from his obituary in the *Athenaeum,* 21 April 1860; also *WWW.*
12. Major Felix's papers are at Alnwick Castle, Northumberland.

13. For Lord Prudhoe, see *DNB* and *WWW*. A typescript of his journals is in the GIA. The originals are at Alnwick Castle, Northumberland.

14. Anthony Charles Harris is especially noted for several important papyri with which his name is associated. Wilkinson made some notes from his papers that F. Ll. Griffith considered "of no little interest and value" (Griffith to Miss Selima Harris, 4 November 1891, BL, Add MSS 56273:24). It has even been suggested that Harris anticipated Mariette in the identification of the Saqqara Serapeum (Jaromír Málek, "Who Was the First to Identify the Saqqara Serapeum?" *Chronique d'Egypte* 58 [1983]:65–72).

15. For the English Reading Society, see BL, Add MSS 25663:149–150.

16. BL, Add MSS 25614:251–253.

17. Lane-Poole, *Life of Lane*, 19; Robert Hay, however, recorded in his diary that Salt received him "cooly tho' politely" on their first meeting (Hay diary, BL, Add MSS 31054:51).

18. Ahmed, *Edward W. Lane*, 27–28.

19. L. M. A. Linant de Bellefonds (1799–1883), French geographer, explorer, and engineer. A fine draftsman, Linant de Bellefonds made a large collection of sketches and was well known to British travelers. He lived in oriental fashion with an Abyssinian woman by whom he had several children. Eventually he became the Egyptian Minister of Public Works. See *WWW* and Hartleben, *Lettres de Champollion*, 2:78–79.

20. Bierbrier, "The Salt Watercolours," 9; also see Málek and Smith, "Henry Salt's Egyptian Copies and Drawings," 35–52. Some of Salt's sketches are in the possession of the Salt family; others are in the Department of Egyptian Antiquities at the British Museum.

21. Hay diary typescript, 34, GIA.

22. Hay diary, BL, Add MSS 31054:82.

23. Bosworth, "Henry Salt," 80.

24. Hay diary typescript, 130, GIA.

25. Hekekyan Bey conducted the first recorded excavation, 1852–53. His stratigraphy was a result of his geological training. After that, there were no real field records until Sir Flinders Petrie's work, though Auguste Mariette (1821–1881) kept records of what he found.

26. Rhind, *Thebes*, 261–263.

27. Occasionally they may have inadvertantly damaged monuments. For example, their practice of putting squeezes onto painted reliefs was doubtful; and they may have tried to clean sooty fresco surfaces with water, which took the paint off along with the soot, as appears to have happened at Medinet Habu.

28. BL, Add MSS 29813:37, 29820:70, and 29813:12v.

29. Bonomi diary typescript, 25 August 1832, GIA.

30. Tillett, *Egypt Itself*, 14.

31. Ibid.

32. For example, a note attached to Hay's copy of a "section of a brick arched tomb at Gournou. Thebes" reads, "The paintings in this tomb destroyed since 1827" (BL, Add MSS 29821:82). Many similar notes about other monuments could have been added subsequently.

33. Several volumes of his work are given over to Islamic architecture; in regard to village scenes, one British Library manuscript is especially notable (BL, Add MSS 29832).

34. BL, Add MSS 31054:86.

35. Wilkinson to Robert Hay, September 1830, BL, Add MSS 38094: 13–14.

36. Examples of this are numerous, as in the following: Wilkinson's dedication of *Topography of Thebes,* his first major published work, told how Lord Prudhoe helped him by sharing manuscripts and information. In the acknowledgments of *Materia Hieroglyphica* he thanked Burton for "many useful extracts from his own papers," Humphreys for his "kindness," and Major Felix for "valuable materials." Lane, in his manuscript draft "Notes and Views in Egypt and Nubia, Made During the Years 1825, —26, —27, & —28" acknowledged Wilkinson's sharing with him a rare Arabic manuscript (BL, Add MSS 34080:215). Finally, Lord Prudhoe noted, "We found Mr. Wilkinson going to Essouan [Aswan] and got from him the Rosetta Stone and then left Essiout" (Prudhoe journal typescript, Notebook V, 22, GIA).

37. BL, Add MSS 25659:2–4.

38. The editor of Wilkinson's letters to Gell saw fit to omit this reference "as being better left unpublished" (Hall, "Letters to Sir William Gell," 136).

39. E.g., BL, Add MSS 38510:187–190, 191–192.

40. Hay diary, BL, Add MSS 31054:163.

41. Captain Sheffield's account, roughly dated September 1824 but related to events in 1822 (University College London Library, Manuscript Room, UCL35/4); G. B. Greenough to James Burton, London, 25 November 1824 (University College London Library, Manuscript Room, UCL35/4).

42. James Burton to G. B. Greenough, Wadi Araba, 8 August 1831. As it turned out, Wilkinson's map found its way to the publisher Arrowsmith who did nothing with it. Over forty years later, after Arrowsmith and Wilkinson were both dead, it was finally published. Wilkinson's haste therefore accomplished nothing, or at least not what he intended (University College London Library, Manuscript Room, UCL35/2).

43. James Burton to G. B. Greenough, Wadi Araba, 8 August 1831. University College London Library, Manuscript Room, UCL35/2.

44. Hay diary, BL, Add MSS 31054:116.

45. Wilkinson to Robert Hay, 20 May 1832, BL, Add MSS 38094:34–35.

46. Wilkinson to Major General J. Nicolls, Cairo, 13 August 1825, private collection of Robert Lucas.

47. Wilkinson to Sir William Gell, Qena, 4 December 1826, in Hall, "Letters to Sir William Gell," 146.

48. Marsot, *Egypt in the Reign of Muhammad Ali,* 217.

49. Bonomi diary typescript, 25 and 26 May 1833, GIA.

50. Henniker, *Notes,* 34. "Notwithstanding the threat the animals stopped their ears," Henniker added.

51. Bonomi diary typescript, 7 June 1832, GIA; Hay briefly mentions his

snake charmer in the Hay diary, BL, Add MSS 31054:186–191; also see Lane's observations of the charmers in his *Modern Egyptians*, 377–379.

52. Hay diary typescript, 9, GIA.

53. Wilkinson to Sir William Gell, Eastern Desert, September 1828, in Hall, "Letters to Sir William Gell," 156. Edward William Lane prescribed directions for treating ophthalmia and dysentery in Appendix E of his *Modern Egyptians*.

54. Sir Richard Burton, *Personal Narrative of a Pilgrimage to Al-Madinah and Meccah*, 1:386n.

55. Tillett, *Egypt Itself*, 48. The speaker was Kalitza Hay, Robert Hay's wife.

56. Wilkinson to Robert Hay, Gurna, October 1831, BL, Add MSS 38094:25–26.

57. Westcar diary, 14 May 1824, fol. 216, and 25 June 1824, fol. 275.

58. Osman Effendi to Wilkinson, 8 May 1835, Wilkinson MSS, "Letters &c II."

59. Wilkinson to Robert Hay, Gurna, October 1831, BL, Add MSS 38094:25–26.

60. Bonomi diary typescript, GIA. James Burton made an interesting collection of documents about cholera and the plague, including case studies (BL, Add MSS 25663).

61. Halls, *Henry Salt*, 281–294.

62. See chapter 9, p. 125. Dysentery also killed J. L. Burckhardt.

63. Wilkinson to Robert Hay, Gurna, October 1831, BL, Add MSS 38094:25–26.

64. Hay diary typescript, 241–242, GIA.

65. Hay diary, BL, Add MSS 31054:108.

66. BL, Add MSS 29816:132.

67. Tillett, *Egypt Itself*, 23–24.

68. BL, Add MSS 29857:22.

69. Hay diary, BL, Add MSS 31054:114.

70. Lane, *Modern Egyptians*, 373.

71. Lane, *Modern Egyptians*, 190–191. Also see Wilkinson's price guidelines for slaves in his *Topography of Thebes*, 286.

72. Judith E. Tucker, *Women in Nineteenth-Century Egypt*, 168. This fact could resolve the puzzlement of Hay's biographer who had difficulty reconciling Hay's extensive activity in the slave market with the fact that he recorded only one visit to the market in his journal—"Went to the Slave Market with Osman, which must always be a disgusting scene" (Hay diary typescript, 13 December 1824, GIA).

73. Tillett, *Egypt Itself*, 37.

74. Tucker, *Women in Nineteenth-Century Egypt*, 168–169, 171.

75. See Tillett, *Egypt Itself*, chapter 3, "Hay's Marriage."

76. Tillett, *Egypt Itself*, 38–39.

77. Ibid., 39.

78. Ibid., 38.

79. Ibid., 39.
80. Ibid., 38.
81. Ibid., 39.
82. Ibid., 38.
83. Humphreys to Bonomi, Boxing Day, 1834, private collection.
84. In *Modern Egypt and Thebes* (1:522–526) Wilkinson quotes Clot Bey about the conduct of Europeans toward their slaves and the care that should be taken when terminating relations with them.
85. Charles Sheffield's account (notes taken by G. B. Greenough), roughly dated September 1824 and related to events in 1822 (University College London Library, Manuscript Room, UCL35/4).
86. If the latter, it may not have been so extraordinary. Some years later the traveler W. H. Bartlett recounted secondhand a story of a man who callously watched his female slave and his child by her being sold at the slave market (W. H. Bartlett, *The Nile Boat*, 133–134).
87. Sir Willliam Gell to Wilkinson, Naples, 25 June 1823, Wilkinson MSS, "Letters &c."
88. Sir William Gell to Wilkinson, Naples, 5 March 1824, Wilkinson MSS, "Letters &c." Gell refers to Ismael Gibraltar, an old friend and Turkish naval officer who was the father of Sadic Gibraltar whom Wilkinson met on Malta.
89. Sir William Gell to Wilkinson, Naples, 10 August 1824, Wilkinson MSS, "Letters &c."
90. Sir William Gell to Wilkinson, Naples, 5 July 1825, Wilkinson MSS, "Letters &c."
91. Wilkinson to Sir William Gell, 2 July 1827, in Hall, "Letters to Sir William Gell," 146.
92. Wilkinson to Sir William Gell, 2 July 1827, in Hall, "Letters to Sir William Gell," 157.

7. Life among the Tombs

1. Belzoni, *Narrative*, 37–38. More prosaic, but also to the point, are Wilkinson's words: "However slight may be the interest felt by a stranger who only visits Egyptian monuments to satisfy the curiosity generally entertained for distant objects, none can look upon the remains of Thebes without feeling persuaded of the grandeur of the city they once adorned, or the skill of the artists who directed their execution" (*Topography of Thebes*, 163).
2. Percy E. Newberry, *Report on Some Excavations in the Theban Necropolis during the Winter of 1898–9*, 1.
3. Floor plans of the tomb are in Norman de Garis Davies, *The Tomb of Nakht at Thebes*, 19; Bertha Porter and Rosalind L. B. Moss, *Topographical Bibliography of Ancient Egyptian Hieroglyphic Texts, Reliefs, and Paintings*, Vol. 1, *The Theban Necropolis*, 160; and Richard Lepsius, *Denkmäler aus Aegypten und Aethiopien*, 3:257. Lepsius's plan shows Wilkinson's par-

titions and additions. The tomb is no. 83 according to the numbering system now used; Wilkinson numbered it 64.

4. Porter and Moss, *Topographical Bibliography*, 167.

5. Davies, *Tomb of Nakht*, 11.

6. Wilson, *Signs and Wonders*, 31–32. Wilkinson made a sketch or watercolor of his view with the note, "View from the court before the tomb I lived in at El Qoorneh." This is mentioned in Seymour de Ricci, "An Album of Drawings by Sir J. G. Wilkinson" in *Studies Presented to F. Ll. Griffith*, 474–476. I have been unable to locate this album. Also see in the Robert Hay collection the folios entitled *"Thebes* Panorama Taken from a Mound below My Tomb." In the upper right hand portion of fol. 103 are clearly drawn the towers and walls of the house (BL, Add MSS 29816:103–107).

7. Wilson, *Signs and Wonders*, 31.

8. Greener, *Discovery of Egypt*, 123. De Buissierre may have been referring not to the house at Gurna, but to what was known as "Kasr [Palace] Wilkinson," a tomb in the Valley of the Kings where Wilkinson sometimes lived when he was working there.

9. Wilkinson to M. Stanhope Badcock, Thebes, 28 June 1827, in Wilkinson MSS, "Eastern Desert to Thebes 1826."

10. Newberry, *Report*, 3.

11. Greener, *Discovery of Egypt*, 107.

12. Henniker, *Notes*, 136.

13. Hay diary typescript, 30 July 1827, GIA.

14. Lane's manuscript draft "Notes and Views in Egypt and Nubia, Made During the Years 1825, —26, —27, & —28," BL, Add MSS 34081:270.

15. BL, Add MSS 29857:95; Hay diary typescript, 25 November 1826, GIA; Lane notebooks, Notebook no. 14, 4 November 1827, Lane collection, GIA; Hay diary typescript, 30 July 1827, GIA.

16. Hay diary typescript, 3 August 1827, GIA.

17. With the note "The residence of Rᵗ Hay Esq. at Thebes." BL, Add MSS 29816:130.

18. BL, Add MSS 31054:129.

19. Robert Blake, *Disraeli's Grand Tour: Benjamin Disraeli and the Holy Land 1830–31*, 92.

20. G. A. Hoskins, *Visit to the Great Oasis of the Libyan Desert*, 16.

21. *WWW*, s.v. "Giovanni d'Athanasi." Somewhat altered, Yanni's house still stands today. Yanni should not be confused with the businessman, antiquity dealer, and sometime diplomat Giovanni Anastasi.

22. Lane's manuscript "Notes and Views in Egypt and Nubia, Made During the Years 1825, —26, —27, & —28," BL, Add MSS 34081:268–269.

23. "I knew him well during more than two years residence at Thebes," Wilkinson wrote years later of Triantaphyllos. Wilkinson MSS, "MSS. 1854–55," item no. 23.

24. *WWW*, s.v. "Piccinini."

25. Newberry, *Report*, 2–3.

26. Edward William Lane's manuscript draft "Notes and Views in Egypt

and Nubia, Made During the Years 1825, —26, —27, & —28," BL, Add MSS 34081:234.

27. Wilson, *Signs and Wonders*, 31. Many *gurnawi* still live in the tombs, much as they did in Wilkinson's time.

28. Belzoni, *Narrative*, 158–159.

29. Ibid., 159.

30. Rhind, *Thebes*, 277–278.

31. Belzoni, *Narrative*, 159.

32. Rhind, *Thebes*, 278.

33. Hay dairy, BL, Add MSS 31054:135–136.

34. Bonomi diary typescript, 30 July 1831, GIA.

35. Hay diary, BL, Add MSS 31054:142–143.

36. Reeve, *Men of Eminence*, 1:77. It should be pointed out that the accounts of the observers cited above may have been unduly critical. Giovanni d'Athanasi (Yanni), who knew the *gurnawi* well, considered them not so much irreligious as unsuperstitious and held them in higher esteem than he did the other Arabs of the region: "They are most industrious workmen, and not indolent, as has been falsely reported of them. M. Belzoni, for instance, was strangely mistaken in them—he did not observe them properly" (Giovanni d'Athanasi, *A Brief Account of the Researches and Discoveries in Upper Egypt etc.*, 132). During my visits to Gurna, I found them a very attractive group of people. Many still sell purported antiquities.

37. Hay diary, BL, Add MSS 31054:92–93.

38. BL, Add MSS 25638. Wilkinson's numbering system is no longer used, having been replaced by one established by Arthur Weigall around the beginning of the twentieth century.

39. Amelia Edwards, *A Thousand Miles up the Nile*, 415.

40. "An extraordinarily careful and valuable survey of ancient Thebes," H. E. Winlock wrote of the map, (*Excavations at Deir El Bahri 1911–1931*, 168). Edward William Lane, who also made a map of Thebes, assessed Wilkinson's map as follows: "Those who desire a more detailed plan of Thebes, will do well to procure Sir G. Wilkinson's, the accuracy of which is most admirable as it is indeed a surpassing monument of exactness & of patience; & I state my opinion of it with confidence as I often watched the progress of its execution, & saw the [   ] applied in cases in which most persons would have considered the eye fully satisfied" (Lane's manuscript draft "Notes and Views in Egypt and Nubia, Made During the Years 1825, —26, —27, & —28," BL, Add MSS 34081:164v. Lane's map is in BL, Add MSS 34088:50).

41. Wilkinson to Robert Hay, 29–30 December 1830, BL, Add MSS 38094:17–18.

42. Frederick Catherwood to Robert Hay, 28 February 1835, BL, Add MSS 38094:77–78.

43. Burton's map is in BL, Add MSS 29815.

44. Many of his rubbings as well as some squeezes are in Wilkinson MSS, "Portraits of Kings & Other Rubbings from the Monum^ts Thebes." But most of Wilkinson's rubbings and squeezes are in the Department of Egyptian An-

tiquities at the British Museum. See Rosalind Moss, "Rubbings of Egyptian Reliefs Made in 1826 by Sir J. Gardner Wilkinson," *Journal of Egyptian Archaeology* 62 (1976): 108–109.

45. *Topography of Thebes,* 258n.

46. Romer, *Valley of the Kings,* 101–102.

47. Wilkinson, *Topography of Thebes,* 101n, 121.

48. Ibid., 122–123.

49. For Wilkinson's work in the Valley of the Kings, also see Romer, *Valley of the Kings,* especially chapter 10.

50. Bierbrier, *The Tomb-builders of the Pharaohs,* 132–133.

51. As he reaffirmed in his *The Egyptians in the Time of the Pharaohs: Being a Companion to the Crystal Palace Egyptian Collections,* v.

52. Wilkinson, *Topography of Thebes,* 127.

53. Percy E. Newberry, *The Life of Rekhmara, Vezîr of Upper Egypt under Thothmes III and Amenhetep II (circa B.C. 1472–1448) with Twenty-two Plates,* 11. Rekhmire's tomb is no. 100 according to the system used today.

54. Jill Kamil, *Luxor: A Guide to Ancient Thebes,* 147.

55. Wilkinson, *Topography of Thebes,* 151–152. In his "Topographical Survey of Thebes, Tápé, Thaba or Diospolis Magna by G. Wilkinson Esq.," Wilkinson noted of the "Hill of Shekh Abd el Qoorneh": "The principal Tombs are N°s 1. 5. 11. 16. 17. 31. 33. 34 & above all, 35" (Wilkinson MSS).

56. Frédéric Cailliaud, *Voyage à Méroé, au Fleuve Blanc, au-delà de Fâzoql dans le Midi du Royaume de Sennâr, à Syouah et dans Cinq Autres Oasis: Fait dans les Années 1819, 1820, 1821 et 1822.* Cailliaud mentions meeting Wilkinson at Gurna (3:305).

57. Wilkinson, *Topography of Thebes,* 156.

58. Incomplete letter from Wilkinson to Sir William Gell, undated but 1833, Wilkinson MSS, "Letters &c."

59. Some of Wilkinson's drawings of the tomb appear in *MCAE,* most notably the scene of the foreigners (vol. 1., plate 4), but the scene in the revised edition of *MCAE* (1878) is from one of Joseph Bonomi's drawings; also see Newberry, *Rekhmara,* 12.

60. Kamil, *Luxor,* 139.

61. Davies, *Tomb of Nakht,* passim.

62. Lise Manniche, *Lost Tombs,* passim.

63. Charles F. Nims, *Thebes of the Pharaohs,* 177.

64. G. A. Hoskins, *A Winter in Upper and Lower Egypt,* 204–208.

65. Wilson, *Signs and Wonders,* 94.

66. E. A. Wallis Budge, *By Nile and Tigris,* 25n. 1.

67. Edward Hogg, *Visit to Alexandria, Damascus, and Jerusalem,* 2:328.

68. Lane's Travel Journal 1833, 39, Lane collection, GIA. For Auad, also see *WWW,* s.v. "Auad"; and Wilkinson, *Handbook for Travellers in Egypt,* 325, 338.

69. Richard Lepsius, *Letters from Egypt, Ethiopia, and the Peninsula of Sinai,* 271. Amelia Edwards noticed the house on her 1873–74 tour. Edwards, *A Thousand Miles up the Nile,* 454. One finds scholars living in

the tomb as late as 1909. Joseph Lindon Smith, *Temples, Tombs, and Ancient Art,* 108. In Alan H. Gardiner and Arthur E. P. Weigall, *A Topographical Catalogue of the Private Tombs of Thebes,* plates 3 and 4 show the northeast tower and part of the northern wall still standing.

8. "One Seems Tied Down to It for Life"

1. Wilkinson to M. Stanhope Badcock, Thebes, 28 June 1827, Wilkinson MSS, "Eastern Desert to Thebes 1826."

2. Wilkinson to Sir William Gell, Eastern Desert, September 1828, in Hall, "Letters to Sir William Gell," 159.

3. James Burton to G. B. Greenough, Wadi Araba, 8 February 1831, University College London Library, Manuscript Room, UCL35/2.

4. Wilkinson to M. Stanhope Badcock, Thebes, 28 June 1827, Wilkinson MSS, "Eastern Desert to Thebes 1826."

5. Thomas Young to M. Stanhope Badcock, 17 June 1828, Wilkinson MSS, "Letters &c II."

6. Wilkinson to Sir William Gell, undated but probably 1828, in Hall, "Letters to Sir William Gell," 161.

7. Thomas Young's memorandum in his own hand is in Wilkinson MSS, "Letters &c II."

8. There is an unbound copy of this in the Wilkinson MSS. Otherwise the only copy of it I have seen is the Italian translation, Orlando Felix, *Note sopra le dinastie de'faraoni con geroglifici, preceduti dal loro alfabeto e raccolti in Egitto nel 1828.*

9. J. G. (Sir Gardner) Wilkinson, *Materia Hieroglyphica, Containing the Egyptian Pantheon and the Succession of the Pharaohs, from the Earliest Times, to the Conquest by Alexander, and Other Hieroglyphical Subjects, with Plates, and Notes Explanatory of the Same.*

10. Ibid., iv.

11. Ibid., 82.

12. Ibid., 72.

13. "Wilkinson on Hieroglyphics," *Fraser's Magazine for Town and Country* 2 (October 1830): 332.

14. *Edinburgh Review* 138 (January 1839): 316.

15. Wilkinson, *Topography of Thebes,* v.

16. A letter from Major Felix as recounted by Joseph Bonomi to Robert Hay, 3 March 1832, BL, Add MSS 38094:31.

17. Wilkinson to Sir William Gell, Cairo, 3 October 1832, Wilkinson MSS, "Letters &c."

18. Wilkinson to Robert Hay, Cairo, 26 March 1833, BL Add MSS 38094: 59–60.

19. Wilkinson's article was not really superseded until the publication of G. Schweinfurth, *Die Steinbrüche am Mons Claudianus in der ostlichen Wüste Aegyptens,* and T. Barron and W. F. Hume, *Topography and Geology of the Eastern Desert of Egypt, Central Portion.* Other classic works on the Eastern Desert include Weigall, *Travels in the Upper Egyptian Deserts;*

G. W. Murray, *Dare Me to the Desert;* L. A. Tregenza, *The Red Sea Mountains of Egypt,* and *Egyptian Years.*

20. Wilkinson to Robert Hay, 20 May 1832, BL, Add MSS 38094:34–36.

21. Edward William Lane to Wilkinson, undated, Wilkinson MSS, "Eastern Desert & [   ] 1823. J.G.W."

22. For discussion of this manuscript, see chapter 9, pp. 133–134.

23. Wilkinson to Robert Hay, Thebes, n.d., BL, Add MSS 38094:53–55. Wilkinson's reference to "my present" is probably to his map of Thebes, which he was considering publishing at his own expense. In *Topography of Thebes* Wilkinson observed, "I hope that Mr. Hay, who has the most accurate drawings of the sculptures of any one who has ever visited Egypt, will have resolution enough to publish them; though I fear he will not be inclined to incur a great and gratuitous expense" (*Topography of Thebes,* 258n).

24. Tillett, *Egypt Itself,* 43.

25. Ibid., 13.

26. Hall, "Letters to Sir William Gell," 142, 154, 159.

27. Leitch, *Thomas Young* 3:392.

28. E.g., Wilkinson MSS, "English, Coptic, and Hieroglyphic Vocabulary. I. G. Wilkinson 1828."

29. BL, Add MSS 25614:251–253.

30. These were sketchbooks 5 and 6, which are not among the Wilkinson MSS. For details about the sketchbooks, see the Appendix.

31. His conclusions were eventually published in his articles "On the Nile, and the Present and Former Levels of Egypt," *Journal of the Royal Geographical Society* 9 (1839):431–441, and "Remarks on the Country between Wady Halfeh and Gebel Berkel, in Ethiopia, with Observations on the Level of the Nile," *Journal of the Royal Geographical Society* 20 (1850):154–159.

32. Wilkinson to Major General J. Nicolls, Cairo, 13 August 1825, private collection of Robert Lucas.

33. Tillett, *Egypt Itself,* 26.

34. BL, Add MSS 29858:113.

35. Wilkinson to Robert Hay, 29–30 December 1830, BL, Add MSS 38094:17–18.

36. Wilkinson to Robert Hay, 10 November 1831, BL, Add MSS 38094:27–28.

37. Wilkinson to Robert Hay, Cairo, 15 April 1832, BL, Add MSS 38094:32–33.

38. Wilkinson to Robert Hay, 30 May 1832, BL, Add MSS 38094:34–36.

39. Tillett, *Egypt Itself,* 50–52.

40. Wilkinson to Robert Hay, undated but 1832, BL, Add MSS 38094:53–55.

41. Wilkinson to Sir William Gell, undated but probably 1828, in Hall, "Letters to Sir William Gell," 160.

42. Major Felix to Wilkinson, Wadi Halfa, 25 January 1829, Wilkinson MSS, an unmarked envelope containing some letters from Major Felix.

43. Tillett, *Egypt Itself*, 47. Burton's knowledge of the encounter with Champollion may have been secondhand, because an examination of his movements make it difficult to see how he could have been present at that time.

44. Tillett, *Egypt Itself*, 46–47.

45. Ibid., 47–48.

46. Baron von Bunsen to Sir William Gell, in Hall, "Letters to Sir William Gell," 137. My translation.

47. "I have always regretted not finding in Egypt this learned and great amateur of hieroglyphic studies" (Hartleben, *Lettres de Champollion*, 2 : 56; my translation).

48. Some sketches of it, flying the French flag, are in BL, Add MSS 29827 : 18 et seq.

49. BL, Add MSS 25663 : 88.

50. Wilkinson to Robert Hay, Thebes, 26 June 1831, BL, Add MSS 38094 : 21–22.

51. Wilkinson to Robert Hay, Gurna, October 1831, BL, Add MSS 38094 : 25–26.

52. Details about Lebas's removal of the obelisk are in the Bonomi diary typescript in the GIA; also see Jean Baptiste Apöllinaire Lebas, *L'Obélisque de Luxor: Histoire de sa translation de Paris*. The illustration of the removal is in Wilkinson's *Topography of Thebes*, facing p. 168.

53. Wilkinson to Robert Hay, Cairo, 15 April 1832, BL, Add MSS 38094 : 32–33.

54. Wilkinson to Sir William Gell, Cairo, 3 October 1832, Wilkinson MSS, "Letters &c." Also see Wilkinson's comments in Jean Lacouture, *Champollion: Une Vie de Lumières*, 471–472.

55. A torn letter from Sir William Gell to Wilkinson, 10 April 1832, Naples, Wilkinson MSS, "Letters &c."

56. Wilkinson to Sir William Gell, Cairo, 3 October 1832, Wilkinson MSS, "Letters &c."

57. Wilkinson to Robert Hay, Gurna, October 1831, BL, Add MSS 38094 : 25–26.

58. This is on one of the long rolls in the Wilkinson MSS.

59. Wilkinson to Robert Hay, n.d., BL, Add MSS 38094 : 53–55.

60. Wilkinson to Robert Hay, Cairo, 15 April 1832, BL, Add MSS 38094 : 32–33.

61. Wilkinson to Robert Hay, 15 January 1833, BL, Add MSS 38094 : 56–57.

9. England Again

1. Wilkinson to Sir William Gell, an incomplete letter, undated but 1833, Wilkinson MSS, "Letters &c."

2. Wilkinson MSS, some loose sheets labeled "1833—Leaving Egypt—June 1."

3. Wilkinson to Robert Hay, May 1834, BL, Add MSS 38094 : 73–74.

4. Sir William Gell to Wilkinson, Naples, 9 September 1834, Wilkinson MSS, "Letters &c."

5. Clay, *Sir William Gell in Italy*, 130.

6. Ibid., 141.

7. BL, Add MSS 38094:73–74. For Wilkinson's election to the Athenaeum, see Humphry Ward, *History of the Athenaeum Club*, 126.

8. Bury, *Lady-in-Waiting* 2:238.

9. Ward, *History of the Athenaeum Club*, 115.

10. Arthur Griffiths, *Clubs and Clubmen*, 96–97.

11. Ibid., 98.

12. F. R. Cowell, *The Athenaeum: Club and Social Life in London 1824–1974*, 42.

13. James Burton to Robert Hay, 1 January 1836, BL, Add MSS 38094: 93–94.

14. *The London Review*, 1862, a biographical notice entitled "Sir Gardner Wilkinson, D.C.L., F.R.S.," clipping, Wilkinson MSS, "Sir Gardner Wilkinson Life. Etc."

15. Sir William Gell to Wilkinson, 9 September 1834, Wilkinson MSS, "Letters &c."

16. Frederick Catherwood to Robert Hay, 28 February 1835, BL, Add MSS 38094:77–78.

17. George Paston, *At John Murray's: Records of a Literary Circle 1843–1892*, 1–23; also, Samuel Smiles, *A Publisher and His Friends*.

18. For Lane's book see this chapter, p. 139, and chapter 10, pp. 158–159.

19. Frederick Catherwood to Robert Hay, 21 March 1835, BL, Add MSS 38094:79–80.

20. See Edward William Lane to John Murray, 12 January 1836, copy; Edward William Lane to John Murray, 31 March 1836, copy; and John Murray to Richard Lane, 11 January 1837, all in the Lane collection, GIA.

21. The notes and the first draft of the manuscript are in the GIA. The second draft is in the Bodleian Library, Department of Western Manuscripts, MS Eng. misc. d. 234. A third draft entitled "Notes and Views in Egypt and Nubia, Made During the Years 1825, —26, —27, & —28," is in BL, Add MSS 34080–34088.

22. Wilkinson to Robert Hay, May 1834, BL, Add MSS 38094:73–74.

23. "Catalogue of Egyptian Antiquities presented to the British Museum by John Gardner Wilkinson. 1834," British Museum, Department of Egyptian Antiquities. Apparently he retained part of his collection and later included it in his donation to Harrow School.

24. Wilkinson to the Keeper of the Department of Egyptian Antiquities, 25 July 1835, Letter no. 5796, British Museum, Department of Egyptian Antiquities.

25. Occasionally he took the initiative and suggested purchases to the museum, as when Giovanni Anastasi offered his collection for £6,000, which Wilkinson considered a good price, considering what the museum had paid for Salt's last collection the year before, a purchase about which Wilkinson apparently was not consulted. "If the Trustees had the intention

of purchasing a large Collection, this should be the one," the secretary of the committee reported him as saying. Even so, the committee declined to buy it (Minutes of the Committee, 15:4252 and 4772, Archives, British Museum). This and other material from this collection is quoted by courtesy of the Trustees of the British Museum.

26. Wilkinson to Mr. Forshall, Secretary of the Department, 21 May 1838, Letter no. 5799, British Museum, Department of Egyptian Antiquities.

27. Minutes of the Committee, 16:4771–4772, Archives, British Museum.

28. Wilkinson to Samuel Birch, 22 December 1865, copy, Wilkinson MSS, leather satchel.

29. Wilkinson to Robert Hay, 17 March 1836, BL, Add MSS 38094:97–98. For details of Osman's death, see Fulgence Fresnel to Edward William Lane, 13 November 1835, Lane collection, GIA.

30. Wilkinson to Robert Hay, May 1834, BL, Add MSS 38094:73–74.

31. Two incomplete drafts for this are among the Wilkinson MSS.

32. Sir William Gell to Wilkinson, "Napsholes" [Naples], 4 November 1834, Wilkinson MSS, "Letters &c." Gell refers to Edward Bulwer-Lytton's *The Last Days of Pompeii* (1834). Bulwer-Lytton had consulted Gell when he was doing the research for his novel and later dedicated it to Gell in gratitude for his assistance.

33. Sir William Gell to Wilkinson, Naples, 9 September 1834, Wilkinson MSS, "Letters &c."

34. Sir William Gell to Wilkinson, 4 November 1834, Wilkinson MSS, "Letters &c."

35. *MCAE* 1:ix–x.

36. Wilkinson to Robert Hay, 17 March 1836, BL, Add MSS 38094:97–98.

37. Frederick Catherwood to Robert Hay, 2 May 1835, BL, Add MSS 38094:81–82.

38. Tillett, *Egypt Itself*, 65.

39. BL, Add MSS 38094:31.

40. James Burton to Robert Hay, 1 January 1836, BL, Add MSS 38094:93–94.

41. Wilkinson sketched many of the animals before he left Egypt. Wilkinson MSS, "Cairo 1833."

42. Sir William Gell to Wilkinson, Naples, 9 September 1834, Wilkinson MSS, "Letters &c."

43. Wilkinson to Robert Hay, 17 March 1836, BL, Add MSS 38094:97–98.

44. Ahmed, *Edward W. Lane*, 39.

45. Frederick Catherwood to Robert Hay, 2 May 1835, BL, Add MSS 38094:81–82.

46. See John L. Stephens, *Incidents of Travel in Central America, Chiapas, and Yucatan;* and *Incidents of Travel in Yucatán*, 2 vols. (London: John Murray, 1843); and Victor W. von Hagen, *Maya Explorer: John Lloyd Stephens and the Lost Cities of Central America.* Also see Frederick Catherwood, *Views of Ancient Monuments in Central America, Chiapas and Yucatán.*

10. *Manners and Customs of the Ancient Egyptians*

1. Even conventional travelogue accounts were called on to provide more detailed information of this kind about the people whom the traveler had observed; for example, John Murray refused to publish Herman Melville's *Typee* (1846) until the author inserted three chapters about the life-style and customs of the Marquesan islanders.

2. *WWW*, s.v. "(Sir) John Gardner Wilkinson."

3. Wilkinson MSS, "Journey in Nubia," 149.

4. Edward William Lane, *An Account of the Manners and Customs of the Modern Egyptians*, 1.

5. *Topography of Thebes*, xx.

6. Wilkinson, *MCAE*, 1:218.

7. Ibid., 4:12.

8. Ibid., 1:95.

9. Ibid., 4:131–132.

10. Ibid., 1:94.

11. Ibid., 1:41. The date 2320 B.C. was a revision of Wilkinson's earlier estimate of 2201 B.C.

12. E. A. Wallis Budge, *The Mummy: A Handbook of Egyptian Funerary Archaeology*, 2d ed. (Cambridge: Cambridge University Press, 1925), 14.

13. Wilkinson's British colleagues in Egypt also doubted the excessive antiquity of Egypt; e.g., Lord Prudhoe to Wilkinson, Turin, 2 July 1837, Wilkinson MSS, an unlabeled envelope.

14. One example among many is Wilkinson's recounting of the story of Amasis and Polycrates in which Amasis attempts to save Polycrates from the baneful effects of excessive good fortune (*MCAE*, 3:111).

15. Ibid., 1:52.

16. Ibid., 1:52n.

17. Ibid., 1:vi.

18. Wilson, *Culture of Ancient Egypt*, 305.

19. John A. Wilson, "The Present State of Egyptian Studies," in *The Haverford Symposium on Archaeology and the Bible*, ed. Elihu Grant, 215.

20. *MCAE*, 1:245.

21. See Herodotus 2.164 and Diodorus Siculus 1.73.

22. *MCAE*, 1:237.

23. Ibid., 1:249.

24. Ibid., 1:247–248.

25. Ibid., 1:253.

26. Wilson, *Culture of Ancient Egypt*, 307–308.

27. *MCAE*, 4:3–4.

28. *Topography of Thebes*, xiv.

29. Wilkinson's second caste had other subdivisions besides the military. These were the farmers, husbandmen, gardners, huntsmen, and boatmen (*MCAE*, 1:282).

30. Ibid., 1:288.

31. Ibid., 1:288–289.

32. Ibid., 2:pl. 6 (facing p. 106).

33. Ibid., 3:158.

34. Ibid., 3:161.

35. Hollis S. Baker, *Furniture in the Ancient World*, 292.

36. *MCAE*, 3:87–88.

37. Ibid., 2:401–402.

38. Ibid., 2:366.

39. Ibid., 2:365–366.

40. Ibid., 4:243.

41. Ibid., 4:246.

42. Ibid., 4:162, 163.

43. Wilson, *Culture of Ancient Egypt*, 305–306.

44. *MCAE*, 5:439.

45. Ibid., 4:227.

46. Ibid., 4:215.

47. Ibid., 4:201–203.

48. Ibid., 4:269. Though apparently not ritual sacrifices to a god, there were a small number of extraordinary incidents in which servants were interred with their masters; of these, however, Wilkinson was unaware.

49. *MCAE*, 5:14.

50. *MCAE*, 4:176.

51. "If, as I have observed in a previous work," Wilkinson wrote, referring to *Materia Hieroglyphica* (part 1, pp. 1–2), "the sons of Ham taught their descendents, the early inhabitants of Egypt, the true worship of one spiritual and eternal Being, who had disposed the order of the universe, divided the light from the darkness, and ordained the creation of mankind, the Egyptians, in process of time, forsook the pure ideas of a single Deity, by admitting his attributes to a participation of that homage which was due to the Divinity alone" (*MCAE*, 4:236). This follows an approach developed in the previous century by the orientalist Sir William Jones in his addresses to the Royal Asiatic Society (George Stocking, *Victorian Anthropology*, 22–23).

52. *MCAE*, 4:236.

53. Ibid., 4:178.

54. Wilkinson MSS, "Journal—1841 Continued: 1842 Egypt, Rosetta, Tripoli, England—to 1843—."

55. *MCAE*, 4:244, 297–298.

56. Ibid., 4:212–213.

57. Ibid., 1:xi.

58. In the later editions volumes 1 and 2 of the second series are numbered 4 and 5, as they are in these notes. There was also a sixth volume of additional illustrations.

59. Wilkinson, *The Egyptians in the Time of the Pharaohs*, vi. In the Wilkinson MSS there is a packet labeled "Rest of cuts of Anc Egns not wanted."

60. *Quarterly Review* 63 (January 1839):121.

61. Frederick Catherwood to Robert Hay, 7 August 1835, BL, Add MSS 38094:91–92.

62. Joseph Bonomi to Robert Hay, 24 December 1836, BL, Add MSS 38094:105–106.

63. Joseph Bonomi to Robert Hay, 13 June 1841, BL, Add MSS 38510: 173–174.

64. Samuel Rogers to Wilkinson, 14 April 1841, Wilkinson MSS, "Letters &c II."

65. Wilson, *Signs and Wonders*, 32.

66. *Quarterly Review* 63 (January 1839):120.

67. *Athenaeum 533* (13 January 1838):32–33.

68. *Edinburgh Review* 68 (January 1839):315–317. According to *The Wellesley Index to Victorian Periodicals 1824–1900*, the review was written by James Browne.

69. *Gentlemen's Magazine*, March 1842, pp. 235–246.

70. John David Wortham, *The Genesis of British Egyptology*, 39–42, 100.

71. T. W. Heyck, *The Transformation of Intellectual Life in Victorian England*, 25; also Amy Cruse, *The Englishman and His Books in the Nineteenth Century*, chap. 9.

72. *Quarterly Review* 59 (July 1837):165.

73. Ahmed, *Edward W. Lane*, 107.

74. Edward William Lane to John Murray, 15 April 1842, Lane collection, GIA.

11. Sir Gardner Wilkinson

1. Wilkinson to the secretary of the Royal Geographical Society, Paris, 6 November 1837, Archives of the Royal Geographical Society (hereafter RGS).

2. Wilkinson MSS, "Journal 1838 Spain, Rome, Pisa."

3. Joseph Bonomi to Edward William Lane, Rome, 27 December 1838, BL, Add MSS 25658:67–68.

4. Joseph Bonomi to James Burton, Rome, 1 January 1839, BL, Add MSS 25658:69–70.

5. James Haliburton [Burton] to Robert Hay, 27 June 1839, BL, Add MSS 38094:120–121.

6. The *DNB* says 28 August; 25 August according to the *London Times*.

7. David Cecil, *Melbourne* (1939; reprint, London: Constable, 1965), 345.

8. *DNB*, s.v. "Sir John Gardner Wilkinson."

9. Wilkinson to the secretary of the Royal Geographical Society, October 1839, RGS.

10. James Haliburton [Burton] to Robert Hay, 22 October 1839, BL, Add MSS 38094:120–121.

11. Wilkinson to Robert Hay, London, May 1834, BL, Add MSS 38094: 73–74.

12. Wilkinson to Robert Hay, London, 17 March 1836, BL, Add MSS 38094:97–98.

13. Tillett, *Egypt Itself*, 85.

14. This wording was suggested by Lane to Hay (quoted in Tillett, *Egypt Itself*, 85).

15. Robert Hay, *Illustrations of Cairo.* A second edition that included the text was printed the following year.

16. Wilkinson to Robert Hay, Cairo, 22 January 1842, BL, Add MSS 38094:158–159.

17. Tillett, *Egypt Itself*, 87.

18. Sir Gardner Wilkinson, *Three Letters*, 3.

19. Ibid., 7.

20. Marsot, *Egypt in the Reign of Muhammad Ali*, 243.

21. Ibid., 237–238.

22. Ibid., 243.

23. Frederick Catherwood to Robert Hay, 2 May 1835, BL, Add MSS 38094:81–82.

24. Marsot, *Egypt in the Reign of Muhammad Ali*, 211.

25. Wilkinson, *Three Letters*, 35.

26. Wilkinson to Lady Lovelace, "On the Nile," 18 May 1842, Bodleian Library, Department of Western Manuscripts, MS. Dep. Lovelace Byron 175, fols. 12–13.

27. Frances Baroness Bunsen, ed., *A Memoir of Baron Bunsen*, 1:464.

28. The following is by no means a complete list: Honorary Member, American Ethnological Society; Hon. Mem., American Oriental Society; Corresponding Mem., Archaeological Society of Edinburgh; Hon. Mem., Architectural Society of Oxford; Vice-president, British Archaeological Association; Vice-pres., Cambrian Archaeological Association; Mem., Egyptian Institute of Alexandria; Hon. Mem., Egyptian Society of Cairo; Corr. Mem., Entomological Society; Hon. Mem., Ethnological and Oriental Societies of America; Hon. Mem., Ethnological and Oriental Societies of New York; Mem. Ethnological Society of London; Vice-pres., Lincoln Diocesan Archaeological Society; Hon. Mem., Oriental Society of Paris; Hon. Mem., Oxford Architectural Society; Corr. Mem., Royal Academy of Turin; Corr. Mem., Royal Asiatic Society (Bombay branch); Corr. Mem., Royal and Imperial Academy of Vienna; Corr. Mem., Royal Imperial Academy of Sciences of Vienna; Hon. Mem., Royal Institute of British Architects; Mem. of the Council, Royal Geographical Society; Hon. Corr. Mem., Royal Society of Literature; Mem. of the Council, Syro-Egyptian Society (later merged into the Society of Biblical Archaeology).

29. Wilkinson's obituary notice in the *Daily Telegraph*, clipping, Wilkinson MSS, "Wilkinson."

30. Wilkinson to the secretary of the Royal Geographical Society, 16 May 1840 and 4 May 1841, RGS.

31. "Mr Burton would be a proper candidate but I certainly think Dr Barth if alive should have the gold medal if it is to be given to merit" (Wilkinson to the secretary of the Royal Geographical Society, undated but received at the Royal Geographical Society 22 March 1855, RGS.

32. Wilkinson to [　　], 7 June 1854, RGS. Wilkinson also refereed Barth's

"Account of Two Expeditions in Central Africa by the Furanys," which was published in volume 23 of the society's journal.

33. Wilkinson to the secretary of the Royal Geographical Society, March 1840, RGS.

34. Material relating to the White River Society is in BL, Add MSS 25652:1–27.

35. In a manuscript copy of Wilkinson's map, he shows the White River more or less drying up in the Mountains of the Moon (Wilkinson MSS, leather satchel).

36. A printed copy of the circular is in BL, Add MSS 25652:9.

37. W. G. Romaine to G. W. [A.?] Hoskins, Marseilles, 10 May 1839, BL, Add MSS 25652:2.

38. Such data as were gathered were reported in the *Bulletin de la Société Geographique de Paris*, second series, vols. 17–18, (1842).

39. Edmund W. Gilbert, *British Pioneers in Geography*, 101 et seq.

40. John Murray IV, *John Murray III, 1808–1892: A Brief Memoir*, 8.

41. A notable example is Amelia Edwards, who wrote *A Thousand Miles up the Nile*.

42. Captain Basil Hall to Wilkinson, HMS *Cyclops*, 30 April 1842, Wilkinson MSS, "Letters &c." Another idea that Wilkinson toyed with was a fictional story about ancient Egypt. The draft of it is in Wilkinson MSS, Miscellaneous papers.

43. See Nikolaus Pevsner, *Some Architectural Writers of the Nineteenth Century*, 18–21.

44. BL, Add MSS 25614:191 et seq; BL, Add MSS 25657 contains some of Burton's notes about the pointed arch.

45. Wilkinson to the secretary of the Royal Institute of British Architects, Lucerne, 22 June 1849, Wilkinson MSS, "MSS. 1849–50."

46. Wilkinson to Lady Lovelace, Rome, 3 November 1849, Bodleian Library, Department of Western Manuscripts, MS. Dep. Lovelace Byron 175, fols. 70–71.

47. *WWW* says that Wilkinson visited Egypt in 1842, but he arrived there in 1841. For this trip, see his manuscript journal entitled "Journal 1841–1842," Journal 56, GIA.

48. Wilkinson journal entitled "Journal 1841–1842," Journal 56, fols. 56–59, GIA.

49. Tillett, *Egypt Itself*, 20.

50. Clay, *Lady Blessington*, 65.

51. Edward William Lane to Robert Hay, Hastings, 7 January 1842, BL, Add MSS 38510:179–180.

52. Wilkinson to Robert Hay, Cairo, 22 January 1842, BL, Add MSS 38094:158–159.

53. Wilkinson to Lady Lovelace, "On the Nile," 18 May 1842, Bodleian Library, Department of Western Manuscripts, MS. Dep. Lovelace Byron 175, fols. 12–13.

54. Wilkinson to Robert Hay, Cairo, 1 April 1842, BL, Add MSS 38094:162–163.

266 Notes to Pages 170–177

55. "Compte rendu des fondateurs de l'Association Littéraire d'Egypte," in BL Add MSS 56285, folded into the manuscript in front of fol. 20.

56. Wilkinson to Robert Hay, Cairo, 1 April 1842, BL, Add MSS 38094: 162–163.

57. Wilkinson to T. J. Pettigrew, Upper Egypt, 22 March 1842, in BL, Add MSS 56230, unfoliated.

58. Wilkinson, "Journal 1841–1842," Journal 56, GIA.

59. Herodotus 2.138.

60. James Baikie, Egyptian Antiquities in the Valley of the Nile, 19.

61. Wilkinson to T. J. Pettigrew, Cairo, 17 December 1841, BL, Add MSS 56230, unfoliated.

62. Sir Gardner Wilkinson, "Some Account of the Natron Lakes of Egypt; in a Letter to W. R. Hamilton, Esq.," Journal of the Royal Geographical Society 13 (1843): 113–118. It is dated, "On the Nile," 18 January 1842.

63. Wilkinson MSS, "Journal 1841 Continued: 1842 Egypt, Rosetta, Tripoli, England—to 1843—."

64. Wilkinson to T. J. Pettigrew, Beirut, 18 May 1844, in BL, Add MSS 56230, unfoliated.

65. Wilkinson to Robert Hay, "On the Nile," 13 January 1844, BL, Add MSS 38094: 182–183.

66. Wilkinson MSS, unlabeled bound volume, mostly of essays by Wilkinson.

67. Wilkinson MSS, "1843–4."

68. Wilkinson to Robert Hay, "On the Nile," 13 January 1844, BL, Add MSS 38094: 182–183.

69. Daniel Highford Davall Burr (1811–1885) of Aldermaston Court, Berkshire, J.P., D.L. He was married in 1839 to Anne Margaretta, daughter of Captain Edward Scobell, R.N. See Warren R. Dawson's notes, BL, Add MSS 56326.

70. Wilkinson to an unidentified correspondent, "Sea of Marmora," 28 June 1844, GIA.

71. Wilkinson, Dalmatia and Montenegro: With a Journey to Mostar in Herzegovina, and Remarks on the Slavonic Nations; the History of Dalmatia and Ragusa; the Usmocs; &c. &c.

72. For this trip, see Wilkinson MSS, "1844"; also, Wilkinson MSS, Sketchbook 20 and Sketchbook XV, among others.

73. Wilkinson, Dalmatia and Montenegro, 1: 444.

74. Ibid., 1: 421–422.

75. Ibid., 1: 476.

76. Ibid., 2: 79.

77. Ibid., 2: 65–67.

78. Ibid., 2: 85–86.

79. Wilkinson to T. J. Pettigrew, Malta, 13 April 1845, in BL, Add MSS 56230, unfoliated.

80. Ibid.

81. Sir Gardner Wilkinson, "On Saracenic Architecture." Transactions of the Royal Institute of British Architects, 1st ser. 2 (1860–1861): 226.

82. James Burton to his father, London, 20 January 1825, University College London Library, Manuscript Room, UCL35/4.

83. Sir Gardner Wilkinson, "On Saracenic Architecture," 226.

84. Wilkinson's notes and sketches of Kairouan are in Wilkinson MSS, "Sicily & Tunis 1845."

85. Wilkinson, *Dalmatia and Montenegro*, 2:242.

86. Sir Gardner Wilkinson, *Dalmatien und Montenegro* (Leipzig: G. Mayer, 1949).

87. Draft of Wilkinson's essay, "On the Decrease of the Level of the Nile, and on Egyptian Fortification," sent to the Royal Society of Literature in a letter dated Lucerne, 20 June 1849. Wilkinson MSS, "MSS. 1849–50." It was published in *Transactions of the Royal Society of Literature* 4 (1853): 93–108.

88. Wilkinson MSS, "Journal 1849," 76.

89. Wilkinson MSS, "1849."

90. Sir Gardner Wilkinson, "Remarks on the Country between Wady Halfeh and Gebel Berkel, in Ethiopia, with Observations on the Level of the Nile," *Journal of the Royal Geographical Society* 20 (1850): 154–159.

91. Wilkinson MSS, "1848–9"; "1849"; "Journal 1849"; "MSS. 1849–50"; "No 1–1849 Hieroglyphics Egypt—Turin—Wilkinson"; "No II—1849 Hieroglyphics Egypt—Ethiopia from Semneh to Thebes Wilkinson"; Sketchbook 26; and Sketchbook XVIII.

92. Wilkinson to T. J. Pettigrew, Lucerne, 2 July 1849 [?], BL, Add MSS 56230, unfoliated.

93. J. H. Breasted's copy of the papyrus from Wilkinson's edition of *The Fragments of the Hieratic Papyrus at Turin*, University of Chicago, Oriental Institute, Director's Library.

94. Sir Gardner Wilkinson, *The Fragments of the Hieratic Papyrus of Kings at Turin*, 3.

95. Wilkinson to Lady Lovelace, Lucerne, August 1849, Bodleian Library, MS. Dep. Lovelace Byron 175, fols. 65–66.

96. Wilkinson, *Hieratic Papyrus*, iii–v; Wilkinson to Lady Lovelace, Turin, 18 September 1849, Bodleian Library, MS. Dep. Lovelace Byron 175, fols. 67–69.

97. Wilkinson MSS, "1849."

98. Besides those mentioned, Wilkinson prepared several other essays during the 1840s, among them: "On an Early Mosaic in St. Mark's, Representing the Removal of the Body of the Evangelist to Venice," which was published in the *Journal of the Archaeological Association;* "Inscription Illustrating the Legends of the Coins of Vaballathus," which was read to the numismatic society 24 December 1846; "Rome in 1848–49," which John Murray printed as a pamphlet; and "An Etruscan Tomb at Cervetri, the Ancient Caere," which was also prepared for the Archaeological Association.

99. Wilkinson to T. J. Pettigrew, Lucerne, 2 July 1850, in BL, Add MSS 56230, unfoliated.

12. A Gentleman Scholar

1. P. W. Clayden, *Samuel Sharpe, Egyptologist and Translator of the Bible,* 65.

2. Ibid.

3. Besides various pages in Wilkinson's sketchbooks, see the envelope entitled "Houses Visited by Sir. G. Wilkinson" in the Wilkinson MSS. For Calke Abbey and Wilkinson's involvement with it, see Howard Colvin, *Calke Abbey, Derbyshire: A Hidden House Revealed.*

4. Reginald Stuart Poole to Wilkinson, 10 February, year illegible but 1856 or 1857, BL, Add MSS 50952:188–193.

5. Wilkinson to Lady Lovelace, Tunbridge Wells, undated, Bodleian Library, Department of Manuscripts, MS. Dep. Lovelace Byron 175, fols. 31–32.

6. Wilkinson to Lady Lovelace, Maple Durham, Reading, 6 October (no year), Bodleian Library, Department of Manuscripts, MS. Dep. Lovelace Byron 175, fols. 63–64.

7. Dorothy Stein, *Ada: A Life and a Legacy,* 32.

8. Doris Langley-Levy Moore, *Ada, Countess of Lovelace: Byron's Legitimate Daughter* (London: John Murray, 1977), 321.

9. Stein, *Ada: A Life and a Legacy,* 224. Her bequests to Wilkinson and Babbage were strangely small. She left Wilkinson her copy of the *Penny Cyclopaedia* and Babbage simply "a book." Moore, *Ada, Countess of Lovelace,* 386.

10. Gell mentions him in one of his letters to Wilkinson, 4 November 1834, Wilkinson MSS, "Letters &c."

11. Wilkinson to Charles Babbage, 11 February 1865, BL, Add MSS 37199: 211–213. Letters to Wilkinson may be found in the Wilkinson MSS. Copies of letters from Wilkinson to Anthony Cumby and many of the others also are in the Wilkinson MSS; letters to Professor Carrara are in BL, Add MSS 38650:103–162; for letters to Reginald Stuart Poole and T. J. Pettigrew, see BL, Add MSS 50952, and BL, Add MSS 56230, respectively. Unfortunately, most of the Babbage letters are missing from the Wilkinson MSS. Their absence may be explained by a letter from Babbage's son to Lady Wilkinson dated 5 August 1878 (Wilkinson MSS, "Letters &c. III"), in which he requests the loan of his father's letters. For some reason, only a few of Wilkinson's letters are in the Babbage correspondence in the British Library. A biography of Babbage is Anthony Hyman, *Charles Babbage;* also see Babbage's autobiographical *Passages from the Life of a Philosopher* (London: Longman, Green, Longman, Roberts, & Green, 1864).

12. Hekekyan Bey to Miss Selima Harris, Cairo, 31 December 1861, in a large folder in the Wilkinson MSS.

13. Wilkinson to Lady Lovelace, 6 January 1850 and 20 July 1850, Bodleian Library, Department of Manuscripts, MS. Dep. Lovelace Byron 175, fols. 73–74, 79–82.

14. Wilkinson to T. J. Pettigrew, Lucerne, 2 July 1849, in BL, Add MSS 56230, unfoliated.

15. Wilkinson to Lady Lovelace, 20 July 1850, Bodleian Library Department of Manuscripts, MS. Dep. Lovelace Byron 175, fols. 79–82.

16. A copy of the prospectus is in the correspondence of the Department of Egyptian Antiquities of the British Museum, Letter no. 5806. John Murray's house printed the book.

17. Asa Briggs, *Victorian Cities* (Harmondsworth: Penguin, 1963), 44, 141; Tillett, *Egypt Itself*, 92; and Joseph Bonomi to Robert Hay, 4 August 1842, BL, Add MSS 38094:166–167.

18. Joseph Bonomi to Lady Wilkinson, 13 March 1862, Wilkinson MSS, "Letters &c. I."

19. Lady Wilkinson to Joseph Bonomi, copy, 16 March 1862, Wilkinson MSS, "Letters &c. I."

20. Tillett, *Egypt Itself*, 97.

21. Ibid., 98.

22. Wilkinson to Lady Lovelace, Aldermaston, 20 July 1850, Bodleian Library, Department of Western Manuscripts, MS. Dep. Lovelace Byron 175, fols. 79–82.

23. Wilkinson MSS, "1850."

24. See Owen Jones and Joseph Bonomi, *Description of the Egyptian Court.*

25. Sir Gardner Wilkinson, *On Colour.*

26. Robert L. Herbert, "A Color Bibliography," *Yale University Library Gazette* 49, no. 1 (July 1974):13.

27. Also less tasteful than the Italians—though not the Germans, he carefully noted (*On Colour*, v–vi).

28. Wilkinson to Lady Lovelace, Aldermaston, 20 July 1850, Bodleian Library, Department of Western Manuscripts, MS. Dep. Lovelace Byron 175, fols. 79–82.

29. Wilkinson, *On Colour,* 16.

30. Ibid., 21–22.

31. Sir David Brewster, a review of *On Colour* in the *North British Review*, February–May 1860, pp. 126–158.

32. E. T. Cook, *The Life of John Ruskin*, 2 vols. (New York: Macmillan, 1911), 2:73; Joan Evans and John Howard Whitehouse, eds., *The Diaries of John Ruskin*, 3 vols. (Oxford: Clarendon Press, 1956–59), 2:488; Raymond E. Fitch, *The Poison Sky: Myth and Apocalypse in Ruskin* (Athens: Ohio University Press, 1982), 523; and Dinah Birch, *Ruskin's Myths* (Oxford: Clarendon Press, 1988), 76n.

33. John Ruskin to Wilkinson, 24 December 1858, Wilkinson MSS, "Letters &c. I."

34. John Ruskin to Wilkinson, undated, Wilkinson MSS, "Letters &c. I."

35. Wilkinson to John Ruskin, 9 January [1859], copy, Llanover, Wilkinson MSS, "Letters &c. I."

36. John Ruskin to Wilkinson, n.d., Wilkinson MSS, "Letters &c. I."

37. John Ruskin to Wilkinson, 31 December 1858, in Wilkinson MSS, "Letters &c. I." In a letter to his father two months later, Ruskin wrote, "My consent to give these two addresses was not merely in good nature; the

publication of Sir Gardner Wilkinson's book had forced me to think carefully over some essential principles which it contradicted, and which were not clearly enough stated in any of my books. I wanted to announce these as soon as I could to stop misunderstanding and the mischief of part of Wilkinson's book, which otherwise would have gone on doing harm for another year." Wilkinson's book was, Ruskin continued, "excellent in almost all points" but gave "too much indulgence to that old idea that nature is to be idealised or improved when it is brought down to manufacture or to decoration" (Cook, *Life of John Ruskin* 1:437–438).

38. Sir Richard Burton, *Personal Narrative of a Pilgrimage to Al-Madinah and Meccah*, xix.

39. Byron Farwell, *Burton* (London: Longman, Green and Co., 1963), 100; Fawn M. Brodie, *The Devil Drives* (New York: Norton, 1967), 105, 349n.5; and Edward Rice, *Captain Sir Richard Francis Burton* (New York: Charles Scribner's Sons, 1990), 202.

40. Wilkinson to the secretary of the Royal Geographical Society, June 1854, Letter no. 30, RGS.

41. Wilkinson to the secretary of the Royal Geographical Society, March 1854, Letter no. 32, RGS.

42. Wilkinson to the secretary of the Royal Geographical Society, March 1855, Letter no. 17, RGS.

43. Rawlinson, Preface, *The History of Herodotus*, vii.

44. Stanley Lane-Poole, ed., *Selections from the Prose Writings of Jonathan Swift* (London: Kegan Paul, French & Co., 1884), xii.

45. Wilkinson wrote that Dr. Whewell was obliged to withdraw before the examination (Wilkinson MSS, "MSS. 1854–55").

46. Wilkinson MSS, "MSS. 1854–55."

47. Wilkinson, *Handbook for Travellers in Egypt*, 91.

48. Robert Hay to an unidentified correspondent, BL, Add MSS 29859:32–33. James Burton also felt that the obelisks of Alexandria were much decayed, that the ones at Luxor were much better (undated copy of a letter from James Burton to John Ward, BL, Add MSS 25658:48–49).

49. Wilkinson to Samuel Birch, 22 December 1865, copy, Wilkinson MSS, leather satchel.

50. Several works describe Cleopatra's Needles and the other obelisks. See Iverson, *Obelisks in Exile*; two popular books that have recently appeared are Labib Habachi, *The Obelisks of Egypt: Skyscrapers of the Past*, and R. A. Hayward, *Cleopatra's Needles*.

51. Wilkinson to Samuel Birch, 22 December 1865, copy, Wilkinson MSS, leather satchel.

52. Hayward, *Cleopatra's Needle*, 25.

53. See the pertinent material in Wilkinson MSS, "Letters &c. I" and his letter to T. J. Pettigrew on the subject, n.d., BL, Add MSS 56230, unfoliated.

54. Harriet Martineau, *Eastern Life, Present and Past*, 2:34–38.

55. Wilkinson to T. J. Pettigrew, Sea View, Ryde, undated, BL Add MSS 56230, unfoliated. Ostriches had only recently disappeared from Egypt as well (Patrick F. Houlihan, *The Birds of Ancient Egypt*, 1).

56. Wilkinson to T. J. Pettigrew, Sea View, Ryde, 31 July, no year but 1848 or 1849, BL, Add MSS 56230, unfoliated.

57. Harriet Martineau to T. J. Pettigrew, 5 August 1848 or 1849, Wilkinson MSS, "Letters &c. II."

58. Wilkinson to Harriet Martineau, Egypt, 1849, copy, Wilkinson MSS, "Selections from Books Letters & MSS."

59. Harriet Martineau to Wilkinson, 15 August 1849, Wilkinson MSS, "Letters &c. II."

60. Many of Wilkinson's letters to newspapers are in Wilkinson MSS, "MSS. 1849–50," MS no. 5 et seq.

61. Wilkinson to T. J. Pettigrew, Sea View, Ryde, 31 July, no year, BL, Add MSS 56230, unfoliated.

62. Wilkinson to T. J. Pettigrew, Beirut, 18 May 1844, in BL, Add MSS 56230, unfoliated.

63. Wilkinson to the secretary of the Royal Geographical Society, Calke Abbey, Derbyshire, 21 April 1859, RGS.

64. Wilkinson MSS, "1863 = 1875 to the end."

65. For an account of the debate, see Donald K. Grayson, *The Establishment of Human Antiquity.*

66. Wilkinson to Charles Babbage, 11 February 1865, BL, Add MSS 37199: 211–213.

67. His letters to Sir Charles Lyell dating from 1861 to 1863 are in the Edinburgh University Library, Department of Manuscripts, E 60/3.

68. *Athenaeum* (9 June 1860): 791.

69. The Reverend Thomas D. Allan to Wilkinson, 18 June 1860, Wilkinson MSS, "L. Letters &c."

70. Wilkinson to the Reverend Thomas D. Allan, 19 June 1860, Wilkinson MSS, "L. Letters &c."

71. See John Wigley, *The Rise and Fall of the Victorian Sunday.*

72. Wilkinson to John Heap at the National Sunday League, 16 July 1860, Wilkinson MSS, "L. Letters &c."

73. Wilkinson, *On Colour,* 193–195.

74. *North British Review,* February–May 1860, p. 152.

75. Edward Miller, *That Noble Cabinet: A History of the British Museum,* 139.

76. Ibid., 207.

77. Wilkinson MSS, "L. Letters &c." The prospectus is dated July 1860.

78. Wilkinson MSS, "Journal 1853–56."

79. Wilkinson to the P & O Company, Worthing, 5 October 1855, BL, Add MSS 42577: 320.

80. Wilkinson MSS, "Journal 1853–56."

81. Ibid.

82. See Jaromír Málek, "New Reliefs and Inscriptions from Five Old Tombs at Giza and Saqquara," *Bulletin de la Société d'Egyptologie, Genève* 6 (1982): 58–61.

83. Dated 25 May 1856, it is among the Wilkinson MSS. This was the basis for his essay, "The Apis-Tablets in the Louvre," which he sent to Regi-

nald Stuart Poole and which appeared in the *Monthly Review* in 1856.

84. Wilkinson to T. J. Pettigrew, Sea View, Ryde, 1848, BL, Add MSS 56230, unfoliated.

85. George Wilson to Wilkinson, 28 July 1859, Wilkinson MSS, "Letters &c I."

86. E. F. Davidson, *Edward Hincks: A Selection from His Correspondence with a Memoir*, 98.

87. Wilkinson to T. J. Pettigrew, undated but mid-1850s, in BL, Add MSS 56230, unfoliated.

88. Budge, *By Nile and Tigris*, 26n.

89. Walter de Gray Birch, *Biographical notices of Dr. Samuel Birch*, 54.

90. Wilkinson to an unidentified correspondent, date illegible, National Library of Scotland, Department of Manuscripts, 583, no. 873, fols. 326–327.

91. E.g., Wilkinson to Samuel Birch, 22 December 1865, copy, Wilkinson MSS, leather satchel.

92. Samuel Birch to Wilkinson, British Museum, 21 April 1847, Letter no. 5804, British Museum, Department of Egyptian Antiquities.

93. Minutes of the Committee, 28:9408, Archives, British Museum.

94. All of them are in the Wilkinson MSS.

95. BL, Add MSS 31054:147.

96. The Syro-Egyptian Society, of whose council Wilkinson was a member, later merged into the Society of Biblical Archaeology (Dawson's notes, BL, Add MSS 56285:169).

97. Tillett, *Egypt Itself*, 97.

98. Ibid., 98.

99. Reginald Stuart Poole to Wilkinson, 19 August 1851, BL, Add MSS 50952:87–90.

100. Tillett, *Egypt Itself*, 99.

101. Ibid., 103.

102. Wilkinson to Robert Hay, Cairo, 22 January 1842, BL, Add MSS 38094:158–159.

103. James Haliburton (Burton) to T. J. Pettigrew, 11 January 1842, in BL, Add MSS 56229, unfoliated.

104. BL, Add MSS 25613–25675.

105. Edward William Lane to Wilkinson, Hastings, 12 February 1850, Wilkinson MSS, leather satchel.

106. Lane-Poole, *Life of Lane*, 113 et seq.

107. Ahmed, *Edward W. Lane*, 40.

108. Tillett, *Egypt Itself*, 93.

109. Von Hagen, *F. Catherwood, Architect-Explorer of Two Worlds*, 56.

110. Joseph Bonomi to Robert Hay, 9 June 1848, BL, Add MSS 38094:187–188.

111. *WWW*, s.v. "Joseph Bonomi."

112. Although not one of the British travelers in Egypt, the fate of Giovanni d'Athanasi, or Yanni, might also be noted, for he was closely associated with them. In the late 1850s, Wilkinson wrote of him to Samuel Birch, "I have been applied to by the Greek Giovanni d'Athanasi to relieve his dis-

tress &c & he tells me he has some pieces of antiquity (Egyptian) which he thinks the British Museum might be disposed to purchase." Then, a couple of years later, Wilkinson later wrote of d'Athanasi to another correspondent: "He was assisted with money by several gentlemen in England, who had known him in Egypt when in Mr. Salt's employ, & among the number by myself, but particularly by Mr Hay who contributed very liberally to his support, until at last having made further unwise speculations he ended his days in a London Work House" (Wilkinson to Samuel Birch, undated but probably either 1857 or 1858 or perhaps 1859, British Museum, Department of Egyptian Antiquities, Letter no. 5848; and Wilkinson to Mr. Hood, 15 June 1860, copy, Wilkinson MSS, "MSS. 1854–55").

113. Tillett, *Egypt Itself*, 98.

13. Brynfield

1. Some of his sketches of British archaeological sites are quite good. They have scales, directions, and sometimes even show aerial perspective; many are colored (e.g., Wilkinson MSS, "Journal 1856–60").

2. Wilkinson MSS, "Book of British Camps, &c"; *Archaeologia Cambrensis* 7, 4th series (1876):66.

3. *Archaeologia Cambrensis* 15, 3d series (1869):447. Notable among his article-length contributions was "The Menvendanus Stone," *Archaeologia Cambrensis* 2, 4th series (1871):140–157. Another of his efforts in Celtic archaeology was *Carn Brea, near Redruth, Cornwall*, originally prepared for the Royal Institution of Cornwall.

4. Robert Lucas, *A Gower Family: The Lucases of Stouthall and Rhosili Rectory*, 79; also see Lucas's "Great Aunt Caroline," *Journal of the Gower Society* 24 (1973):22–29, and his *Rhossili*.

5. Wilkinson, *On Colour*, 353–354.

6. Two undated letters from Lady Lovelace to Wilkinson, Wilkinson MSS, "Letters &c. II."

7. For example, Wilkinson to Lady Lovelace, Bodleian Library, Department of Western Manuscripts, MS. Dep. Lovelace Byron 175, fols. 38–39.

8. Hyman, *Babbage*, 234–235.

9. Wilkinson MSS, "Poetry Selections."

10. Wilkinson MSS, "Poetry."

11. Lucas, "Great Aunt Caroline," 26. Another of her publications was *The Church of England Not Descended from the Church of Rome*.

12. BL, Add MSS 28512:258.

13. Wilkinson MSS, Sketchbook 39.

14. Ibid.

15. Lucas, "Great Aunt Caroline," 27.

16. Wilkinson to Thomas Lewis, Tenby, 22 March, no year but around 1860, Wilkinson MSS, miscellaneous papers.

17. Wilkinson to Charles Babbage, 11 September 1866, BL, Add MSS 37199:325–326.

18. Sir Gardner Wilkinson, "Avenue and Carns about Arthur's Stone in

Gower," *Archaeologia Cambrensis* 1, 4th series (1869):22–45, 117–121.

19. For example, Wilkinson MSS, Sketchbook XXVI.

20. Wilkinson to Charles Babbage, 11 September 1866, BL, Add MSS 37199:325–326.

21. Wilkinson MSS; also see "M.S.S. Cabinet," "Sketchbook N° xxxiii: Collections, & Book, of Memoranda. of Fossils &c in Cabinet," and other catalogs in the Wilkinson MSS.

22. The catalog is in the archives of Harrow School. The Egyptological portion of the collection was cataloged again some years later by Budge in *Catalogue of the Egyptian Antiquities from the Collection of the Late Sir Gardner Wilkinson.* The classical collections were cataloged by Cecil Torr, *Catalogue of Classical Antiquities from the Collection of the Late Sir Gardner Wilkinson.* Torr frequently quotes verbatim from Wilkinson's catalog, adding little and losing some. Another of Wilkinson's catalogs among the Wilkinson MSS is fuller than the one he made for Harrow.

23. Wilkinson MSS, leather satchel.

24. See Jasper Gaunt and D. C. Kurtz, "Corpus Vasorum Antiquorum: Harrow" (Manuscript).

25. J. D. Beazley, *Attic Red-Figure Vase-Painters,* 2d ed., 3 vols. (Oxford: Clarendon Press, 1963), 1:272–278, 2:1641, *Paralipomena: Additions to Attic Black-Figure Vase-Painters and to Attic Red-Figure Vase Painters,* 2d ed. (Oxford: Clarendon Press, 1971), 304, 353–354, 511.

26. Wilkinson MSS, miscellaneous papers. I am grateful to Jasper Gaunt who pointed out this detail to me and explained the overall significance of Wilkinson's bequest to Harrow School.

27. Copy in the private collection of Robert Lucas.

28. *Anthenaeum* (23 December 1871).

29. Wilkinson MSS, "1863 = 1875 to the end."

30. Ibid.

31. Wilkinson to Charles Babbage, 11 February 1865, BL, Add MSS 37199:211–213.

32. John Murray to Wilkinson, 2 June 1863, Wilkinson MSS, "Letters &c," and Wilkinson to John Murray, 5 June 1863, copy, Wilkinson MSS, "Letters &c."

33. Wilkinson to Charles Babbage, 11 September 1866, BL, Add MSS 37199:325–326.

34. Wilkinson MSS, "1863 = 1875 to the end"; also, Wilkinson to Charles Babbage, Tenby, 11 February 1865, BL, Add MSS 37199:211–213.

35. Private collection of Robert Lucas.

36. This manuscript is among the Wilkinson MSS.

37. *Tenby Observer* (31 January 1867).

38. Wilkinson to Albert Way, 24 January 1867, copy, in Wilkinson MSS, "Letters &c. III."

39. *Archaeological Journal* 24 (1867):79.

40. Wilkinson MSS, "Letters &c III."

41. Albert Way to Wilkinson, 15 February 1867, "Letters &c III."

42. Circular printed by George Chater, Wilkinson MSS, "Letters &c III."

43. Edward William Lane to Wilkinson, Worthing, 19 March 1875, Wilkinson MSS, "Letters &c." Lane died on 9 August 1876, less than a year after Wilkinson, working almost to the last; Bonomi died at his desk at the Sir John Soane Museum on 3 March 1878.

44. In Lady Wilkinson's hand, Wilkinson to General Sir Thomas Biddulph, Calke Abbey, 23 August 1875, copy, Wilkinson MSS, a loose volume of papers.

45. Wilkinson MSS, "1863 = 1875 to the End."

46. *The Welshman*, 12 and 14 November 1875.

47. Granted on 31 March 1876. Frederic Boase, *Modern English Biography*, 3:1353–1354.

48. A copy of the prospectus for "Desert Plants of Egypt Described and Drawn from Nature by Sir Gardner Wilkinson D.C.L., F.R.S." is among the Wilkinson MSS. Another is in the Department of Egyptian Antiquities, British Museum.

49. Unlike the first edition, the title of the revised edition begins with the article *The*.

50. Lucas, "Great Aunt Caroline," 28. The set is now in the private collection of Robert Lucas. Apparently Lady Wilkinson initially wanted to dedicate the revised edition of *Manners and Customs of the Ancient Egyptians* to Queen Victoria, but the queen declined (General Sir Thomas Biddulph to Lady Wilkinson, Buckingham Palace, 23 June 1876, private collection of Robert Lucas).

51. Wilkinson MSS, "Heads of a Subject," Lady Wilkinson's biographical manuscript.

Epilogue

1. Adolf Erman, *Agypten und Ägyptisches Leben im Altertum*, 2 vols. (Tübingen: H. Laupp, 1885). This was translated into English in 1895.

2. James H. Breasted, *A History of Egypt from the Earliest Times to the Persian Conquest*.

3. For men of letters, see John Gross, *The Rise and Fall of the Man of Letters*.

4. Charles K. Wilkinson, *Egyptian Wall Paintings: The Metropolitan Museum of Art's Collection of Facsimiles*, 13.

5. Margaret S. Drower, *Flinders Petrie: A Life in Archaeology*, 203.

6. Ibid.

7. Wilkinson, *Egyptian Wall Paintings*, 15.

8. Correspondence relating to the loan is in the GIA.

9. A. J. Youel, "Saved for the Nation . . . the Magic of Calke," *National Trust*, Autumn 1984, p. 26.

Selected Bibliography

Ahmed, Leila. *Edward W. Lane.* London: Longman, 1978.

d'Athanasi, Giovanni. *A Brief Account of the Researches and Discoveries in Upper Egypt etc.* London: John Hearne, 1836.

Azim, Michel. "Karnak et sa topographie." *Göttinger Miszellen* 113 (1989): 33–46.

Baikie, James. *A Century of Excavation in the Land of the Pharaohs.* New York: Fleming H. Revel, n.d.

———. *Egyptian Antiquities in the Valley of the Nile.* New York: Macmillan, 1932.

Baines, John, and Jaromír Málek. *Atlas of Ancient Egypt.* Oxford: Phaidon Press, 1980.

Baker, Hollis S. *Furniture in the Ancient World.* New York: Macmillan, 1965.

Barron, T., and W. F. Hume. *Topography and Geology of the Eastern Desert of Egypt, Central Portion.* Cairo: National Printing Department, 1902.

Bartlett, W. H. *The Nile Boat.* London: Arthur Hale, 1849.

Belzoni, Giovanni Battista. *Narrative of Recent Operations and Discoveries within the Pyramids, Temples, and Tombs, and Excavations in Egypt and Nubia.* London: John Murray, 1821.

Bierbrier, M. L. "The Salt Watercolours." *Göttinger Miszellen* 61 (1983): 9–12.

———. *The Tomb-Builders of the Pharaohs.* London: British Museum Publications, 1982.

Birch, Walter de Gray. *Biographical Notices of Dr. Samuel Birch.* London: Trubner & Co., 1886.

Blake, Robert. *Disraeli's Grand Tour: Benjamin Disraeli and the Holy Land 1830–31.* New York: Oxford University Press, 1982.

Boase, Frederic. *Modern English Biography, Containing Many Thousand Concise Memoirs of Persons Who Have Died Since the Year 1850 Etc.* 3 vols. Truro: Netherton and Worth, 1901.

Bosworth, C. E. "Henry Salt, Consul in Egypt 1816–1827 and Pioneer Egyptologist." *Bulletin of the John Rylands University Library of Manchester* 57, no. 1 (Autumn 1974):69–91.

Bratton, F. Gladstone. *A History of Egyptian Archaeology.* London: Robert Hale, 1967.

Breasted, James H. *A History of Egypt from the Earliest Times to the Persian Conquest.* New York: Scribner's, 1905.

Bruce, James. *Travels to Discover the Source of the Nile, in the Years 1768, 1769, 1770, 1771, 1772, and 1773.* 5 vols. Edinburgh: G. G. J. and J. Robinson, 1790.

Bryant, Philip H. M. *Harrow.* London: Blackie & Son, 1936.

Budge, E. A. Wallis. *Catalogue of the Egyptian Antiquities from the Collection of the Late Sir Gardner Wilkinson.* Harrow: J. C. Wilbee, 1887.

———. *Cleopatra's Needles.* London: Religious Tract Society, 1926.

———. *By Nile and Tigris.* London: John Murray, 1920.

———. *The Rosetta Stone in the British Museum.* London: Religious Tract Society, 1929.

Bunsen, Frances Baroness, ed. *A Memoir of Baron Bunsen.* 2 vols. London: Longmans, Green, and Co., 1868.

Burton, James. *Excerpta Hieroglyphica.* Cairo: By the Author, 1825–28.

Burton, Sir Richard F. "Giovanni Battista Belzoni." *Cornhill Magazine* 42 (July 1880):36–50.

———. *Personal Narrative of a Pilgrimage to Al-Madinah and Meccah.* 2 vols. 1855. Reprint. New York: Dover, 1964.

Bury, Lady Charlotte. *The Diary of a Lady-in-Waiting.* 2 vols. London: John Lane, 1908.

Butler, H. Montagu. "Harrow Benefactors and Benefactions." In *Harrow School,* edited by Edmund W. Howson and George Townsend Warner, 135–152. London: Edward Arnold, 1898.

Cailliaud, Frédéric. *Voyage à Méroé, au Fleuve Blanc.* 4 vols. Paris: Imprimierie Royale, 1826.

Carré, Jean-Marie. *Voyageurs et écrivains français en Egypt.* 2d ed. 2 vols. Paris: Imprimerie de l'Institut Français d'Archéologie Orientale, 1956.

Catherwood, Frederick. *Views of Ancient Monuments in Central America, Chiapas and Yucatán.* London: Vizetelly Bros., 1844.

Cesaretti, Maria Pia. "Sir John Gardner Wilkinson a Deir el-Hagar." *Discussions in Egyptology* 14 (1989):17–30.

Clay, Edith, ed. *Lady Blessington at Naples.* London: Hamish Hamilton, 1979.

———. *Sir William Gell in Italy: Letters to the Society of Dilettanti, 1831–1835.* London: Hamish Hamilton, 1976.

Clayden, P. W. *Samuel Sharpe, Egyptologist and Translator of the Bible.* London: Kegan, Paul, Trench & Co., 1883.

Clayton, Peter A. *The Rediscovery of Ancient Egypt: Artists and Travellers in the 19th Century.* London: Thames and Hudson, 1982.

Colvin, Howard. *Calke Abbey, Derbyshire: A Hidden House Revealed.* London: National Trust, 1985.

Conner, Patrick. *The Inspiration of Egypt.* Brighton: Brighton Borough Council, 1983.

Cowell, F. R. *The Athenaeum: Club and Social Life in London 1824–1974.* London: Heinemann, 1975.

Cruse, Amy. *The Englishman and His Books in the Nineteenth Century.* New York: Thomas Y. Crowell, 1939.

Culler, A. Dwight. *The Victorian Mirror of History.* New Haven: Yale University Press, 1985.

Davidson, E. F. *Edward Hincks: A Selection from His Correspondence with a Memoir.* Oxford: Oxford University Press, 1933.

Davies, Nina M. "Birds and Bats at Beni Hasan." *Journal of Egyptian Archaeology* 35 (1949): 13–20.

Davies, Norman de Garis. *The Rock Tombs of El Amarna: Part I. The Tomb of Meryra.* London: Gilbert and Rivington, 1903.

———. *The Tomb of Nakht at Thebes.* New York: Metropolitan Museum of Art, 1917.

Dawson, Warren R. *Charles Wycliffe Goodwin, 1817–1878.* Oxford: Oxford University Press, 1934.

———. "The First Egyptian Society." *Journal of Egyptian Archaeology* 23 (1937): 259–260.

Dawson, Warren R., and Eric P. Uphill. *Who Was Who in Egyptology.* 2d ed. London: Egypt Exploration Society, 1972.

Denon, Vivant. *Voyages dans la Basse et la Haute Egypte.* London: Samuel Bagster, 1807.

Dickens, Charles, ed. *Life of Charles J. Matthews.* London: Macmillan, 1879.

Disher, Maurice Willson. *Pharaoh's Fool.* London: William Heinemann, 1957.

Drower, Margaret S. *Flinders Petrie: A Life in Archaeology.* London: Victor Gollancz, 1985.

Edwards, Amelia B. *A Thousand Miles up the Nile.* Rev. ed. London: George Routledge and Sons, 1890.

Edwards, I. E. S. *The Pyramids of Egypt.* Harmondsworth: Penguin, 1947.

Fagan, Brian M. *The Rape of the Nile: Tomb Robbers, Tourists, and Archaeologists in Egypt.* New York: Charles Scribner's Sons, 1975.

Felix, Orlando. *Note sopra le dinastie de'faraoni con geroglifici, preceduti dal loro alfabeto e raccolti in Egitto nel 1828.* Firenze: Tip. Celli e Ronchi, 1830.

Festugière, A. J. *La révélation d'Hermès Trismégiste.* 4 vols. Paris: Librarie Lecoffre, 1944.

Gardiner, (Sir) Alan H. *Egypt of the Pharaohs: An Introduction.* Oxford: Clarendon Press, 1961.

Gardiner, Alan H., and Arthur E. P. Weigall. *A Topographical Catalogue of the Private Tombs of Thebes.* London: Bernard Quaritch, 1913.

Gaunt, Jasper, and D. C. Kurtz. "Corpus Vasorum Antiquorum: Harrow." Manuscript.

Gautier, Henri. "Un précurseur de Champollion au XVIe siècle." *Bulletin de l'Institut Français d'Archéologie Orientale* 5 (1906):65–86.

Gell, Sir William. *The Geography and Antiquities of Ithaca.* London: Longman, Hurst, Rees, and Orme, 1807.

———. *Pompeiana.* 2 vols. London: Rodwell and Martin, 1817–19.

———. *The Topography of Troy and Its Vicinity.* London: Longman and Rees, 1804.

Gell, Sir William, and Antonio Nibby. *Le mura di Roma disegnate da Sir W. Gell: Illustrate con testo e note da A. Nibby.* Rome: Presso Vincenzo Poggioli Stampatore Camerale, 1820.

Gilbert, Edmund W. *British Pioneers in Geography.* Newton Abbot: David & Charles, 1972.

Glanville, S. R. K. *The Growth and Structure of Egyptology.* Cambridge: Cambridge University Press, 1947.

Grayson, Donald K. *The Establishment of Human Antiquity.* New York: Academic Press, 1983.

Greener, Leslie. *The Discovery of Egypt.* London: Cassell, 1966.

Griffiths, Arthur. *Clubs and Clubmen.* London: Hutchinson and Co., 1907.

Groenewegen-Frankfurt, H. A., and Ashmole, Bernard. *Art of the Ancient World.* Englewood Cliffs, N.J.: Prentice-Hall, 1972.

Gross, John. *The Rise and Fall of the Man of Letters.* London: Macmillan, 1969.

Habachi, Labib. *The Obelisks of Egypt: Skyscrapers of the Past.* New York: Scribner's, 1977.

Hagen, Victor W. von. *F. Catherwood: Architect-Explorer of Two Worlds.* Barre, Mass.: Barre Publishers, 1968.

———. *Frederick Catherwood Arch*ᵗ. New York: Oxford University Press, 1950.

———. *Maya Explorer: John Lloyd Stephens and the Lost Cities of Central America.* Norman: University of Oklahoma Press, 1947.

Hall, H. R. "Letters of Champollion le Jeune and of Seyffarth to Sir William Gell." *Journal of Egyptian Archaeology* 2 (1915):76–87.

———. "Letters to Sir William Gell from Henry Salt, (Sir) J. G. Wilkinson, and Baron von Bunsen." *Journal of Egyptian Archaeology* 2 (1915): 133–167.

Hallett, Robin, ed. *Records of the African Association 1788–1831.* London: Thomas Nelson and Sons, 1964.

Halls, J. J. *The Life and Correspondence of Henry Salt.* 2 vols. London: Richard Bentley, 1834.

Hartleben, Hermine. *Champollion: Sein Leben und sein Werk.* 2 vols. Berlin: Weidmann, 1906.

———, ed. *Lettres de Champollion le Jeune.* 2 vols. Paris: Ernest Leroux, 1909.

Hay, Robert. *Illustrations of Cairo.* London: Tilt and Bogue, 1840.

Hayward, R. A. *Cleopatra's Needles.* Buxton: Moorland, 1978.

Henniker, Sir Frederick, Bart. *Notes during a Visit to Egypt, Nubia, the Oasis, Mount Sinai, and Jerusalem.* London: John Murray, 1822.

Herbert, Robert L. "A Color Bibliography." *Yale University Library Gazette* 49, no. 1 (July 1974): 3–49.

Heyck, T. W. *The Transformation of Intellectual Life in Victorian England.* New York: St. Martin's Press, 1982.

Hogg, Edward. *Visit to Alexandria, Damascus and Jerusalem.* London: Saunders and Otley, 1935.

Hoskins, G. A. *Visit to the Great Oasis of the Libyan Desert.* London: Longman, Rees, Orme, Brown, Green, & Longman, 1837.

———. *A Winter in Upper and Lower Egypt.* London: Hurst and Blackett, 1863.

Houlihan, Patrick F. *The Birds of Ancient Egypt.* Warminster: Aris & Philips, 1986.

Hyman, Anthony. *Charles Babbage.* Princeton: Princeton University Press, 1982.

Iversen, Erik. *The Myth of Egypt and Its Hieroglyphs in European Tradition.* Copenhagen: G. E. C. Gad, 1961.

———. *Obelisks in Exile.* 2 vols. Copenhagen: G. E. C. Gad, 1968.

Jomard, Edmé François, ed. *Description de l'Egypte.* 24 vols. Paris: Imprimerie de C. L. F. Panckoucke, 1809–1813.

Jones, Owen, and Joseph Bonomi. *Description of the Egyptian Court.* London: Bradbury and Evans, 1854.

Kamil, Jill. *Luxor: A Guide to Ancient Thebes.* 2d ed. London: Longman, 1973.

Lacouture, Jean. *Champollion: Une Vie de Lumières.* Paris: Bernard Grasset, 1988.

Lane, Edward William. *An Account of the Manners and Customs of the Modern Egyptians.* 1836. Reprint. London: J. M. Dent & Sons, 1954.

———. *Cairo Fifty Years Ago.* Edited by Stanley Lane-Poole. London: John Murray, 1896.

Lane-Poole, Stanley. *Life of Edward William Lane.* London: Williams and Norgate, 1877.

Lebas, Jean Baptiste Apöllinaire. *L'Obélisque de Luxor: Histoire de sa translation de Paris.* Paris: Carilian-Goeury et V^r Dalmont, 1839.

Leitch, John, ed. *Miscellaneous Works of the Late Thomas Young.* 3 vols. London: John Murray, 1855.

Lepsius, Richard. *Denkmäler aus Aegypten und Aethiopien.* 12 vols. Leipzig: J. C. Hinrichs'sche Buchhandlung, 1960.

———. *Letters from Egypt, Ethiopia, and the Peninsula of Sinai.* Translated by Leonoraa and Joanna B. Horner. London: Henry G. Bohn, 1853.

Levine, P. J. A. *The Amateur and the Professional: Historians, Antiquarians and Archaeologists in Nineteenth-Century England, 1838–1886.* Cambridge: Cambridge University Press, 1986.

Lucas, Caroline Catherine (Lady Wilkinson). *The Church of England Not Descended from the Church of Rome.* Swansea: Herbert Jones, 1855.

Lucas, R. L. T. *A Gower Family: The Lucases of Stouthall and Rhosili Rectory.* Lewes: Book Guild, 1986.

————. Rhossili. Cambridge: D. Brown & Sons, 1989.

————. "Great Aunt Caroline." Journal of the Gower Society 24 (1973): 22–29.

McNaught, Lewis. "Henry Salt: His Contribution to the Collections of Egyptian Sculpture in the British Museum." Apollo 108 (October 1978): 224–231.

Madden, Richard Robert. Egypt and Mohammed Ali. London: Hamilton, Adams, & Co., 1841.

————. The Literary Life of the Countess of Blessington. New York: Harper & Brothers, 1855.

————. Travels in Turkey, Egypt, Nubia, and Palestine in 1824–7. 2 vols. London: Henry Colburn, 1829.

Madox, John. Excursions in the Holy Land, Egypt, Nubia, Syria, &c. 2 vols. London: Richard Bentley, 1834.

Málek, Jaromír. "A Graffito of Year 17 of Amenemhet II at el-Hósh." Göttinger Miszellen 24 (1977): 51–52.

————. "New Reliefs and Inscriptions from Five Old Tombs at Giza and Saqquara." Bulletin de la Société d'Egyptologie, Genève 6 (1982): 58–61.

Málek, Jaromír, and Mark Smith. "Henry Salt's Egyptian Copies and Drawings." Göttinger Miszellen 64 (1983): 35–52.

Manniche, Lise. Lost Tombs: A Study of Certain Eighteenth Dynasty Monuments in the Theban Necropolis. London: Kegan Paul International, 1988.

————. The Tombs of the Nobles at Luxor. Cairo: American University in Cairo, 1987.

Marsot, Afaf Lutfi al-Sayyid. Egypt in the Reign of Muhammad Ali. Cambridge: Cambridge University Press, 1984.

Martineau, Harriet. Eastern Life, Present and Past. 3 vols. London: Edward Moxon, 1848.

Maundeville, Sir John [pseud.]. The Voiage and Travaile of Sir John Maundevile, K^t. London: J. Woodman, D. Lyon, and C. Davis, 1725.

Mayes, Stanley. The Great Belzoni. London: Putnam, 1959.

Meinardus, Otto F. A. Monks and Monasteries of the Egyptian Deserts. Cairo: American University in Cairo Press, 1961.

Miller, Edward. That Noble Cabinet: A History of the British Museum. London: Andre Deutsch, 1973.

Mitchell, Timothy. Colonising Egypt. Cambridge: Cambridge University Press, 1988.

Montobbio, Luigi. Giovanni Battista Belzoni: La vita i viaggi le scoperte. Padova: Edizioni Martello, 1984.

Moore, Doris Langley-Levy. Ada, Countess of Lovelace: Byron's Legitimate Daughter. London: John Murray, 1977.

Moss, Rosalind. "Rubbings of Egyptian Reliefs Made in 1826 by Sir J. Gardner Wilkinson." Journal of Egyptian Archaeology 62 (1976): 108–109.

Murray, G. W. Dare Me to the Desert. South Brunswick: A. S. Barnes & Co., 1968.

Murray, John, IV. *John Murray III, 1808–1892: A Brief Memoir.* London: John Murray, 1919.

Newberry, Percy E. *The Life of Rekhmara, Vezîr of Egypt under Thothmes III and Amenhetep II (circa B.C. 1472–1448) with Twenty-two Plates.* London: Archibald Constable and Co., 1900.

———. *Report on Some Excavations in the Theban Necropolis during the Winter of 1898–9.* London: Archibald Constable and Co., 1908.

Nims, Charles F. *Thebes of the Pharaohs.* London: Elek Books, 1965.

Noakes, Aubrey. *Cleopatra's Needles.* London: H. F. & G. Witherly, 1962.

Norden, Frederik Lewis. *The Antiquities, Natural History, Ruins and Other Curiosities of Egypt, Nubia, and Thebes.* London: Royal Society, 1780.

———. *Travels in Egypt and Nubia.* 2 vols. London: Royal Society, 1757.

Paston, George. *At John Murray's: Records of a Literary Circle 1843–1892.* London: John Murray, 1932.

Peacock, George. *Life of Thomas Young, M.D., F.R.S., &c., and One of the Eight Foreign Associates of the National Institute of France.* London: John Murray, 1855.

Pemble, John. *The Mediterranean Passion: Victorians and Edwardians in the South.* Oxford: Clarendon Press, 1987.

Pevsner, Nikolaus. *Some Architectural Writers of the Nineteenth Century.* Oxford: Clarendon Press, 1972.

Pococke, Richard. *A Description of the East and Some Other Countries.* London: W. Boyer, 1743.

Porter, Bertha, and Rosalind L. B. Moss. *Topographical Bibliography of Ancient Egyptian Hieroglyphic Texts, Reliefs and Paintings. I. The Theban Necropolis. Part 1. Private Tombs.* Oxford: Clarendon Press, 1960.

Rawlinson, George, ed. *The History of Herodotus.* 4 vols. New York: Appleton and Company, 1859.

Reeve, Lovell. *Men of Eminence in Literature, Science, and Art,* 4 vols. London: Lovell Reeve & Co., 1863.

Rhind, Alexander Henry. *Thebes, Its Tombs and Their Tenants.* London: Longman, Green, Longman, and Roberts, 1862.

Ricci, Seymour de. "An Album of Drawings by Sir J. G. Wilkinson." In *Studies Presented to F. Ll. Griffith,* pp. 474–476. London: Egypt Exploration Society, 1932.

Romer, John. *Valley of the Kings.* New York: William Morrow, 1981.

Said, Edward. *Orientalism.* New York: Pantheon, 1978.

St. John, James Augustus. *Egypt and Mohammed Ali; or Travels in the Valley of the Nile.* 2 vols. London: Longman, Rees, Orme, Brown, Green, and Longman, 1834.

Sattin, Anthony. *Lifting the Veil: British Society in Egypt 1768–1956.* London: J. M. Dent & Sons, 1988.

Saulnier, M., Fils. *Notice sur le voyage de M. Lelorrain en Egypt: Et observations sur le zodiaque circulaire de Denderah.* Paris: Chez l'Auteur, 1822.

Scaife, C. H. O. "Two Inscriptions at Mons Porphyrites (Gebel Dokhan).

Also a Description, with Plans, of the Stations: Between Kainopolis and Myos Hormos Together with Some Other Ruins in the Neighborhood of Gebel Dokhan." *Bulletin of the Faculty of Arts Fouad I University* 3, no. 2 (1935): 58–104.

Schweinfurth, G. *Die Steinbrüche am Mons Claudianus in der ostlichen Wüste Aegyptens.* Berlin, 1897.

Sherer, Joseph Moyle. *Scenes and Impressions in Egypt and in Italy.* London: Longman, Hurst, Rees, Orme, Brown, and Green, 1824.

Sidebotham, Steven E., et al., "Fieldwork on the Red Sea Coast: The 1987 Season." *Journal of the American Research Center in Egypt* 26 (1989): 131–132.

Smiles, Samuel. *A Publisher and His Friends.* London: John Murray, 1891.

Smith, Joseph Lindon. *Temples, Tombs, and Ancient Art.* Norman: University of Oklahoma Press, 1956.

Stein, Dorothy. *Ada: A Life and a Legacy.* Cambridge, Mass.: MIT Press, 1985.

Stephens, John L. *Incidents of Travel in Central America, Chiapas, and Yucatan.* 2 vols. New York: Harper & Brothers, 1841.

———. *Incidents of Travel in Yucatán.* 2 vols. London: John Murray, 1843.

Stocking, George. *Victorian Anthropology.* New York: Macmillan, 1987.

Tillett, Selwyn. *Egypt Itself: The Career of Robert Hay, Esquire of Linplum and Nunraw, 1799–1863.* London: SD Books, 1984.

Torr, Cecil. *Catalogue of Classical Antiquities from the Collection of the Late Sir Gardner Wilkinson.* Harrow: J. C. Wilbee, 1887.

Tregenza, L. A. *Egyptian Years.* London: Oxford University Press, 1958.

———. *The Red Sea Mountains of Egypt.* London: Oxford University Press, 1955.

Tucker, Judith E. *Women in Nineteenth-Century Egypt.* Cambridge: Cambridge University Press, 1985.

Vaux, W. S. W. "Memoir of Sir Gardner Wilkinson, F.R.S." In an offprint entitled *Address of the Council of the Royal Society of Literature.* April 1876.

Ward, Humphry. *History of the Athenaeum Club.* London: William Clowes & Sons, 1926.

Webster, James. *Travels through the Crimea, Turkey, and Egypt; Performed during the Years 1825–1828.* 2 vols. Henry Colburn and Richard Bentley, 1830.

Weigall, A. E. P. *Travels in the Upper Egyptian Deserts.* Edinburgh: H. Blackwood & Sons, 1909.

Whittaker, Thomas. *The Neo-Platonists.* 2d ed. Cambridge: Cambridge University Press, 1918.

Wigley, John. *The Rise and Fall of the Victorian Sunday.* Manchester: Manchester University Press, 1980.

Wilkinson, Charles K. *Egyptian Wall Paintings: The Metropolitan Museum of Art's Collection of Facsimiles.* New York: Metropolitan Museum of Art, 1983.

"Wilkinson on Hieroglyphics." *Fraser's Magazine for Town and Country* 19, no. 2 (October 1830): 329–333.

Wilkinson, (Sir) John Gardner. *The Architecture of the Ancient Egyptians.* London: John Murray, 1850.

———. "Avenue and Carns about Arthur's Stone in Gower," *Archaeologia Cambrensis* 1, 4th series (1869): 22–45, 117–121.

———. *Carn Brea, near Redruth, Cornwall.* Truro: Heard and Sons, 1860.

———. *Dalmatia and Montenegro: With a Journey to Mostar in Herzegovina, and Remarks on the Slavonic Nations; the History of Dalmatia and Ragusa; the Usmocs; &c. &c.* 2 vols. London: John Murray, 1848.

———. *The Egyptians in the Time of the Pharaohs; Being a Companion to the Crystal Palace Egyptian Collections.* London: Bradbury and Evans, 1857.

———. "An Etruscan Tomb at Cervetri, the Ancient Caere." Archaeological Association. Offprint.

———. *Extracts from Several Hieroglyphical Subjects, Found at Thebes, and Other Parts of Egypt. With Remarks on the Same.* Malta: Government Press, 1830.

———. *The Fragments of the Hieratic Papyrus of Kings at Turin.* London: T. Richards, 1851.

———. *Handbook for Travellers in Egypt.* London: John Murray, 1847.

———. "The Listening Slave and the Flaying of Marsyas." *Transactions of the Royal Society of Literature* 11 (1878): 263–279.

———. *Manners and Customs of the Ancient Egyptians.* 6 vols. London: John Murray, 1837.

———. *Materia Hieroglyphica, Containing the Egyptian Pantheon and the Succession of the Pharaohs, from the Earliest Times, to the Conquest by Alexander, and Other Hieroglyphical Subjects, with Plates, and Notes Explanatory of the Same.* Malta: Government Press, 1828.

———. "The Menvendanus Stone." *Archaeologia Cambrensis: The Journal of the Cambrian Archaeological Association* 2, 4th series (1871): 140–157.

———. *Modern Egypt and Thebes.* 2 vols. London: John Murray, 1843.

———. "Notes on a Part of the Eastern Desert of Upper Egypt." *Journal of the Royal Geographical Society* 2 (1832): 28–60.

———. *On Colour.* London: John Murray, 1858.

———. "On the Contrivances by Means of Which the Statue of Memnon at Thebes was Made Vocal." *Transactions of the Royal Society of Literature of the United Kingdom* 2 (1834): 451–56.

———. "On the Decrease of the Level of the Nile, and on Egyptian Fortification." *Transactions of the Royal Society of Literature* 4 (1853): 93–108.

———. "On an Early Mosaic in St. Mark's: Representing the Removal of the Body of the Evangelist to Venice." *Journal of the Archaeological Association.* Offprint, n.d.

———. "On the Nile and the Present and Former Levels of Egypt." *Journal* of the Royal Geographical Society, 9 (1839): 431–441.

———. "On Saracenic Architecture." Transactions of the Royal Institute of British Architects, 1st ser. 2 (1860–1861): 216–230.

———. Remarks on the Country between Wady Halfeh and Gebel Berkel, in Ethiopia, with Observations on the Level of the Nile." Journal of the Royal Geographical Society 20 (1850): 154–159.

———. Rome in 1848–49. Pamphlet. N.p., n.d.

———. "Some Account of the Natron Lakes of Egypt; in a Letter to W. R. Hamilton, Esq." Journal of the Royal Geographical Society 13 (1843): 113–118.

———. "Survey of the Valley of the Natron Lakes and of a Part of the Bahr-el-Farg." Journal of the Royal Geographical Society 9 (1839): 431–441.

———. Three Letters on the Policy of England towards the Porte and Mohammed Ali. London: John Murray, 1840.

———. Topography of Thebes and General View of Egypt. London: John Murray, 1835.

Williams, John Fischer. Harrow. London: George Bell and Sons, 1901.

Wilson, John A. The Culture of Ancient Egypt. Chicago: University of Chicago Press, 1951.

———. "The Present State of Egyptian Studies." In The Haverford Symposium on Archaeology and the Bible, edited by Elihu Grant. New Haven: American Schools of Oriental Research, 1938.

———. Signs and Wonders upon Pharaoh: A History of American Archaeology. Chicago: University of Chicago Press, 1964.

Winlock, H. E. Excavations at Deir El Bahri 1911–1931. New York: Macmillan, 1942.

Wood, Alexander. Thomas Young, Natural Philosopher, 1773–1829. Completed by Frank Oldham. Cambridge: Cambridge University Press, 1954.

Wortham, John David. British Egyptology 1549–1906. London: David & Charles, 1971.

———. The Genesis of British Egyptology. Norman: University of Oklahoma Press, 1971.

Yates, Francis A. Giordano Bruno and the Hermetic Tradition. London: Routledge and Kegan Paul, 1964.

Index